University of London Historical Studies

III

POLISH POLITICS
AND THE
REVOLUTION OF NOVEMBER
1830

Polish Politics
and the Revolution of November 1830

by
R. F. LESLIE

GREENWOOD PRESS, PUBLISHERS
WESTPORT, CONNECTICUT

Reprinted by permission
of The Athlone Press

First Greenwood Printing 1969

Library of Congress Catalogue Card Number 79-91766

SBN 8371-2416-6

PRINTED IN UNITED STATES OF AMERICA

PREFACE

THE Polish revolution of November 1830 and the war which followed it were the last challenge of the old Poland to the Russian hegemony in Eastern Europe. It was a rash venture which had little chance of success. I cannot think that the lot of the common people would have been improved materially if the Polish gentry, led by men like Adam George Czartoryski, Skrzynecki and others, had in fact succeeded in re-establishing independence with the frontiers of historic Poland. Defeat, however, compelled the left wing of the political class to realize that the people had to be admitted to equality with the gentry. The revolution, therefore, as well as being an epilogue, was also a prelude to the struggle of 1832-64 in which the cause of independence and the emancipation of the people were closely connected. This book touches only upon one episode in the history of Poland in the nineteenth century. The revolutionary effort of the next three decades and its achievements I hope I shall be able to deal with elsewhere in the future.

The book now published represents in part the work done for a Ph.D. thesis of the University of London. It was made possible by the award of a postgraduate studentship by the university in 1948 and by a scholarship granted to me in the same year by the Treasury Committee for Studentships in Foreign Languages and Cultures, which was set up with the object of encouraging the study of Slavonic, African and Oriental problems.

I was fortunate enough to be able to spend two terms in Poland, where I was granted free access to Polish archives and libraries. My especial thanks are due to the staffs of the Instytut Historyczny of the University of Warsaw, the State Archives in Warsaw, the Museum of the Czartoryski Princes in Cracow and the Library of the University of Cracow. I am likewise grateful to the Ministry of Foreign Affairs and the Ministry of Public Education in Warsaw for the very considerable assistance they gave me. Poles are extremely gracious to foreigners who study their literature and history, which, though they rarely say so openly, they feel to be neglected in Western European countries. I hope that this book may make some contribution towards the understanding of the history of the Polish nation.

I must thank also my former teachers, Professor R. R. Betts and Professor S. T. Bindoff for all their help and encouragement, and likewise Professor A. Cobban and Dr. G. H. Bolsover who read the manuscript of this book and suggested many improvements. Mr. G. R. Versey, of the department of Geography, University College, London, drew the maps.

Queen Mary College   R. F. LESLIE
November 1955

CONTENTS

A Note on Pronunciation	x
I. Poland and the Partitions, 1772–1815	1
II. Economic Problems: Peasants and *Szlachta*	51
III. Discontent in Congress Poland and the Revolution of 1830	96
IV. The Break with Russia and the War	134
V. The Failure of Agrarian Reform	172
VI. The Rising in the former Eastern Provinces and the Battle of Ostrołęka	194
VII. The Last Phase of the Insurrection	220
VIII. After the Rising	256
Appendices	
A. The Polish Aristocracy	282
B. The form of the Bill for reform on the State Lands at the end of the debates in the Diet	284
Bibliography	287
Index	303

MAPS

The Polish Republic, 1772	3
The Battle of Grochów: February, 1831	165
The Battle of Ostrołęka: May, 1831	210

A NOTE ON THE PRONUNCIATION OF POLISH WORDS AND NAMES

THE stress in Polish falls almost invariably on the penultimate syllable. An important exception is the word *Rzeczpospolita* ('Republic' or 'Commonwealth') where it falls on the third syllable.

The Polish alphabet is phonetic and words are pronounced as they are spelt. The following guide which shows the main differences between English and Polish sounds will assist the reader in achieving a reasonably accurate pronunciation:

1. Vowels

'a' as in 'f*a*ther'
'e' as in 'm*e*t'
'o' as in 'h*o*t'
'u' as in 'b*oo*t':
'ó' is pronounced in the same way as 'u', this spelling being necessary for philological and other reasons
'i' is long as in 'm*ee*t'
'y' is short as in 'b*i*t'
'-yj-' is the same sound as 'i'

2. Nasal Vowels

'ą' achieves the same sound as in the French 'b*on*'
'ę' as in the French 'Jacob*in*'

3. Diphthongs

'-aj-' as in '*eye*'
'-ej-' as in 'h*ay*'
'-oj-' as in 'b*oy*'
'-uj-' an elongated 'u' as in the French 'L*ouis*'

A NOTE ON PRONUNCIATION
4. CONSONANTS

'c' is 'ts' cf. Potocki (pr. Poto*ts*ki)
'ch' is aspirated as in the Scots 'loch'
'g' is always hard as in 'go'
'gi-' gives the 'g' a slight 'y' sound, 'gy'
'j' is the equivalent of the English 'y', as in *y*ear
'l' as in the English '*l*esson'
'ł' is hard:

>(a) In the Eastern districts and in the theatre it retains 'l' sound as in the English 'wa*ll*'

>(b) In Central and Western Poland it has become a slight 'w', cf. the pronunciation of 'wa*ll*' which is achieved sometimes by English children

'w' is the equivalent of 'v'

Some difficulty may be experienced in distinguishing the difference between the following hard and soft consonants, but it should not be allowed to worry the English reader, a correct pronunciation being possible only after much practice:

SOFT	HARD	
ć, ci	cz	'ch' as in '*ch*ur*ch*'
dź, dzi	dż	'g' as in '*G*eor*g*e', or 'j' in '*j*am'
ś, si	sz	'sh' as in '*sh*op'
ź, zi	ż, rz	's' as in 'plea*s*ure' or 'j' as in the French '*j*our'.

Note should be made that an accented 'n', cf. 'ń', gives the slight nasal sound as in the French 'Boulo*gn*e' or the English 'o*n*ion'.

These pronunciations refer to the modern standardized Polish spellings. Some variety of spelling is evident in the eighteenth and nineteenth centuries. In the footnotes I have retained the spellings which appear on the title pages of the books cited.

Proper Names

Where Polish names occur I keep Polish spellings, but in the case of Russian names I have transliterated them as if from the Cyrillic, even where a transliteration into Polish characters is possible, cf. *Khrapovitsky*, which I prefer to *Chrapowicki*, or *Paskevich* in preference to *Paszkiewicz*.

The spelling of place names is a serious problem, especially where the places were once part of the pre-1772 Poland, but are now part of the U.S.S.R. I have used forms which are familiar to the English reader or ought to present no difficulty. Obviously, *Warsaw* is to be preferred to *Warszawa*, *Cracow* to *Kraków*, *Danzig* to *Gdańsk*, *Brest Litovsk* to *Brześć Litewski* etc. On the other hand, I think *Poznań* is preferable to *Posen*, *Lvov* to *Lwów* (the Polish form), *Lemberg* or *Leopol*, *Toruń* to *Thorn*. Lithuanian names present the greatest difficulty and defy a satisfactory solution.

CHAPTER I

Poland and the Partitions, 1772-1815

THE Polish state suffered partition three times in the eighteenth century and, in spite of a brief revival in a modified form as the Duchy of Warsaw from 1807 to 1813, was once more divided by the Vienna settlement of 1815, but the loss of independence did not make the Poles any the less conscious of their continued identity as a nation. In the second half of the nineteenth century they were forced to accept foreign domination as an unavoidable necessity and did perhaps absorb some of the traditions of that particular country to which they owed their official allegiance, but the memories of the past were too strong to be stifled completely. In the Polish territories there were distinct political, religious, social and economic problems, which arose, not from the partitions by Austria, Prussia and Russia, but from the fact that Poland had had an uninterrupted and separate existence since the tenth century. For this reason emphasis must be placed upon the continuity of Poland's history even after her disappearance as a sovereign state. In their struggles for independence the Poles were seeking to establish a new state upon the foundations which had been laid in the past. The faults of the old Poland which had led to her downfall they wished to correct, but they never lost sight of the community which had existed before the First Partition of 1772.

Poland of the eighteenth century was the *Rzeczpospolita*, a federation of communities united by a single diet and an elected king. In contrast with the other great states of Europe, whose power and efficiency were achieved by the destruction of particularism, the Republic had undergone a process of extreme decentralization which had strengthened regional privileges and circumscribed the authority of the Crown. The Republic consisted of two distinct portions, the *Korona*, or Kingdom, which was divided into two great provinces, Wielkopolska and Małopolska, and the Grand Duchy of Lithuania. The Kingdom was administered under Polish common law in many of its palatinates, but Royal Prussia, annexed from the Teutonic Order in 1466, retained its own distinct law. In the east the position was more complicated. All Lithuania had been joined in permanent union with the Kingdom in 1569, but under varying conditions. The southern provinces of the Grand Duchy, the *województwa* or palatinates of Volhynia, Kiev and Bracław (Lower Podolia), had concluded a separate union and became part of Małopolska in the Kingdom itself, but continued to be governed by the Second Lithuanian Statute of 1569. The northern provinces retained the title of the Grand Duchy of Lithuania, using as a code of law the Third Lithuanian Statute of 1588. In the far north lay Kurland, a province owing allegiance to the Kingdom and the Grand Duchy jointly and enjoying the semi-independent status which Ducal or East Prussia had had before its cession in full sovereignty to the Elector of Brandenburg. In spite of this extreme diversity there was among the nobility or *szlachta* a strong sense of unity based upon their extensive privileges and freedoms and upon their common culture and religion.

By the eighteenth century the *szlachta*, who were at the outset drawn from all groups of the community irrespective of their race or creed, were for the most part Polish by speech and Roman Catholic by religion, but the same cannot be said for the mass of the population. The native Polish elements were almost all Roman Catholics and likewise the native Lithuanians who were concentrated in the Duchy of Samogitia and to some extent in the area of Vilna. There had been a strong Lutheran and Calvinist movement in the sixteenth century, but it had lost ground owing to the superiority of the Jesuit system of education and because the nobility's interest in religious dissent declined when once they had won their political and economic privileges. The Protestant element in Poland was strongest in Western Poland where there had been a considerable German settlement. The problem of religious dissent however was most serious in the eastern provinces where the White Russian and

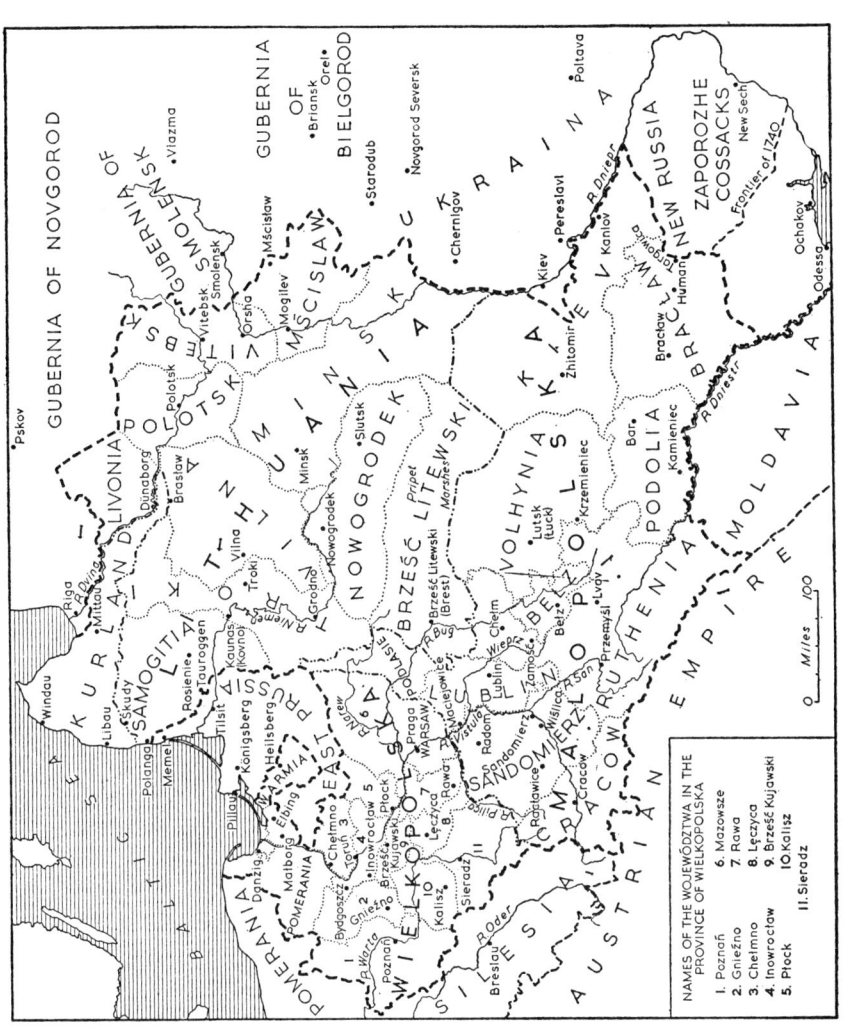

The Polish Republic, 1772

Ruthenian population had originally owed allegiance to the Orthodox Church. The attempt of the Polish Crown to enforce the principle of *cujus regio ejus religio* took the form of the Union of Brest (Brześć Litewski) of 1595, by which the Orthodox communities retained their liturgy, but acknowledged the supremacy of the pope in Rome. The compromise of the Union succeeded in its initial purpose of binding the *szlachta* of the east more closely with their fellows in the west, but it had only slight influence among the peasantry. For the *szlachta* conversion to the Roman Church was relatively easy, because the Roman Catholic seminaries and schools alone provided a modern education, while Roman Catholicism was a passport to political office and favour. The continual passage of the *szlachta* from the Uniate Church to Roman Catholicism had the serious consequence of separating the natural leaders of the people from the mass of the population and introducing an irritation additional to the mutual antagonisms of lords and peasants. The adoption of the Polish language emphasized still further the distinction between the upper and lower ranks of society in the east, but it would perhaps be unwise to stress factors of language before 1848, because the Polish nobles of Lithuania, White Russia and Ruthenia were proud of their local affinities, much as the Protestant landowners of Ireland came to be proud of being Irish. More often than not the *szlachta* had an adequate command of the peasants' language, and the Polish which they spoke contained many words retained from the speech of the people and soft intonations which distinguished their accent from the harder tones of Poland proper. Religious differences were of greater importance. Where the *szlachta* had religion in common with the people, as they had in the western half of the Kingdom and in Samogitia, there was no serious conflict with the clergy. In the Uniate districts of the east on the other hand the nobles could hardly avoid favouring the Roman priests at the expense of the Uniate popes. The result was that the Uniate priests came to stand as intermediaries between the *szlachta* and the people, throwing their influence on one side or another according to the degree of favour shown them. If the noble had the good sense to protect the Uniate Church relations were good, but too often the Polish gentry considered the Uniates to be little better than the schismatic Greeks, an attitude which was encouraged by the Roman Catholic Church and schools. In addition to the Roman Catholics and the Uniates there were also the Orthodox Christians, for the Greek Orthodox Church never entirely lost its hold. The Union of Brest was not accepted from the outset by all the Orthodox bishops and their clergy. The Orthodox bishop of Przemyśl, Innocenty Winnicki, agreed privately in 1681 to accede to the Union, but it was not until 1692 that he was able to make a public declaration of his conversion. Józef Szumlański, bishop of Lvov, agreed to join the Union in 1677, but formal amalgamation was postponed until 1700 and disputes among the clergy of the diocese were brought to a close only in the 1730's. The bishopric of Łuck acceded to the Union in 1701 because the Uniate metropolitan, Leon Załęski, was willing to confirm the archimandrite, Dionyzy Żabokrzycki, in the see, whereas the Orthodox metropolitan of Kiev considered him unsuitable owing to the irregularities of his past life. At the same time the remnants of the Orthodox Church received great encouragement from the revival of the Russian state and the frequent passage of Russian troops through the territories of the Republic in the eighteenth century did much to sustain their cause. Prince Sylwester Czetwertyński, who became Orthodox bishop of Mogilev, openly appealed to Peter the Great for aid and succeeded in obtaining confirmation of his appointment in 1720 from Augustus II largely through the Russian government's help. His successor, Józef Wolczański, followed in the same tradition. Ablest of all was Georgy Konissky, who became bishop of Mogilev in 1754, and who never ceased to urge upon Russia the need for obtaining toleration of Orthodoxy within the Republic. In the same way the bishops of Pereslavl in southern Russia were not backward in assisting Orthodox communities across the border in Poland. Legally Russia's case for intervention was strong. In 1686 by the so-called Grzymułtowski treaty the Republic and Russia had agreed, among other things, to toleration of their respective religious minorities, though it was not until 1710 that the Polish diet in the stress of war could be brought to confirm this arrangement. Russia could therefore argue that the four Orthodox bishoprics which had existed in 1686 must be maintained.

The Poles from their side gave some provocation. Roman Catholic opinion, which even in the eighteenth century was so strong that it looked upon the annual pilgrimages to Kiev, in which Orthodox and even Uniate Christians took part, as the equivalent of high treason, saw to it in 1717 that dissenters were forbidden by law from holding public services or establishing new churches, and that in 1733 they were excluded from the diet, tribunals and all public offices.

It was the enforcement of toleration by Russia in February 1768 on the basis of the conditions which existed in 1717 which led in the first instance to the troubles which produced the first partition of Poland in 1772. From that time Orthodoxy began to regain its strength in the east, and the Uniate Church, losing adherents to Roman Catholicism or to Orthodoxy, began to decline. Catherine II skilfully used Roman Catholic differences after 1772 to weaken the loyalties of the Poles themselves in the territories acquired by the First Partition. Siestrzencew, the Roman Catholic bishop of White Russia, was encouraged to make himself in all but name independent of Rome and was in fact created archbishop of Mogilev by Ukaz in January 1782, though papal confirmation eventually followed in 1784. Siestrzencew for his part did everything in his power to weaken the Uniate Church. In the same way, the great Jesuit centre at Polotsk, protected by Catherine II after the suppression of the Society of Jesus in 1773, used its influence to promote Roman Catholic loyalty towards Russia.[1] The Polish diet of 1788–92 gave up the effort to suppress Orthodoxy and chose instead to attempt the creation of an independent Polish Orthodox Church, a step which aroused the bitter opposition of the Roman Catholic and Uniate clergy. This church was to be connected with the Patriarchate at Constantinople, which gave it recognition in 1790, and to be governed by an archbishop metropolitan and three diocesan bishops, but the scheme came to nothing, for with the Second and Third Partitions the Russian state was able to place all its resources at the disposal of the Russian Orthodox Church in the annexed areas. The Russian policy of incorporating all Uniate parishes of less than

[1] For details of this problem see M. Loret, *Kościół katolicki a Katarzyna II, 1772–84* (Cracow–Warsaw, 1910).

100 hearths in neighbouring parishes, whether Uniate or Orthodox, coupled with vigorous propaganda for reconversion to Orthodoxy, weakened the position of the Poles in these areas, even though under Paul I there was some relaxation of pressure. Thus the eighteenth century saw the beginning of the process by which the Polonized gentry of Lithuania, White Russia and Ruthenia became foreigners in their homeland, though not of any corresponding growth of national consciousness among the mass of the people.[1] Prayers for the monarch enforced by the Russian government left the people in no doubt where their official loyalties ought to lie, no matter what their form of religious observance. Everywhere the loyalty of the peasants to the monarch, whether Prussian, Austrian or Russian, was in fact to be a serious obstacle to Polish insurrections which counted upon mass popular support.

As important as religion in giving Poland its peculiar social system had been the commercial development of the fifteenth and sixteenth centuries which, so far from encouraging, had actually inhibited the growth of a strong native urban middle class. In the early modern period Poland had concentrated upon the export of raw materials and grain to Western Europe. The *szlachta*, who were the principal primary producers, had had little patience with the towns of the hinterland, which sought to confine commerce to the ancient trade routes and impose tolls and dues upon it. In contrast with the states of Western Europe Poland adhered to the principle of free trade, which was the policy of the landlord everywhere in Eastern Europe. The Polish nobility secured virtual exemption from both municipal tolls and state customs and obtained the right to send their produce to the sea without serious hindrance. In consequence, only those cities, which lay at the mouths of the navigable rivers and

[1] As a rough rule it may be assumed that proper names with the adjectival ending *-ski* or its modifications indicate a native Polish noble origin, cf. Raczyński, Walewski, Potocki, etc. The stem of the surname indicates the manor from which the family originally came. Names ending in *-(i)ewicz* are of White Russian descent, cf. Tyszkiewicz, Naruszewicz, Niemcewicz. Names which appear to be non-Slavonic, cf. Radziwiłł, Sapieha, Polytełło, are usually Lithuanian in origin. There are of course many exceptions, cf. the Ruthenian family of princely Lithuanian descent, the Czartoryskis. For details of Polish families and their origins reference should be made to T. Żychlinski, *Złota księga szlachty polskiej*, the relevant volumes of which are a mine of information.

became entrepôts of the export trade, retained their importance. These were the ports of Riga, Memel, Königsberg, Elbing and Danzig, of which only Danzig owed allegiance to Poland at the time of the Second Partition; these cities were German rather than Polish in their outlook. The Polish towns of the hinterland were for the most part confined to serving the needs of the local market. Even the relatively large cities like Poznań, Cracow, Lvov, Vilna and Warsaw had an administrative rather than a commercial significance. It is true that in Warsaw, which began to expand in the eighteenth century and contained in the first half of the nineteenth century, alone of all the Polish towns, a population of more than 100,000 inhabitants, there were some banking firms of German origin, but these were not large enough to provide the old Polish state with substantial loans and were, in fact, to be ruined in the financial crisis caused by the Second Partition of 1793. The majority of the Polish towns, whether they were royal boroughs or owned by private persons, were usually little more than large villages engaged as much in agriculture as in trade. Within the towns the Christian element was only a fraction of the population, owing to the heavy admixture of Jews. The Jews had found their way into Poland during the Middle Ages, mainly as refugees from persecution in Germany. Owing to the rule that only Christians could hold land they were unable to become farmers and remained a caste of traders, differing from the rest of the community by their Yiddish speech and by their religion. They fulfilled almost all the trading functions of the country and made themselves indispensable to noble and peasant alike, spurning no commercial transaction however small. There was a saying in Poland that 'every man has his Jew'. About ten per cent of the population, but concentrated in the urban centres, they gave Polish municipal life a predominantly Jewish character. Able and willing to operate for lower profits than the Christian tradesmen, they depressed the status of the native bourgeoisie, but were themselves too distinct to adopt the political aspirations of a *tiers état*. The Polish Republic was fundamentally a noble society in which the middle class could play only a minor role.

The population thus may be said to have been divided into

five social groups; the *szlachta*, the clergy, the Christian bourgeoisie, the Jews and the peasants, though there were other small groups of distinct religious or ethnic character.[1] At the head of the community stood the privileged orders, the *szlachta* and the upper ranks of the Roman Catholic clergy, who were drawn from the *szlachta* and exhibited no fundamental difference of outlook from them. It was the ideas, political concepts and traditions of the *szlachta* which determined the course of Polish history. The *szlachta* and the clergy elected the king, had sole representation in the diets and provincial dietines, and alone had the right to political office. The constitutional life of Poland had been bedevilled since the seventeenth century by the *Liberum Veto*. This was a concept that the deputies to the central diet were empowered to vote only in accordance with the instructions which they had received from the dietines; if matters were raised which had not been discussed and voted on in the dietines, the deputies were obliged to break off negotiations and take no further part in the debates. Because unanimity had to be obtained in the central diet, the secession even of one deputy brought its proceedings to an end. In other words, the objection of an individual could and did frustrate any attempt at introducing new legislation. An exception must be made of those occasions when the diet met under the rules of the 'Confederation' which excluded from the outset the use of the *Liberum Veto*, but Confederation diets normally met only to settle civil commotions and disturbances.

[1] Any estimate of the population of the eve of the partition of 1772 must necessarily be approximate in the absence of reliable figures, but the conclusions of T. Korzon, *Wewnętrzne dzieje Polski za Stanisława Augusta, 1764–1794*, 2nd ed. (Cracow-Warsaw, 1897), i, 320, for the year 1791 after the losses of 1772, are generally recognized to be sound. Korzon put the total population at 8,790,000. Of these there were 10,000 Roman Catholic and 40,000 Uniate and Orthodox clergy. The *szlachta* amounted to 725,000, of whom 318,000 were landed proprietors and 407,000 without land. The Christian bourgeoisie are given as 500,000, of whom 150,000 were Protestants. There were 900,000 Jews. There was a total of 6,365,000 peasants, of whom 3,465,000 were Roman Catholics, 2,600,000 Uniates and 300,000 Orthodox. Their economic categories were as follows: 10,000 were 'Hollanders' holding their lands on long leases; 190,000 belonged to the king's personal estates and 840,000 to the public estates or *starostwa*; 921,300 were serfs on ecclesiastical lands and 3,404,700 on noble estates. Korzon refers to 1,000,000 'free peasants', by which I interpret him to mean that they had no land or belonged to those small communities which had never suffered enserfment. There were besides 100,000 Greeks and Armenians, 50,000 Tartars and 100,000 Old Believers.

Presiding over this aristocratic republic was the king, whose function was to represent the state to the outside world and discharge the routine details of the administration. This was a task which the Saxon kings of Poland, Augustus II (1697–1733) and Augustus III (1733–63), performed without much enthusiasm, preferring the charms of their electorate, where their word was law, to the rough and tumble of Warsaw. In the first half of the eighteenth century Poland did not offer a field of activity for a vigorous monarch. Augustus II owed his continued kingship to Russian support against the anti-king, the Polish nobleman, Stanisław Leszczyński, whom Charles XII of Sweden had sought to place on the throne. On the death of Augustus II in 1733, Leszczyński made a second attempt to win the crown of Poland, but Russia again intervened to uphold the election of Augustus III. The price which the Saxon kings paid to Russia was the continuation of the old constitutional system in Poland; Russia had no wish to see a strong state in Poland which might threaten the security of her western frontiers. Nor did the weakness of the Crown offend Polish sentiment. The Poles could declare that nowhere else in Europe had government by consent received such full expression. The Poles could argue that they feared no princely despotism, but enjoyed a Golden Liberty which ought to excite the admiration and envy of the whole world.

During this period of Saxon rule, however, some sections of Polish opinion began to realize that legislative inertia and political weakness might bring dire consequences in their train. Attention was gradually turned to the need for reform. The attachment of the *szlachta* to the traditional concepts of Golden Liberty demanded that at all costs the principles of freedom and equality should be maintained and that on no account was the king to obtain autocratic powers. The varying interpretations which the *szlachta* placed upon the terms, liberty and equality, can only be understood against the background of Polish conditions. Within the noble order there were divisions and differences of wealth which account for the different definitions of freedom.

The most important section of the *szlachta* was the aristocracy, who were indeed almost too august to be referred to as *szlachta* at all, though in theory they enjoyed no special privileges which marked them off from the rest of the nobility. Some recognition, it is true, was given to their pre-eminence by the existence of a Senatorial Order sitting as an upper house in the diet in distinction from the Equestrian Order sitting in the lower house, but this represented a distinction between the high officers of state and the mass of the *szlachta*. For practical purposes however the aristocrats, owing their power to great latifundia lying for the most part east of the Vistula, ruled the state. It was between these great landlords that the struggle for political power was waged. They secured for themselves the principal offices of state, obtained the richest benefices of the church for their relatives and clients, and divided among themselves the *starostwa*, public estates attached to the administrative appointment of *starosta*, or sheriff.

From 1717 to 1764 the Republic was distracted by the rivalry of two great clans, the Potockis and the Czartoryskis, each side seeking predominance in the counsels of the Crown and a monopoly of royal patronage. Franciszek Salezy Potocki was famous for his wide possessions in Ruthenia and resentful of interference by the Crown in what he considered almost an autonomous principality. He was known to his contemporaries as the *Królik Rusi*, which may be translated idiomatically as the 'Uncrowned King of Ruthenia'. To his son Stanisław Szczęsny (i.e. Felix) Potocki he transmitted the same concept of semi-independent and almost regal dignity. There were, besides, cadet branches of this family known as the 'poor Potockis', by which was meant that their possessions, though substantial, could not compare in size with those of the senior branch. The Czartoryskis were no less conscious of their importance. Though their great territorial position was of recent origin, they traced their ancestry back to the grand duke of Lithuania, Gedymin, through Korygiełło, a younger brother of Władysław Jagiełło, the first Lithuanian king of Poland. For this reason they considered that a member of their clan might well be elected king of Poland, though they found it convenient to associate their private ambition with a plan of constitutional reform. The Potockis on the other hand stood forth as the defenders of the Polish traditions, as the 'Patriotic Party' against the upstart

'Family', as the Czartoryskis were called. The turning point in the struggle was the election of August Czartoryski's nephew, Stanisław August Poniatowski, as king of Poland in 1764, with the support of Catherine II, not so much because of the physical strength he had presumably exhibited as a lover of the empress, as because of the political weakness which he was expected to show as king of Poland. The Potockis had no love for a Poniatowski of the Czartoryski connection, while the Czartoryskis themselves privately considered that their kinsman was a *parvenu*, not of the Gedymin line and not very well off at that, and would have much preferred the election of the head of the family, Prince August. After the First Partition of 1772 the Czartoryskis and the Potockis drew closer together by the conclusion of a marriage alliance. In 1772 Ignacy Potocki, a junior member of the clan in one of its poorer lines, was married off to Elżbieta Lubomirska, granddaughter of Prince August Czartoryski, who had withdrawn from active politics on the election of Stanisław August; his place at the head of the faction had been taken by Prince Stanisław Lubomirski, his son-in-law and the father of Ignacy Potocki's bride. This marriage was an attempt to rehabilitate the unpopular Czartoryskis by identifying them with the Potockis, who enjoyed great prestige as the Patriotic Party, though the Czartoryskis continued to entertain what may be termed 'Orleanist pretensions', which were to be revived as late as the mid-nineteenth century. Ignacy Potocki, who was to make his name as a leader in the diet of 1788–92 and to be regarded almost as a national hero, in fact began his political career as a member of an aristocratic *fronde*.[1]

Only slightly less powerful were the other great clans.[2] The Zamoyskis, descendants of the great chancellor, Jan Zamoyski, and still based upon the fortress of Zamość which he had built, were a formidable power with which to reckon. There were also the Sanguszkos, who like the Czartoryskis were descended from Gedymin. The Radziwiłłs were eminent enough for one of their family to marry a Hohenzollern princess. The Sapiehas, the Sułkowskis, Raczyńskis, Tyszkiewiczs, Pacs, Platers,

---

[1] For a balanced view of Ignacy Potocki's early career, see K. M. Morawski, *Ignacy Potocki*, Cz. I (1750–1788) (Cracow-Warsaw, 1911), pp. 66–7.
[2] See Appendix A for a sample of aristocratic interrelationships.

Branickis, Rzewuskis, and others were families with extensive properties, which enabled them to attract clients and build up powerful followings with which to dominate the political life of the old Republic.

An unfortunate feature of aristocratic intrigue was the tendency to seek aid of foreign powers to augment the party influence. In a country in which the eastern and western frontiers lay on no definite geographical feature, diplomatic orientations were necessarily of great importance. Before the eighteenth century the main cause for difference was whether Poland should follow a French or an Austrian alliance, but the rise of Russia and Brandenburg-Prussia added two more possibilities. What was originally a matter of state came to be seen in the light of family interests. The inclination to seek foreign support was especially strong when the Saxon dynasty depended so openly upon Russia and when the Potockis and the Czartoryskis were evenly balanced within the state. Poles thus became connoisseurs of diplomatic combinations and could see the resurrection of Poland in the most unlikely associations of the powers. In fact, no Polish political programme was ever complete without its diplomatic slant, nor was there ever an international event from which Polish politicians did not see some hope of gain for their country, often thinking that Poland was the hub of European politics. It was the magnates who bequeathed to the national tradition the belief that salvation could be obtained by diplomatic dexterity, as if success might be miraculously achieved as a conjurer produces a rabbit from a hat.

The most important element after the magnates were the well-to-do landed proprietors of the second rank, the *zamożna szlachta*. The term *szlachta folwarczna* is often used and describes their position even better, indicating the possession of a *folwark* (German *vorwerk*) or demesne. Nobles of this type held between one and four villages and were most powerful in the western half of the Kingdom, especially in Wielkopolska, where there were only a few aristocratic estates. In the eighteenth century this medium gentry exhibited little independence of the aristocracy. They supported the interest of a local magnate and in return obtained a monopoly of the lesser provincial offices. They were restricted in their outlook to the politics of the locality and confined themselves to a life of bucolic oblivion, except when the magnitude of disaster roused them forcibly from their lethargy. The style of their dress was even in the second half of the eighteenth century distinctly Asiatic in appearance, an effect which was emphasized by the practice of shaving the head at the sides so that only a tuft was left on the crown, in contrast with the aristocrats who had begun to copy French fashions and the peasants who allowed their hair to grow to the shoulders. Little can be said of the medium gentry, except that they were boorish and provincial, a country squirearchy of a type which in England writers delighted to portray both for their vices and their virtues.

The largest in numbers and the poorest in wealth were the petty *szlachta*, who had little or no property and who included well over half the total noble class. There was a large concentration of rural petty *szlachta* in the north of the Kingdom, especially in the former Duchy of Mazowsze, which had been joined to the Polish Crown in 1525, and in the *województwo* of Podlasie and the Lithuanian areas just over the boundary, but there were scattered islands of them throughout the Republic. The petty *szlachta* who remained on the land generally lived in villages composed entirely of noble holdings.[1] They were almost indistinguishable from the peasants except for their pretensions and their ability to read and write, and, as some Polish writers added unkindly, by reason of their worse drunkenness. In some areas it is obvious that Polish was not their native speech, but they rejected Lithuanian or Ruthenian, considering that Polish was a mark of superiority. Sometimes they performed occasional

[1] An active propagandist during the diet of 1788–92, Father F. S. Jezierski, wrote a pamphlet *Jarosza Kutasińskiego herbu Dęboróg szlachcica łukowskiego Uwagi nad stanem nieszlacheckim w Polszcze* (1790), in which, to make his pleas for the non-noble classes more effective, he represented himself as being born in one of these districts and therefore as having the background and prejudices of a petty noble. 'My father, being the head of the family and the master of the house, was the lord of an inheritance on which he sowed nine *korce*, three *ćwierci* and six *garnce* of rye. He worked the land himself and when he had bought iron, tools, boots and salt was free of all other needs for his household. Our village settlement, belonging in hereditary right to 47 *szlachta*, had 80 villages like itself. Altogether they covered many square miles of country in which there was not a peasant or a townsman, only *szlachta*' (pp. 11–12). A *korzec* (pl. *korce*) contained in 1819, when it was stabilized, 128 litres or 3.5215 bushels, and was subdivided into 4 *ćwierci* and 32 *garnce*.

labour services for a superior lord like the peasants themselves. Distinct from the village *szlachta* were the sons of relatively well-to-do proprietors whose fathers could not provide them either with the land to sustain their dignity or the money to purchase the lease of a manor; for them there was no alternative but to find employment. In the first half of the eighteenth century there were few outlets for this noble proletariat. Some were absorbed into the administration of the estates of magnates and substantial landlords. The church was able to take a few, but the *szlachta* always showed a marked disinclination to become parish priests, because the parochial clergy, even of the Catholic Church, were recruited in the main from the peasants whose poverty, outlook and social inferiority they shared. There was therefore at the bottom of Polish society a noble element with little or no property which was ever seeking employment worthy of its rank. The petty *szlachta* were democratic to the extent that they wished for a wider distribution of wealth in their own favour, but they went no further than this. They were above all conscious of the rank which the possession of a coat of arms conferred upon them. The king was seen as head of the commonwealth, the *szlachta* its breast, the people its limbs, which the *szlachta* set in motion, but without independent action of their own. All civic virtues were found in the *szlachta*, whose occupation was politics and war, though the military functions of the nobility had long since declined. For the *szlachta* trade and industry were degrading, and it was not until the eighteenth century that the restrictions on entry into commerce and the crafts were formally removed. Within the caste there was supposed to be complete equality; *Szlachcic w swoim ogrodzie równy wojewodzie*—'the noble in his plot is the equal of the Palatine'—was the ideal to which the petty nobles all clung. There was little feeling that this equality should be shared with the lower ranks of society. One of the most unpopular acts of the Austrian monarchy, when it came into possession of Galicia in 1772, was the patent of 13 June 1775 establishing a social hierarchy for its Polish subjects. Two orders were created from the *szlachta*, the Magnates from the aristocracy, and the *Ritterschaft* from the medium gentry provided that they paid a minimum land tax of 300 crowns. The lower ranks of the *szlachta* were to be excluded from all voice in Galician affairs, an act which was considered to strike at the very heart of the ancient Polish tradition of equality within the caste and to reduce the poor *szlachta* to the level of the people.

Attachment to this theoretical equality was bound to have its effect upon politics. By comparison with Poland, British society was hierarchical in the extreme. Poles in their hearts considered that all opinions were of equal validity. Every Pole desired to play a role in politics in order to achieve a distinction which would mark him off from his fellows. Speeches tended to be grandiloquent, but usually devoid of more than the simplest meaning; the oratorical style found its way also into political pamphlets. The emphasis upon individual achievement accounts for the marked preference in Polish historiography until recent years for biographical study, disentangling the mass of recrimination and establishing whether or not the subject was justified in his actions. In the modern history of Poland there has been a remarkable instability in the personnel of politics; in periods of crisis individuals flit across the scene and hold the stage for the moment only. It was natural that members of the great aristocratic families, always ready to hand and held together by close ties of blood, should reappear time and time again at the head of affairs and represent a factor of permanence, but in the nineteenth century they were extremely sensitive to the accusation that they were seeking exclusive control of the country. They were conscious that the lesser *szlachta* had a strong argument when they asserted that many of Poland's misfortunes were due to the narrow oligarchical political system of the old Republic. In consequence even the aristocrats began to defer to the doctrine of *szlachta* equality in practice as well as in theory. This was all part of the change in the climate of opinion produced by the Partitions.

The transformation of the Polish gentry's political consciousness proceeded very slowly in the eighteenth century. This was not necessarily due to lack of public spirit, but rather because Poland had been overwhelmed by a series of disasters in the previous hundred years and time was needed for material as well as moral recovery. The victory of Gustavus Adolphus over the Polish armies in 1627 had been the beginning of a long period of turmoil and devastation. Sobieski's relief of Vienna was one of the few bright episodes amid the disasters of Cossack risings and Swedish invasions, culminating in the Great Northern War which left the Republic exhausted and unable to assert herself against foreign domination. The Dumb Diet of 1717 saw Poland firmly attached to Russia and her weakness was confirmed during the War of the Polish Succession. There was a general realization that in the first instance an army ought to be created to enable the Republic, if not to stand alone, at least to be an ally whose wishes would have to be consulted; but the raising of a large army was not possible without a new system of taxation such as would be suspect to a nobility which had little money to spare and which was obstinately attached to its immunities and privileges. The unsuccessful anti-king, Stanisław Leszczyński, was the first to suggest the army of 100,000 men which became an axiomatic plank of every political programme in the second half of the century.[1] On the death of Augustus III in 1763 the Czartoryski faction tried to carry a measure of moderate reform, but ran up against the opposition of Catherine II, who combined with Frederick II to secure the election of Stanisław August Poniatowski in 1764, but only with the preservation of the old constitution and the *Liberum Veto*. Though there was considerable opposition within the country to any reform carried by the Czartoryskis, the First Partition of 1772, giving to Prussia Ermeland, Royal Prussia, the Netze District and parts of Wielkopolska, to Austria the broad tract of Małopolska along the line of the Carpathians which received the name of Galicia, and to Russia all Polish territory north of the Dvina and large areas of White Russia up to the Dniepr and the valley of the Druc, was sufficient evidence even for the die-hard *szlachta* that the Republic was in a sorry condition.

The great issue of the years 1767–8 immediately before the First Partition had been that of toleration. The Russians and the Prussians in 1767 induced the Polish dissenters to form the Confederations of Słuck and Toruń and the Roman Catholics the Confederation of Radom, all of them in defence of their religions, and then engineered on 26 February 1768 the

[1] Cf. his book, *Głos wolny wolność ubespieczaiący* (1733), pp. 107–19.

C

Committee of the Diet's scheme for complete toleration for the dissenters. The Roman Catholics, believing themselves cheated, announced the Confederation of Bar on 29 February. Underlying their religious hostility to toleration was the fear of the political aims of the Czartoryskis and the new king, Stanisław August, whom they suspected of aiming at hereditary monarchy. The slogan of the Confederation was 'Freedom and the Church'. Its leader, Adam Krasiński, bishop of Kamieniec, declared the throne vacant since the death of Augustus III and insisted that it must in future be regulated according to the old system—*par succession, mais jamais le royaume héréditaire*. In the period of confusion which followed, rendered the more terrible by a peasant jacquerie in the Ukraine, the Czartoryskis abandoned Stanisław August, of whom, in any case, they had been only lukewarm supporters, and adopted an attitude of neutrality for fear of compromising themselves for ever with the mass of the *szlachta*. Stanisław August, deserted by his kinsmen and denounced as a tyrant by the Confederation of Bar, could do nothing but agree to carry on the Russian policy of toleration and break once and for all with his family.

The powers partitioned Poland at their convenience in 1772, but for Russia the results were not entirely satisfactory. Russian policy in the eighteenth century wavered between two courses, on the one hand the domination of all Poland by a system of indirect control, and on the other piecemeal annexations in the eastern territories of the Republic. The former involved the obligation of military intervention as far as the borders of Brandenburg, while the latter had the advantage of limiting Russia's commitments, for which there were always strong arguments when the Russian army was involved in war with Turkey. The Russo-Turkish war, which opened in 1767 and ended only in July 1774 with the treaty of Kutchuk-Kainardji, made it difficult to maintain an hegemony in Poland. The Partition of 1772 was therefore a victory for the annexationist policy, but with the termination of the Turkish war the old policy of indirect control was soon resumed. In March 1775 the *Rada Nieustająca*, or Permanent Council, was established, consisting of eighteen senators and eighteen deputies of the diet, the majority of whom were subservient to the Russian interest. It

POLAND AND THE PARTITIONS 19

supervised five departments, foreign affairs, police, war, justice and finance, and controlled the actions of the king. This was the first modern government which Poland had obtained, but the circumstances of its erection did not increase the popularity of Stanisław August Though the diet in September 1774 insisted upon the principle that the throne was elective and that no sons or grandsons of the previous monarch might become king, Stanisław August's record of collaboration with Russia and the composition of the Council created the impression that the king was nothing more than a creature of Catherine II. Catherine was determined that the new régime in Poland should be reasonably efficient and be able to maintain order. Under the Permanent Council the army was reorganized on Prussian lines and used frequently for distraint of taxes, an unheard of innovation, which kept alive the old fear that there was danger of absolute monarchy. No less worrying was the possibility of oligarchy, of which the seeds seemed present in the Permanent Council. In the quiet years of 1775–88 considerable confusion of thought was evident among the Polish opposition, but two points of view were to emerge, the reactionary which saw a solution in a return to the conditions of Golden Liberty, and the progressive, which desired the regeneration of the Republic by internal reform. The only point of agreement between the two was the wish to free Poland from Russian tutelage.

The party of the great magnates was naturally anxious to return to the old system, but it lacked homogeneity and could not produce a programme which consisted of more than personal grievances. The Hetman Branicki wanted the restoration of his powers over the army and the humiliation of the king's agent, General Komarzewski, into whose hands the effective command had been entrusted. Stanisław Szczęsny Potocki was anxious to maintain his position in Ruthenia, while Adam Kazimierz Czartoryski inherited the pique of his family that a Poniatowski had been preferred for the throne and, as a great Podolian landlord and General of the Podolian Lands, he too had an interest in the restoration of the old system. Ignacy Potocki, at this stage still thinking in the traditional terms of aristocratic intrigue, could conceive of opposition as a family affair. The Dogrumova scandal of 1784 is an indication of the character of this aristocratic faction. Dogrumova, in spite of her Russian name an Italian lady who was born Anna Maria de Neri, warned Adam Kazimierz Czartoryski that General Komarzewski and the councillor, Ryx, were engineering a plot to kill him and that the king was the ultimate inspiration of their designs. Branicki and Ignacy Potocki egged on Czartoryski to indict Komarzewski and Ryx, but the plot was revealed to be a complete fabrication and Czartoryski was heavily fined, though not before he had taken the opportunity in true aristocratic style to complain to the Prussian and Austrian courts that Stanisław August was plotting his downfall. The failure of this legal action served only to make the magnates more determined than ever to settle accounts with the king.

The opportunity for an attack on the royal administration came with the meeting of the diet in 1788. The death of Frederick II on 16 August 1786 was the starting-point for a new venture of Russia against Turkey in collaboration with Austria. Stanisław August tried to use the occasion of Joseph II's meeting with Catherine II at Kaniov to present a plan of reform for the Republic and achieve at the same time an increase of Polish territory at the expense of Turkey, in return for sending the reformed Polish army to fight side by side with the Russians. His reception on 6 March 1787 was cold and formal, and granted then only after he had been forced to kick his heels in Kaniov for seven weeks. In August 1788 Turkey declared war on Russia to forestall attack, but Catherine's final refusal of reform in Poland in June 1788 showed that even in a position of some difficulty she intended to uphold the arrangements of 1772–5. In the west however the settlement of the affairs of the United Provinces and the conclusion in June 1788 of the Triple Alliance of Britain, Prussia and the Dutch revealed a combination of the powers which might lend its support to Poland and enable her to defy Russia. When the diet assembled in the autumn of 1788 it needed only some slight encouragement for the reactionary opposition to throw off the Russian yoke. It came on 13 October when the Prussian ambassador offered the Republic a formal alliance. On 20 October the enlargement of the army to an establishment of 100,000 men was triumphantly voted. On 3 November the War Department of the Permanent

POLAND AND THE PARTITIONS 21

Council was abolished and the military administration taken over by a commission of the diet. On 18 December General Komarzewski was dismissed and on 19 January 1789 the Permanent Council itself was overthrown to complete the work of destruction. The reactionaries had achieved their end, but had raised for themselves the awkward question of the future organization of the state. The diet had assembled under the rules of a Confederation and there was no fear that the *Liberum Veto* would disrupt its proceedings, but only on 7 September 1789 was a committee to discuss constitutional reform appointed and that under the chairmanship of the bishop of Kamieniec, Adam Krasiński, leader of the Confederation of Bar, a fact which did not promise substantial changes. The reactionaries sat down to rule the roost and to wait for what would emerge from the machinations of Prussian diplomacy. Prussia concluded a formal alliance with Turkey in January 1790 and with the Republic in March, the implication being that Austria would be forced to surrender Galicia to Poland, while Poland in her turn would cede Toruń and Danzig to Prussia for her services. All this was to reckon entirely without consideration of the public discussion and enthusiasm which the issue of reform had raised. New elements were appearing to make suggestions for the better government of Poland which were little to the taste of the great feudalists.

Beyond the narrow circle of traditionally important political interests a new spirit was emerging, encouraged by the educational reforms of the quiet years. Poland was not left entirely untouched by the intellectual ferment in Western Europe. A Polish translation of Mably's *Traité de la législation* was published in 1783 and in 1784 a translation of Rousseau's *Discours sur l'origine de l'inégalité*, a title provocative to the Polish mind. The influence of western ideas was most apparent among the intelligentsia of lowly origin, especially among the priests. In 1785 the priest Stanisław Staszic startled Polish society with his pamphlet, *Observations on the life of Jan Zamoyski*.[1] Staszic's aim

---

[1] The full title in Polish is *Uwagi nad życiem Jana Zamoyskiego Kanclerza i Hetmana W.K. do dziesiejszego stanu Rzeczypospolitej przystosowane*, of which there is a good annotated edition by S. Czarnowski (*Biblioteka Narodowa*, Serja I, No. 90, Cracow, 1926). Some authorities give its actual date of publication as 1787.

was to give direction to the vague desires for reform felt by the younger generation by referring to the achievements of Jan Zamoyski, the great chancellor of the reigns of Stefan Batory and Zygmunt III, who was always thought of as the champion of the small man, though he himself built one of Poland's largest fortunes on the basis of his command over the lesser *szlachta*. Staszic called into question the whole structure of Polish society and pleaded for new principles which would end once and for all the stagnation of political life. Though he had little personal influence upon the course of events, his ideas were taken up by an active group of propagandists led by Father Hugo Kołłątaj, which took the name of *Kuźnica* or 'the Forge'. Kołłątaj and his friends showed that the much-vaunted principle of *szlachta* equality no longer had much foundation in fact. As much as the peasants and the townspeople, the mass of the *szlachta* was excluded from political rights. Only the aristocrats and the landed gentry had any rights at all. When the dietines met they summoned the lesser *szlachta* to support them, treating them as brothers, calling them equals and plying them with liquor, but in all else ignored them.[1] The plan of the Forge was to call in the lower ranks of the *szlachta* to redress the balance in the state and save the Republic from the anarchy to which the aristocracy had reduced it.[2] Therefore Poland needed an hereditary monarchy which would owe nothing to the aristocracy and would not be obliged to sign away its powers at each

[1] F. S. Jezierski published a pamphlet, a commentary in the form of question and answer upon the political condition of Poland, *Katechizm o tajemnicach rządu polskiego* (Warsaw, 1790), which is reproduced in part in *Kuźnica Kołłątajowska—Wybór Źródeł*, ed. B. Leśnodorski (*Biblioteka Narodowa*, Serja I, No. 130, Breslau, 1949). 'Question: How does equality work out among the noble order in the provinces of Małopolska? Answer: The great lords have vast inheritances and the great *starostwa* and on them they have tenant *szlachta* who by reason of their poverty, simplicity and duties in no wise differ from the serfs. The great men order them to the dietine as if to a corvée, there to elect their nominee as a representative or deputy, and when the other side offers resistance to fight it out in the usual manner, just as it is done in this country in disputes in frontier districts. To this *szlachta* commune at the dietine they liberally distribute spirits and mead and call them "Milords! Brothers! Vivat Equality and Freedom!" Thus once more *szlachta* equality makes its appearance' (p. 10).

[2] Staszic was most violent of all in his condemnation of the aristocracy in another pamphlet of this period, *Przestrogi dla Polski* (*Biblioteka Narodowa*, Serja I, No. 98, Cracow, 1926), pp. 76–7.

election. The *Liberum Veto* was an archaism which had been used to block all legislation. The diet ought to sit permanently and conceive itself as having the duty to pass laws rather than to protect liberties and privileges. Other reformers could point to the example of England, a country which managed to enjoy liberty and freedom under a strong monarchy. Many of the institutions of England might be adapted with slight modification to Polish conditions and thus produce the stability which Poland urgently needed.[1] Above all, the propagandists emphasized the need for a strong standing army, such as might have made the Partition of 1772 impossible, and enthusiastically approved the creation of the army of 100,000 men. The prospect that this army would afford employment to the lesser *szlachta* was not overlooked, as Staszic wrote in his Observations: 'If it should seem to the *szlachta* to be unfair that they have to be at once the citizens and soldiers of their country, which indeed is the foundation of Freedom, and yet it were not agreed to distribute the royal lands among the serving soldiers of our land, then you have no alternative, but of necessity to create a standing army.'[2] No less anxious for the poor *szlachta* was Wojciech Turski, who evolved a scheme whereby the rich were to be compelled to marry not the rich but the poor, considering that 'such a law would heal the worst evil of the commonwealth, shield us from the overweening power of the wealthy landlords and free the poor *szlachta* from serving in the houses of the lords, that is, from the service of an equal by an equal'.[3]

The tone of the reformers was threatening and it was plain that, though they had not won the ear of all the *szlachta*, at least the deputies of the diet were being shaken out of their narrow provincialism. There seemed a possibility that the whole fabric of Polish society would be destroyed and the noble class split into two hostile groups. The extreme wing of the conservative camp was beside itself with anxiety; men like Seweryn Rzewuski and Stanisław Szczęsny Potocki, two of the greatest landlords of

[1] Interest in England owed much to the influence of the court, for Stanisław August was an ardent anglophil. A court pamphlet of the period is I. L. Łobarzewski, *Zaszczyt wolności polskiey angielskiey wyrównaiący* (Warsaw, 1789).
[2] *Uwagi* (1785), p. 124.
[3] *Myśli o królach, o sukcessyi, o przeszłym i przyszłym rządzie* (Warsaw, 1790), pp. 26-7.

the Republic, protested against the principle of hereditary succession to the throne, but their arguments had much in common with those of the reformers, that Freedom was their aim, which in their opinion could only be achieved under an elective system. Rzewuski painted a terrifying picture of what a hereditary monarch might do; what else could the Poles expect but that he would

establish a new educational system so that the youth would acquire mental habits hostile to Freedom; incite the serfs in order to suppress the noble order with the aid of the peasants and place the yoke on the necks of both; extort taxes to destroy the landlords and weaken leading personages and affluent families to prevent the more powerful citizens from being able to come to the rescue of Freedom; question hereditary rights and noble property in order to get everyone enmeshed in the law; use influence in the courts to get his opponents under his thumb and fill the army with foreigners, persons with no sympathy for Liberty, and have them at his call to suppress Freedom?

The *Liberum Veto* was the only means of safeguarding *szlachta* democracy.[1] That a great nobleman should protest in this way and laud the principle of Freedom played into the hands of the propagandists. They turned to a historical analysis of elective kingship and produced arguments to show that it was an innovation of the magnates themselves at the time of the death of the last Jagiellonian king, Zygmunt August, in 1572.[2] Father Jezierski went still further into the past and invented a theory that the original Sarmatian inhabitants of Poland, a pure and simple people loving peace and free from sin, had been conquered by the Slavonians, a kindred people, but strong in war, who imposed upon them the institution of serfdom, so that the position of the privileged classes was founded on nothing but naked force. Jezierski did not live to pursue his Rousseauesque arguments, nor was it within the realm of practical politics to talk of the sovereignty of the people in Poland. The position taken by the reformers was that the people had natural rights, but that political rights were reserved to the propertied classes. Kołłątaj saw three orders in the state, the *szlachta*, the bour-

[1] *O sukcessyi tronu w Polszcze Rzecz Krótka* (Amsterdam, 1789), pp. 14–15, 19–20 n.
[2] F. S. Jezierski, *O bezkrólewiach w Polszcze y o wybieraniu królów* (Warsaw, 1790), pp. 7, 52–4. For an academically stronger but less effective conservative reply, see *Rozwagi o królach polskich, bezkrólewiach, elekcyach i sukcessyi tronu* (Warsaw, 1790).

geoisie and the peasants.¹ The peasants had no property² so that political rights could be demanded only for the bourgeoisie in order to unite them with the *szlachta*. In the first instance the bourgeoisie meant the heads of the banking firms in Warsaw, but ultimately it included all the Christian inhabitants of the petty townships of the provinces, many of whom were described as *mieszczanie-rolnicy*, or bourgeois farmers. Under the influence of Dekert, the burgomaster of Warsaw, who was in close contact with Kołłątaj, a congress of 141 royal towns was organized in November 1789 to press for the extension of constitutional privileges to themselves. The conservatives realized that this attempt to create a third estate on the French model might lead to the enfranchisement of a section of the population almost as large as the *szlachta* itself. To meet this danger they tried by the issue of no less than 422 patents of nobility in November 1790, to buy off the leading representatives of the bourgeoisie, a mass creation hitherto unheard of in the history of the Republic which in the sixteenth century had taken precautions to prevent the ennoblement of commoners.³ There was in all this an element of panic, for the conservatives were watching events in France and feared a similar development in Poland.⁴ Their efforts to detach the leading financiers did not succeed. On 18 April 1791 the reformers carried through a bill granting the townspeople equal rights with the *szlachta*, though it is important to remember that this freedom was limited to the inhabitants of the royal towns and that no attempt was made to interfere with the rights of landed proprietors in their own towns. The reformers had no wish to alienate the substantial *szlachta* unnecessarily.

By the spring of 1791 it was becoming imperative that the Poles should resolve their own internal differences.⁵ The

---

¹ Cf. *Kuźnica Kołłątajowska*, pp. 36–7, an excerpt from Kołłataj's *Listy Anonima*.
² I deal with this question in Chapter II.
³ Cf. *Volumina Legum*, ii, 971, Constitutions of 1578, No. 35. The grant of nobility could take place only in the diet or on the field of battle where a soldier had shown exceptional bravery.
⁴ The propagandists were quick to counter this conservative move in an appeal to the bourgeoisie not to desert the cause of humanity and surrender the Republic once more to oligarchical anarchy, cf. *Głos na prędce do stanu mieyskiego* (Warsaw, 1790), a pamphlet usually attributed to F. S. Jezierski.
⁵ The diplomatic background is dealt with in R. H. Lord's well-known study, *The Second Partition of Poland* (Cambridge, Mass., 1915).

Prussians had failed to extort Galicia from Austria, but in July 1790 had concluded the Convention of Reichenbach which was only an agreement that Austria should make no annexations at the expense of Turkey. The Swedes had withdrawn from war against Russia by the Peace of Varëla of August 1790 and in the spring of 1791 the Younger Pitt was compelled to abandon his design of forcing Russia to give up Ochakov. It could only be a question of time before Russia, free from her commitments in the south, would turn once more against Poland. It was clear too that Prussia could not be put off with a marriage of Stanisław August to a Hohenzollern princess, or alternatively with the designation of the elector of Saxony as king-elect with the obligation of contracting a similar marriage alliance in Berlin, but that she would demand the cession of territory in Western Poland, Danzig and Toruń, at least, as the price of supporting Poland against Russia, a course which would never be agreed to in the diet. Ignacy Potocki, with his own political career at stake decided to dissociate himself and his followers from the right wing of the oligarchical faction led by the Hetman Branicki, Seweryn Rzewuski and Szczęsny Potocki and to save his face by carrying through a measure of reform in alliance with the king, Stanisław August.[1]

The king's behaviour during the sessions of the diet had been moderate in the extreme and helped to dispel many of the fears that he aimed at making himself a despot. It was clear that he could attract the votes of a substantial section of the diet, especially after the elections of November 1790 when the number of deputies was doubled. A coalition therefore of the so-called Patriotic Party and the supporters of the king had a reasonable chance of pushing through a new constitution. At first, Stanisław August was suspicious of Ignacy Potocki's offer of friendship, but at length he accepted the alliance. In the winter of 1790–1 secret discussions were held in the castle in Warsaw and the draft of a new constitution prepared. Outwardly it was to appear that the king was the principal author of it, but in fact he was compelled to accept Ignacy Potocki's thesis that the monarch could be only the titular head of the

---

[1] For a critical view of Ignacy Potocki at this stage, see W. Kalinka, *Konstytucya trzeciego maja* (*Kwiecień-Czerwiec, 1791*) (Lvov, 1888), pp. 43–4.

state, the chairman of a council of ministers as he has been under the Permanent Council. In return Stanisław August was allowed a voice in the discussion of the details of the new settlement.[1]

The position of the reforming party was one of great difficulty. The debates in the diet during 1790 had shown that a variety of opinion existed on the precise details of a new constitution, while on the other hand there was no means of assessing the attitude of the mass of the *szlachta* in the provinces. The success of the bill for reform in the royal towns was encouraging, but the bill was not an infringement of noble rights, except in so far as it pointed the way to reform in the private towns by a voluntary surrender of privileges, and its passage was not a true reflection of the upper classes' state of mind. Fearing that they could not convince the diet, the reformers decided to stage a *coup d'état*, hoping that the lack of political organization among their opponents would make resistance impossible and that the new constitution would be accepted as a *fait accompli*. The *coup* was timed for Easter 1791 because during the holiday the deputies would drift off to their homes and would be slow in returning. It was secretly arranged that the supporters of reform should remain in Warsaw and vote the new constitution through the diet before their opponents returned. Out of 500 senators and deputies only 182 were present in the city, but of these 110 were in favour of reform. Ignacy Potocki and his party took the opportunity to bring before the diet the danger of renewed partition and urged that a new constitution was the only means of saving the Republic. The reform bill was there and then presented and passed amid scenes of great enthusiasm, along with some protests. When the other members of the diet returned the new constitution was already in existence.

In many ways the Constitution of 3 May 1791 seemed to be a complete break with the past. Legalized rebellion in the form of the Confederation was abolished. The *Liberum Veto* and

[1] Potocki and his friends were afterwards to place the blame for delay in the years 1788–90 upon the 'Moscow Party' with whom they declared the king was allied, for the purpose of glossing over their own failure to press for an early solution, cf. *O ustanowieniu i upadku konstytucyi polskiey 3-go maia 1791* (Metz, 1793), i, pp. 66–7.

elective kingship were abandoned. The throne after the death of Stanisław August was made hereditary in the person of the elector of Saxony and his male heirs. Otherwise the new constitution was a compromise solution which owed much to the settlement of 1775, avoiding the danger of personal government; the king was to rule in collaboration with a council of ministers (*Straż Praw*) and all his acts were to be countersigned by one of the ministers. The function of the king in council was to conduct the relations of the state with foreign powers and watch over the administration, which consisted of four commissions, of education, police (by which was meant internal affairs), war and finance. Though the members of the Chamber of Deputies had plenary and not legatine powers, the Senate retained a temporary veto. The franchise was given as before to the landed proprietors, their sons and relatives, and to leaseholders, provided that they paid taxes, in other words to all except the poorest of the *szlachta*; the right to vote in elections was granted to other persons if they paid 100 *złp* in taxes annually, a substantial figure which excluded all except the richest of the Christian bourgeoisie. Twenty-four representatives of the towns were admitted to the diet, though without the right of voting. The Jews remained without privileges. The principle that the state might intervene in the relations of landlords and serfs was established, though the machinery to make this effective was not defined.[1] Altogether, the Constitution of 1791 did little to alter the political balance in the Republic and left the upper ranks of the *szlachta*, as before, masters of the state.

Nevertheless some progress had been made towards satisfying the aspirations of the lesser *szlachta*. This was particularly evident in the military reforms of the period. In 1788 the diet gave its authority for the levy of 100,000 men, though the army never reached more than 65,000. In 1789, however, the method of recruiting was reformed and a measure of selective conscription for 7–8 years was applied. At the same time a commissariat was created. In the tiny army of 1791 are to be found the seeds of the militarism which became so strong a characteristic of the Polish gentry in the nineteenth century. In the place of the old general muster and the military units assembled by

[1] See Chapter II.

POLAND AND THE PARTITIONS 29

commissions of array was brought into being an army which, though small and incapable of fighting on two fronts, was a professional force, moderately well-officered and efficient by contemporary standards. Most significant of all, its officers and N.C.O.s were drawn from the lesser *szlachta* and therefore from the most radical element in Polish society. The army officers and with thém the literary men of the capital were ardent supporters of the Constitution, but the intervention of the powers was to dash to the ground the high hopes they entertained for the future.

The final dismemberment of the Republic was carried out in circumstances which had a profound effect upon the mentality of the Poles throughout the nineteenth century. The reception of the Constitution in the provinces was in the first instance mixed. The reformers had counted on taking the local *szlachta* by surprise and on being able to convert them and stir their patriotism when once they had recovered from the shock produced by the loss of their traditional privileges and had examined the new situation. In this they succeeded in the sense that the provincial *szlachta* did not break out into armed rebellion, but their attitude was cool. The dietines voted their thanks to the king for the Constitution, but half of them refused to swear their adherence to it.[1] The oligarchical party headed by Branicki, Rzewuski and Potocki, knew that they could not raise a spontaneous revolt against the Constitution, but that if they secured the aid of Catherine II they would be able to rally a large body of *szlachta* in the Ukraine and Lithuania. Under the protection of Russia therefore they organized the Confederation of Targowica in 1792. Their calculations proved correct, for they were joined by the lukewarm nobility of the east who looked upon themselves as rising in the sacred cause of Liberty. Much was made of the fact that the Constitution had in fact disenfranchised many of the poorer nobility.[2] The passing of the new constitution by a trick offended Polish sentiment which still

[1] Cf. W. Smoleński, *Ostatni rok sejmu wielkiego*, 2nd ed. (Cracow, 1897), pp. 60–1, for the attitude of Lithuania. A detailed study of Volhynia is C. Nanke, *Szlachta wołyńska wobec konstytucyi trzeciego maja* (Archiwum Naukowe, Dz. I, t. iii, Lvov, 1907).
[2] Cf. *Zbiur wszystkich druków Konfederacyi Targowickiey y Wileńskiey*, (1792), Cz. i, pp. 39–40.

adhered to the principle of unanimity and the supporters of the Confederation pleaded that they were only upholding the good old cause. Little did they realize the danger to which their action submitted the state. Prussia, who had in 1790 guaranteed the integrity of the Republic, and Russia, free from her commitments in the south, combined to reimpose foreign control and take what they wanted of Polish territories. In 1793 the Republic lost to Prussia almost all of Wielkopolska and to Russia all its provinces east of a line running in the north from a point on the Dvina near Dünaborg almost due south to where it met the Austrian frontier on the river Zbrucz, a tributary of the Dniestr. All that was left to the Republic was a meaningless tract of land including parts of Central Poland and the western half of Lithuania. The hatred of the lesser *szlachta* was directed as much against the men who had played into the hands of foreign enemies by adhering to the Confederation of Targowica, as it was against the faithless ally, Prussia, and Catherine II. Many of the followers of the Confederation realized too late the damage which their folly had done. The Constitution of 1791 had taken away many of their privileges, but this deprivation was as nothing compared with the humiliation of renewed partition and the disintegration of the Republic. For the moment all was confusion, but in the course of time the uncertain reception of the reforms of 1791 was forgotten and they came to be in the Polish national mythology not the work of intrigue and fraud, but the symbol of the community's regeneration from which there could be no going back. To call an opponent a 'man of Targowica' was the vilest insult in the political vocabulary of the Polish language.

This was however a long-term development. In 1793 the upper ranks of the *szlachta* were still at sixes and sevens and could produce no positive policy. The lesser *szlachta*, who had everything to gain from reform, even under the narrow constitution of 1791, were not disposed to accept the Second Partition without a stuggle and for the first time emerged as an independent factor in Polish politics, their patriotism roused and never again to be quenched by undue respect for the august families. Whatever else the Confederation did, it destroyed the divine right of the aristocracy to a monopoly of political power.

Allegiance to the national cause replaced the system of interest groups attached to the heads of the great noble households. By implication even those aristocrats who had not been party to the Confederation were discredited. In 1793, as in 1772, many magnates discovered that their estates fell outside the boundaries of the Republic and to save as much as possible from the disaster they were often prepared to bow and scrape before the partitioning powers. The king, Stanisław August, had acquiesced in the proceedings of the diet of Grodno which gave its unwilling approval to the partition under the compulsion of foreign bayonets. The bourgeoisie, too few and too timid for independent action and ruined by the events of 1792–3, wanted nothing better than the restoration of stability. The lesser *szlachta*, convinced that in moments of crisis the aristocrats would prefer their own private interest to the welfare of the state, saw themselves as inheriting the cause of Poland.

The insurrection of 1794 was thus the work of the small men, anxious to take advantage of the feelings of humiliation and indignation which were current in the country. They saw that the reduction of the army's size would soon make insurrection more difficult; recruiting officers of foreign powers had appeared to enlist the disbanded soldiers, whose loyalties, being regimental rather than national, could not be appealed to when once they had been dispersed. Two problems worried the left wing, the question of new political forms and the best moment for the rising. One group, the more moderate, wished to re-establish the constitution of 1791; the other, outraged by the conduct of the king in acceding to the Confederation of Targowica, demanded the abandonment of the monarchical principle and urged the creation of a republic. The men of 1791 were in favour of careful planning and waiting for the right moment for insurrection, while the republicans wanted to begin the revolt at the earliest opportunity. In the end, it was the mass arrests of 5 March 1794, an attempt at a proscription of its opponents by the new puppet government, which set off the revolt. Many of the revolutionary leaders were arrested and confessions led to more arrests. On 12 March a subordinate commander, Madaliński, called upon his cavalry brigade to revolt, but obtaining a weak response was forced to flee into Prussia. The group of

Polish leaders gathered in exile at Leipzig, Ignacy Potocki, Kołłątaj and the soldier, Kościuszko, was compelled to act. The fact that Kościuszko was chosen to lead the revolt which began in Cracow on 24 March 1794 is significant; he was the one Polish commander who had distinguished himself in the defence of the Republic in 1792. Under the old system supreme command fell to one of the great aristocrats, but in 1794 it was Kościuszko, a petty noble, who alone could inspire confidence. Nevertheless, Kościuszko himself made it clear that he had no intention of overthrowing the social order; in a letter to the Princess Czartoryska he wrote: 'God sees that we are not starting a French revolution.'[1]

It was not long before Kościuszko discovered that the left wing of the movement was not to be put off with the strict observance of legal forms. When he won his first success at Racławice on 4 April, where his peasant levies particularly distinguished themselves, the citizens of Warsaw and more especially the lower classes among them were emboldened to show their adherence to the insurrection. On 17 April there was a popular rising. Owing to the general bankruptcy of the Republic many of the leading families had given up living in the city. In consequence there was severe unemployment in Warsaw and the attitude of the craftsmen towards the upper classes, especially the members of the puppet government, was threatening in the extreme.[2] The insurgent council in the city found that it could not satisfy the demands of the lower classes led by the extreme left wing. Kościuszko attempted to solve the question by the creation of the Supreme National Council with himself as head, but the left wing continued to press for a more radical attitude and in particular the punishment of the men of Targowica. One result was the prompt trial and execution of four leaders of the Confederation. A radical touch was given to the rising by the manifesto of Połaniec, a call to the whole people to rise in which promises of economic justice were held out to the peasants.[3] Later, under the impression of defeat at

---

[1] T. Korzon, *Kościuszko*, 2nd ed. (Cracow-Warsaw, 1906), p. 331.
[2] For an excellent account of conditions in Warsaw in 1794 see W. Tokarz, *Warszawa przed wybuchem powstania 17 kwietnia 1794* (Cracow, 1911).
[3] See below, Chapter II.

POLAND AND THE PARTITIONS 33

Rawka and the fall of Cracow to the Prussians, which confined Kościuszko's field of action to the immediate vicinity of Warsaw, there were more popular demonstrations leading to the execution without trial on 27–28 June of nine of the extreme conservative party. The movement became so dangerous that Kościuszko detailed a whole cavalry brigade to restore order. 947 arrests were made, though 726 were subsequently found not guilty and only 5 of the ringleaders hanged. When Kościuszko was wounded and taken prisoner at Maciejowice on 10 October, the moderates, distressed by the violence of the lower classes and fearing Kołłątaj who had by now acquired the reputation of being the Polish Robespierre, secured the nomination of their own Wawrzecki as the head of the Supreme National Council. When the Russians stormed Praga and Warsaw fell there were many moderates as well as conservatives who thought that they had been delivered from the danger of bloody revolution and would probably have been more grateful to the Russian army if it had not been for its excesses at Praga.[1]

The memory of 1791 and 1794 long continued to trouble Poland. On the one hand it was felt that these years had seen a process of moral and political recovery which had been frustrated by domestic reaction and foreign intervention; even the conservatives felt guilty for their part in the Confederation of Targowica and many of their descendants were to show fine courage in the campaigns and revolutions of the future in an effort to wipe out what they considered a stain on the family name. On the other hand the memory of violence and passions displayed by the Warsaw insurgents of 1794 was indelible. The propertied classes feared the unruly elements of the city and were apprehensive of the lesser *szlachta*'s tendency to hang political opponents without trial. The radicals for their part continued to believe that in moments of supreme danger when the holy cause of independence was at stake summary executions and even lynchings were permissible. All Poles were

[1] Cf. Alexander Linowski's memoir, *Kołłątaj w rewolucyi kościuszkowej* (Leszno, 1846), pp. 29–31, 56, 82. The radical account of the revolution is J. Zajączek, *Histoire de la révolution de Pologne* (Paris, 1797). Zajączek accused the substantial proprietors of being only lukewarm for the insurrection, cf. pp. 89, 96, 99–100, 112–13, and considered that Kościuszko had been altogether too lenient in his treatment of backsliders, cf. p. 191.

D

united in the common aim of restoring their country's greatness, but they never ceased to be suspicious of one another's methods. Acute divisions almost invariably were to reveal themselves in moments of crisis and the pattern of 1794 to be repeated more than once. Revolutions were to be begun by individuals or isolated groups, the radicals to get the upper hand for the moment, and the conservatives to combat their extremism in the face of resolute enemy pressure when even a unified national movement had only small chance of success. Underlying Polish politics was always the question which side was to rule when independence had been won.

The Third Partition of 1795, which finally destroyed the Polish state, was the parting of the ways for the Poles. There was no longer even a small portion of independent Polish territory in which they could rebuild the Republic, for Austria, Prussia and Russia each took their share of what had been left in 1793. The western frontier of Russia in 1795 bore some resemblance to the later Curzon line except where Austria was already in possession of Galicia, but it is difficult to argue that Russia was concerned only to advance to the limit of areas where Orthodoxy might restore its influence. Large numbers of native Lithuanian Roman Catholics in Samogitia and elsewhere were embraced by the Russian empire, nor did Catherine II press claims to Uniate districts west of the Bug in the land of Chełm. A geographical and strategic explanation of the new frontier is as good as any. It ran in the north from the Prussian border, then along the line of the Niemen as far as Grodno whence it took the shortest possible route through the primeval forest of Białowieża to the river Bug, and passed along it to where it met the Galician frontier of 1772. It was a frontier which required the minimum of definition and surveying. The same use of river lines may be seen in the distribution of the remaining Polish territories between Prussia and Austria. Austrian Western Galicia was embraced by the rivers Bug, Vistula and Pilica with small modifications. The suburb of Praga was naturally part of Warsaw and a small triangle of territory east of the Vistula was given to Prussia to allow it to remain attached to the capital, while at the sources of the Pilica contours offered a better line of demarcation than the river.

Russia therefore took almost all Lithuania of 1569 and only a small part of the Kingdom of Poland, principally the eastern half of the *województwo* of Podolia, which was ethnically akin to the provinces of Volhynia, Kiev and Bracław, and portions of Podlasie and the eastern part of the land of Chełm, where the native Polish elements were similarly not strong. In terms of the ideologies of the nineteenth century Russia took no territories which were predominantly Polish and only a very small area which was Roman Catholic, the Duchy of Samogitia and that mainly native Lithuanian. It cannot be said that the Russian annexations destroyed a natural economic region. Parts of Volhynia it is true were accustomed to send grain down the Bug and thence by the Vistula to Danzig, but the Prussian interpretation of the commercial treaty with the Republic of 1775 had already subjected this trade to considerable obstruction, while on the other hand the Russian advance to the line of Dniestr in 1792 made the peaceful development of the Polish Ukraine possible and opened the way to the Black Sea for the landlords of the southern group of eastern provinces. By and large the new Russian provinces lost and gained very little by the changes, but for the Russian administration there were two complications. The loyalties of the Polish *szlachta* of the east could not be changed at will. The Poles continued to think of themselves as belonging to a different social and political system, insisting that they belonged to the West and had been nurtured in a civilization superior to that of the barbarian east. At the same time the Russian empire was in danger of being penetrated by the large Jewish population in the annexed territories and the Russian government became fearful that the commercial features of Polish life would be reproduced in Russia herself. It was for this reason that the imperial government attempted in the nineteenth century to confine its Jewish subjects to the areas annexed from the Republic or provinces freshly acquired from the Turks, a policy which tended to perpetuate the Polish appearance of Western Russia.

By contrast the division of Poland proper between Austria and Prussia was clearly artificial. The acquisition by Prussia of a large area of Polish territory from the Niemen in the northeast to the tip of Upper Silesia in the south no doubt benefited those regions in the sense that they were embraced within the Prussian economic system and no longer subjected to the same extent to the harsh treatment of customs officials in the shipment of grain and timber to the Baltic ports, but Austrian dominion over Galicia and Western Galicia effectively destroyed the economic unity of the Vistula valley. It is difficult to see how this division could have had any permanence. The history of Prussia and Poland might have taken a different turn if it had not been for the Napoleonic wars. Prussia already contained a large Slavonic population in Silesia and the Mazurian districts of East Prussia before 1772. In 1795 she was as much a Slavonic as a German state and might but for the disasters of 1806 have succeeded to all the Polish claims.

This suggestion is by no means as fantastic as it might seem at first sight, for there was always an inclination among the Poles to seek the restoration of the Republic by appealing to the self-interest of the partitioning powers. After 1795 the aristocrats turned for aid to the countries in which the majority of their properties fell, though at the same time trying to keep a foot in the other two camps if their subsidiary interests were at stake. They dangled before the three monarchies the possibility of a reconstituted Polish Republic which any of them might append to their hereditary dominions whether by direct dynastic link or through a cadet branch of their royal houses which would be accepted as the ruling family of Poland. The aristocrats realized that the *szlachta* by themselves, only 7–8 per cent of the population of Poland, could never succeed in recovering independence. From the social point of view the lesser *szlachta* had in 1794 shown a distressing tendency to seek a solution in radical reform. Reliance on foreign aid therefore seemed to the conservatives to offer a safer and surer means of restoration. Szczęsny Potocki in Hamburg maintained a correspondence with Catherine II and Zubov, though keeping other possibilities open by attending banquets in honour of the French Revolution. Adam Kazimierz Czartoryski courted Vienna, though his two sons, Adam George and Konstanty, resided in St. Petersburg as sureties of his good behaviour in Podolia. Polish magnates flocked to Moscow in 1797 to pay their respects to Paul I on the occasion of his coronation. The Prussian court was not without its Polish suitors. Even Jan Dąbrowski in February 1796, before he went into exile to command Polish legions in the service of France, submitted a plan to Prussia for an attack upon Austria to dispossess her of the two Galicias as she had been robbed of Silesia; the king of Prussia was to become king of Poland on the basis of the Constitution of 1791, raise a Polish army and attack Russia.

For the lesser *szlachta* the collapse of the Polish state was a disaster. The partitioning powers of necessity brought their own administrative systems to Poland. Their armies offered but a few opportunities for the mass of the Polish gentry. Those who were compromised in the events of 1794, for the most part lesser *szlachta* with a sprinkling of well-born names, could do little but emigrate and they were followed by many for whom there was no future in Poland. One group, of diverse social origins and even more diverse political opinions, established itself in Venice, where it pleaded for a pro-Austrian orientation. It pressed for peace between France and Austria to permit Austria to ally herself with Sweden and Turkey and to restore Poland under a Hapsburg dynasty. This concept may have been fanciful, but the reasons of the radical wing were interesting; they preferred Austria because Josephism was more thorough and far-reaching than the principles professed by Kościuszko's Supreme National Council. They thought it was undesirable that the two progressive powers of Europe, Austria and France, should waste their time in fighting one another. The Venice group did its cause little service when in August 1795 it established a 'Paris Deputation', which burst in on the Convention in September and by forcing attention to the Polish question in this importunate manner alienated the sympathies of many deputies. The folly of the Deputation strengthened the position of the milder 'Polish Agency' under the lawyer Barss, which took its stand on the moderate constitutionalism of Kościuszko. The Deputation, having failed in France, turned its attention to building up a network of organizations in Poland, but the 'Central Committee at Lvov' had only slight success. In emigration a small section broke away to form the 'Society of Polish Republicans', but it was evident that extreme radicalism was losing its momentum. That is in some measure a result of the changing character of the French Revolution itself. The petty *szlachta*, for all their pretensions provincial in outlook and radical not so much by conviction as through ambition, were discovering a new world undreamed of in Poland. Wherever they went they found states of a new type, with large armies and large bureaucracies. The organization of France was particularly impressive, offering endless opportunities of employment. French constitutionalism with its façade of consultation, the apparatus of reporting debates, its discipline and strength, seemed to offer the Poles everything they wanted. The petty *szlachta*, more clearly convinced than ever of the error of the Republic's extreme particularism, were converted to the worship of the state. The old regional loyalties, as far as the most active section of the Polish *szlachta* was concerned, were subjects for sentimental reflection, but no longer of practical validity. Etatism, centralism and power, which had seemed the very negation of the Polish traditions before 1791, came to dominate the thoughts of the *émigrés* and caused them to see salvation in the strengthening of the government and the expansion of the army rather than in social reconstruction. Idealization of the liberty of the individual was replaced by insistence on the liberty of the whole community with but slight regard for the interests of its separate members.

The efforts of the post-1794 emigration were necessarily military. Large numbers of Galician peasants conscripted by Austria were taken prisoner by the French armies and after some hesitation it was agreed that they should be employed as auxiliary troops in the service of the puppet government set up in Lombardy. They were organized into legions by *szlachta* officers under the command of General Jan Dąbrowski, but though there was in the early stages much egalitarianism in these formations the tasks which they were asked to perform were not the best training for exponents of liberty. The legions did in fact from time to time fight in the line, often against Austrian regiments which contained large Polish contingents, but their main task was internal security in Italy, where they were frequently called upon to put down peasant disturbances. The attitude of Dąbrowski was that only Bonaparte could assist Poland and that all his instructions ought to be carried out to the letter in order to establish a claim upon his gratitude, for which reason he encouraged his officers to observe a rigid discipline and not to question their orders. As Bonaparte's reputation grew, so the Poles more and more pinned their hopes upon him and many of the radicals shook off their idealism and became little more than condottieri in the service of France. The respect of the Poles for Bonaparte survived even the San Domingo affair of 1802. In order to get rid of an element which complicated his relations with Russia and a force which in 1801–2 mutinied on several occasions to obtain arrears of pay, he shipped off 6,000 officers and men of the Polish legions to San Domingo to suppress the negro revolution on the island. Many Polish officers left French service before the troops were transported and took the opportunity of the peace to go home. Others remained behind, their immediate hopes disappointed, but without their faith in Napoleon shattered, to form the nucleus for new legions when the renewal of war, this time in Germany, brought more Polish soldiers, conscripted into the armies of Austria, and later Prussia, within the grasp of the French.[1] The formation of the legions, whether in Italy or on the Rhine, was never the spontaneous response of the Polish people to the national cause, but the expansion of small cadres of *szlachta*. In these circumstances a distinct type of professional officer began to emerge which thought in authoritarian terms. One of the most famous of them was Józef Zajączek, who became more and more conservative with his advancement in the hierarchy of command until it was almost forgotten that in 1794 he was one of the most radical of Kościuszko's supporters. Chłopicki, Kossecki, Różniecki are but a few of those whose names spring to mind, who, though of petty *szlachta* origin, were ultimately to be renowned for their services to conservatism. Pride in one's rank was always strong in Polish society. Before the partitions there were only a few

---

[1] The Polish national anthem is derived from a popular tune of this period. One verse still contains a reference to Napoleon:
   'Przejdziem Wisłę, przejdziem Wartę
   Będziem Polakami,
   Dał nam przykład Bonaparte,
   Jak zwyciężać mamy.'
(We will cross the Vistula, we will cross the Warta, we will be Poles again. Bonaparte gave us an example how we have to conquer!)

hereditary titles in Poland, mainly of Lithuanian origin, or granted by foreign princes, the pope and the emperor, and the Poles had scrambled for the appointments which carried with them life titles, *wojewoda*, *starosta* and others. The partitioning powers had attempted to regularize the position of the more important *szlachta* by the mass creation of counts, so that the title of count came to be a target of petty *szlachta* abuse, indicating as it did successful collaboration with the enemy. Under the command of Napoleon Polish officers revelled in their new military ranks and gloried in the number of their medals, the marks of men who had not ceased to fight for their country. Proud of their achievements in the cause of Poland the military came to think of themselves as a superior caste for whom the rest of the community had to work.[1] This feeling was doubly strong because the civilian population naturally manifested its strong appreciation of the efforts of officers abroad when they reappeared in 1806 with the French army which overran Prussian Poland. There never was a Polish youth who at some stage did not wish himself to become an officer and share in this glory. Personal bravery and pride in the possession of a uniform should not however be identified with love of discipline. The old conception of *szlachta* equality, too firmly rooted to be lost entirely, remained. As every Pole was entitled to formulate his own individual policy for Poland, so every Polish officer saw himself as a commander-in-chief whose brilliant strategy and tactics, preferably at the head of the largest possible formation, would win the battle for independence. Every Pole yearned to play an outstanding role in his country's history and leave some memorial of his endeavours. In moments of success *szlachta* officers were capable of fine courage, but temporary setbacks for Polish arms were often attended by disputes and intrigues. From the Polish point of view no battle was ever lost because of the enemy's superiority, but because faulty disposition of their own troops or individual failure at critical moments had thrown the army out of gear. Generals who had failed to achieve success would put themselves at the head of renewed attacks to prove that at least their personal bravery was not to be questioned.

[1] Cf. J. U. Nemcewicz's unflattering opinion of Prince Józef Poniatowski's behaviour, *Pamiętniki 1811–1820* (Poznań, 1871), i, 172.

Napoleon recognized that the Poles were good soldiers as long as their discipline held, but when it broke officers were inclined to form a dietine and discuss the unsuccessful battle. The conflict of the conservative elements, based for the most part on the landed gentry who had stayed at home, and the *émigré* groups, which returned to the homeland with Napoleon, had by 1806 lost much of its bitterness. Conservative opinion had changed in the years of peace between France and Russia from 1800 to 1805. The aristocracy and the substantial *szlachta* had been able to take stock of the situation and, though they considered Napoleon an upstart, they saw that at least he was unlikely to permit revolutionary excesses. Indeed, he might do what the monarchies of Austria, Prussia and Russia had shown little inclination for, reconstruct the Republic in its old frontiers. It was this factor which forced Alexander I to enter into the game of competing for the support of the Poles when he arrived in Poland in 1805 and after the Tilsit settlement to negotiate with the leaders of the Polish *szlachta* in Western Russia. When in 1807, by agreement with Alexander I, Napoleon created the Duchy of Warsaw in the main from Prussia's annexations under the Second and Third Partitions, he was obliged to seek a solution which would satisfy both the upper ranks of society, men like Prince Józef Poniatowski, who took their stand upon the Constitution of 1791, and the representatives of the lesser *szlachta*, who though shorn of much of their radicalism wanted a French-style constitution and the introduction of French law, which they regarded as an essential condition of their advancement. Zajączek wrote to Napoleon in December 1806: 'Il faut à ce pays une constitution française, un code civil et criminel français et surtout un roi français. La dernière constitution de Pologne de 1791 est insuffisante pour son bonheur.'[1] He also urged Napoleon to place his trust in the radical Kołłątaj rather than in the aristocrats.[2] Hopes were current also that Napoleon would reward his Polish adherents with gifts from the public estates.[3] The enmity which the upper ranks of the

[1] 'Z korespondencyi Generała Zajączka 1806, 1807, 1811 i 1812', A. M. Skałkowski, *O cześć imienia polskiego* (Warsaw-Lvov, 1908), p. 342.
[2] *Ibid.*, pp. 344–5.
[3] *Instrukcye i depesze rezydentów francuskich w Warszawie, 1807–1813*, ed. M. Handelsman (Cracow, 1914), i, 7.

privileged classes showed towards Zajączek and Dąbrowski,[1] and pressure from Alexander I inclined Napoleon to a conservative solution. The territories of the Duchy were given to the king of Saxony as duke of Warsaw, because so weak a prince could give offence neither to Russia nor to Prussia. The effective control of the Duchy under an authoritarian constitution, supervised by a resident minister and the French military commander, was given over to the Polish conservatives. The introduction of French law was a gesture to the lesser *szlachta*, which in effect surrendered nothing to them. The liberty of the subject and equality of all men before the law were granted, but side by side with the old social structure. A diet was established, consisting of a senate in which there were six bishops, six *wojewodas* and six castellans, and a chamber of deputies composed of 60 members elected by the *szlachta* and 40 by the commons; the latter were elected by persons with a capital of 10,000 *złp*, which excluded all except the well-to-do. In fact, the deputies elected by the commons were almost all members of the substantial gentry and the few representatives of the bourgeoisie had no influence at all. The deputies held their places for nine years, one-third retiring every three, so that violent changes in the composition of the diet were unlikely to take place, while initiative in legislation rested with the ruler. Moreover, liberty of the press was curtailed so that the radical elements of Polish society might be kept under close control. The lesser *szlachta* were to be satisfied with the creation of a large army, but it was soon discovered that the Duchy of Warsaw, even when it was enlarged by the addition of Western Galicia and the district of Zamość in 1809, was too poor to support 100,000 men under arms. For financial reasons it was arranged that more legions should be raised to serve against the Spaniards and the British in the Iberian peninsula, though most of these troops were transferred to the Eastern European theatre for the campaign of 1812.

The Napoleonic *débâcle* in Russia and the advance of the Russian armies into central Poland in the spring of 1813 brought the collapse of Polish hopes, which had been so high in 1812 that the diet had formed a Confederation with the

[1] *Ibid.*, p. 10.

object of recreating the Republic of Poland. The Polish armies were swept along with the remnants of the Grand Army, and the politicians and aristocrats, who had enthusiastically joined the Confederation, quickly revealed that they had lost faith in Napoleon and transferred their hopes to Alexander I whose friendship with the younger Czartoryski, Adam George, seemed to offer the possibility that something might be salvaged from the wreck. The army publicly announced that for honour's sake it would remain with Napoleon to the last, though many of its officers subsequently resigned their commissions on a variety of pretexts. When honour had been satisfied the Polish troops swore allegiance to Alexander I and returned to form the nucleus of the army of the Kingdom of Poland established in 1815. Thus the traditions and training of the military caste in post-war Poland remained Napoleonic. The achievements upon which the Polish officer corps could pride itself had been won against the powers which after 1815 continued to occupy Poland. This was of little account to the professional officers, most of whom wanted nothing more than to retire at the end of their service with a pension, but it was a constant reminder to the Polish public that the Vienna settlement was imposed from without and was as much a forcible partition as the Partitions of 1772, 1793 and 1795. The sight in Warsaw of Polish officers who had entered Moscow with Napoleon was an encouragement to the younger generation to believe that Moscow might again be taken and with more lasting success.

The novelty of the 1815 settlement of Europe was that the Poles obtained international recognition of their subjection. The territories of the Duchy of Warsaw were partitioned by Prussia and Russia. The western half of Wielkopolska was given to Prussia under the name of the Grand Duchy of Posen, while the rest of the Duchy with the exception of Cracow fell to Russia and was given the title of the Kingdom of Poland, a separate political unit joined to Russia by the link of a common monarch. During and after the revolution of 1830-1 the Poles were to argue that the final act of the Congress of Vienna of 9 June 1815 gave them certain definite freedoms and that if the partitioning powers did not observe them the other signatory powers ought to intervene on behalf of the Poles. Article I of the Final Act was rather a statement, not so much of the rights of the Poles, as of the position of the powers.[1] Alexander I granted a constitution to Congress Poland in 1815, which stipulated in its first article that the Kingdom was bound to Russia by an indissoluble link. Outside the Kingdom the Poles were to enjoy representative institutions in accordance with the constitutional systems which applied in Russia, Prussia and Austria. This meant local diets in Prussia and Austria and provincial assemblies of the nobility in Russia. The partitioning powers assumed that, if they made these arrangements, which were entirely at their own discretion, they were entitled to the loyal co-operation of the Poles. This view was to deny a tradition which in Poland stretched back to the Middle Ages, to the concept of *diffidatio* and the confederation. The Poles continued to suppose that with the non-observance of a clause of the Vienna settlement all their obligations were automatically dissolved and that they had the right to obtain a settlement of their affairs by a European Congress, in its way, an international Confederation diet establishing new conventions and rules for the monarch, or even removing him altogether. Only this habit of mind can explain the Polish insistence upon rights which the Vienna settlement did not give. The signatory powers were under no obligation to intervene in Polish affairs, and indeed, had little right to intervene, if the Poles violated the first clause of the Final Act; the right of intervention in Polish affairs really amounted to little more than the power to demand that the Poles be treated in a humane manner. A good case could have been made for enforcing freedom of commercial intercourse between the various portions of the pre-1772 Republic, a stipulation which

---

[1] 'Le Duché de Varsovie, à l'exception des Provinces et Districts, dont il a été autrement disposé dans les Articles suivans, est réuni à l'Empire de Russie. Il y sera lié irrévocablement par sa constitution, pour être possédé par sa Majesté l'Empereur de toutes les Russies, ses Héritiers et ses Successeurs à perpétuité. Sa Majesté Impériale se réserve de donner cet État, jouissant d'une administration distincte, l'extension intérieure qu'elle jugera convenable. Elle prendra avec ses autres Titres celui de Czar, Roi de Pologne, conformément au Protocole usité et consacré pour les Titres attachés à ses autres possessions.'
'Les Polonois sujets respectifs de la Russie, de l'Autriche et de la Prusse obtiendront une Représentation et des Institutions Nationales, réglées d'après le mode d'existence politique que chacun des gouvernements auxquels ils appartiennent jugera utile et convenable de leur accorder.' *B. & F.S.P.*, 2 (1814–15), p. 11.

was not observed, with the consequence that the free city of Cracow established in 1815 became a centre of the contraband trade for the entire area, but in all else the signatory powers' rights were vague. In the long run the Poles were not really concerned with international rights, whether their own or the partitioning powers', for the Polish national ideal of independence throughout the length and breadth of the pre-1772 Republic was the very negation of the 1815 settlement. If appeal was made at all to the Vienna treaty, it was made because the semi-independent Congress Kingdom offered a base for future operations and therefore had to be defended.

The constitution for the Kingdom of Poland, which was drawn up under the general supervision of Adam George Czartoryski and promulgated in 1815, has often been regarded as a mark of Alexander I's liberalism. In fact, the aim of Alexander in granting Poland representative institutions was not to conciliate all groups of the population, but rather to bind the propertied classes closely to him. There was no better method of achieving this than by taking over with some alterations the system which was in force in the Duchy of Warsaw in 1813. The constitution of 1815 bore a close resemblance to the constitution which Napoleon drew up for the Duchy in Dresden in 1807. It established a diet which consisted of a senate composed of the nominees of the Crown, subject to the qualification that they were over 35 years of age and paid a land tax of over 2,000 *złp*;[1] and a chamber of deputies which drew its members from the medium landlords.[2] In theory the whole body of the nobility and the bourgeoisie was represented, but in practice property qualifications and the division of the country into territorial constituencies effectively reduced the influence of all except the most important *szlachta*. Each palatinate, or *województwo*, was divided into districts (*obwody*) and subdistricts (*powiaty*).[3] For

---

[1] The exchange equivalent of the Polish *złoty* (abbr. *złp*) was about 6d. in British money, though owing to the low level of Polish prices its purchasing power was double that amount. 1 *złp* = 30 *grosze* (abbr. *gr*) in this period.

[2] The French text of the constitution is given in *B. & F.S.P.*, 19 (1831–2), pp. 971–85.

[3] Reference is made here to the territorial divisions which existed from 1816 to 1842 and the administrative organization laid down in *Dziennik Praw Królestwa Polskiego*, i, 115–20, 383–4, and ii, 31–80. In 1844 after interim arrangements for two years the country was divided into 5 *gubernii*.

electoral purposes the constituency of the nobility was the subdistrict. The advantage which the substantial proprietors enjoyed under the 1815 constitution may easily be seen if the total number of persons of noble descent is broken down into its constituent portions. It was estimated that the population of the Kingdom in 1830 was 4,137,634 inhabitants of both sexes;[1] in 1827 there were, according to Rodecki, 301,971 persons of *szlachta* status, of whom 62,593 were heads of families.[2] Most of the *szlachta* belonged either to the class of petty gentry or to the large body of public officials and administrators of estates. The rural petty *szlachta* were concentrated in the *województwa* of Płock, Podlasie and Augustów, the north-eastern corner of the Kingdom, where there were 30,733 heads of families out of a total of 32,490 persons of this category for the whole country, which amounted to roughly half of the total number of heads of noble households. 21,126 heads of families are accounted for by the public officials and estate administrators, about a third of the total *szlachta* caste. With about five-sixths of the *szlachta* belonging to a depressed class, or dependent upon an employer for their livelihood, it follows that the number of independent voters, upon whom some form of electoral pressure could not be placed, was very small in the noble constituency. The number of substantial proprietors was almost the same as the number of rural communes, which totalled 5,373. By a decree of the viceroy of 30 May 1818 patrimonial justice was enforced on private and public lands.[3] The landlord, or in the case of the government estates the leaseholder, became *de jure* the *wójt*, an office corresponding to that of a justice of the peace, of his own lands, provided that they constituted a commune of at least 10 hearths, or households.[4] It is therefore reasonable to assume that the

---

[1] J. Słowaczyński, *Polska w kształcie dykcyonarza historyczno-statystyczno-jeograficznego opisana* (Paris, 1833–8), p. 215. Too great a reliance should not be placed on Polish statistics which are never reliable before the 1850's. Słowaczyński arrived at this figure by taking the figure for the end of 1831 and adding the estimated war losses suffered during the insurrection of that year.

[2] F. Rodecki, *Obraz jeograficzno-statystyczny Królestwa Polskiego* (Warsaw, 1830), Tablica iii.   [3] *Dziennik Praw Królestwa Polskiego*, vi, 34–41.

[4] Petty noble villages often linked themselves together to achieve a commune of ten households, thus preserving control over their own affairs, cf. the appendix listing rural communes in the district of Lipno in W. H. Gawarecki, *Opis topograficzno-historyczny ziemi dobrzyńskiey* (Płock, 1825).

number of landlords capable of wielding political influence by virtue of their social standing could not have been more than 5,373. The practical working of the constitution even in the large noble constituencies of the north of the kingdom ensured that only substantial proprietors were returned as members of the diet.

The representatives elected by the non-noble constituencies were in the main of the same social standing. There were fewer constituencies for the non-noble electors because the electoral unit was the district and not the subdistrict; 77 deputies were returned by the *szlachta* and 51 by the commons, which made certain that the nobility would in any case have a predominant voice in the diet. The non-noble franchise, which embraced men of property who paid the land tax or who had a minimum capital of 10,000 *złp*, together with persons distinguished by their intellectual attainments or social functions, men of letters, priests, schoolteachers and others, was too narrow to permit the election of persons whose interests differed from those of the *szlachta*. At the same time, the Polish towns, with the exception of Warsaw and one or two other places,[1] remained, as they had in the eighteenth century, in some degree of dependence upon the ground landlord. In 1830 there were 453 places classed as towns, of which 242 were owned by private persons and 211 by the government.[2] Most of them contained less than 4,000 inhabitants and the few voters in them could easily be influenced at election time.[3] In general it was the practice for the commons to elect landowners of noble status. The chamber of deputies must therefore be considered the medium of expression only of the upper ranks of the *szlachta*. A further safeguard against any infringement of the landed gentry's interests was the equal legislative power of the senate, composed of the very large landed proprietors.

[1] Warsaw had a population of 139,654 in 1830, cf. F. M. Sobieszczański, *Rys historyczno-statystyczny wzrostu i stanu miasta Warszawy do 1847* (Warsaw, 1848), p. 300.
[2] J. Słowaczyński, *ibid.*, p. 215.
[3] Szaniecki records that in the town of Pinczów in the 1820's there were 6,000 persons of whom 4,000 were Jews and without rights. The town was required to render 300 days labour services to the landlord each year, chiefly during harvest. The town had no accounts, while the landlord held the monopolies of the sale of vodka, wine, mead, meal and fish and had the exclusive right of milling, cf. *Pamiętnik Jana Olrycha Szanieckiego*, ed. M. Handelsman (Warsaw, 1912), p. 39.

It was also convenient for Alexander I to take over the French administrative system from the Duchy. At the head of the government was the viceroy, Józef Zajączek, who for all his radical past and connections with the extreme left in 1794, was considered suitable for the post and even dignified with the title of prince, and was to become as years went on the personification of devotion to the Russian connection.[1] The heads of the five ministries, finance, education and religion, justice, internal affairs and war, together with co-opted members, formed the Administrative Council. The function of the Council of State was the approval of drafts of bills to be submitted to the diet. Over all this the tsar's personal commissioner, the senator Novosiltsev, cast his eye, obstructing here and hastening there, without great power, but a nuisance to the Polish ministers, who had to meet his criticisms and justify their actions to the tsar. The medium of contact with the tsar was the secretary of state in the Polish Chancery at St. Petersburg. Important legislation was referred to the diet, but the tsar as king of Poland could legislate by decree, as could the viceroy in less important matters. All ministers and officials were nominated by the Crown. The diet in theory was to meet every two years for a session of one month; one-third of its membership was to seek re-election every two years. There was nothing liberal in all this. It was a constitution under which all effective power was in the hands of ministers appointed by the Crown, but which permitted periodic consultation with the substantial gentry. No more than the constitution of 1807 did it bring within its compass the lesser *szlachta*.

The army was reconstructed under the command of the tsar's brother, the Grand Duke Constantine. In 1830 it consisted of the Royal Guard, composed of an infantry and a cavalry regiment with ancillary services, and an infantry corps of two divisions with a cavalry corps of two divisions also. There were besides a general staff and miscellaneous subsidiary formations.[2] The army amounted in all to about 40,000 men, to which the

[1] A new viceroy was not appointed on Zajączek's death in 1826 and the chairman of the Administrative Council, Walenty Sobolewski, became the head of the administration in Warsaw.

[2] For the organization of the Polish forces in 1830, see B. Pawłowski, *Źródła do dziejów wojny polsko-rosyjskiej 1830–31 r.* (Warsaw, 1930), i, 1–8.

Russian empire contributed a small force attached to the person of the commander-in-chief and maintained out of the Russian treasury. In theory all inhabitants of the Kingdom were liable for service, but there were numerous exemptions so that in fact conscription was selective. The common soldiers were as a rule taken from the strongest of the landless peasantry, but the officers and N.C.O.s were volunteers of *szlachta* origin. Between 1815 and 1830 some 28,000 men were raised in the Kingdom, not enough to cause serious economic disruption nor yet to satisfy the Poles who still yearned for an army of 100,000 men, but more than enough to impose a serious strain upon the Polish treasury. The army absorbed nearly 50 per cent of the revenue of the Kingdom. For all its small size it was a good army; its morale was restored by Constantine after the disintegration of discipline attendant upon the defeat of 1812–13, though it must be admitted this was achieved by spit and polish methods. Constantine succeeded in communicating to it some of his own Russian military pride and reinforced the conception which the Poles derived from Napoleon that an army constituted a state within a state. It was difficult for the civil administration to make much impression upon an army commanded by the monarch's brother, himself an object of some curiosity for having resigned in favour of his younger brother, Nicholas, all claims to the throne, a circumstance which was not clear to the Poles until after Nicholas I's succession in 1825. Though he was a martinet, some Poles privately hoped that he might further the Polish cause, a task for which he had neither the energy nor the inclination.

The Poles could consider themselves fortunate that they had emerged from their ordeal with these slight gains. Indeed, the warmth of the reception which Alexander I received at the first meeting of the diet in 1818 was an indication that the Poles of the Kingdom were genuinely grateful for his efforts on their behalf, but it remained to be seen how the new order of things would work out in practice. The frontiers of Poland could be redrawn at will, but what could not be altered was the Polish community which had existed since the Middle Ages and which still existed in the social sense. The community of spirit among all Poles survived and at the bottom of their hearts they felt that an injustice had been done. A Pole could feel equally at home in Poznania, Galicia, the Kingdom or Western Russia, a sentiment which made the frontiers seem artificial.

Though the old ideal of independence within all the Polish territories remained the same, the Poles of 1815 were not the Poles of 1772. The Polish *szlachta* nation had been a byword in Europe for its particularism and its instability, but by 1815 new elements had been introduced into the national mystique. The state and the army had become objects of veneration, no longer things to be feared. Liberty had become synonymous with national independence, not with individual privilege. In one way the Polish *szlachta* had acquired a new sense of unity and purpose, but there was a fissure within the noble order, between the propertied element, agrarian and conservative in outlook, ready to collaborate with the partitioning powers in quiet years, and the non-propertied section, professional and radical, which found it difficult to accept indefinite dismemberment. Differences were not always to be pushed to extremes, for the poor *szlachta* aspired to become landed gentry, but successive crises were to reveal a cleavage. From 1815 to 1864 Polish politics were complicated by this rivalry within the educated class.

CHAPTER II

Economic Problems: Peasants and *Szlachta*

THE PEASANTS

THE history of Poland might have been altogether different if the Republic had been a naturally wealthy community. The cause of its downfall was as much its poverty as its constitutional weakness, a poverty which afflicted peasants and nobles alike. Even to the middle of the nineteenth century Poland remained a backward country with many relics of the medieval social structure. The peasants of all regions which had been embraced by the Republic before 1772 lived in circumstances of extreme misery. Western European writers often referred to them as the 'slaves' of the landlords. One of the arguments put forward for the enactment of the British Corn Laws in 1815 was the fear that Polish wheat, produced by slave labour, might undercut home-grown wheat. In the eighteenth century Coxe could comment upon the abject poverty and begging of the peasants of Central Poland and refer to them as 'cringing and servile'.[1] In the nineteenth century there was little change in their situation; Harro-Harring, himself sympathetic to the Polish cause, wrote in 1831: 'The Polish serf is in every part of the country extremely poor, and of all the living creatures I have met with in this world, or seen described in books of natural history, he is the most wretched. He is in a worse condition than the Russian serf, who is at least maintained by his master... in return for the cudgellings which he receives.'[2]

[1] W. Coxe, *Travels into Poland, Russia, Sweden and Denmark* (London, 1784), i, 169, 234.

[2] P. Harro-Harring, *Poland under the dominion of Russia* (London, 1831), pp. 255–6. Harring was not absolutely right here because the lord was in certain circumstances required to aid the peasant, see below, pp. 64–5, but his comment indicates the impression which Polish conditions made upon the outside observer. For a favourable comparison of the Russian with the Polish peasant, see *Rozprawa o przyczynach ciemnoty niektórych osób duchownych stanu niższego i o ciemnocie ludu wieyskiego* (Cracow, 1816), p. 43.

In Western Europe serfdom began to disappear from the fifteenth century onwards, but in Eastern Europe, and especially in Brandenburg, Poland and Russia, an altogether different social and economic development occurred. There serfdom was intensified, and the freedom of the peasants restricted during the period when in Western Europe the condition of the people was improving. The deterioration of the Polish peasants' lot is attributed to the expansion of the grain trade in the fifteenth and sixteenth centuries, the golden age of the Polish *szlachta*. Up to the middle of the fifteenth century the prevailing form of payment to the lord was the money rent. In the codification of Polish law by Kazimierz the Great of 1347 the peasants had definite rights against the lords.[1] In Małopolska one peasant could leave each village annually and in Wielkopolska two. By a statute of 1496 however they were for practical purposes tied to the soil.[2] From the fifteenth century the statute books are studded with regulations for the control of labour and the restitution of fugitive serfs. At first labour dues were light, consisting of eight to twelve days' service a year, but under the statute of Bydgoszcz-Toruń of 1520 the *szlachta* were authorized to exact one day per week from each peasant *łan*, the Polish equivalent of the virgate.[3] In the second half of the sixteenth century the *szlachta* exploited this initial gain to the full. The Polish currency, though stable enough in itself until the seventeenth century when debasement was practised on a large scale, was undermined by the influx of precious metals from the new world which made nonsense of traditional money rents. Labour which produced the grain sold in Danzig did not decline in value, and everywhere the *szlachta* increased services to the maximum. The Polish Crown, weak in all its dealings with the

[1] *Volumina Legum*, i, 29, 49–50, 54.   [2] *Ibid.*, i, 259–60.
[3] *Ibid.*, i, 394, 396. Cf. also O. Balzer, *Corpus Juris Polonici*, III (1506–22) (Cracow, 1906), where the two texts are printed side by side. A frequent condition of tenure of the fifteenth century, that the peasants 'work when they are ordered', should not be taken to mean unlimited labour services. This condition usually applied in areas where demesnes were not highly developed and services so slight that they were not worth defining, cf. M. Baruch, *Pabianice, Rzgów i wsie okoliczne* (Warsaw, 1903), pp. 117–18, for a good example of this. S. Orsini-Rosenberg, *Rozwój i geneza folwarku pańszczyźnianego w dobrach katedry gnieźnieńskiej w xvi w.* (Poznań, 1925), *passim*, regards undefined labour services as a mark of an underdeveloped demesne economy.

ECONOMIC PROBLEMS: PEASANTS

nobility, was able to do very little to protect the interests of the peasants even on the estates under its own supervision.[1] As early as the 1510's it was disclaiming the power to intervene on noble lands. Detailed evidence is lacking for conditions on private estates, but complaints which came before the courts which dealt with the crown lands show that there were cases here where leaseholders were exacting six days a week from the *łan* by the end of the sixteenth century. More and more land was taken into the demesnes, whether by purchase of the *sołectwa*—fields given to the contractors who had established villages for the lords under German law, by the assumption of lapsed peasant holdings, or by assarting from the waste; there is little evidence of evictions, for in a country where labour was in short supply dispossession of the peasants was uneconomic.[2] Labour services tended to be most severe in Central Poland where access to the entrepôt was relatively easy,[3] and declined towards the periphery of the state where the possibility of flight and the likelihood of war made peasants less willing to tolerate excessive burdens and the lords more cautious of undertaking heavy capital expenditure.[4] The political troubles of the second half of the seventeenth century and the first half of the eighteenth did little to improve the condition of the peasants. Cossack risings and Swedish invasions devastated the country and the Polish forces themselves were not backward in looting villages. The after-effects of war, plague and famine, added to the confusion. The population declined and holdings fell vacant.[5]

[1] Cf. I. T. Baranowski, 'Zmienne koleje statuta toruńskiego', *Przegląd Historyczny*, XVI (1913), 220 and 294 *seq.*

[2] From this expansion emerged the conventional medieval agrarian structure, villages without demesne lands, demesnes without peasants, or villages with both; the unit of exploitation was the 'key' (*klucz*) in which demesnes and peasant lands were integrated.

[3] In Royal Prussia where transport costs were low the practice was to use hired labour, cf. J. Rutkowski, 'Pańszczyzna i praca najemna w organizacji folwarków królewskich za Zygmunta Augusta', *Roczniki Historyczne*, IV (1928), 38 *seq.*, in contrast with estates up country where ready money was needed to cover the expenses of shipment.

[4] The flight of the peasants was a highly organized business. Nobles who needed labour sent out agents to attract peasants and assisted them in their flight, cf. S. Śreniowski, *Zbiegostwo chłopów w dawnej Polsce jako zagadnienie ustroju społecznego* (Warsaw, 1948).

[5] Cf. J. Rutkowski's analysis of royol estates in Red Russia, 'Przebudowa wsi w Polsce po wojnach z połowy xvii wieku', *Kwartalnik Historyczny*, XXX (1916), 323-4.

Land reverted to scrub, which produced neither grain nor timber. To keep as much land as possible under cultivation the nobility was forced to maintain the already high labour services. The peasants often could not be granted as much land as they held before the wars, for they would need more time to devote to the demesnes. The size of the peasant holdings, which even in the sixteenth century was diminishing, continued to decline in the eighteenth. Legally the period of transformation and resettlement following the wars was a misfortune for the peasants. Long-established conventions and customs were obscured and documents defining tenures were often lost or simply fell out of date.

It would be unwise to suppose a uniformity of conditions in Poland at the end of the eighteenth century any more than in the sixteenth. The incidence of labour dues and terms of tenure varied from region to region. Here and there were isolated communities which enjoyed remarkably good conditions. Nevertheless, the mass of the peasants were serfs whose lives were governed by certain well-defined legal and economic circumstances. In the legal sense the peasant was subject to all the limitations upon his personal freedom which were common to serf societies. The Polish word *poddaństwo* differed in practice very little from the German *leibeigenschaft*.[1] The peasant was tied to the soil. He could not change his lord, though he himself might be transferred from one holding to another. The peasants on the smaller private estates were worse off than those on the royal lands and on some aristocratic and ecclesiastical properties where attempts were made from time to time to impose restraints upon the leaseholders,[2] but everywhere the legal position of the peasant was bad enough. It was assumed from the wording of Article IV of the Act of Confederation of 1573 that

---

[1] J. Rutkowski, *Poddaństwo włościan w xviii wieku w Polsce i niektórych innych krajach Europy*, Prace Komisji Historycznej (Poznań, 1921), i, 69, maintained that the position of the peasants was by no means exceptional and was even more favourable than in some other countries; the evidence of travellers who had the opportunity of seeing with their own eyes Polish and other conditions would seem to suggest that materially the peasants in Poland were the worst off in Europe.

[2] The Czartoryski estates were notoriously underexploited in the eighteenth century, cf. I. T. Baranowski, 'Z dziejów gospodarki rolnej w Polsce,—Dobra puławskie pomiędzy I-ym a II-im rozbiorem', *Ekonomista*, VII (1907), 235.

ECONOMIC PROBLEMS: PEASANTS 55

the lord had the right of punishing his serfs with death.[1] It was only in 1768 that the lord was explicitly deprived of the *jus vitae et necis*; at the same diet the lord was for the first time made liable for the death penalty if he himself murdered a peasant; for which up to that time he had paid a *główszczyzna* or wirgild.[2] Some idea of the petrification of Polish society may be obtained from the fact that even in the eighteenth century free men commended themselves to a lord and entered into serfdom.[3]

A distinction must be drawn between legal serfdom and tenure by labour services, a distinction which the Poles themselves did not find easy to make. The incidence of labour services appears to have changed very little from that which prevailed in the sixteenth century. Money rents still existed, side by side with labour dues; they were not necessarily the sign of regions which were emerging from the feudal economy, for in the eastern districts of Lithuania which were notoriously backward they were often more frequent than in central Poland.[4] Peasants in the Duchy of Samogitia maintained a rare degree of independence up to the time of the Russian occupation in 1794, especially in the district of Telsze.[5] In this case proximity to the sea and the ability to market grain in Polanga and Memel seems to have enabled them to pay money rents. At the beginning of the nineteenth century the principle which operated in the sixteenth, that labour services tended to be lower in the frontier

[1] *Volumina Legum*, ii, 842.
[2] *Konstytucye seymu extraordinaryinego w Warszawie*, Warsaw, 1768, Articles XIX and XX, p. 94. Doubts have been expressed whether in fact the right of capital punishment was ever exercised, for it was not in the interest of the landlord to reduce the size of the labour force; B. Baranowski, 'Czy szlachta w xvii i xviii wieku mogła chłopów karać śmiercią?' *Państwo i Prawo*, III (1948), z. 12, p. 87, believes that capital punishment was normally imposed by the urban courts to which the *szlachta* referred serious peasant offences.
[3] J. Łukaszewicz, *Krótki . . . opis miast i wsi w . . . powiecie krótoszyńskim* (Poznań, 1869), i, 291 and ii, 127, cites two cases, one as late as 1764; the motive was to avoid prosecution in the courts.
[4] W. Wieczorek, *Z dziejów ustroju rolnego Wielkiego Księstwa Litewskiego* (Poznań, 1930), gives details of 1200 villages of Lithuania in 32 districts. In 1043 villages, containing 7,205 peasant holdings, 46 per cent of the land was held by money rents and 54 per cent by labour services (p. 39). No less than 680 villages investigated fell within the *województwo* of Vitebsk, the most easterly of the Polish provinces.
[5] Cf. F. Wrotnowski, *Zbiór pamiętników o powstaniu Litwy w r. 1831* (Paris, 1835), 'Pamiętnik Onufrego Jacewicza', Nota A, 'O stanie włoscian w powiecie telszewskim na Żmudzi przed rokiem 1794', p. 130.

areas, seems to hold good. The core of the problem was central Poland, though the advance of the Russian state to the Black Sea and the appearance of orderly government as the Turks were pushed back brought the same conditions to the southern Ukraine in the second half of the eighteenth century. The principal personal service was the performance of a number of days' service a week on the arable land of the lord (*pańszczyzna*). This service consisted of labour which required animals (*pańszczyzna ciągła* or *sprzężajna*), of manual labour only (*pańszczyzna piesza*), or of a mixture of both. A day with animals was reckoned in some districts as having twice the value of a day without, or in others as having one and a half times the value. Carting services were especially important in districts which produced grain for the export market. In some places, for example Lithuania, the peasants were under the obligation to abandon their own work, leaving only one woman in the house, and assist the lord in moments of sudden necessity (*gwałty*). Extra days in seasons of heavy work, whether as part of the normal schedule of services, or as compulsory hired labour were the rule throughout Poland; in the latter case, wage rates had often not changed since the beginning of the seventeenth century, and here manorial records could be exploited to the full by the lord, if he had them. There were besides many obligations to provide gifts in kind (*daniny*), consisting of eggs, poultry or delicacies like mushrooms, berries and even hops which grew wild in the woods. The time taken to gather wild fruits might vary from year to year according to their plentifulness. Obviously an assessment of the weight of labour services cannot be measured from the services on the arable land of the manor alone. The variety of miscellaneous labour services in Poland leaves the impression that there could not have been a more thorough exploitation of the peasants' physical resources.

It was customary to assume four or five different types of peasant landholders. The most important services, those of ploughing and carting, were rendered by the 'full-peasants', while beneath them was a class of 'half-peasants', holding only half as much land and rendering in theory only half the dues of a full-peasant. Lower in the social scale were the smallholders, tilling only a quarter or less of the land held by a full-peasant, and known by a variety of names, for whom the term 'quarter-peasant' may suffice. At the bottom were the householders who held no land, or at the most a few drills of potatoes or perhaps a thin strip of corn, and who earned a living by day labour. Beyond the peasant householders were the peasants who held neither land nor house, living either in the bothies provided by the manor, or in the houses of the landed peasants themselves, if they employed labour.[1] The function of the landless peasantry becomes clearer when the number of days' labour services is considered. In the first half of the nineteenth century it was thought normal and reasonable to ask of the full-peasant ploughing and other services requiring the use of animals up to 5–6 a week, or if animals were not used 10–12 days a week. For other types of peasants there was a sliding scale in proportion to this maximum. The half-peasant for example rendered only half these dues. In general it is true to say that the full peasants and the half-peasants rendered services with animals, while the quarter-peasants and the cottagers provided only manual labour; because ordinary manual labour was assessed as having only half the value of services with animals, the quarter-peasant might render up to four days a week and the cottager two days. Obviously, a full-peasant who celebrated Sundays and all the saints' days of the Roman Catholic or Uniate calendar could not by himself provide 5–6 days a week with animals or 10–12 days without animals. The explanation is that the unit for the assessment of services was not the individual peasant, but the peasant household. Opinions varied on the number of persons the family group of the full-peasant ought to contain. One writer, J. Sołtykowicz, writing in 1814–15 when the peasant question was under discussion and therefore likely to be overstating his case, urged that the ideal household of the full-peasant ought to consist of eight persons: the peasant,

---

[1] Much depends upon local custom in the description of the different categories of peasants. The full-peasant was usually called a *całorolnik*, or even plain *rolnik*, though some writers mean the same when they use the ancient term *kmieć*; the half-peasant was called *półrolnik*. Below these classes terms are confused; there were many gradations between the quarter-peasant and the peasant holding only a messuage in which his house stood; the difference between a *zagrodnik* and an *ogrodnik* will not always be easy to determine, so that extreme caution is needed in large-scale statistical analysis.

his wife, a ploughman, and his assistant, a serving girl, a cowherd, and a shepherd; while the labour value of the peasants' children might be reckoned as the equivalent of that of one able-bodied man.[1] To maintain this household he demanded two ploughs with enough animals to draw them, one team to perform labour services on the demesne, and the other to till the land of the peasant. The assumption was that the full-peasant ought to be able to devote himself entirely to his own land, sending others to perform his services.[2] The peasant question cannot be seen entirely from the point of view of the husbandmen who held land. The landless peasants were an integral part of the system. The organization of labour services was such that they were performed to a large extent by the peasants' labourers, who naturally did not bring their masters' best animals with them. In these circumstances there could be little thought of improving agricultural techniques on the demesnes. Manorial cultivation was geared to the standards of the lowest strata among the peasants. The function of the manor up to the time of the Second and Third Partitions and the wars, when the provincialism of Polish society was broken down and landed proprietors began slowly to realize the possibilities of improved husbandry, was limited to the supervision and organization of labour services. The manor, though it was in most cases the owner of the peasants' beasts, only in very rare circumstances at the beginning of the nineteenth century maintained its own draught animals, with the result that peasant lands were generally better manured than the demesnes. The lord often delegated the management of his lands to a steward and himself led the parasitical life of a round of entertainment and pleasure.

[1] *O przyczynach wewnętrznych i naybliższych tudzież zewnętrznych i dalszych nędzy naszych włościan* (Cracow, 1815), p. 40.
[2] F. Skorzewski, writing at the same time, held similar views, though he stated that in the lower reaches of the Vistula the full-peasants employed apart from their own families only two hired labourers and a serving girl; 'In the departments of Poznań, Bydgoszcz and Kalisz the full-peasant never used to perform draught services, but sent his ploughman instead. He never performed his dues with all his beasts, but sent horses and oxen to do the tasks of the manor always keeping some beasts to himself for his own use. And yet many have waxed indignant that the Polish peasant had to work from Sunday to Sunday without rest.' *Uwagi nad polepszeniem stanu włościan* (Bydgoszcz, 1814), pp. 7–8.

ECONOMIC PROBLEMS: PEASANTS 59

Even if the full-peasant did not himself perform services, it was not always possible for the manor to find men willing to occupy the largest holdings in the village. The essential condition for the full-peasant was that he should be able to find the labour necessary for the performance of the heavy labour dues. Owing to the high rate of infantile mortality in a country ravaged by smallpox, the number of peasant children who lived to adult years was often small.[1] Hired labour had in any case to be sought outside the family when peasants' children were under age. If the full-peasant failed to find enough labour he was unable to perform the heavy duties demanded by the manor. It is for this reason that in the last quarter of the eighteenth century and at the beginning of the nineteenth, writers were complaining that farmers of the full-peasant type were increasingly difficult to find, especially in Western Poland, with the important political consequence that the gap between the landed nobility and the peasants was widening, though modern research had shown that this feature was equally present in the sixteenth century. Villagers preferred to take holdings of the half-peasant type which did not require so much labour to maintain and for which at a pinch the services might be found from within the family. From the lord's point of view an obvious extension of this principle, if he wished, was to get rid entirely of full-peasants and half-peasants, centralize all draught animals at the manor and employ only hired labour for the ploughing services, but this was not an easy policy to carry out. New steadings had to be built and owing to lack of capital this transformation was not often possible. Where lords consciously employed this policy they waited for a full- or half-peasant holding to fall vacant and then incorporated it into the demesne rather than undertake wholesale evictions. In fact, the old system survived very little changed up to the 1830's.

Propagandists were interested in what ought to be the area of arable land a peasant of each class ought to hold. The general assumption was that the full-peasant held 30 morgs,

[1] 'In our country it happens that a woman will give birth to as many as twenty children and will not rear more than three, four or five of them.' 'About three-quarters of the children in the villages will die of smallpox and the other quarter will lie sick for a very long time.' *O poddanych polskich* (1788), pp. 68–9n.

the half-peasant 15 morgs and the quarter-peasant 4–7 morgs.¹ The councillor of state, Brodzki, speaking in the diet of the Kingdom of Poland in 1831, declared: 'We have a certain scale, that for the maintenance of one family is needed a definite area of land, at least 15 morgs in extent. There may be exceptions to this . . . but the general principle always remains.'² Sołtykowicz thought that a family of eight persons, with the task of providing six days a week with animals ought to have 60 morgs; this calculation was made on the basis of a peasant's having to maintain two plough teams.³ On the Czartoryski estates in Central Poland which were reorganized after 1815 on what were considered generous terms the full-peasant received 36–43 morgs, the half-peasant 13–17 morgs and the quarter-peasant, described as a *chałupnik*, 2·66 morgs.⁴ In the 1840's one writer complained that in England 22 morgs sufficed to feed one agricultural family and three non-agricultural families, while in Poland 705 morgs sufficed to maintain only 42 rural families, i.e. an average of 17 morgs a family.⁵ Fifteen morgs, the size of the half-peasant family holding, may reasonably be taken as the minimum which could sustain the household without obliging any of its members to seek paid employment elsewhere.

The really important question however was the distribution of peasants of each type on estates, which would be determined by the labour requirements of the manor, according to the number of plough teams needed to keep the demesne under

¹ The Polish *mórg* is the equivalent of the acre or the *arpent*, the amount of land which could be ploughed in one day. There were several types of morg in Poland, the most common being the Magdeburg morg, the Culm morg and the morg of New Polish Measurement, the last two differing very little. 30 morgs of New Polish Measurement equalled 29·06 morgs Culm. The morg of New Polish Measurement was 55·987 *ares*, the Prussian or Magdeburg 25·532 *ares*, and the morg used in Galicia 57·546 *ares*. The English acre was 40·467 *ares* and the Russian *diesiatin* 109·25 *ares*. Reference is made here to the Polish morg. For conversion tables for all Polish measurements and weights see J. Kolberg, *Porównianie teraźniejszych i dawnieyszych miar i wag w Królestwie Polskiem używanych* (Warsaw, 1819).
² *Dyaryusz sejmu z r. 1830–1*, ed. M. Rostoworowski (Cracow, 1907–12), ii, 577.
³ *O przyczynach . . . nędzy naszych włościan*, p. 45.
⁴ Konstanty Krompolc, *Sposób urządzenia włościan w dobrach Konińskiey-Woli dziedzicznych J. O. Xięcia Imci Adama Czartoryskiego* (1816), p. 7. The artificial figure for the quarter-peasant represents a conversion from Magdeburg to New Polish morgs.
⁵ 'Odwiedziny w Klemensowie i gospodarstwo michalowskie w roku 1844–5', *Roczniki Gospodarstwa Krajowego*, vii (Rok iv), Nr. II, 1845, p. 262.

ECONOMIC PROBLEMS: PEASANTS 61

cultivation and the manual labour to fulfil subsidiary tasks. The total of substantial peasants was always small relative to that of the lesser peasants. In a property of Count Jan Zamoyski, of 4,000 morgs in extent of which 2,800 were in the hands of the peasants, there were before its reorganization in the 1840's 21 full-peasants with 30 morgs, 102 quarter-peasants with 6 morgs, and 62 substantial cottagers with 1–4 morgs.[1] In the sixteenth century this social stratification received the recognition of the state in the subsidy law of 1564, levied in place of the obligation to serve in person, where the various categories of peasants were taxed in accordance with their means, the professional day-labourers, who were regarded then as the enemies of society, being the most heavily burdened class.[2] The difference between Poland of the sixteenth and Poland of the nineteenth century was that a growing population in the nineteenth century was beginning to press heavily on the land and that subdivision of peasant holdings was to reduce all but a few to the position of quarter-peasants. This process was however not much in evidence until after 1815 when peaceful conditions and a decline of the death rate made an increase in the population possible.

All accounts seem to show that there was little to praise in the Polish countryside. Writers of the late eighteenth and early nineteenth centuries almost invariably mention as the chief characteristic of the Polish and Ruthenian peasants their dislike of the lords. The peasants had developed a habit of mind which the *szlachta* found extremely irksome. They adopted an attitude of passivity and stupidity and refused to render the lord assistance beyond what was absolutely unavoidable. 'To work

[1] *Ibid.*, p. 284. A. C. von Holsche, *Geographie und Statistik von West-, Süd- und Neu-Ostpreussen* (Berlin, 1800–7), ii, 436–80, gives figures which would indicate that the process of parcelization and proletarianization was more advanced in the western areas than in Central Poland; in the Prussian department of Poznań in 1800 there were 7,415 full-peasants, 11,426 half-peasants, 11,076 quarter-peasants, 5,944 'eighth-peasants', 9,656 cottagers, 14,985 hired men, 14,721 farmers' boys, 20,882 ploughmen and 19,324 serving girls in a total rural population of 422,499, by contrast with the department of Warsaw where there were 12,069 full-peasants and 12,461 half-peasants in the much smaller rural population of 236,865. Holsche, *ibid.*, iii, 158–9, gives figures for West Prussia, but these do not agree with the figures given in the anonymous brochure, *Beitrage zur Beschreibung von Süd- und Neuostpreussen* (1803), i, 48. [2] *Volumina Legum*, ii, 661–3.

as you work on the demesne' was a saying for the lazy execution of a task in both Poland and in Russia. It is not difficult to imagine why this situation should have arisen. Stewards in particular, often men of little or no education and drawn from the brutalized petty *szlachta*, were sometimes merciless in their exactions, whether to impress the lord with their conscientiousness, or to obtain some profit for themselves from the system. The Polish equivalent of 'What the eye does not see, the heart does not grieve' was the expression 'The steward may hang the peasant for all the lord knows'. The nobility frequently responded to the peasants' hostility and go-slow tactics by keeping them at their labours for as many hours as possible. Other more enlightened manors discovered that by giving the peasants set tasks, on the completion of which they were free to go home, a form of agricultural piece-work, the labour services were performed more quickly.

A frequently voiced complaint of the *szlachta* was that the peasants were drunken and so corrupt by nature that effort to improve their lot was wasted. It is true that vodka was the only pleasure of their lives and that they drank it in large quantities, even administering it to their children as medicine. On the other hand the peasants' inclinations were encouraged by the proprietors themselves. One of the feudal rights of the lord was the monopoly of the distilling and sale of spirits on the manor.[1] In the fluctuating conditions of trade in the eighteenth and nineteenth centuries large stocks of grain were left on the hands of the *szlachta* who rather than let it rot used it for distilling and brewing. Galicia was famous for its rural distilleries and Galician politics before the 1840's turned very largely on the Austrian government's excise policy. It was in the interest of the lords to encourage their peasants to drink as deeply as possible. While on the one hand the lords might be ready enough to consider the reduction of full- and half-peasant holdings, there was not the least desire to reduce the number of peasants on estates, partly because a reserve of manual labour was essential and partly because evictions would leave fewer mouths to drink the manorial vodka. Some landlords tried to encourage peasants from other estates to buy their spirit by

[1] First granted in 1496, *Volumina Legum*, i, 269–70, and confirmed in 1768.

lowering the price or improving its potency,[1] which accounts for the not infrequent condition of tenures that peasants should buy no other vodka but their lords'.[2] Vodka had other uses. Proprietors normally had very little ready money and often paid their hired labourers in the form of vodka tickets which could be traded in the local inn, which was the property of the lord though usually leased to a Jew. This extreme form of truck payment accentuated what was already a social evil.[3] In the 1830's and 1840's with the resurrection of the public conscience the Church took the lead in establishing temperance societies throughout Poland, much to the annoyance of the landlords. Ludwik Górski could write: 'Some opponents of distilleries do not wish to understand that they were in some districts almost the only means of raising the standard of agriculture'.[4] From the point of view of the more enlightened propagandists the drunkenness of the peasants was caused by an inborn feeling of despair. They condemned the system of tenure and urged that only an improvement in the peasants' material conditions could develop that elementary self-respect which would make education a desirable attainment.

In all discussions of the relations of lords and peasants an important part was played by historical arguments. From the eighteenth century onwards attempts were made to discover what had been the original status of the peasant. One school of thought argued that the peasants were never the owners of their holdings, but had received them from the *szlachta*; to explain this state of affairs the theory of Norse conquest was developed, while those who rejected the crudity of this conception could nevertheless insist that the peasants were descendants of unfree people, slaves or prisoners of war whom the *szlachta* or their predecessors had settled on the land. Others insisted that the peasants were originally freeholders who had been deprived of

[1] J. Gluziński, 'Włościanie z okolic Zamościa i Hrubieszowa', *Archiwum domowe do dziejów i literatury krajowej* (Warsaw, 1856), p. 426.
[2] I. T. Baranowski, *Materyały do dziejów wsi polskiej* (Warsaw, 1909), p. 42.
[3] Cf. the complaints of the village of Pogorzel in 1789, *ibid.*, p. 52.
[4] 'O obecnym stanie gospodarstwa wiejskiego w Rawskiem i dalszym onego kierunku', *Roczniki Gospodarstwa Krajowego*, vi (1845), 127, though he went on to describe the effects in his own district of Rawa, where there were 11 deaths from drunkenness and allied causes in 1839, 18 in 1840, 33 in 1841 and 24 in 1842, in a total population of about 60,000, *ibid.*, pp. 160–1.

their rights by the *szlachta*, a theory supported by the undoubted belief of the peasants that they had definite rights to the soil. One difficulty was that there is not a single law to show that the *szlachta* were ever considered to have complete ownership of peasant lands, nor yet a statute defining the property rights of the peasants. The *szlachta* from the outset were concerned not with land ownership, for in a sparsely populated country like medieval Poland there was before the nineteenth century plenty of land for cultivation, but with their rights over the persons of the peasants, *poddaństwo* or serfdom, the right to control the labour which was in short supply. Conceptions of private property in land are comparatively modern in Poland.[1] Lords and peasants had mutual obligations, the peasant to support the noble in his political and military functions, the noble to protect and organize the peasant. There were many relics of the older society even in the nineteenth century. Throughout Poland the lord was regarded as having the obligation to come to the aid of the peasant in the event of harvest failure, or if a beast or building were destroyed by lightning. In the early nineteenth century the disadvantages of this custom were becoming apparent to the landlords. In the period before harvest when food was short, a period for which in Poland there is a special word, *przednówek*, the peasants customarily went to the manor for assistance. Often they took little trouble to husband their supplies, reckoning entirely on the aid of the lord. As late as 1849 J. Gołuchowski, a spokesman of the die-hard school of landlords, could see in this custom the real cause of the peasants' poverty; the charity of the lord encouraged the peasants to be wastrels.[2] The peasants were extremely anxious to establish their claim to the aid of the manor. They are said to have resisted proposals for the abolition of serfdom for fear that with it would disappear the duty of the lord to aid them in times of distress, their only form of social security; with this was coupled a fear lest emancipation should mean exclusion from the woods and pastures to which they felt the lord had a strong claim.[3] An

---

[1] Cf. H. Grynwaser, *Kwestia agrarna i ruch włościan w Królestwie Polskim w l-ej połowie xix wieku, Pisma*, ii (Breslau, 1951), 27.
[2] *Kwestya włościańska w Polsce* (Leipzig, 1849), p. 12.
[3] W. Surowiecki, *Uwagi względem poddanych w Polszcze* (Warsaw, 1807), p. 34.

extreme example perhaps was the custom of one estate on the Wielopolski lands, where a peasant on transfer from his holding to a larger plot was pushed and beaten to his new house; this custom had the approval of the peasants themselves, for it bore witness to the fact of compulsion and gave them the power to plead, if they failed to make a living in a new holding, that they had accepted transfer against their will and therefore had the right to ask the lord to make good the wrong he had done.[1]

The question of rights to the soil became acute only in the eighteenth century when ideas current in Western Europe filtered into Poland and among them the conception of universal personal freedom. Freedom for the Polish peasants meant the abolition of serfdom and with it of every means the *szlachta* had of compelling men to work on the demesne. Faced with the danger that the entire economy might be disrupted, Polish theorists maintained that the *szlachta* had complete ownership of the soil and that only the persons of the peasants were to be free. The peasants were to be forced to perform all the old duties whether by payment in kind, labour or money, and that by their economic dependence upon the lord. In place of the system of mutual obligation was to be substituted the relationship of landowner and tenant. The exact form of tenure was open to dispute. Those who claimed the maximum for the *szlachta* insisted that the rights of the landlord were absolute and that he might arrange and organize his estate at will. Enlightened thinkers like Staszic considered that the peasants could not be evicted arbitrarily and that the peasant was the hereditary tenant of his lands, so long as he fulfilled his obligations to the lord.[2] Staszic maintained also that there was a division between noble and peasant land and that peasant holdings might not be taken into the demesne.[3] Kołłątaj and his school were more representative, leaving these matters open for fear of antagonizing the *szlachta* whom they hoped to win over for the policy of political reform. In 1788 Kołłątaj wrote of the peasant:

He has no land, but he has industrious hands with which he can feed

[1] *Pamiętnik Jana Olrycha Szanieckiego*, p. 36.
[2] *O statystyce Polski krótki rzut wiadomości* (Cracow, 1809), p. 18.
[3] *Przestrogi dla Polski*, p. 147.

himself and enrich his lord. Let the lords be obliged according to their needs to make contracts with the peasants, as each may think best for himself, whether for rents or for work, provided that the rent or the work depends upon an honest assessment of the pure income of the land granted. Such contracts are acts of free will and both sides ought to observe them conscientiously.... Thus future legislation ought to preserve two essential conditions; the freedom of the peasant's person and the property rights of the landlord.[1]

The first public recognition by the *szlachta* of the need to resolve this question came in the Constitution of 1791, when some consideration of peasant rights could hardly be avoided. The question had been raised much earlier in 1776 when Andrzej Zamoyski had been commissioned to compile a new civil code in place of the muddle of statutes and privileges which passed in Poland for law. When his project was presented to the diet in 1780 it was in spite of its caution rejected. Though he proposed only that peasants who were born and bred in the same village were to have hereditary rights, while those who had come to villages from outside were to hold by contract, and did not touch the question of patrimonial jurisdiction or labour burdens, it seemed to the deputies that it was an unwarranted attempt at interference with the rights of the manor.[2] The words of the king's decision express the spirit of the opposition: 'We signify that we do not wish it ever again to be brought before any diet.'[3] In 1791 an attempt had to be made to bring Polish legislation into line with that of more enlightened countries. The great peasant disturbances of 1768 in the Ukraine left the Polish *szlachta* in the east in constant dread of another outbreak. In 1789 a brutal murder of a landlord in the Ukraine revived feelings of insecurity. In the years

---

[1] From *Listy Anomima* (11 October 1788), reprinted in *Kuźnica Kołłątajowska*, pp. 33–4.
[2] Cf. W. Heinosz, 'Stanowisko prawne ludności wieśniaczej w Zbiorze Praw Sądowych A. Zamoyskiego', *Roczniki dziejów społecznych i gospodarczych*, v (1936), 69 *seq*. who emphasizes the agrarian aspects of this code in contrast to M. Bobrzyński, 'Zbiór Praw Andrzeja Zamoyskiego', *Szkice i studja historyczne* (Cracow, 1922), ii, 376–92, who argued that Zamoyski had exceeded his parliamentary instructions, and W. Smoleński, 'Przyczyny upadku projektu Andrzeja Zamoyskiego', *Pisma historyczne* (Cracow, 1901), i, 369–77, who saw in its rejection the reactionary role of Russia.
[3] *Konstytucye sejmu wolnego ordynaryinego* (1780), p. 31.

ECONOMIC PROBLEMS: PEASANTS 67

1788–90 there were sporadic disturbances throughout the Republic which could not be ignored.[1] The fact that the new constitution was supposed to be a mark of Polish regeneration required at least some formal recognition of the *szlachta*'s willingness to make concessions to the people. In Article 2 it was assumed that the *szlachta* had complete property rights, but in Article 4 the reformers offered the peasants the protection of the courts: 'The peasant population we receive under the protection of the law and the government of the country, ordaining that from this time onwards any manner of freedoms, donations or agreements which the landlords have in fact arranged with the peasants of their estates shall constitute a common reciprocal contract. . . .'[2] For the peasants, if they were aware of the diet's good intentions, the Constitution was meaningless. What was meant by the protection of the law was not clear, for Polish law had never been codified and remained obscure. Likewise, the really important problems of security of tenure, the burden of labour services and immediate patrimonial jurisdiction were not considered at all. The reformers' concessions to the peasants seem a vague expression of good-will, so framed that no offence would be given to the extreme school of conservatives.

The timidity of the Polish reformers appears in its proper perspective when it is remembered that from 1772 parts of Poland had been annexed to Austria and had been subject to Austrian law, and that in Galicia the legislation of Maria Theresa and Joseph II had already gone a long way towards finding a solution which did no injustice to the peasants. In 1775 it was ordered that peasants were not to perform duties above the norms recorded in the old inventories. In 1782 Joseph II established a provisional limitation of labour services to a maximum of three days a week with animals for full-peasants and three days without animals for half-peasants. At the same time, absolute serfdom or *leibeigenschaft*, which Polish sophistry considered not to exist in Galicia, was abolished and with it limitations upon free marriage and prohibitions against

[1] The official report on the Ruthenian disturbances, *Relacya deputacyi do examinowania sprawy o bunty oskarżonych na seymie 1790 roku* (Warsaw, 1790), saw the matter as a manifestation of religious hostility instigated by the popes under Russian pressure.
[2] *Konstytucje polskie 1791–1921*, ed. M. Handelsman (Warsaw, 1926), pp. 39–40.

engaging in industry and trade. This and other edicts were codified in the Robotpatent for Galicia of 1786, framed in the spirit of the Robotpatent for Bohemia of 1785. This law may have been uneven in its effects owing to local variations; in the circle of Bochnia six days a week with animals had been the rule, but in the eastern districts, specially in the circle of Stanisławów, services had often been below the maxima laid down in the patent.[1] What influence Austrian legislation had upon peasants in the Polish districts bordering upon Galicia is not clear,[2] but Młodecki, who lived near Sandomierz on the Vistula, opposite the Galicia of 1772, could write in his appreciation of Joseph II's work: 'The peasants of the left bank of the Vistula, spurning a homeland which up to that time had been but a burden to them, crossed in crowds to the right bank.'[3] Whatever the truth may be in this matter the 84 paragraphs of the Robotpatent of 1786 form a striking contrast with the one article of the Polish constitution of 1791.

The vagueness of this clause did not escape contemporary criticism. One concession which the diet granted was the decree of 24 April 1792 recognizing the hereditary rights of peasants on the royal lands, but bringing no relief to the serfs on private estates. The desperate conditions of the rising of 1794 under Kościuszko extracted from the patriots a more concrete policy. Kościuszko called upon the people to rise and in his manifesto of Połaniec of May 1794 laid down the principle that henceforth the peasant was a free man enjoying the protection of the law. A whole series of concessions was announced, to last for the duration of the insurrection, after which they would receive formal statutory authority. Serfs performing 5–6 days' service a week received a remission of two days, while those who performed 3–4 days were remitted one. Peasant volunteers were not to be liable for services during their absence in the army and were guaranteed security of tenure. Landlords and officials who

---

[1] Cf. the complaint of I. L. Czerwiński, *Okolica zadniestrska między Stryiem i Łomnicą* (Lvov, 1811), p. 108.

[2] W. Tokarz, writing on the basis of the administrative survey of Galicia in 1783, declared that he discovered no evidence of immigration into Galicia from the Republic to take advantage of better conditions, *Galicya w początkach ery józefińskiej* (Cracow, 1909), pp. 240–1.

[3] *O polepszeniu teraźnieyszego stanu włościan polskich uwagi* (Warsaw, 1815), p. 17.

attempted evictions were to be prosecuted in the courts.¹ The manifesto did not differ much from Joseph II's legislation. No attempt was made to overthrow the serf economy, which the circumstances of an insurrection would not have allowed, but at least Kościuszko was willing to grant the peasants security of tenure and seek an alleviation of services, which no other Polish leader or group had ever seriously attempted before. The consequence was that the peasants rallied to the cause of Poland, a response which the revolts of the nineteenth century never obtained.

The final partition of 1795 can hardly be said to have brought additional hardships to the Polish peasants. The extension of Austrian rule to Western Galicia would indeed seem to have been an advantage to the peasants of that area. The Prussian government attempted at first to govern in accordance with Polish law, using the private compilation of Trębicki as a guide,² but the attendant confusion led to the introduction of the Prussian *Allgemeine Landrecht* in the annexed territories in 1799. The Prussian code, translated into Latin for the benefit of the Poles, still recognized the modified condition of serfdom, *Unterthänigkeit*, but it expressly forbade the lord to sell the peasant without his holding or to make any change in his material conditions which would leave him worse off than he had been before.³ Because the government made the landlords responsible for the maintenance of good order among the peasantry, there was little tendency towards eviction during the period of Prussian occupation. Moreover, the terms of trade were very much in favour of the landlords in the years 1800–5 when Prussian neutrality had the effect of attracting large orders for grain from the powers engaged in hostilities. Naturally, there was little inclination for eviction in Prussian Poland while the old methods of cultivation paid handsome profits.

It was the creation of the Duchy of Warsaw in 1807 which brought about a catastrophic change in the relations of Polish landlords and peasants. The Duchy of Warsaw was required to

[1] *Tadeusz Kościusko, jego odezwy i raporta*, ed. L. Nabielak, new edition (Cracow, 1918), pp. 172–9.
[2] A. Trębicki, *Prawo polityczne i cywilne Korony Polskiey y Wielkiego Xięstwa Litewskiego*, 2 vols. (Warsaw, 1789–91).
[3] *Jus Borussico-Brandenburgicum Commune* (Berlin, 1797–1800), ii, 281–2.

receive French institutions and in a decree of 17–21 December 1807, in elaboration of Article 4 of the constitution which declared that all citizens were equal before the law, it was announced that the peasants had complete freedom of movement and that they might not be kept on their holdings against their will.[1] In a supplementary decree of January 1808 the *Code Napoléon* was declared the legal basis of the Duchy from 1 May 1808[2] and was extended to Western Galicia and the district of Zamość after the war of 1809. The *Code Napoléon* had been drafted to give recognition to social and economic relationships which had emerged in France; in the eyes of French lawyers 'ownership is the right to enjoy and dispose of things in the most absolute manner, providing they are not used in a way contrary to law and regulations'. This conception took no account of the system of dual ownership adhered to in practice rather than in theory in Poland, but insisted that there could be only two conditions of tenure, ownership and tenancy, the latter being a freely negotiated contract between the tenant and the owner. In this way the landlords of the Duchy became the absolute owners of their estates and the peasants were left to make what terms they could with their masters.[3] The peasants of the Duchy lost the small element of security which the partitions had given them. Fashionable theories seemed to assure the landlords that this state of affairs was justified. Physiocratic doctrines demanded an organization of the state in the interests of the landed class, while Adam Smith appeared to condemn interference in matters pertaining to private property as an interference with the law of nature. For those landlords who wished to reorganize their estates on modern lines there were neither moral nor legal obstacles. New methods were becoming known and much might have been done to improve cultivation by the reallocation of peasant holdings and the consolidation of the demesnes.[4] Not all landlords were in

---

[1] *Dziennik Praw Księstwa Warszawskiego*, i, 10–12.   [2] *Ibid.*, i, 46–7.
[3] The authorities were well aware that this would be the result of introducing the Code, cf. H. Grynwaser, *Kwestia agrarna, Pisma*, ii, 38–41.
[4] Contemporary writers speak of the two- or three-field system as being universal, but there might be even within the normal village intensive and extensive agriculture in certain fields, cf. W. Styś, *Drogi postępu wsi* (Breslau, 1947), pp. 141–2. For a detailed study of agrarian techniques based on conditions in 117 selected

ECONOMIC PROBLEMS: PEASANTS 71

fact enthusiastic for the *Code Napoléon*, fearing that the peasants' new freedom might denude estates of labour.[1] The old idea that the wealth of an estate might be measured in terms of its number of peasants necessarily survived while the landlords lacked the capital to improve their methods. Debt and political preoccupations did not encourage attempts at modernization. These were conditions which existed in the Duchy of Warsaw, but much the same may be said of the other parts of Poland. Galicia of 1772 was crippled by war, inflation and state bankruptcy. Here the only outstanding changes took place in the district of Tarnopol, which was ceded to the Russian Empire by the treaty of Schönbrunn of October 1809. In this area the Polish lords, free from the irksome Josephine administration until 1815 when Austrian rule was restored, took the opportunity to carry out evictions. In the north-east Lithuania was devastated by the passage of French and Russian armies during the campaign of 1812–13. Of all the Polish territories only the Ruthenian provinces of the south-east, which were incorporated in the Russian empire, enjoyed much prosperity during the Napoleonic Wars owing to the rapid expansion of the Odessa trade. On the whole little occurred between 1791 and 1815 which can be said to have improved materially the lot of the peasants.

Before the creation of the Congress Kingdom in 1815 a committee of inquiry was set up in Warsaw to consider what steps ought to be taken to better the condition of the peasants, of which the guiding spirit as in drawing up the constitution was Prince Adam George Czartoryski, but the inquiry broke down amid a flood of contradictory advice and suggestion.[2] Alexander I, anxious to conciliate the *szlachta* and not unwilling to inherit

Galician villages, see J. Fierich, 'Kultury rolnicze, zmianowanie i zbiory w katastrze józefińskim, 1785–7', *Roczniki dziejów społecznych i gospodarczych*, xii (1950). In eastern Galicia run-rig was disappearing only at the end of the eighteenth century, cf. R. Rozdolski, *Wspólnota gminna w b. Galicji Wschodniej i jej zanik* (Lvov, 1936); in villages of this type the same social stratification of the peasantry existed as in the three-field village.

[1] Cf. *Instrukcye i depesze rezydentów francuskich w Warszawie, 1807–1813*, i, 308.

[2] A full account may be found in Z. Kirkor-Kiedroniowa, *Włościanie i ich sprawa w dobie organizacyjnej i konstytucyjnej Królestwa Polskiego* (Cracow, 1912), chapter x. A representative selection of opinion may be found in S. Kieniewicz, *Przemiany społeczne i gospodarcze w Królestwie Polskim 1815–1830* (Warsaw, 1951), pp. 197–207.

the centralized Napoleonic system, agreed to the retention of the *Code Napoléon*. The record of the government after 1815 reveals nothing which in any way benefited the peasants. By an order of 30 May 1818 it was laid down that the *wójt* of the rural commune was by law the owner of the property in which the commune fell.[1] The only control over the appointment was that the ministry of internal affairs should confirm it. The enforcement of patrimonial jurisdiction and the fact that the peasant required a passport to move from place to place, provided by the landlord in his capacity as *wójt*, meant that serfdom was as complete as it ever had been. The government did not normally interfere in the landlord's dealings with his peasants, except on occasions when it assisted him against the more recalcitrant of them. From time to time *szlachta* agitators who took up the cause of the peasants appeared in the courts to plead against injustices. The best known case is that of the lawyer Rupiński, who was commissioned by the peasants on the estates of Teresa Tyszkiewiczowa, Marshal Poniatowski's sister, in the region of Mariampol. The peasants accused the administrator, Linowski, formerly an adherent of Kościuszko, of raising dues, locating farm servants on peasant lands, increasing the number of inns unnecessarily, preventing the collection of fuel and manipulating the collection of taxes, but the viceroy, Zajączek, replied by placing Rupiński in prison, from which he was released only on the personal order of the tsar.[2] The authorities put a stop to protests from government lands by ordering in April 1824 that the responsibility for verifying the complaints of illiterate peasants lay with the person who drew up their depositions. Since the tenant of the manor held the rolls there was little possibility that the veracity of statements could be established. Discussion in the Council of State in September–October 1822 when reform on the government lands was considered came to nothing; reorganization of these estates had been attempted, but the peasants had offered resistance. In 1825, as a result of the decision to use Crown lands as security for the newly created

---

[1] *Dziennik Praw Królestwa Polskiego*, vi, 34–41.
[2] S. Askenazy, 'Trybun gminu', *Dwa stulecia—XVIII i XIX* (Warsaw, 1901–10), ii, 371–420. H. Grynwaser's researches reveal that there were other men like Rupiński, cf. *Przywódcy i burzyciele włościan, Pisma*, iii.

Land Credit Society, the regulation which permitted government peasants to purchase their lands was cancelled, lest inconvenient freeholds reduce the value of estates if ever they were surrendered to the Society for sale.[1] The minister of finance, Lubecki, regarded government estates as unproductive and from the moment of taking office in 1821 decided not to waste time with them, but capitalize them for the purpose of financing industrial development.[2] In 1828 he at length obtained authority to sell government estates,[3] a course which caused some humanitarians to object that it surrendered peasants who enjoyed good conditions to the caprice of private landowners, and others less idealistic to plead that the marketing of so much land would succeed only in reducing the value of real estate. In the diet of 1830, which was to sit throughout the revolution of 1830–1, J. O. Szaniecki, a petty *szlachta* radical who had made a fortune as a lawyer under the Duchy of Warsaw, presented through a friend, for he himself was too ill to attend the session, a petition for agrarian reform and the recognition of the peasants' property rights, though with due compensation for the landlords. The suggestion was received with derisive scorn by the deputies. The marshal of the diet was almost forced to close the sitting owing to the noisy protests of the members. Even afterwards in 1831 when the proceedings of the diet were published the petition was omitted from the records and survived only because Szaniecki had it published in the press.[4] The diet agreed with Count Jan Ledóchowski: 'There is no such thing as serfdom in our country. The peasants may move from place to place. They may come to agreements to compound for labour services. So there is absolutely no point in a petition for the abolition of labour services.'

In Congress Poland the old system continued as before. As luck would have it there has survived from this period one complete memoir of a peasant, Kazimierz Deczyński, the son of a peasant farmer and the schoolteacher in his native village, a

---

[1] *Dziennik Praw Królestwa Polskiego*, ix, 352–4.
[2] *Korespondencya Lubeckiego z ministrami sekretarzami stanu Ignacym Sobolewskim i Stefanem Grabowskim*, ed. S. Smolka (Cracow, 1909), i, 110.
[3] *Dziennik Praw Królestwa Polskiego*, xii, 169–80.
[4] *Pamiętnik Jana Olrycha Szanieckiego*, pp. 59–60.

government property in the *województwo* of Kalisz.¹ His account is a full description of the cruelties perpetrated by the tenant of the estate. It is a chronicle of beatings and violence against which there was no redress. When at length Deczyński complained to the treasury in Warsaw, making with the connivance of the notary a list of the old duties and the duties exacted by the leaseholder, an inquiry was conducted by the district commissioner in collaboration with the *wójt*, the very tenant against whom the complaints were made, and very naturally the decision went against the peasants. Deczyński for his pains was selected for conscription by the *wójt* and sent off to Warsaw with a covering letter to state that he was a dangerous agitator. Whether or not Deczyński's memoir is representative of conditions throughout the Congress Kingdom it is difficult to establish, but it is at least clear that the Kingdom cannot be considered as a splendid experiment pregnant with hope of a better future. In the years 1815–30 the administration was in the hands of Poles and though perhaps it was not left in undisturbed control by the tsar's commissioner, Novosiltsev, it was usually the Polish solution, dictated by the interests of the Polish *szlachta*, which in the end obtained approval in St. Petersburg. There was no large body of public opinion which was willing to raise a finger on behalf of the peasants. The comment of Gołębiowski is typical of the late 1820's: 'It is still not time to change them into rent-payers and the state of the country and experience confirms this, but perhaps the moment is not far distant when with the revival of the towns by industry and the whole of the country by internal trade the peasant also will recognize the object and usefulness of labour and will not need compulsion to it.'² In 1830 it was still considered necessary to conquer *szlachta* prejudice against the peasants and one Żukowski actually issued a pamphlet with this aim.³ There the matter rested when the revolution of November 1830 broke out.

There was no reason why Alexander I or Nicholas I should

---

[1] K. Deczyński, 'Opis życia wieśniaka polskiego', first published in M. Handelsman, *Żywot chłopa polskiego na początku xix stulecia* (Warsaw, 1907), which was considered so detrimental to the national cause that when Deczyński attempted to print it in France in the 1830's it was suppressed for fear of the harm it might do.
[2] L. Gołębiowski, *Lud polski, jego zwyczaje, zabobony* (Warsaw, 1830), p. 9.
[3] L. Żukowski, *O pańszczyźnie* (Warsaw, 1830).

ECONOMIC PROBLEMS: PEASANTS 75

have taken an interest in the conditions of peasants in Poland, for there was little pressure on them to improve the lot of the Russian peasantry. The Prussian government was in an altogether different position. In Prussia personal serfdom had been abolished by the decree of October 1807 and the main principles of economic emancipation had been laid down in 1811. The task of the Prussian administration in 1815 was to adapt the system to be applied in the German provinces to the Grand Duchy of Posen and the regency of Marienwerder which had been exempted from the scheme of 1811 on account of its local peculiarities. In the German districts only those farmers were embraced by the scheme who were settled on holdings registered as peasant land in the taxbooks. Peasants holding by hereditary right were entitled to two-thirds of their land, while those who held by temporary right or contract obtained only one-half. The execution of this decree was difficult enough in the German provinces. A regulation of 1816 limited its operation to those peasants who performed services with animals and excluded the smaller peasants, and only in 1821 were details of compensation for the landlords finally settled.

In the Grand Duchy of Posen it was not at first clear whether Prussian law or the *Code Napoléon* was valid. In 1815 the Polish landlords anticipated the application of the edict of 1811 to Poznania and used this legal confusion to carry out evictions; some 1,500–2,000 peasants are said to have been affected.[1] To prevent social disruption the Prussian government, while promising that the Polish regions would receive special treatment and that the *szlachta* would be consulted, in 1819 reintroduced the *Allgemeine Landrecht* and put an end to evictions.[2] The *szlachta* offered resistance to emancipation by every means in their power, some even advancing the curious argument that the edict of 1811 had been a concession to French ideas and that reforms on these lines would perpetuate French influence. The governor, Zerboni, who held large estates in the Polish areas, tended to side with the landlords. The viceroy, Antoni Radziwiłł, used all his influence at court to uphold the position of the

---

[1] A. Michalski, 'Włościanie i ich regulacya', *Biblioteka Warszawska*, 1845 (iii), 355.
[2] *Gesetz-Sammlung für die königlichen preussischen Staaten* (1819), p. 153.

szlachta under the *Code Napoléon*, but in the end continual discussion and consultation began to disrupt the economic life of the Grand Duchy and Radziwiłł, with the onset of the crisis of the 1820's, consented to the government's scheme which was issued as an edict on 8 April 1823.[1]

The solution in the Polish areas followed the general pattern for the German provinces, but in some senses the terms of emancipation were different. Only those peasants who performed services with animals or who used or needed a plough on their holdings were covered by the reform, but no distinction was made between the legal nature of holdings, whether they were held by hereditary right or by contract, or whether by written agreement or verbal. Labour services might be retained for a maximum of 24 years, but were limited to three days a week. Farm buildings with their messuages passed into the peasants' possession. It was granted that a freely negotiated contract of emancipation might be concluded by the two parties, provided that the lord did not take more than one-half of the peasant's land in compensation, and then only if the residue was sufficient for the employment of a pair of strong oxen. Where no agreement could be reached the state authorities were to enforce a settlement in accordance with an elaborate compilation of the rights of all kinds which the lord and the peasant surrendered to one another. Clapham has referred to this measure as 'an interesting case of calculated humanity'.[2] Undoubtedly the scheme was more generous than for the German provinces and did excite, owing to the willingness of Prussian officials to supervise its operation, the bitter criticism of the Poznanian gentry, but by the 1840's a note of satisfaction was evident and there were thoughts of applying it to the Congress Kingdom.[3] The Poznanian landowners had continued to agitate against the decree of 1823 and in 1836 extracted the concession that only those peasants who performed services with animals and who held not less than 25 morgs Magdeburg might be liable for

---

[1] *Ibid.* (1823), pp. 49–73.
[2] *The Economic Development of France and Germany, 1815–1914* (Cambridge, 1923), p. 44.
[3] Cf. P. Łubieński, *O uregulowaniu stosunków włościańskich w W.Ks. Poznańskiem i potrzebie zastosowania tegoż do Królestwa Polskiego* (Leipzig, 1843).

regulation.[1] Up to 1840 only 23,750 peasant holdings in the Grand Duchy had been regulated; these holdings amounted to 1,309,192 morgs Magdeburg, while 148,715 morgs of peasant land had been surrendered to the landlords by way of compensation. For the mass of the Poznanian peasants who were neither full- nor half-peasants there was no improvement.[2] Labour services, gifts in kind and compulsory labour at fixed rates survived in new forms; in the district of Odolanów, for example, there were peasants who for a plot of land less than one morg worked three days a week.[3] On some estates peasants were required to work all week at fixed labour rates. The creation of a substantial independent peasantry was achieved only at the cost of depressing the standards of the smaller peasants to lower levels than those of their fellows in the Congress Kingdom.

In the other Polish areas there were no comparable developments. Galicia, far removed from the sea and economically one of the most backward regions, stagnated. In Lithuania however the landlords seem to have appreciated the significance of events in Poznania and the Kingdom, the more so because of changes in Estonia and Kurland in 1816–18 where schemes of emancipation disadvantageous to the peasants had been approved by Alexander I. Relations between lords and peasants in Lithuania were not good. Landlords wished to increase labour services in order to wipe off arrears on debts which the peasants owed to the manors. Some scheme of emancipation on the lines of those existing in the Baltic provinces or under the *Code Napoléon*

[1] For a critical view of Poznanian emancipation see A. Krzyżtopor (pseudonym of Tomasz Potocki), *O urządzeniu stosunków rolniczych w Polsce*, 2nd ed. (Poznań, 1859), esp. pp. 224–5. A good short outline is W. Jakóbczyk, *Uwłaszczenie chłopów w Wielkopolsce w xix w.* (Warsaw, 1951). The genesis of emancipation is dealt with in M. Kniat, *Dzieje uwłaszczenia włoscian w wielkim księstwie poznańskim*, 2 vols. (Poznań, 1939–48); the second volume is unfortunately incomplete owing to the author's death in a concentration camp.

[2] W. Jakóbczyk, 'Z dziejów proletariatu rolnego w Poznańskim w połowie xix w.', *Przegląd Zachodni*, II/12 (1952), 595, estimates that 2·5 per cent of the population owned 67·35 per cent of the land in 1859. *Opisanie historyczno-statystyczne Wielkiego Księstwa Poznańskiego*, ed. J. N. Bobrowicz (Leipzig, 1846), pp. 44–8, states that there were 122,207 hearths in 1837, of which 30,889 were officially urban.

[3] K.G., 'O cząstkowych statystyczno-przemysłowo-rolnych opisach w W. Księstwie Poznańskiem', *Roczniki Gospodarstwa Krajowego*, II (1843), 13.

would have been to the advantage of the lords, but in spite of the agitation of the district assemblies in Lithuania Alexander I was not willing to listen to Polish requests, no doubt fearing assimilation of Lithuanian to Central Polish conditions.[1]

The peasant problem must inevitably engage the attention of historians of Poland, whose judgment of the attitude of the *szlachta* can hardly fail to be severe, but it would be unwise to suppose that it was merely a question of oppression of the poor by the rich. The poverty of the landlords themselves to a large extent determined their unsympathetic approach to the needs of the common people. The plight of the peasantry was only one aspect of the agrarian crisis of the nineteenth century.

The *Szlachta*

The landed proprietors of Poland emerged from the Napoleonic Wars almost overwhelmed by a crushing burden of debt. Poland was not a rich country and recuperation from the devastation of the war years was naturally slow. The position of the landed gentry was not made any easier by the fluctuation of the grain trade before and after 1815. Though Poland's chief port, Danzig, remained an integral part of the state from 1772 until 1793, it was cut off from the hinterland by Prussia's annexations under the First Partition. The Prussian government used its control of the lower reaches of the Vistula to place every obstacle in the way of the export of Polish produce. The Prussian aim was in part to increase the customs revenue, and in part to protect the landlords of Brandenburg-Prussia from Polish competition. The control of Stettin, Königsberg and Memel and the virtual control of Danzig meant that Polish trade to the Baltic depended entirely upon the good will of the authorities in Berlin. The official 12 per cent *ad valorem* duty agreed under the commercial treaty of March 1775 was always much higher in fact owing to the arbitrary valuation of Polish cargoes by Prussian officials. In consequence the grain trade slumped with serious results for Polish finances; in the absence of ready sources of credit at home the Polish government had in

---

[1] Henryk Mościcki, 'Sprawa włościańska na Litwie w pierwszej ćwierci xix wieku', *Odbitka z Biblioteki Warszawskiej* (1908), saw Alexander's refusal as evidence of his deviation from liberal ideas, but this is to ignore economic problems.

ECONOMIC PROBLEMS: *SZLACHTA* 79

the end to seek the aid of Dutch loans.[1] With the Prussian occupation of large tracts of Polish territory in 1793–5 the situation was reversed. The Polish provinces of Prussia no longer suffered from the exactions of the customs officers and obtained unimpeded access to the sea. On 5 April 1795, by the treaty of Basel, Prussia withdrew from the war against France and remained neutral until 1806. During the years 1795–1805 Prussian, and therefore Polish, grain was much in demand in Western Europe. Poor harvests in Great Britain especially sent shipmasters to Danzig in search of grain. Polish landlords under the dominion of Prussia began to enjoy an unprecedented prosperity. One landlord in Western Poland recalled that 'we had to count the money on the floor for want of room on the tables'.[2] The landed *szlachta* took full advantage of the increased demand and inflated prices. In 1791, 12,119 lasts of wheat were exported from Danzig. Exports rose in 1796 to 26,881 lasts, in 1800 to 40,864 lasts and maintained that level up to 1805. The average price of a quarter of wheat in 1791 was only 35s. 5d., but it reached 76s. in 1800 and 80s. 6d. in 1801. Prices in Warsaw were not as high because prices in Danzig included the cost of shipment down the Vistula and drying in the granaries. The usual method of transport was the raft which could not keep out water and allowed the grain to germinate if it were not attended to. Nevertheless there were increases in Warsaw prices; in 1800 the quarter of wheat cost on an average 47s. 10½d., and in 1801 33s. 9½d., which compared very favourably with an average price of less than 20s. in 1791.[3] The natural result of the boom was feverish speculation in landed estates

[1] For details of the Prussian trade war against Poland see J. A. Wilder, *Traktat handlowy polsko-pruski z roku 1775* (Warsaw, 1937). For a contemporary view see T. Czacki, *Refleksye nad uszkodzeniem dla kraiów polskich wynikaiącym z zaniedbywania handlu ochodzącego z mnieyważenia porzuconey nad Gdańskiem opieki* (1790), esp. pp. 6–7.
[2] F. S. Gajewski, *Pamiętniki (1802–1831)* (Poznań-Lvov, 1912), i, 11. To some extent the peasants also benefited, cf. F. Skarbek, *Pamiętnik Seglasa* (Warsaw, 1845), p. 87.
[3] I take these figures from W. Jacob, *Report on the Trade in Foreign Corn and on the Agriculture of the North of Europe*, 2nd ed. (London, 1826), appendix 13a, pp. 164–6, which gives information supplied from Prussian sources by Alexander Gibsone, the British consul at Danzig, and appendix 22, p. 178, which gives figures for Warsaw. More detailed figures for Warsaw prices may be found in S. Siegel, *Ceny w Warszawie w latach 1701–1815* (Lvov, 1936), and for Danzig in T. Furtak, *Ceny w Gdańsku w latach 1717–1815* (Lvov, 1935).

with borrowed money. At the time of the Republic's collapse native Polish banking firms had been bankrupted,[1] but in Berlin there was a surplus of funds for investment. In Prussia land prices were relatively high, but in Poland they were low. From the Prussian point of view there was considerable inducement to invest in the Polish area. For their part Polish landlords were equally disposed to accept Prussian money, because the Warsaw rate of interest was at its lowest 5 per cent,[2] while Berlin financiers could offer mortgages at rates varying from 2 per cent to 4 per cent. Polish landowners and speculators hastened to take advantage of these conditions. The Prussian government and semi-official institutions, veterans' funds and educational establishments as well as private bankers were able to invest large sums in the new territories. It is almost impossible to determine how much was invested by Prussians in these years, but Strzeszewski, the most recent historian of this episode, declares that it was about 150,000,000 złp of which two-thirds belonged to the Prussian government itself.[3] Polish Prussia was therefore much more seriously affected than the German districts. Land values are said to have risen 30 per cent in Brandenburg-Prussia and nearly 100 per cent in the Polish provinces.

With the deterioration of Franco-Prussian relations in 1805 it was natural that Prussian creditors and banks, well aware that Polish troops were serving with Napoleon and that if an opportunity arose the Poles would rise against Prussia, should begin to call in their investments. A crisis was averted only by Prussian defeat at Jena in 1806 and the occupation of the Polish provinces. When the governing commission, set up on the order of Napoleon, began its work in the occupied provinces on 18 January 1807, the most pressing task was to find a solution of the debt question. The director of justice, Feliks Łubieński, submitted a plan for a moratorium which was signed on 30 January.[4] Landlords were given a respite until January 1808. Napoleon, though ready to make concessions to the Poles, was

[1] See W. Kornatowski, *Kryzys bankowy w Polsce 1793 roku* (Warsaw, 1937).
[2] S. Siegel, *op. cit.*, p. 170.
[3] C. Strzeszewski, *Kryzys rolniczy na ziemiach Księstwa Warszawskiego i Królestwa Kongresowego, 1807–1830* (Lublin, 1934), p. 125.
[4] *Materyały do dziejów Komisyi Rządzącej z r. 1807*, ed. M. Rostworowski (Cracow, 1918), i, 508–13, Wyrok względem moratoriów.

ECONOMIC PROBLEMS: *SZLACHTA* 81

a man of business and aimed at making them pay at least part of the costs of the campaign. By the treaty of Tilsit almost all Prussia's gains under the Second and Third Partitions, with the exception of Toruń which was retained, and the district of Białystok, which was annexed to Russia, were bestowed upon the king of Şaxony and given the title of the Duchy of Warsaw, but in the first instance these areas were surrendered to Napoleon personally who then disposed of them as his private property. Though the actual territory was granted to the king of Saxony, Napoleon reserved to himself the disposal of Prussian state assets. The so-called *amty*, Prussian crown lands formed of the Polish *starostwa*, were handed over on condition that grants already made from them to French generals and other officers were upheld, but debts due to the Prussian state were for the moment retained by Napoleon; credits of private Prussian citizens remained their own and were not subject to confiscation. Napoleon's aim was to mobilize his assets as quickly as possible. On 10 May 1808 the convention of Bayonne was concluded by which Prussian state credits were ceded to the Duchy in return for a lump sum to be collected and paid into the French treasury within three years.[1] The real difficulty was the varying estimates of the total value of Prussian state credits. The sum demanded under the convention was 20,000,000 *fr.* at 5 per cent interest; the French government calculated that Prussian credits amounted to 43,366,220 *fr.* 51 *cent.*, with 4,000,000 fr. interest outstanding. From the French point of view the Duchy was endowed with a substantial sum,[2] but Polish estimates were very much lower than the French.[3] Difficulties arose in deciding what was a Prussian state credit and what was purely a private credit which under the terms of the Tilsit treaty and the Franco-Prussian convention of 8 September 1808 was not liable for confiscation. Some debtors claimed that they had never been paid the sums they were alleged to owe, or that they had not been paid in full. An

[1] Martens, *N.R.*, i, 71–4.
[2] Napoleon thought that it was 60,000,000 fr., *Correspondance de Napoléon, 1807*, xv, no. 13007, 8 August 1807.
[3] F. Skarbek, *Dzieje Xięstwa Warszawskiego* (Poznań, 1860) i, p. 213 n. put the total at 29,969,030 fr. 60 cent., but the ministry of justice thought it was even lower.

G

added cause for discontent was the declaration in the Kingdom of Prussia of a moratorium on 1 December 1807 which was to last until 24 June 1810. Polish debtors compared the action of Napoleon very unfavourably with this lenient decree and complained that if they had known that they were to be treated as Napoleon had treated them they would never have taken out the loans in the first place. One means of evasion was simple. Debtors demanded the mortgage deeds on the ground that otherwise they might be faced with the danger of having to pay twice. This meant careful inquiry in Prussia and led to protracted and difficult lawsuits.

Apart from the purely legal aspects of collection there were complications which resulted from the new territorial division and the Duchy's participation in the French system of alliances. The *szlachta* of the Duchy no longer enjoyed the advantages which had come their way within the neutral Prussian Kingdom. Agricultural produce could no longer be exported, but was requisitioned at the French intendant general's rates for the supply of the French forces in the Duchy and the new Polish army which was being created. By the Fontainbleau decree of 18 October 1810 all powers in diplomatic relations with France were required to accede to the Continental system.[1] Severely hit already by exclusion from the wider market and now with little prospect that the export trade would again flourish, the landlords were required to pay heavy taxes for the maintenance of the new state and the army. From 1806 to 1813 conditions were as bad as the previous years under Prussian rule had been good. Properties were sold for ridiculously low prices until the promulgation of a decree fixing two-thirds of an estate's estimated value as the minimum price in the case of sale to pay off debts.[2] Worse still was to come. The failure of 1812 brought in the early spring of 1813 a Russian army into Central Poland,

[1] For the Polish edicts complying with Napoleon's order see *Dziennik Praw Księstwa Warszawskiego*, ii, 434–60.

[2] *Ibid.*, iii, 351 *seq.* The decree was issued after the notorious affair of Załęze Małe, a property which sold in 1796 for 27,850 *złp* and resold in 1800 for 45,000 and for 50,000 in 1805; the purchaser was unable to pay the vendor in full and was ued in 1808 for 11,829 *złp* 4 *gr.* with interest outstanding. The property was put up for auction and bought by the vendor for 12,500 *złp* from which the debt was subtracted, cf. F. Czermiński, *O towarzystwie kredytowem ziemskiem w Królestwie Polskiem*, i, 33–4.

which treated the Duchy as occupied enemy territory. The difficulty of drawing upon supplies from Russia meant that the Duchy was compelled to supply almost all the needs of the Russian troops. In spite of these adverse conditions under the Duchy and during the Russian occupation of 1813–15, the Polish landlords were able to escape, to some extent, from repaying their debts until 1822. This was especially true in relation to debts owed to the state. On 30 May 1808 the king of Saxony, as duke of Warsaw, ordered the collection of sums due under the terms of the Bayonne convention, but very little money was forthcoming. A decree of 8 October 1808 ordered administrative distraint with compulsory sale of properties where debtors continued to refuse payment. The French resident, Serra, insisted that the sums could be collected, in spite of the opposition of Łubieński, now minister of justice.[1] The French foreign minister, Champagny, declared that credits of certain Prussian institutions also came within the terms of the convention.[2] In spite of French pressure it was clear that in view of the universal distress some measures of relief were needed. A moratorium on private debts was declared for one year by the decree of 18 June 1810,[3] which was extended again in 1811 and 1812.[4] The Bayonne debts were treated separately. Three schemes were evolved for collection; the general stagnation of trade which even the French were forced to admit meant that in fact the Bayonne debts could not be collected within three years. A decree of 16 April 1810 conceded a postponement of payment for ten years,[5] while a second decree of January 1811 granted those who wished to join the scheme a term of 41 years for repayment, for which a state credit institution was set up with the object of funding landed debt.[6] For those who did not wish to join the 41-year scheme a plan for 16-year period of repayment was devised at a lower rate of interest, 3 per cent instead of 5 per cent.[7] The disaster of 1812 nullified these efforts to solve the question

[1] *Instrukcye i depesze rezydentów francuskich w Warszawie, 1807–1813*, i, 124, 28 December 1808.   [2] *Ibid.*, i, 134–6, 31 January 1809.
[3] *Dziennik Praw Księstwa Warszawskiego*, ii, 224.   [4] *Ibid.*, iii, 313–14; iv, 331–2.
[5] This decree is not printed in the *Dziennik Praw* and is known only from the preamble of a subsequent decree.   [6] *Ibid.*, iii, 174–91.
[7] *Ibid.*, iii, 347–8, 21 June 1811.

and the Russian temporary government set up in Warsaw in 1813 decreed a further moratorium until the settlement of the whole issue by the peace treaty. In 1815 all sums ceded to Napoleon by the treaty of Tilsit reverted to the Prussian state.[1]

The position of the Polish landlords in 1815 was little short of desperate. The aim of the Russo-Prussian convention of 30 March 1815 which restored the Bayonne sums was to smooth out their difficulties. It was agreed that there should be a six-year moratorium on all debts owed to Prussia and Prussian subjects by citizens of the new Kingdom of Poland, at the rate of 4 per cent interest per annum. At the expiry of the moratorium creditors could claim annually one quarter of the total debt. In other words, a collection was foreseen which was slightly more lenient than the original Napoleonic scheme for settlement within three years. Polish lawyers sought some relief in the interpretation of these terms, pleading that the quarter after the initial repayment was in fact 25 per cent of the residue of the debt and not of the original total. By a decree of 16 July 1817 Alexander extended the moratorium on all private debts incurred before 20 June 1815 to 1 January 1821, which was confirmed at the first meeting of diet on 26 April 1818.[2] This moratorium was continued at the next meeting of the diet until 24 December 1821, the date on which the moratorium on Prussian debts ceased.[3] The real crisis came in 1822 when the whole problem of agrarian debt, whether owed privately within the Kingdom or due to the Prussian government and subjects, was reopened. The plight of the *szlachta* was aggravated by the onset of an economic crisis in this year.

In the first few years after 1815 the gravity of the situation was not apparent. In 1816, 12,821 lasts were exported from Danzig, 21,142 in 1817 and in 1820 as many as 30,001. It seemed for the moment that the prosperity of 1800–5 might return. Prices were high and the burden of debt might have

---

[1] *Dziennik Praw Królestwa Polskiego*, ii, 480. The Russo-Prussian convention of 30 March 1815, with the additional article, ii, 484–93.

[2] *Ibid.*, iii, 381–8, and v, 407–8.

[3] *Ibid.*, vii, 102–4, Law of 12 October 1820. As far as debts owed to the treasury were concerned however courts were to begin their activity on 1 January 1818, *ibid.*, iii, 170–5, cancelling the moratorium on debts to the state of 7 February 1816, *ibid.*, i, 222–8.

been easy to bear if they had remained at that level, but in 1821 only 10,281 lasts were exported from Danzig and in 1822, the year when the moratoria ceased, exports fell to 2,571 lasts and the average price of a quarter of wheat to 31s.; stocks in the granaries, which had been as low as 2,436 lasts in 1815 rose by 1824 to 22,296.[1] The grain market had collapsed completely. Polish historians often see the British Corn Laws as one factor in Polish distress, but this can hardly be taken seriously. The whole of Europe after 1815 was open to the grain merchant. The essence of the Polish complaints was that prices did not maintain the abnormally high levels of the years 1800–5 when the demands of almost all Europe were concentrated upon Prussia; in 1815 the grain trade reverted to pre-war conditions and this was disguised until 1822 by exceptionally poor harvests in Western Europe. Land values in Poland fell in sympathy with grain prices. Landowners who had hastened to take advantage of the boom years now found, as in 1807, that they had to repay mortgages which had been taken up when land values and prices were high. Mortgages often exceeded the current market values of estates. The Polish landlord was in a position in which he could neither hold on nor let go. Czermiński reproduced a document from the archives of the Land Credit Society formed in 1825 which shows the extent of agrarian debt in the Congress Kingdom in 1823; the total value of all estates in the Kingdom was placed at 799,006,048 *złp* 2 *gr* and mortgages burdening them at 505,989,335 *złp* 26 *gr*.[2] The incidence of debt however was uneven; estates valued at 130,941,483 *złp* 19 *gr* were encumbered to the extent of 230,083,445 *złp* 29½ *gr*. The part of the Kingdom of Poland which up to 1809 had been incorporated in the Austrian Empire, the *województwa* of Cracow, Sandomierz, Podlasie and Lublin, had experienced the full weight of Austrian taxation and the currency crisis of the later period of the Napoleonic wars, but were not as heavily burdened as the former Prussian portions. Strzeszewski's conclusion is that the former Prussian areas had a total debt of 406,199,000*złp* and the former Austrian 178,659,000 *złp* before 1830.

[1] W. Jacob, *Report on the Trade in Foreign Corn*, pp. 164–6.
[2] F. Czermiński, *O towarzystwie kredytowem*, I, 192–3.

The same pattern of poverty may be found in the western provinces of Russia. Tremendous losses were sustained in Lithuania during the passage of the French and Russian armies in 1812–13; incomplete returns for the *Gubernii* of Vilna and Grodno show a loss of 131,814 horses and 399,952 head of cattle and draught oxen, though there may be some exaggeration here.[1] In the southern provinces of Western Russia the Polish landlords suffered from the post-war fluctuations. Trading conditions at Odessa were exceptionally good in the years 1816–17 when exports totalled 79,674,300 roubles and imports 41,182,310. The price of the quarter of wheat was 45s. 11d. in 1816 and 49s. 11d. in 1817, but fell to 13s. 6d. by 1825. According to William Jacob the cost of production in the Polish regions and transport charges to the coast required a minimum price of 20s. 6d. a quarter. After 1818 the Polish landlords of the interior began to run into debt; '... Half the farmers of land have been already ruined, whilst the proprietors, not being able to subsist on the low income derived from their estates, are loading them with debts which they are unable to discharge; and ... all the courts of the country are filled with the business of liquidation and sequestration.'[2] The Polish landlords, producing soft wheat which could be milled into fine grade flour, unlike the farmers of the Black Sea coastal region who grew hard wheat which could be made into macaroni, vermicelli and spaghetti eaten in the Mediterranean areas, could never estimate the demands of Western Europe, especially Great Britain, and often found that they were left with large stocks of grain on their hands. In Western Poland times were equally hard; Jacob was informed by the Prussian authorities that of 262 estates in the province of West Prussia, 2,048,000 acres in extent, 195 were encumbered with mortgages and in 71 cases sequestration had been applied for the non-payment of debts.[3]

The appearance of the agrarian crisis in its full force in 1822 was bound to complicate the relations of Russia and Prussia.

[1] Cf. J. Iwaszkiewicz, 'Rejestracja i indemnizacja strat na Litwie po r. 1812', in *Likwidacja skutków wojny w dziedzinie stosunków prawnych i ekonomicznych w Polsce* (Warsaw, 1917), ii, tabela generalna, i and ii.
[2] W. Jacob, *Tracts relating to the Corn Trade and Corn Laws* (London, 1828), 'Notices respecting the Commerce of the Black Sea and of the Sea of Azoff', p. 11.
[3] *Report on the Trade in Foreign Corn*, p. 153.

ECONOMIC PROBLEMS: *SZLACHTA* 87

Under the terms of the Russo-Prussian treaty of 3 May 1815 it was agreed to allow as free as possible a passage of goods through the two portions of the former Republic, imposing only such dues as might be necessary for the maintenance of river banks and roads. Article XXIX of the treaty declared: 'Quant au commerce de Transit il sera parfaitement libre dans toutes les parties de l'ancienne Pologne. Il sera soumis au peàge le plus modéré...'[1] By the commercial agreement of 1818 a small transit custom on Polish grain was imposed, while Prussian goods were allowed access into the Congress Kingdom and thus into the Russian Empire, at reasonable rates.[2] The dues imposed by Prussia on Polish grain amounted to $3\frac{1}{2}$ *Rth.* on the last of wheat, $1\frac{1}{6}$ *Rth.* on rye, 1 *Rth.* on barley, $\frac{2}{3}$ *Rth.* on oats and 3 *Rth.* on pease. Russian tariffs were revised on 2 December 1819 to take effect from 1 January 1820 and the Kingdom of Poland and the Empire were joined in a customs union. In this way a period of comparatively free trade between Prussia and Russia was inaugurated, but from the Russian side the reception of this agreement was mixed. In Eastern Europe free trade was the policy of the landowners, but Russian manufacturers realized the danger of Prussian competition and began to agitate for a readjustment of tariffs. In 1822 Alexander I decided to revert to the protectionist system from the end of March; the customs union with the Congress Kingdom was dissolved and temporary regulations instituted for Russo-Polish trade until a fresh agreement could be arranged. In the same way a fresh commercial treaty with Prussia had to be negotiated. The Prussians for their part chose to show the strength of their position by raising the transit custom on Polish goods; their hostility reached its height in the new tariff for the seven eastern provinces of the Kingdom issued on 10 April 1823, which imposed a transit duty of 10 thalers on every last of grain and pease passing the Prussian frontier to the sea, by English standards of no great significance, but enough to give Prussian grain an advantage over the grain of the Congress Kingdom. Prussian retaliation completed the sum of Polish landowners' misfortunes.

[1] F. Martens, *Recueil de traités et conventions conclus par la Russie*, iii, annexes 2, p. 347. [2] *Ibid.*, vii, 328–69.

From the Russian side the Congress Kingdom received better treatment. In 1822 a twenty-year agreement was reached between the Kingdom and the Empire.[1] A customs duty of 1 per cent on goods manufactured from native Polish materials and of 3 per cent for goods produced from foreign materials was imposed by Russia. The export of wool and sugar to the Empire was forbidden for three years, while tariffs of 15 per cent and 25 per cent respectively were to operate on the import into Poland of these products from the Empire during the same period. No dues were imposed upon other raw materials or upon goods and materials imported to the Kingdom through the Baltic ports of Libau and Riga. To assist the passage of goods from the north a canal was put under construction to link the Vistula with the Niemen, though W. Jacob was sceptical of the practicability of diverting Polish grain to the Dvina; it was a long journey and facilities for drying did not exist at Riga. The main advantage however of the agreement was that it gave an opportunity for the development of the Polish cloth industry and with it for the expansion of sheep farming, as an alternative form of income for the landlords. From this time Łódź, which in the early 1820's was only a small village, began to expand into a great textile centre producing cloth for the eastern European market; in 1821 it had only 112 houses and 799 inhabitants, but by 1829 there were 369 houses and 4,273 inhabitants, an abnormal increase for a Polish town in this period, and by the 1850's the town was well on the way to becoming one of the largest, though not the most beautiful of Polish cities. The more immediate problem was the tariff war between Russia and Prussia which caused Polish imports from Prussia to fall by 50 per cent and exports by 25 per cent, and it was only on 11 March 1825 that a convention was drawn up to solve the dispute.[2] The new transit rates were not as low as those of 1818, but were a reduction on the rates of 1823. One thaler was levied on the last of rye, barley and oats and 4 *Rth.* on the last of wheat and pease passing from Congress Poland to Prussia. On the other hand a protective tariff was imposed on manufactured goods coming into Congress Poland in order to

---

[1] *Polnoe Sobranie Zakonov Rossijskoi Imperii* (1st Series), xxxviii, no. 29,149. 1/13 August 1822. [2] F. Martens, *op. cit.*, viii, 1–46.

encourage native industrial enterprise and sheep farming. In other words the policy of free trade was abandoned and in its place was adopted a plan of industrial expansion and concentration upon the eastern market.

It had been Alexander I's intention that Congress Poland should be an independent political unit, but when the landlords could not pay their taxes as a result of the adverse balance of trade and deflation which kept prices at a low level it was apparent that financial stability would be difficult to achieve; up to that time the budget had always shown a deficit except in 1817. In a rescript of 25 May 1821 Alexander I questioned the whole principle of the Kingdom's independent existence and asked whether or not some reorganization ought to be made. The Polish administration could offer no solution and Alexander I took matters into his own hands and appointed Prince Ksawery Lubecki minister of finance on 31 July 1821.

Lubecki was a Lithuanian Pole who in 1812 had been a follower of the group of Lithuanian nobles who rejected the advances of Napoleon; in 1813 he was a member of the temporary government of the Duchy of Warsaw and had been employed on the negotiation of the liquidation treaties which wound up the tangled affairs of the Duchy. He therefore enjoyed the full confidence of the tsar and was well versed in the financial affairs of the Kingdom, but it was equally clear that a man with this record would have little sympathy for emotional nationalism. Nor was he the type of man the *szlachta* admired, and that is probably why he was regarded as being little more than a Russian nominee. He was not a reformer, but took the Congress Kingdom as he found it and tried to preserve it. He approached the problem with no preconceived opinions and indeed his first act was the anticipation of the first quarter's revenue of 1822 by a drastic collection in 1821.[1] When he did not obtain the money he needed he resorted to military distraint, a measure which did not increase his popularity. As his experience grew he began to realize the nature of the problem and threw his energies into the exploitation of the Russo-Polish commercial agreement of 1822. Congress Poland was a debtor

[1] For his appeal to the public see S. Smolka, *Polityka Lubeckiego przed powstaniem listopadowem* (Cracow, 1907), pp. 95–8.

community and money left the country in settlement of debts in Prussia or to buy goods from abroad; the failure of the wheat trade meant that foreign currency was not available for imports.

If it were not for the supply of Russian money advanced for the Polish army, together with that coming in to pay Russian troops, for the amusements of the Grand Duke and the frequent visits of the King which also bring money into the country, as well as the entertainments in Warsaw of the many Poles with incomes drawn from estates in Russia and spent here, we should have seen the last of our money.[1]

Only a policy of economic self-sufficiency could cure the crisis of deflation.

Lubecki could combine this policy with measures designed to conciliate the landlords. As far as finance was concerned he saw to it that no additional burdens were imposed on the substantial *szlachta*, keeping the land tax constant at 16,000,000 *złp* throughout his administration, but imposing taxes on the articles of consumption. Imported goods were more heavily taxed than domestic products; indirect taxation produced 26,766,057*złp* in 1821 and 44,978,981 *złp* in 1829. The salt monopoly was especially oppressive for the peasants, because they normally consumed large quantities of salt like all men obliged to perform heavy physical labour.[2] By these means Lubecki succeeded in balancing the budget, though he never collected arrears of taxation. Expenditure rose from 60,356,586*złp* in 1821 to

[1] *Korespondencya Lubeckiego*, i, 144–5, letter to Sobolewski, 24 January 1822. In his appreciation of the situation, 'Coup d'oeil financier sur le Royaume', of 4 October 1823, *ibid.*, i (Dodatki), 395–9, he wrote: 'On verra que, depuis 1815 sur 56,990,361 (i.e. Polish *złp*) frappés à l'effigie du Souverain, à peine y en a-t-il un quart en circulation, tandis que le reste s'est entièrement écoulé chez l'étranger, au point qu'aujourd'hui même il faut donner un intérêt considérable en sus des sommes que l'acquisition des certains produits nous arrache, et que notre monnaie a un cours on ne peut plus défavorable, lorsque l'argent prussien a gagné à Varsovie jusqu'à 5 et 6% tant il était rare, et que celui d'Autriche s'est élevé jusqu'à 7% au dessus de sa valeur intrinsèque.'

[2] M. Ajzen, *Polityka gospodarcza Lubeckiego, 1821–1830* (Warsaw, 1932), pp. 39–47. Lubecki also exploited the *czopowy*, a tax on vodka distilled and sold in towns, which did not enjoy the exclusive privileges of the landed gentry. Here he was falling into line with Russian practice, cf. *Korespondencya*, i, 41. Monopolies of tobacco and colonial products also played a part in his fiscal schemes.

ECONOMIC PROBLEMS: *SZLACHTA* 91

86,612,843 *złp* in 1829.[1] His chief worry was the maintenance of the army which absorbed nearly 50 per cent of the revenue. It was for this reason that he was anxious to create an armament industry within the country, as yet another means of solving the financial crisis. Barzykowski declared that Lubecki once said to his friend, Ludwik Plater that 'three things are necessary for Poland—(1) schools, that is, education and intelligence, (2) industry and trade, that is, wealth and plenty, and (3) arms factories. Possessing these things, even in association with Moscow, she will succeed in maintaining her independence in its entirety...'[2] This passage is often interpreted to mean that Lubecki was at bottom hostile to Russia, but it is quite clear that he ruled out all thoughts of more armed uprisings.[3] His whole work depended upon the assumption of friendly and peaceful relations with Russia. Without the Russian market the Kingdom could not maintain its independence; hostility to Russia would destroy the agreement of 1822 which was beginning to give the Kingdom a favourable balance of trade with the Empire.

It was only in 1825 that the problem of landed debt could be dealt with; the crisis of 1822 produced such discontent that no useful purpose could have been served in calling the diet, though Lubecki was aware at the outset that some attempt must be made to settle the landlords' affairs.[4] In 1825 the diet gave its approval to the charter of the Land Credit Society modelled on the 'Landschaft' of Poznania.[5] Under the scheme of funding

[1] J. Bloch, *Finanse Rosji xix wieku* (Warsaw, 1883), iii deals with Polish finances in this period.
[2] S. Barzykowski, *Historya powstania listopadowego* (Poznań, 1883–4)i, 113.
[3] L. Sapieha, *Wspomnienia* (*z lat od 1803 do 1863*), ed. B. Pawłowski (Lvov, 1912), pp. 86–7, states that Lubecki believed in close collaboration with Russia and penetration of the Russian administration. 'He used to cite the example of the Chinese who, conquered by the Tartars, nevertheless succeeded in obtaining such power that they became the masters of their rulers.' [4] Cf. *Korespondencya*, i, 78–9.
[5] *Dziennik Praw Królestwa Polskiego*, ix, 185 *seq*. The Lithuanian landlords wanted a similar institution, but the authorities as ever avoided any assimilation of Lithuania to the Kingdom and declared that the facilities offered by the Bank of St. Petersburg sufficed; the bank issued loans on the basis of the tax system to a maximum of 150 roubles a soul which was valued at 175 roubles. Cf. H. Mrozowska, 'Project wprowadzenia Towarzystwa Kredytowego Ziemskiego w Wilnie w r. 1830,' *Księga pamiątkowa ku uczczeniu 25-letniej działalności prof. M. Handelsmana* (Warsaw, 1929).

landed debt the debtor was to be free of his obligations after twenty-eight years; creditors accepted payment in bonds upon which they drew an annual interest of 4 per cent and which they could sell in order to realize their capital. An indication of the success of the scheme is the rise in the course of bonds on the Warsaw market from 74·5 in 1826 to 97·5 in 1830, which must also be a sign of the growing prosperity of the country.[1] There were however some features of the scheme which were not entirely satisfactory. Only debtors who paid over 100 *złp* land tax were included and bonds might be issued only up to three-fifths of the value of an estate. In 1829 bonds to the value of 148,000,000 *złp* had been issued, but of this sum 52,800,000 *złp* were accounted for by mortgaging of government lands; the bonds issued to private landlords amounted to only one-fifth of the total private debt of 1823. It would therefore seem that only a minority of the landlords benefited before 1830. Similarly, the mortgaging of public lands meant that government estates might be sold, for which reason it was necessary to cancel the privilege the government peasants had of buying their freeholds which by creating enclaves would otherwise have reduced the value of estates. The Land Credit Society was limited in its scope and did some positive harm.

Lubecki's hope was that the Society would free Polish capital. It was commonly supposed that there was much money in Congress Poland, which the *szlachta* kept at home under the bed, and which might be mobilized in its turn if a bank were established. The project of a bank was not realized without searching criticism from the Russian minister of finance, Kankrin, but at length Nicholas I gave approval to its charter on 29 January 1828 and the Bank of Poland came into existence with an authorized capital of 30,000,000 *złp*, guaranteed by the state. In spite of government departments' opposition all state funds were to be lodged in it.[2] Men after Lubecki's own heart were given executive positions, Ludwik Jelski becoming president, and Józef Lubowidzki, brother of the vice-president of the city of Warsaw, its vice-president; on the board of directors

---

[1] For the course of the Society's bonds see *Korespondencya*, ii (Dodatki), 482–7.
[2] The charter is given in *Dziennik Praw Królestwa Polskiego*, xii, 119–53. H. Radziszewski, *Bank Polski* (Warsaw, 1910), deals with the early history of the bank.

was Henryk Łubieński, son of Feliks Łubieński, minister of justice under the Duchy of Warsaw and brother of General Tomasz Łubieński, who was an active director of the Land Credit Society. These were men who were prepared to break with the *szlachta* tradition that it was loss of caste to engage in trade.[1] Firmly in control of the Bank of Poland Lubecki ceased to be merely the minister of finance and became for practical purposes the prime minister of Congress Poland, an eminence which did not endear him to the *szlachta*. The dislike of Lubecki was as great as the private deposits in the bank were small. In 1829 only 1,900,000 *złp* were obtained from this source, partly because of the general lack of confidence in banks owing to the financial collapse of 1793, and partly because there was little ready money to deposit. There was still a tendency for the *szlachta* to spend their money in what was termed 'typically Polish hospitality', which was a polite expression for drunkenness and extravagant living—*soûl comme un polonais* as the French still say, though the Russians had long since set higher standards in these matters. Owing to its limited resources the note issue of the Bank was only 16,000,000 *złp* in 1829. The chief success of the Bank was in its attempt to take the grain trade out of the hands of petty Jewish factors. Its discount rate of 6 per cent compared very favourably with the rates offered by moneylenders and private banking agencies in Warsaw.

Lubecki turned to the only sources of money he could find, the government estates and loans. State lands were already mortgaged to some extent and on 31 August 1828 Lubecki obtained permission for their sale.[2] It was afterwards declared that he abandoned the peasants of these lands to the mercies of the private landowners and had thrown away the assets of the state, but *szlachta* annoyance was in some measure due to the jealousy which the profitable bargains made by men like Gliszczyński and Wężyk, both to be prominent in 1830, aroused, and to the fact that the sale of so much land tended to reduce

[1] The correspondence of Tomasz Łubieński with his father, Feliks, edited by R. Łubieński, *General Tomasz Pomian hr. Łubieński* (Warsaw, 1899), 2 vols., and T. W. Łubieński, *Henryk Łubieński i jego Bracia* (Cracow, 1886), are valuable sources of information for the activity of this family of noble business men who saw in economic reconstruction a means of rehabilitating Poland.

[2] *Dziennik Praw Królestwa Polskiego*, xii, 169–80.

the value of real estate. To some extent the state properties, which were notoriously underexploited, were more attractive to speculators than deposits in the Bank of Poland, but only 16,000,000 *złp* were obtained by alienations before the revolution of 1830. The impossibility of obtaining large sums from within the Kingdom drove Lubecki to seek loans and on 25 January 1829 an agreement was signed with the Berlin banking firm of S. A. Fraenkel for a loan of 42,000,000 *złp* at 5 per cent repayable in twenty-five years, of which one-third was allotted to the Bank and the remainder placed in the account of the ministry of finance.[1] Lubecki was able to do very little with this money because the revolution broke out in November 1830 which caused Polish credits in Berlin to be sequestrated, but it is clear from his tour of the Congress Kingdom in September–October 1824 that he had long been planning to develop the metallurgical industries of Poland. What he was able to do in the short time he had these funds at his disposal indicates that he intended to develop also the facilities of Warsaw. The Bank made a loan of 5,000,000 *złp* for the development of quays and other public needs. Lubecki intended to improve the water supply of the city and in January 1830 obtained permission to construct granaries. All this activity shows that he hoped to make Warsaw an emporium of the goods of east and west and establish the city's importance as a trading centre. Some caution is necessary in assessing the work of Lubecki, for the sums at his command were small, though in relation to the poverty, the country, and the size of the budget his schemes were bold. These were only the beginnings of industrialization and commercial expansion, but they were enough to show that Congress Poland was on the way to recovery from the disasters of the Partitions and the war years.

There was little in the economic and social policy of the government which suggests deliberate victimization of the Polish ruling class by Russia, though Russia still had large claims upon the Kingdom, dating from the administration of the Temporary Government of 1813-15, which remained unsettled and might have led to an increase in taxation. Economic policy had almost no effect upon the events which led up to the

[1] *Ibid.*, xii, 312-22.

revolution of November 1830, though the poverty of the country was important for the course of the war in 1831. A country with only 4,000,000 inhabitants and no armaments industry, dependent upon outside sources for military stores, for which however it did not have the foreign currency to pay, could not hope to challenge the Russian Empire. When its economy was beginning to be concentrated upon the eastern market, war against Russia meant commercial disaster. The substantial gentry on the whole accepted the Russian connection and had little wish to overthrow it. The improvement of the country, though slight, was noticeable and a source of satisfaction. It was the younger generation which was not content with the parish-pump politics of Congress Poland and continued to dream of the greatness of the Republic extending from Danzig to the Carpathians and from Brandenburg to the Dvina and Dniepr. The grandeur that was Poland contrasted too forcibly with the narrow confines of the present.

CHAPTER III

Discontent in Congress Poland and the Revolution of 1830

AFTER 1831 Polish exiles, who were then the only articulate section of the Polish nation and whose propaganda has coloured interpretations of the rule of Alexander I and Nicholas I, represented the revolution of November 1830 as the logical outcome of Russian misgovernment in the Congress Kingdom.¹ On the other hand, the responsible Polish leaders in Warsaw during the years 1815–30 were willing enough to accept the Russian connection and wanted nothing more for the moment than to overcome the difficulties of post-war reconstruction. The substantial *szlachta* could hardly complain that the administration was unsympathetic to their material needs. Nevertheless, in spite of everything which the administration did to conciliate Polish feeling, there remained below the surface a consciousness of the greatness of Poland in the past. In Warsaw it was felt that Congress Poland, formed out of a portion of the Duchy of Warsaw, offered a basis for the restoration of the Republic. Most Poles hoped that Alexander I would unite the former eastern provinces to the Kingdom and undoubtedly obtained the impression that he had promised as much in his speeches to the diet in 1818, but neither the opening speech of 27 March nor the closing address of 27 April 1818 reveals anything so definite.² The Poles clearly read their own aspirations into them and took at their face value the many charming compliments which Alexander paid them at official receptions.

¹ This view was expressed at the very outset of the November revolution by K. A. Hoffman in his *Wielki tydzień Polaków* (Warsaw, 1830), the theme of which he expanded in *Rzut oka na stan polityczny Królestwa Polskiego pod panowaniem rossyiskiem* (Warsaw, 1831).
² For the texts see *B. & F.S.P.*, 5 (1817,1818), pp. 1114–20.

Some sections of the Polish public assumed that the constitution which Alexander I had granted the Kingdom in 1815 gave them rights against the monarch himself. Undoubtedly, the constitution was not strictly observed; the budget was never submitted to the diet, nor was the diet itself called every two years, as indeed the constitution laid down. Alexander I obviously hoped that the Polish deputies would assume an attitude of disciplined restraint and co-operate with the administration. This was to expect too much of the *szlachta*, reared in the traditions of the eighteenth-century diets and confederations, and anxious to make on all occasions flowery but often meaningless speeches.

Parliamentary opposition first raised its head in the *województwo* of Kalisz under the leadership of the brothers Niemojowski, Wincenty and Bonawentura.[1] The Niemojowskis had both received their education in Germany where they came under the influence of French ideas, especially those of Benjamin Constant. Their programme, closely modelled on the conceptions of Constant, was the strict observance of the constitution of 1815. From the outset they tried to build up among the deputies from their *województwo* a group which would be able to act in concert in the diet. Their political methods were traditionally Polish. Meetings of the local *szlachta* were organized in the houses of the leaders, to which they were attracted by the liberal quantities of liquor provided by the Niemojowskis. Indeed, the drunkenness of the Niemojowskis was a matter of some notoriety, and that in Poland where vast quantities of liquor were habitually consumed.[2] At these gatherings a programme of opposition was worked out. Wincenty Niemojowski's

---

[1] The fullest account of the parliamentary history of the Congress Kingdom is H. Więckowska, *Opozycja liberalna w królestwie kongresowem*, *Rozprawy Historyczne Tow. Nauk. Warsz.*, iii z. 2, 1925. For the diet of 1825, see R. Przelaskowski, *Sejm Warszawski roku 1825*, *Rozprawy Historyczne Tow. Nauk. Warsz.*, vii z. 2, 1929.

[2] A distant relative, Jan Nepomucen Niemojowski, wrote that this opinion of them was completely unjustified, *Wspomnienia*, ed. S. Pomarański (Warsaw, 1925), pp. 33–4, but H. Braunsteinowa, who had access to the family papers, declares them to be full of references to drinking bouts, 'Charakterystyka Braci Niemojowskich w dobie Królestwa Kongresowego', *Przegląd Historyczny*, xxiii (1921–2), 78. Certainly Wincenty in his pamphlet, *Głosy posła kaliskiego na seymie królestwa Polskiego* (Poznań, 1818), p. 11, showed great interest in the taxation of billiard halls, coffee shops and restaurants.

H

argument was that under the terms of the constitution the deputies were entitled to voice their opposition and he encouraged them to do so, irrespective of the merits of measures under discussion. Wincenty declared himself in 1818 against a bill to settle boundary disputes between property owners.[1] In 1825 his friends raised difficulties when the bill to establish a Land Credit Society came before the diet, a factious opposition which turned the more sober deputies against them. In the eyes of the public however the Kalisz group seemed to be the defenders of Polish liberties. Gangs of students and journalists thronged the public galleries of the diet in 1818 and 1820, applauding obstructive speeches with enthusiasm. Applause in Poland could only have the effect of encouraging the deputies to further flights of verbosity. The unhelpful attitude of the Niemojowskis gave direct offence to Alexander I. It was Wincenty Niemojowski's defence of Radoński, a landowner who had taken part in the Neapolitan rising of 1820, which caused his downfall. Radoński was arrested by the viceroy Zajączek on his return to Poland and Niemojowski announced his intention of raising the matter in the diet. The Grand Duke Constantine called Niemojowski to the Belvedere Palace and told him that he was guilty of *lese majesté* and that in future he must not reside in the same place as the tsar; this meant that though elected to the diet he could not attend its meetings if the tsar were present. Steps were taken also to exclude his brother, Bonawentura, by questioning the validity of his election. In defiance of instructions Wincenty Niemojowski attempted to take his seat but was stopped at the toll gates of Warsaw and sent back to his estate where he was confined under house arrest at the tsar's pleasure on the direct order of Nesselrode. The government for its part made every effort to avoid sterile debates. Pressure was put on the electors to choose deputies favourable to the administration. Alexander I himself intervened in the question and on 13 February 1825, before the assembly of the diet in May, issued the Additional Article to the Constitution, by which only the first and last sittings of the diet were to be open to the public; it was frankly stated in the preamble that the measure was designed to prevent deputies

---

[1] F. Siarczyński, *Diéte du Royaume de Pologne* (Warsaw, 1818), p. 66.

THE REVOLUTION OF 1830 99

from playing to the gallery.[1] This decree was issued apparently without the knowledge of the viceroy or the ministers. It is impossible not to detect in Polish objections a certain chagrin that the deputies would no longer be able to exercise their oratorical prowess, but it was hardly 'equivalent, in some measure, to a suppression of the Constitutional Charter itself', as Szymon Askenazy wrote.[2] Undoubtedly, Alexander I achieved his immediate purpose, but by removing the public from the galleries he gave the radicals to believe that he was not prepared to observe the letter of the constitution and might in future make other alterations. At the same time, the secrecy of debates shielded the deputies themselves from public criticism. The deputies were thought of as the defenders of Polish liberties, though in fact they offered opposition on only one question, the reform of the marriage laws.

Alexander I's policy from the outset was to conciliate powerful vested interests in the Kingdom. In addition to the substantial gentry he hoped to win over the clergy, who objected strongly to the marriage laws introduced under the Duchy of Warsaw and who claimed for themselves complete jurisdiction over divorce. Alexander I was willing to transfer to the Church complete control over marriage, but when bills were introduced in the diet they met with strong opposition in the Chamber of Deputies. The revision of the Civil Code was the special province of the diet. Opposition on this question gave the impression that the diet was a bastion against reaction. Neither the administration nor the Church desired the spread of liberal ideas in Poland. It soon became clear that Polish journalists intended to interpret the freedom of the press in the widest possible terms. In 1819 the government imposed a censorship, first upon periodical literature and later upon all printed matter.[3] At the same time prefects were appointed to observe the behaviour of students in the newly created university of Warsaw. In 1821 the Voltairean Stanisław Kostka Potocki, brother of Ignacy Potocki, was dismissed from his post as minister of religion and education and his place taken by the obscurantist Stanisław Grabowski, a natural son of Stanisław

[1] *Dziennik Praw Królestwa Polskiego*, ix, 91.   [2] *Cambridge Modern History*, x, 455.
[3] *Dziennik Praw Królestwa Polskiego*, vi, 327-9, 362-3.

August Poniatowski. By royal decree the ministry was reorganized and the direction of ecclesiastical affairs and education brought more and more under the influence of the bishops and the clericals.[1] Grabowski and his assistant, Szaniawski, an ex-radical with a revolutionary past, became two of the most unpopular men in the Kingdom for their efforts to control the spread of liberalism. Expenditure on education was severely curtailed, with the approval of the ministry of finance which wished to husband its meagre resources for other purposes.[2] The government's policy was bound to arouse the hostility of the advanced sections of public opinion. Up to this time the tendency of all governments, whether Polish, Prussian or that of the king of Saxony had been to promote secular education. The official reaction occurred at the very time when the younger generation was beginning to come under the influence of Romanticism in literature, the doctrine of the complete freedom of the spirit.

The younger generation in Poland had come to manhood after the great struggles of the past and felt itself limited by the narrow confines of the Congress Kingdom. It looked back to the Republic with regret and idealized the attempt of Napoleon to recreate it. The older generation talked longingly of the old days, but without conviction. Nevertheless pictures of Napoleon hung in the manor houses. It is easy to understand why Napoleon, himself a petty nobleman who had risen from obscurity to an imperial throne, who had humbled the absolutist monarchies which had partitioned Poland, could not have failed to appeal to the petty noblemen of Poland. It was Napoleon the soldier, rather than Napoleon the organizer and codifier who appealed to their imagination. As in France, so in Poland Bonapartism had little connection with the rationalism of the eighteenth century. It was rather a nostalgia for the glory and battles of the past, a sentiment easily acquired by a nobility which felt itself humiliated by the partition of its country and frustrated in the straightened circumstances of defeat.

[1] *Ibid.*, vi, 174–229 for the reorganization of the ministry.
[2] For the decline of education see M. Manteufflowa, *J. K. Szaniawski—Ideologja i działalność, 1815–1930* (Warsaw, 1936), pp. 56–113. University education seems to have been maintained; at Warsaw there were usually about 600 students attending courses, *ibid.*, p. 97 n.

THE REVOLUTION OF 1830 101

Hero-worship of Napoleon was strengthened by new literary modes. As social life in Warsaw returned to normal after the disorganization of the war years the new generation of writers and critics began slowly to fall under the sway of German romanticism. Even classical writers were not insensitive to the past. Julian Niemcewicz, a deputy of the diet of 1788-91, a follower of Kościuszko, the very personification of the eighteenth century, published in 1816 his *Śpiewy historyczne z muzyką i rycinami*, a glorification of Polish achievements, written in verse of a classical model, but of immediate appeal to the Polish intelligentsia. By 1819 this work had gone into three editions and made Niemcewicz the lion of the Warsaw salons.[1] Romanticism in the true sense of the word infiltrated into Poland through articles in foreign newspapers. The search for a new means of expression was presented cautiously to the public by the reviews and translations of Kazimierz Brodziński, but Poles were at first slow to realize the implications of the new movement. The classicists managed to uphold their view that the past served only to provide the modern world with the inspiration of its great men's lives. When Adam Mickiewicz, a Lithuanian Pole, first published his attempts at adapting the poetic methods of Schiller and Byron in Vilna in 1822-3 under the title of *Poezje Adama Mickiewicza*, the event passed unnoticed in Warsaw. It was not until 1825, when Franciszek Dmochowski gave his work attention in the press, that Mickiewicz began to enjoy popularity in the Kingdom, and then only among the younger generation. Mickiewicz's early work is important rather for its social effect than for its quality. The first volume of his *Poezje, Ballady i Romanse* contributed little to European literature as a whole, but it was distinguished by the fact that the ballads were not mere copies or translations of foreign poems, but creations of an original Polish flavour. The poems of the second volume, *Grążyna*, the story of a Lithuanian Amazon who gave all her worldly possessions for the fatherland, and *Dziady*, the story of frustrated love and despair, demonstrated that the movement with which the younger generation

[1] The attentions given to Niemcewicz went to his head; Skarbek, usually a reliable observer, says that he was 'spoilt by the women like a delicate child'. *Pamiętniki* (Poznań, 1878), p. 123.

was familiar in foreign literature, had found its place in Poland. The classicists were not slow to defend themselves. Their attacks on Mickiewicz encouraged him to renew his efforts and before 1830 he had produced his *Sonety Krymskie*, *Konrad Wallenrod*, a poem particularly provocative of patriotic feeling, and *Oda do Młodości*. It is for the literary historian to assess the merits of these poems, but in the political sense their importance is very great. The older generation, steeped in the ideas of the eighteenth century and for the most part willing to accept the Russian connection in spite of irritations, defended the classical point of view. Even the Kalisz group, hostile as it was to the government, provided a champion, Wincenty Niemojowski himself, to defend the classical models; the Kalisz group associated constitutional government with France, the home of the classical forms which had influenced Polish literature before 1815, and where now Romanticism was associated with the reactionary Chateaubriand. The younger generation however was won for Romanticism, which set before them the ideal of a strong, free individual, struggling against fate and dying gracefully in his hour of defeat. Romanticism was an appeal to action. It encouraged the young men to look forward to the day when they might once more hew out a Poland in its old frontiers. Moreover, denied an active part in the politics of the country, the young men of Congress Poland could under cover of literary criticism and discussion propagate the idea of the uprising against continued partition. As long as they confined themselves to the academic aspects of Romanticism they could evade censorship.

The result was a flowering of Polish artistic genius. Mickiewicz was a Lithuanian Pole. Poles were especially conscious of the separate character of Lithuania, with its own laws and institutions. Its population was sparser than that of the Congress Kingdom. It was a country with many medieval customs and superstitions, touched to a lesser extent than the Kingdom by the advance of civilization. It was the perfect setting for the romantic poem, far away from the crowds and the streets, its landscape wild and awe-inspiring. It was only natural that the Poles living south of the Pripet marshes in Volhynia, Podolia and the Ukraine should similarly seek to express their own past

THE REVOLUTION OF 1830 103

in prose and poetry. The south-eastern regions were the land of the Cossacks, of the wars against the Tartars and of the struggle against Turkey in defence of Christendom. Three writers, Antoni Malczeski, Bogdan Zaleski and Seweryn Goszczyński, set themselves to do for the Ukraine what Mickiewicz had done for Lithuania. Similarly the literary critics strove to discover the principles of the new idioms. Maurycy Mochnacki began his literary career in the newspapers *Dziennik Warszawski* and *Gazeta Polska* by examining the sources of inspiration in Polish poetry. The test of a national poetry, he wrote, was its originality, the means to which Germans had already shown the way; he urged that the poet should seek his inspiration in the spirit of the Middle Ages, the pristine purity of Slavonic legend and in the Scandinavian mythology. He condemned outright the devotion to French models and in his first monograph he put forward the claim that the romantic was the national literature.[1] The quickened interest in the past added importance to the study of history. The first modern Polish historian made his reputation in this period, Joachim Lelewel, himself closely connected with the former eastern provinces, having been educated at Vilna, and become a teacher at Krzemieniec in Volhynia and eventually a lecturer and professor of history at Vilna. Ousted from his post through the hostility of the Russian authorities because his lectures were glorifications of Poland where the Russians wished for emphasis upon loyalty to St. Petersburg, he had removed to Warsaw to engage in historical research. Lelewel, in contrast to the strictly chronological approach of the eighteenth-century historian Naruszewicz, tried to raise historical study above the level of narrative. He was interested in factors in Polish history in order to explain the rise and fall of the state. In 1829 he published a popular history in Warsaw which enjoyed an extraordinary success;[2] 2,000 copies, a large number for this period, were sold in the first five months, which caused it to be reprinted in 1830, and in the same year a second edition with maps was offered for sale. This work made as great an impression upon the Polish nation as Niemcewicz's *Śpiewy Historyczne*. Lelewel, an

[1] *O literaturze polskiej w wieku xix* (Warsaw, 1830), p. 135.
[2] *Dzieje Polski Joachim Lelewel potocznym sposobem opowiedział.*

attractive lecturer, became the idol of the younger generation which regarded him as the very embodiment of the national virtues, an adoration which made him doubly suspicious to the older generation which was already alarmed by his connections with student disturbances in the University of Vilna, though he had enough popularity with the *szlachta* to get himself elected in 1828, before the publication of his history, as a deputy for Żelechów in Podlasie. Besides this development in poetry and history there was no less important an advance in music, the aspect of the cultural flowering of the period best known in Western Europe. Polish musicians began to investigate the nature of the national folk music and their research laid the foundation for the work of Chopin, who was at this time a youth learning to play the pianoforte in Warsaw and who in 1830, before the rising, was to leave Poland to make his reputation in the West.

The influence of the Romantic movement upon the Polish mind was enormous. The radical *szlachta* had already adopted as their ideal the concept of a strong national state which Romanticism with its appeal to the past could only emphasize. Moreover, it gave encouragement to individualism and pleaded that the purpose of the knight errant of the present was to win by his efforts, unaided if need be, the battle to restore the Republic. His reward, the creation of the modern Polish state, was not the less attractive for the difficulties it presented. Insistence upon the capacity of the individual for decisive action fitted exactly the temperament of the *szlachta* with their long tradition of revolution and confederation. It reinforced the belief that the most noble occupation of man was war and extolled prowess in battle to the exclusion of the more solid qualities of the administrator and business man. This intellectual climate did not encourage among the younger generation respect for Lubecki, the aristocrat who thought in terms of industry and trade. Patriotism was measured by professions of devotion to the national cause. Discussion of social and economic realities found little place in the thoughts of the radical youth who laid stress upon the essential Polonism to which all should be faithful and by which all should be judged. In nineteenth-century Poland politics came to be regarded as the outlet of young men,

THE REVOLUTION OF 1830 105

as if they were the sole arbiters of the moral attitude to be adopted towards national problems. Thus the political aspirations of schoolboys and university students were a serious factor with which the leaders of the older generation were always obliged to reckon. In the 1820's, as the young Romantics became more assertive, parents attempted to shield their sons from their own irresponsibility. The fashion among the wealthy families was to ship off their sons to a foreign university and let them vegetate in a more sedate intellectual atmosphere. Tomasz Łubieński sent his son to Edinburgh, where the young Andrzej Zamoyski and his cousin, Leon Sapieha, also studied; Wincenty Krasiński dispatched abroad his son, Zygmunt, who was to become one of Poland's greatest Romantic poets, but these young aristocrats were quite exceptional. The majority of the young *szlachta* was educated within Poland and had little knowledge of life elsewhere.

Warsaw was not only the capital of the Kingdom of Poland. It was the centre for young men from all over the area of the former Republic. It was the chief station of the army and the *szlachta* flocked there to take employment as soldiers. The hub of the literary world, Warsaw held attractions which could not be found in the other Polish centres, Vilna, Kiev, Lvov, Cracow and Poznań. The influx of young men was especially noticeable from Galicia, where the Austrian government had never forgiven those families in Lvov and its surrounding districts which had risen in support of Prince Józef Poniatowski's invasion of 1809.[1] In Warsaw there gathered many poverty-stricken intellectuals, anxious to assert their claims and impatient of restraint.

The constitution of the Congress Kingdom, like that of the Duchy of Warsaw, did not permit any form of open political association which might have absorbed the energies of the younger generation. Instead, they were to seek self-expression in secret societies, for which the masonic lodges of eighteenth-century Poland provided a model. Freemasonry itself was

---

[1] This was the motive of the Mochnackis' migration, cf. J. Gollenhofer, *Polityczna strona działalności Maurycego Mochnackiego* (Cracow, 1910), p. 13. Cf. also M. Toczyński, *Pamiętniki* (Cracow, 1873), p. 57, who saw no future for himself in Galicia.

disliked by the ecclesiastical authorities, not because it was philanthropic in intention, but because of its Voltairean outlook and because of the influence which the grand master of the Polish lodges, the free-thinker, Stanisław Kostka Potocki, had in its counsels. After 1815, though the government to some extent accorded freemasonry official tolerance, the authorities attempted to control its activities and keep it under supervision. In 1820 the chief of the gendarmerie, General Różniecki, took the place of Potocki as grand master until the lodges were suppressed in 1821 in Russia and in Poland. At the same time the Jesuits were suppressed in Russia, and the great centre at Polotsk dispersed, with a consequent extension of Jesuit influence in Galicia, where the majority of its members moved. The result of the Russian government's hostility to the more or less open forms of association was that the Poles were driven to gather in clandestine groups. Contact with German universities had already produced some effect in Poland. A number of insignificant associations had been formed: *Panta Koina* (1817), *Powszechny Związek* (The General Association) (1819), *Wolni Lechici* (Free Lachs, i.e. Poles) and *Wolni Polacy* (Free Poles) (1820). The aims of these societies were simple; they professed to be animated by a desire for freedom, a feeling of patriotism and a hatred of despotism. They proclaimed the freedom of all nations and their own right to express the spirit of the Polish nation. From the point of view of political theory they rarely went beyond the dogma that government was an agreement between the people and the head of the state. They were modelled on and had the same significance as the *Burschenschaften* in Germany. The government viewed with alarm the growth of radicalism among the young generation. In an effort to prevent students from making contact with dangerous ideas current abroad young men were forbidden to study outside the Kingdom without the permission of the authorities; the grounds given were that a satisfactory education could be had in the new university in Warsaw. Permission to study abroad was granted only on the recommendation of the ministry of religion and education.[1] An attempt had been made previously to discourage study abroad by forcing the holders of foreign diplomas

[1] *Dziennik Praw Królestwa Polskiego*, vii, 361–4, 9 April 1822.

THE REVOLUTION OF 1830 107

and degrees to submit their qualifications for consideration by the government; the penalty for failure to conform with this order was exclusion from posts in the public administration.[1] The government in fact found it very difficult to control illegal political activity. An edict was issued on 6 November 1821 forbidding all secret societies in the Kingdom,[2] but this measure could have had the effect only of frightening the more timid youth from clandestine organizations. The resources of the Kingdom were not large enough to support an efficient police force capable of investigating all the acts of private citizens. The uniformed police under the command of General Różniecki was scattered throughout the countryside and had the duty rather of enforcing the decisions of the commissioners of the *województwa* than of looking for crime. The frontiers were guarded by Cossack patrols. Constantine himself maintained a secret police organization for the collection of information which seems to have had only two capable detectives. The adjutant of the grand duke, an Englishman, General Fanshaw, assisted by the general *à la suite*, Gendre, was responsible for the supervision of the army. Novosiltsev, the tsar's commissioner, had a fund for financing his own private investigations. Other police organizations were the Russian gendarmerie under Baron Sass and the municipal police controlled by the vice-president of Warsaw, Mateusz Lubowidzki. The activity of the police seems to have been remarkable for the multiplicity of its organizations rather than for the number of policemen employed. The whole apparatus was co-ordinated in August 1821 by a central body, the Central Office of Police for Warsaw and the Kingdom. Askenazy estimated that about 500,000 *złp* or £12,500 sterling per annum was expended on all branches of the secret police.[3] At the same time he is careful to point out that police funds were often a means of supplementing the meagre salaries of officials; the salary of Lubowidzki was only 9,000 *złp*. In 1831 about 200 secret agents were known by name and at the most there could have been only about 400 persons employed by the government. These agents were not paid officials, but men of every class of society, criminals, counts, Jews, Germans and

[1] *Ibid.*, vi, 342, 19 June 1819. [2] *Ibid.*, vi, 259–61.
[3] S. Askenazy, *Łukasiński* (Warsaw, 1908), i, 328.

foreign merchants resident in Warsaw, who received a payment for information they provided. Sometimes they were the creditors of General Różniecki, who, when they became too pressing, were put on the secret police pay roll. The detectives seem to have waited for denunciations rather than to have searched for information. Not all their activity was concerned with criminal or political matters. Constantine required a report on all activity of interest in Warsaw; because he was too exalted in rank to talk scandal and gossip with his officers he had to obtain information by other means. Reports were submitted to him of quite casual events, the Jewess who had recently returned from Vienna with new fashions, students playing billiards and lowering the tone of the university, the activities of bawdy women, the plight of widows for whom some small charity would not be out of place, and many other insignificant details.[1] On some days, so boring was life in Warsaw, there was nothing to enliven the Grand Duke's breakfast. Constantine often seems to have thought that the police exaggerated events in order to justify their own existence.

Students' associations seemed to be of little importance and did not attract the attention of the Polish police until the Prussian police forwarded information in December 1821 that Polish students in Berlin had formed a group called *Polonia*, which had connections with a similar group in Warsaw. Mauersberger, the leader of *Panta Koina* in Warsaw realizing that he was liable for indictment under the edict of 6 November 1821 forbidding secret societies, decided to make a clean breast of the whole affair, asserting that *Panta Koina* had already been dissolved.[2] The affair called for a special commission of inquiry

[1] 'La maquerelle Jasińska, femme du joueur de profession, qui fut transporté de Varsovie, tient depuis quelques jours un bordel dans la rue Longue Nr. 579 au premier étage tout près des fenêtres de S.E. mr. le général Blumer. Les filles de ce bordel sont couchées tout le jour dans les fenêtres et attaquent les passants; ce qui est une chose très inconvenable dans une rue principale et ses voisins se plaignent beaucoup à cause de cela, parceque ces inconvénients donnent de mauvais exemples à leurs enfants. Outre cela ce bordel est posé vis-à-vis des fenêtres de la caserne de la garde des Grenadiers près de l'arsenal,—ce qui donne occasion que les sous-officiers et les cadettes de cette garde restent presque toute la journée dans ce bordel, et on y fait souvent de bruits pendant le jour et pendant la nuit.' *A.A.D., Raporty policji tajnej*, 13/25 April 1823.

[2] *Panta Koina* seems to have seen its task partly to support the work of Alexander I in restoring Poland, see A. Kraushar, *Panta Koina, Miscellanea Historyczne*, xv (War-

but was not taken seriously by the authorities. Some concern was however felt in May 1823 when there were student disturbances in Vilna, where the commissioner Novosiltsev was sent to restore discipline. This event brought Adam George Czartoryski, the curator of the University, once more before the public eye. After 1815 he had been passed over and given no responsible office; he had indeed been guilty of a public indiscretion by fighting a duel in 1817 with Count Ludwik Pac over the Princess Anna Sapieha, a slip of a girl whom Czartoryski subsequently married. In 1823 Czartoryski resolved to make an appeal to Alexander I for a more liberal treatment of the university students in both Lithuania and Warsaw. Taking advantage of the presence of the tsar in Wołosowce during October–November 1823, he made a personal intervention, raising not only the question of the students at Vilna, but also of the observance of the Polish constitution and of granting Constantine increased powers in his capacity as commander-in-chief in Western Russia. At the end of his interview he asked to be relieved of his post as curator of Vilna, and Alexander I granted his request, though allowing him to resign only on 17 April 1824. This incident was of some importance, for Czartoryski, hitherto regarded as an adherent of the Russian connection from having been Alexander's foreign minister and an opponent of Napoleon, was thought to have changed his mind. Young radicals saw in his action a confirmation of their own feeling, that Alexander I had moved away from his original liberalism.

The preoccupation of the administration with the misdeeds of students distracted its attention from a far more serious conspiracy which had been formed under the very nose of Constantine himself. Major Waleryan Łukasiński, an officer of the 4th Infantry Regiment, a unit which received the especial approval of Constantine for the excellence of its drill and for that reason was not suspected by him of disloyal activity, had

saw, 1907), 22–4, for an alleged speech of Mauersberger. Some idea of the seriousness of the offence can be obtained from the fact that Koehler, a student arrested in Berlin, returned to the Kingdom after 1831, set up in practice as a physician, and died in 1871 at the age of 72; evidently the Russian government could be forgiving.

in 1819 formed an association under the name of *National Freemasonry*. This was an attempt to use the masonic organization as a cover for political activity. Unlike the student organizations, National Freemasonry was uninspired by intellectualism, but was military in outlook and composition, conservative and not prepared for hasty action. Łukasiński preferred to bide his time and strengthen his connections. His outlook was not even anti-Russian, because he saw no objection to re-establishing the Republic with the aid of the Russian Empire. It was the action of a group in Western Poland which forced him to take more decisive action. Lieutenant-Colonel Ignacy Prądzyński, already considered a capable staff-officer, in 1821 conceived the idea of abandoning the ritual of freemasonry and founding an association based upon the methods of carbonarism, in which the masonic hierarchical organization was to be replaced by a more democratic system, with elected officers and equality in discussion. He and General Umiński founded the 'Society of Scythemen' after the peasant soldiers who had fought for Kościuszko, but there was little response in Poznania where the landlords were more concerned with the practical problems of peasant emancipation, nor could General Umiński command very much respect.[1] Łukasiński was aware of developments in Poznania, but was taken by surprise when in the spring of 1821 Umiński appeared in Warsaw and demanded his adherence to the new conspiracy. The meeting of the conspirators on 1 May on the outskirts of Warsaw was a comic opera affair. Umiński arrived late, dressed in extravagant costume and riding a white horse, attracting the attention of the passers-by. To allay suspicion it was arranged that they should pretend to be in attendance at a duel between Prądzyński and Colonel Kozakowski, one of the adherents of Łukasiński; it was presumed that the police would not interfere in so understandable an

[1] Umiński, brother-in-law of Wincenty Niemojowski, had gambled away a considerable fortune and been forced to resign from the army of the Congress Kingdom when he lost his divisional funds in card games. His reputation was saved by a friend who advanced him money to cover his losses, but he considered it wiser to opt for Prussian citizenship. He resigned ostensibly because he would not serve with Różniecki, the chief of the gendarmerie, and in this way won a golden reputation for himself. He was to be imprisoned by the Prussian government for his conspiratorial activity, but later escaped to serve in the Polish army in 1831.

THE REVOLUTION OF 1830

affair. As they were retiring in the woods to discuss their plans a former officer, Jordan, who was in no way connected with either Umiński or Łukasiński, chanced to meet them and was invited to join in their deliberations. Speeches were made, a new society—The Patriotic Society—was formed and a dramatic oath was sworn to work for the reunion of all the Polish lands and to uphold the constitution. Later in the day it was decided to create seven fields of activity, or 'provinces': Warsaw, Lithuania, Cracow, Poznań, Volhynia, Lvov and the army, in each of which were to be three circles, each subdivided into three to nine communes. Umiński was given command of the Poznań province and promptly refused to join in the central committee's discussions on the ground that he was now a provincial leader; he also had some pressing invitations to card parties which he considered more important. The Poznanian members of the central committee, Prądzyński, Bruno Kiciński and Teodor Morawski, who had thought that they would play the leading role in the conspiracy, withdrew from all part in it when they discovered that they were outnumbered by Poles from the Congress Kingdom. Łukasiński was thus left in supreme control.

During the discussion a number of conspirators had left Warsaw to begin their work in their provinces under the impression that all was well in the central committee. Ludwik Sobański began to organize Volhynia, Podolia and Kiev, uniting the Patriotic Society with another group of conspirators, the *Templars*, which had come into existence independently in Volhynia. A similar organization was set up in Vilna, but in Galicia and Cracow the efforts of the society were a complete failure. No one capable of leading a conspiracy was found in Lvov. In Cracow Pawlikowski, who took over command from Jordan, the officer picked up so casually on 1 May 1821, took no action at all. Umiński did little or nothing in Poznań. Only among the army officers in the Kingdom, Łukasiński's own province, was progress made, though not one person with any claim to national reputation joined the movement. Łukasiński never evolved anything which could be called a political theory. One of his few political ideas was that the constitution of 1815 was the best one for Poland; when Umiński had attempted to uphold the Constitution of 1791, Łukasiński rejected it as reactionary: 'Give us a rest, General! Put away your old piece of furniture. It's nice in a library for those who are curious, but it's not for use. Our constitution is far better.'[1] He preferred even the Dresden constitution. For the rest he had no solution to offer. He certainly had no ideas of social reform; there is no evidence that he wished to break with Russia. The illegality of Łukasiński's activity lay not so much in its intentions as in its existence.

The conspiracy did not prosper. He made the mistake ot entrusting vital negotiations to a certain Sznayder, a man of doubtful worth who was running the risk of prosecution for bigamy and revealed what he knew to the police in order to ingratiate himself with the authorities; so dubious was his integrity that Constantine thought that he was an *agent provocateur*. Łukasiński was called to the Belvedere Palace where he revealed the existence of National Freemasonry which he said had been suppressed, but kept the Patriotic Society a secret. Constantine was apparently satisfied, but owing to one or two inconsistencies in his story removed Łukasiński from the 4th Infantry Regiment and sent him on half pay to the staff of the Uhlan division commanded by the Prince of Wurtemberg. What finally ruined Łukasiński was the treachery of an ex-officer, Nagorski, who had been admitted to the Patriotic Society in Kalisz, and who betrayed its existence for 800 roubles, not to Constantine, but to Novosiltsev. Constantine, who had no particular desire to investigate the past of his officers, was forced to take the matter up. Confirmation of the Patriotic Society's existence came when another ex-officer, Karski, who had gone to Paris with the intention of passing on to join the Greek army but run short of money in a bout of dissipation, reported to the ambassador Pozzo di Borgo that he had been entrusted with letters for the Society's sympathizers in Paris. His confession produced no more than 300 francs from the ambassador for further debauchery and he was forced to agree to return to Poland to make a report to the authorities on the spot. Łukasiński was inevitably arrested with a few of his closer associates and himself sentenced to seven years' hard

[1] S. Askenazy, *Łukasiński*, ii, 54.

THE REVOLUTION OF 1830 113

labour, from which in fact he was never released, dying in prison in 1868. Alexander I issued an amnesty for all acts which occurred before January 1824 in the hope that the matter might be buried for ever, but Łukasiński's reticence had ensured that not all his followers were discovered. Lieutenant-Colonel Krzyżanowski assumed direction of the Society's work.

It had already been noticed in 1823 that the officers of the Russian forces stationed in the Ukraine were dissatisfied, making remarks to the Poles that the existing social order could not be maintained and that radical changes were necessary. The Polish nobility even obtained reports of a Russian secret society, presumably aiming at revolution, but at first no contact could be established. Eventually, as a shot in the dark, Muraviev-Apostol and Bestuzhev-Riumin approached Count Alexander Chodkiewicz in 1823 and asked for information on the state of Polish preparedness. Chodkiewicz did not himself belong to the Patriotic Society, but had some idea of persons likely to belong to secret societies and promised to arrange an interview.[1] It was not until the Kiev Contracts of January 1824, an occasion for business transactions when Poles might legitimately be in Kiev, which still served as a centre for the Polish *szlachta* of the southeast even after its cession to Russia, that Krzyżanowski arrived to discuss collaboration. Some Polish writers have been inclined to defend the attitude adopted by Krzyżanowski, who refused to commit himself and retained full freedom of action, pleading that he had no powers to conclude an agreement. The Russian conspirators were willing to make substantial concessions and would have granted an extension of the Polish frontier to the east, provided that the Polish army maintained an attitude of neutrality and prevented Constantine from intervening in Russia. When conversation turned to the form of government to be adopted there was serious disagreement. The Russians favoured a republican constitution of the American type, but Krzyżanowski declared for constitutional monarchy, fearing legitimist hostility in Prussia and Austria, and refused to condone the assassination of the monarch. Prince Jabłonowski was appointed to continue the talks, but the meeting at the

[1] The official account of the relations of the Decembrists and the Poles may be found in *Donesenie Varshavskavo Sledstvennavo Komiteta*, of 3 December 1827.

I

Contracts in Kiev in January 1825 had the same negative result. In the absence of definite agreement another meeting was called for January 1826. The Russians were in no haste; Bestuzhev told the Poles that a rising might be carried out in five years' time, while Muraviev thought it might be achieved a little earlier. As it was, Alexander I left Warsaw on 14 June 1825 and died unexpectedly at Taganrog on 1 December. The Decembrists rose in revolt to take advantage of the confusion when most of Russia was uncertain whether Constantine, who had foregone his rights of succession to marry the Polish lady, Grudzińska, or the Grand Duke Nicholas would become tsar. The Patriotic Soicety was found completely unprepared and maintained an attitude of passivity while the Decembrists were suppressed, no doubt because the Polish conspiracy existed only on paper. Inactivity did not save Krzyżanowski because once again the inevitable traitor appeared, Prince Jabłonowski, who in hope of saving his estates divulged the conversations between the Poles and the Russians. There was no alternative but to establish a committee of investigation to collect evidence which led in its turn to the arrest of Krzyżanowski and his associates in Warsaw.

Krzyżanowski's trial was a turning-point in Russo-Polish relations. His dealings with the Decembrists were not technically high treason because the Kingdom of Poland and the Russian Empire were two distinct political units. When the government appeared to wish a conviction on the charge of treason the Poles protested that not only was it an injustice to try Krzyżanowski for an offence committed outside the Kingdom, but that the very autonomy of the Kingdom was threatened. Vigorous protests of the aristocracy led to the transfer of the trial to a special court of the diet, which convicted Krzyżanowski on the lesser charge of conspiracy. Though this verdict, supported by Lubecki himself, was upheld by Nicholas I, the damage was done. An affront was given to national feeling. Czartoryski's participation in the proceedings of the court gave the impression once more that even he, whose political career had been built upon the conception of Russo-Polish co-operation, was no longer convinced of Russian good will. At first sight however the trial was not without its advantages for the government, for it appeared that the authorities were in earnest in their efforts to put down conspiracies. Persons prominent in political circles avoided contacts with secret societies even more than before. The consequence of the official leaders' caution was that the direction of conspiratorial activity fell into the hands of men who were too obscure to attract the attention either of the police or anyone else. Of little experience in political affairs, they took upon themselves the task of interpreting the needs of Poland, and, though not light-heartedly, at least with little knowledge of the nature of the opposition or of the price of failure, they prepared to bring their country to the point of revolution. The men who were ready to challenge the Russian connection were the subalterns of the Warsaw garrison, the cadets of the training school and the literary men of the capital. In December 1828 Piotr Wysocki, a subaltern instructor of the cadet school in the Łazienki Gardens, not a mile from Constantine's residence in the Belvedere Palace, formed an association among the cadets under instruction.

There was in the late 1820's plenty of material for Wysocki to bring into his conspiracy, especially among the military. A term of service in the army was a desirable part of a young man's education, on the completion of which he would retire to his native district with a military rank by which he would ever afterwards be known. Advancement however was not easy to obtain. Constantine had declined to employ his Polish army in the Russo-Turkish war of 1828–9 lest its parade ground efficiency be disrupted. The Napoleonic veterans clung to their commissions and blocked promotions. The cadets saw no prospect of advancement and seemed condemned by the stultifying military system to a life of endless parades and instruction.[1] In the early days the commander-in-chief, Constantine, had set himself the task of restoring discipline in the army by imposing his own stiff Russian standards. Undoubtedly he could be

[1] W. Tokarz, *Sprzysiężenie Wysockiego i Noc Listopadowa* (Warsaw, 1925), pp. 16–17, gives a depressing account of the state of affairs in the cadet school. Over one-third of the cadets had served nine years in the army by 1830. Some had served thirteen years. Out of 266 cadets one-third had been in the school for five years or more, a galling experience for young men who thought of themselves entitled by birth to hold commissions, and incredibly boring if it is considered that those cadets who were not commissioned at the end of the course began it all over again.

harsh, and would criticize even high-ranking officers on parade for their lack of proper military bearing. One officer was so humiliated by Constantine's insults that he committed suicide on parade, while others resigned from the army rather than suffer further indignities. One of these was the toughest officer in the Polish army, General Józef Chłopicki, who had served everywhere from Italy to Spain, from Germany to Moscow, and was something of a popular hero in Warsaw, a popularity which was only increased by his determined rejection of Constantine's pleas to rejoin. After his marriage to his Polish wife, Grudzińska, Constantine apparently became much milder in his treatment of his officers. If his administration of the army showed occasional severities, which are common enough in any army, but which were offensive to the Poles who did not take to military discipline of this kind well, it can at least be said in his favour that he also appeared at times to be generous and just. The main source of discontent among the younger elements of the army was the frustrating restrictions of military life and the lack of purpose in an army which existed but was not used. They wanted glory and distinction, very much as the literary men, suffocated by a censorship which applied the tests of the clericals to all writings, wanted freedom from intellectual supervision and liberty to achieve success outside the bounds of conventional literature. The cadets and the literary men met in the cafés and joined forces. Romanticism seemed to express the longings of the cadets also. Seweryn Goszczyński, who was closely connected with artistic circles in 1830, wrote of the literary conspiracy: 'This civilian association had shown above all a literary character. Its field of activity was literature— literature of a new trend, with a spirit different from what had gone before. . . . It freed the Polish spirit from foreign models in the intellectual and moral field.'[1] For all these literary associations there was nothing intellectual in Wysocki and his political programme. Wysocki himself was scarcely educated at all, though in the hours when he was not instructing the cadets in musketry he tried to master Latin and French with little success. He was typical of the petty *szlachta*, provincial in outlook and with little knowledge of the world outside Poland, or

[1] S. Goszczyński, *Noc Belwederska, Dzieła Zbiorowe* (Lvov, 1912), iv, 302–3.

of high politics. He himself had no clear plan of action, but his aims were simple; the members of his group swore to uphold the constitution.[1] There seems no reason to doubt his own subsequent confessions, that he had no intention of launching an attack upon the Russian Empire to win back the lost provinces of the east; still further from his thoughts were ideas of social emancipation or the regeneration of Poland by reform.[2] The conspiracy was an association of men who carried little weight in political circles. From the outset Wysocki sought to attract prominent personages, but found it difficult to interest them. According to Mochnacki three deputies did make contact with him before the diet of 1829, when Nicholas I came to Warsaw for his coronation, with the object of organizing a *coup*, but the majority of the members of the diet were plainly more interested in obtaining the decorations which were to be distributed to mark the occasion.[3] Failure to take action was repeated in May–June 1830 when Nicholas was again present in Warsaw for the meeting of the diet, though the cadets, who had not obtained promotions on the occasion of the coronation, were more than ever anxious to stage a *coup*. It seemed that the *coup d'état* would have to be put off indefinitely when suddenly the whole situation changed in the second half of 1830. Revolution broke out in Paris and a state of suppressed excitement was evident in Warsaw, for France was, for the younger generation, still the France of the Revolutionary epoch and of Napoleon,

[1] *Ibid.*, iv, 296–7.
[2] J. S. Harbut, *Noc listopadowa w świetle i cieniach procesu przed Najwyższym Sądem Kryminalnym* (Warsaw, 1926), pp. 405–84, has reprinted the confessions of Wysocki in Bobruisk and before the supreme criminal court set up to try the conspirators who fell into Russian hands. Wysocki declared that '. . . we had no other plan if we succeeded in disarming the Russian troops stationed in Warsaw at the time than to call upon the Nation, or rather the Diet, and put ourselves in all respects under its orders, but as for making an incursion into the *gubernii* which formerly belonged to Poland and operating there, there was no mention in the plan we drew up.' *ibid.*, p. 477.
[3] M. Mochnacki, *Powstanie narodu polskiego* (Paris, 1834), i, 547 and footnote: Mochnacki relied upon the verbal evidence of his friend, Adam Gurowski. S. Barzykowski, *Historya powstania listopadowego*, i, 256, writes that he questioned Tytus Działyński and Bernard Potocki, two of the persons alleged to have been in touch with Wysocki, who indignantly denied all part in the affair, and questioned whether or not it had ever existed. A. Kraushar, *Spisek koronacyjny z roku 1829 w świetle prawdy historycznej (Miscellanea historyczne*, XXXIII) (Cracow, 1909), finds no evidence for Wysocki's part in a plot in 1829.

which might once again take up a policy of expansion. Even Czartoryski could feel suppressed excitement. Wysocki, urged on by his closest associate, Zaliwski, a swimming instructor in the army, who believed that it was necessary only to begin an insurrection to attract everyone else in Poland to take part in it, was compelled to quicken his preparations and by bringing more members into his conspiracy increased the likelihood of its being discovered.

Nicholas I was no less aware of events in Western Europe. Too much can be made of his ideological preference for legitimism. Undoubtedly he thought that Louis Philippe, for all the folly of Charles X and Polignac, had no right to the throne of France, but what troubled him more was the practical consideration whether France would take up the expansionist policy of the Republic and the Empire. Each advance of the Russian frontier had raised the problem of relations with countries to the west. There was a natural preference for friendly states as neighbours, which gave Russia an interest in maintaining princely particularism within the German Confederation and in suppressing liberalism with its demands for unification which would make Germany strong. Metternich and Nesselrode agreed in July at Carlsbad that the powers ought to combine to prevent France from extending her influence on the Rhine and in Italy, but this did not mean that they were to intervene in the internal affairs of France; Nicholas I thought that by withholding recognition of Louis Philippe he could exert a moral pressure on the French government to manifest its willingness to accept the Vienna settlement. On 18 August he wrote to Constantine:

L'Orleans ne sera toujours qu'un infâme usurpateur. Mais tout cela ne nous donne ni le droit ni le besoin même d'intervenir de force; notre opposition sera *morale*. Mais si, ce qui n'est qu'à prévoir, la France révolutionnaire pense à recouvrer ses anciennes frontières, cela change entièrement nos devoirs, et alors les traités sont là pour nous prescrire à chacun notre rôle, c'est l'épée à la main que la chose doit se terminer, ce dont Dieu nous préserve.[1]

---

[1] *Correspondance de L'Empereur Nicholas I et du Grand Duc Constantin*, ii (1830-1) (*Sbornik Imperatorskavo Russkavo Istoricheskavo Obshchestva*, cxxxii, St. Petersburg, 1911), p. 36.

THE REVOLUTION OF 1830

Nicholas I's plan was that Austria, Prussia and Russia should not leave their attitude towards France open to doubt, but should undertake a partial mobilization to demonstrate their readiness and ability to take prompt action. There was some hesitation in St. Petersburg because the ministers and entourage of the tsar were not all of one mind, Nesselrode believing with Kankrin that war would place too great a strain upon Russian finances unless a British subsidy could be obtained, while Field-Marshal Diebitsch was insisting that war, if it came, could be made to pay for itself.[1] Nevertheless, to discuss the military arrangements of this demonstration of power the tsar's adjutant, Count Orlov was sent to Vienna and Diebitsch to Berlin.[2] Austria and Prussia however did not regard the matter with the same urgency, preferring like Great Britain to recognize Louis Philippe, and to await positive indications of French aggressiveness, and considering also that the Belgian crisis could be solved by the conference to be arranged in London. Diebitsch, who arrived in Berlin on the night of 26/27 August, found that Frederick William III was unwilling to make any immediate decision. In the meantime Nicholas acted as if Prussian cooperation were a foregone conclusion. Steps were taken to put the Russian First Army on a war footing. Chernishev, the minister of war, was ordered to let these preparations be advertised in order that they might act as a deterrent to France, though with the instruction that the expenses of mobilization should be kept down.[3] Troops were to move forward on 22 December. The situation was however altered when Diebitsch reported that Prussia was disinclined to take hasty action. Nevertheless, the outbreak of disorder in Brussels and a wave of riots in Germany affecting Cassel, Brunswick, Leipzig, Aix-la-Chapelle, Hamburg and Dresden seemed so serious that the tsar decided to proceed with mobilization in order to put heart into the German princes who might otherwise waver and adopt

---

[1] N. K. Shilder, *Imperator Nikolai Pervii* (St. Petersburg, 1903), ii, 471 n, quoting Diebitsch's letter of 30 November 1830 to Nesselrode, shows that the party of intervention was thinking in terms of Russian security: 'Si nos finances ne nous permettent pas de défendre la paix de l'Europe, alors elles nous permettront encore bien moins de soutenir quand cette même Europe émancipera la Pologne.'

[2] N. K. Shilder, *ibid.*, ii, 571–4, prints Diebitsch's summary of his instructions.

[3] Shilder, *ibid.*, pp. 575–6.

a supine attitude towards France.¹ At the outset Nicholas had intended to embody the army of the Congress Kingdom in the observation force. On 18 August Lubecki was instructed to explore the administrative problems of putting the Polish army on a war footing. Before he had received news of the Prussian decision not to undertake mobilization Nicholas I wrote to Constantine on 18 October instructing him to make arrangements with Diebitsch for Polish mobilization when he passed through Warsaw on his return from Berlin.² Official orders would arrive from St. Petersburg as a matter of course. Diebitsch however, failing to obtain Prussian collaboration, returned to St. Petersburg direct and wrote to Constantine advising him to suspend preparations, an action which Constantine had already taken when Diebitsch did not arrive in Warsaw on time.³ The financial resources of the Congress Kingdom were so slender that it was inadvisable to impose unnecessary burdens and Nicholas I agreed to an indefinite suspension of mobilization in the Kingdom, instructing the secretary of state Grabowski to apologize to Lubecki for what might turn out to be fruitless effort.⁴ This decision was of enormous importance for the insurrection of 1830. If mobilization had been ordered in Poland the Polish army would have been better able to take the field, or, removed from its normal peacetime stations and set on march for the frontier, would not have fallen under the influence of the revolutionary movement in Warsaw. As it was, the revolution broke out at a time when the Polish troops were unprepared, while Russian troops were moving up to the western frontier of the Empire.

There is very little evidence to show that the leading Polish conspirators rose in revolt in order to prevent the Polish army from being used to quell the French revolution. That was a justification after the event for the purpose of establishing a claim to French sympathy. The truth is that Constantine, who had minimized the danger of a Polish revolution in his letters to

---

¹ *Correspondance*, ii, 62. Nicholas I to Constantine, 9 November 1830.
² *Ibid.*, ii, 55.   ³ *Ibid.*, ii, 57, 59–60, 63.
⁴ 'Sa Majesté a été fort satisfaite de vous voir penser à tout *ce qui se trouvera nécessaire pour le cas de la guerre*, et m'a chargé de vous dire qu'Il [sic] y a pensé, et s'Il n'a point donné encore *aucun ordre*, c'est qu'Il ne voulait pas occasionner des dépenses inutiles.' *Korespondencya Lubeckiego*, iii, 397, Grabowski to Lubecki, 17 November 1830.

Nicholas, had discovered the existence of the conspiracy. The usual phenomenon of denunciation and confession had revealed a plot among the students which clearly had links with the army. Constantine began to investigate the conspiracy with his customary slowness, probably distrusting his own police and suspecting the existence of *agents provocateurs*, but it could only be a question of time before the trail led to Wysocki. Wysocki for his part, even in the late autumn of 1830, could find no one in Warsaw to consult, except the historian, Lelewel, with whom he and his principal lieutenants had an interview on 21 November. Lelewel warned them that a rising could expect success only if it were supported by a foreign power, but the conspirators pointed out that they were in a difficult position: '. . . We declared that we could not withdraw now and that if we did not take up arms we should all be hanged; that we would revolt, for it was always possible to entertain the hope that it might succeed, and we said that we had decided not to abandon our plan now that we had made it.'[1] Lelewel asked for a few days to think the matter over, but on 26 November he again advised them not to undertake an insurrection.[2] As it was there was no alternative for Wysocki but to hasten his plans. The original date for the rising had been 10 December, but the news that Constantine had received instructions from St. Petersburg to draw up a list of suspects and make arrests compelled him to arrange the revolt for 29 November, the day on which public buildings in Warsaw were being guarded by the 4th Infantry Regiment in which the bulk of the conspirators' strength lay.

In this haphazard way, almost with no plan, the rising began. Some of the civilian conspirators had decided that the insurrection had small chance of success and had disassociated themselves from it. Not one prominent person was informed that it would take place when it did. The signal, the burning of a brewery, was bungled; the fire picket put it out. Only fourteen civilians appeared where fifty had been promised for the attack on the Belvedere Palace, which failed because the attackers did not stay long enough to seek out Constantine. Wysocki had roused a handful of cadets for the task of bringing out the rest of the Warsaw garrison, but nowhere could he find a senior

[1] J. S. Harbut, *Noc listopadowa*, p. 410.   [2] *Ibid.*, pp. 410–11.

officer willing to join the revolutionary movement. A number of high-ranking officers, some of them quite popular with the soldiers, were done to death for their refusal to join the rioters.[1] Citizens of the bourgeois class locked their doors and stayed behind them. The whole affair might have petered out in a few hours. Instead, it succeeded in its object for reasons which had not entered into the calculations of the conspirators.

Although Warsaw was not a large city there were in the poorer quarters large numbers of craftsmen, while the nobility resident in the city maintained considerable staffs of servants. Though this was not a proletariat in the modern sense it at least reacted strongly to economic pressures, as indeed it had in 1794.[2] 1830 had been a year of harvest failure in Poland. The *korzec* of rye, the staple food of the lower classes in Warsaw, had risen from 9 *złp* in May to 19 *złp* 5 *gr* in November.[3] Similar rises had taken place for other grains. To the disgust of the artisans the prices of beer and vodka had been raised on 29 November, a Monday and traditionally a day for drunken brawls.[4] A financial scandal in the city's administration had increased the hostility of the lower classes during the autumn to the authorities who had for years been suspected in the popular mind of dishonesty. When once the workmen realized what was afoot in the city it did not take them long to decide whether or not they might join in. If the military were engaged in the movement, the people could rise with impunity. The arsenal was broken open and nearly 30,000 rifles were distributed among the mob.[5] Economic factors may also have some

[1] Including General Maurycy Hauke, the vice-minister of war, father of Julia Hauke who subsequently became princess of Battenberg.

[2] According to F. M. Sobieszczański, *Rys historyczno-statystyczny wzrostu i stanu miasta Warszawy*, pp. 252, 300, out of a total population of 139,654 persons of both sexes in 1830, 30,945 were Jews who can be discounted as a political factor in the rising, and 108,709 were Christians, of whom 54,325 were males. In 1825 the total number of persons of *szlachta* status was 15,306. On this basis a reasonable guess, after the deduction of the upper strata of the bourgeoisie and the male children of the working class too young to appear in the streets, might be about 20,000–30,000 adults capable of taking part in the insurrection.

[3] Table of average prices of food in the markets of Warsaw and Praga, *A.A.D.*, *No. 426 (Ceny Targowe)*, 26 January 1831.

[4] T. Lipiński, *Zapiski z lat 1825–1831*, ed. K. Bartoszewicz (Cracow, 1883), p. 211.

[5] B. Pawłowski, *Źródła do dziejów wojny polsko-rosyjskiej 1830–1831 r.*, i, no. 120, p. 125. According to the ministry of war there were in the arsenal 34,311 rifles at the time of the revolution of which only 5,000 remained on 4 December 1830.

THE REVOLUTION OF 1830

influence upon the conduct of the private soldiers of the Warsaw garrison. Half the soldiers' pay was allotted to the colonel of the regiment for the purpose of buying rations. In periods of constant and generally low prices the colonel could feed his men well and at the same time make a handsome profit, but in 1830 no adjustment of pay had been made to meet the increased cost of food. When the soldiers saw the mob breaking open provision shops and helping themselves to vodka they joined in readily.[1] Discipline quickly broke down and the senior officers lost control over their men. What had begun as a military *coup* had by midnight assumed the proportions of a popular revolution.[2]

Outside the city Constantine was in a position of some difficulty. He could trust his Russian troops, but to use them might be considered a violation of the Kingdom's independence and even an act of war. He was limited to the handful of Polish troops he could gather together, if he refused to use his Russians.[3]

---

[1] It would be unwise to suppose much conscious revolutionary ardour among the peasant soldiers of the Polish army. A. E. Kozmian records how the Grand Duke Constantine in 1816 asked a soldier in which war he had won a medal he was wearing on his chest. On the third time of asking the soldier replied: 'I was standing in the second line, so I did not know with whom they were fighting in the front.' *O kmiotku polskim* (Leszno, 1843), p. 21. This may be only a good story, but it contains a grain of truth.

[2] On the day of the rising there were 8,700 Polish infantry and 850 cavalry with 13 guns stationed in Warsaw; troops of the Russian army numbered 4,400 infantry, 2,250 cavalry and 4 guns. 30,000 armed civilians in the narrow streets of the city would have been a match for all these men even if discipline had not broken down among the Polish troops.

[3] Władysław Zamoyski, his A.D.C. and after 1831 Czartoryski's lieutenant in exile, begged Constantine to send his cavalry into the city to restore order, but Constantine replied: 'De la cavalerie? Je n'en ai point. Ceux-ci sont des Russes et pas un Russe, à moins qu'il n'y soit forcé, pour sa propre défense, ne fera un coup de fusil, ne donnera un coup de sabre dans toute cette affaire. Le crime est de votre côté, je n'y veux donner la main . . . Ces troupes sont ici pour me préserver d'une nouvelle attaque, mais si on approche, eh bien, elles se retireront. Pas un Russe ne se mêlera de cette affaire. Les Polonais l'ont commencé, c'est une affaire polonaise; qu'ils s'arrangent entre eux. On verra maintenant s'ils ont mérité des bienfaits . . . Moi, je ne mêle de rien. Que les Polonais s'arrangent. C'est leur affaire.' W. Zamoyski, *Jenerał Zamoyski* (Poznań, 1910–14), i (1803–30), 376, notes 1 and 2. Nicholas subsequently endorsed the course which Constantine had taken, cf. *Lettres et papiers du chancelier Comte de Nesselrode, 1760–1850* (Paris, 1904–12), vii, 161. There seems to have been a long-standing arrangement dating from the time of Alexander I not to allow Russian troops to become embroiled with the Poles.

Among the leaders of Polish political circles in Warsaw the presence of armed rioters in the streets at first called forth no response; they believed that Constantine would soon restore order. When it became obvious that he had no intention of intervening and that the revolutionaries for their part had not set up an organization to take over the government of the Kingdom, each group after its fashion began to reflect upon what measures ought to be taken to meet the crisis. The aristocrats had no wish to break the connection with Russia, but they feared to stand aside lest the situation get out of control. Their action naturally depended upon the lead given by Adam Czartoryski. Czartoryski, informed by his nephew Władysław Zamoyski, of Constantine's refusal to intervene, was reluctant to become involved, but feared the consequences if a revolutionary government obtained command. He afterwards wrote: 'We were caught in a most inconceivable manner. It would have been to no purpose and quite fruitless to have offered resistance to the movement or to have refused participation in it.'[1] With Lubecki's approval he called an emergency meeting of the Administrative Council, of which he was still officially a member, though he had not attended its meetings for some years, believing that if he lent his own moral authority to the government it might be able to convince the revolutionaries that there were men in control who had the best interests of Poland at heart. When, in an interview with Constantine, Czartoryski and Lubecki learned that Russian troops would not be sent into the city to put down the rising,[2] it was plain that the onus of responsibility had been placed upon the Administrative Council to find its own way out of the difficulties. It was decided to co-opt new members, who would be popular with the mob; the literary lion Julian Niemcewicz,[3] Prince Michał

[1] *Jenerał Zamoyski*, ii, 37. Popiel relates how Zamoyski replied regretfully, 'C'est trop tard!' when he pressed him to get Constantine to use his troops, *Pamiętnik Pawła Popiela* (Cracow, 1927), p. 59.

[2] Leon Dembowski heard that Constantine replied: 'Je suis suis loin de vouloir commettre la même faute, qu'a faite à Bruxelles mon cousin d'Orange. Me battre dans les rues, c'est m'exposer à verser le sang des braves . . . C'est à Vous, Mesieurs, à employer les mesures que Vous jugerez éfficaces pour tranquilliser cette émeute.' *Moje wspomnienia* (St. Petersburg, 1898), ii, 28.

[3] Niemcewicz was utterly opposed to the revolution and condemns it in his diary, *Pamiętniki z 1830–1831 roku*, ed. M. A. Kurpiel (Cracow, 1909), p. 46.

Radziwiłł, whose brother, Antoni, was viceroy of the Grand Duchy of Posen, and who was accordingly some guarantee to the outside world of the Council's respectability, Ludwik Pac, an aristocrat with vast estates and a good war record, Michał Kochanowski, a veteran of 1791, and most popular of all, the hero, General Józef Chłopicki.[1] The first action of the council was to issue a proclamation calling for self-restraint on the part of the Poles and containing a warning that an internecine struggle could have only the most unfortunate results for the country.[2]

The tone of the proclamation did not reflect the spirit of the soldiers and the mob. Looting began again early in the morning on the fashionable Nowy Świat, and a Polish officer who attempted to intervene was shot dead by the soldiery. The students of the university were forming an academic guard. When the Council transferred its place of meeting from the Branicki palace to the Bank of Poland for better security, it was greeted on its way by revolutionary cries and demands for the nomination of General Chłopicki as commander-in-chief, a request which was difficult to fulfil because Chłopicki had been in hiding from the moment the revolution had begun. Steps were now taken to mobilize the propertied classes of the city in support of the Council. Węgrzecki, the former town president from the Duchy of Warsaw, with political views similar to those of the Council, was reappointed with the energetic Tomasz

[1] On the night of 29 November Chłopicki hid himself in the ministry of war, remarking: 'Some half-wits have started a riot for which everyone may pay dearly. We ought not to get mixed up in it, lest we get drawn into this folly against our will.' 'Pamiętnik Alfreda Młockiego', *Zbiór pamiętników do historyi powstania polskiego z roku 1830–1831*, ed. A. Hirschberg (Lvov, 1882), p. 271. It was for this reason that he could not be traced on the morning of 30 November.

[2] D'Angeberg, *Recueil des traités, conventions et actes diplomatiques concernant la Pologne, 1762–1862* (Paris, 1862), p. 763, gives a French translation of this proclamation. '. . . Le Polonais, pourrait-il souiller ses mains du sang de ses frères? Voudriez-vous donner au monde le triste spectacle d'une guerre civile? Votre propre modération seule pourrait vous sauver de l'abîme sur lequel vous êtes placés. Rentrez donc dans l'ordre et la tranquillité; que tous les emportements disparaissent avec la nuit qui les a couvert de son voile! Songez à l'avenir de cette patrie, qui a passé par tant de malheurs! Éloignez d'elle tout ce qui pourrait mettre son existence en danger. Quant à nous, notre devoir sera de veiller à la sûreté, à l'execution des lois et aux libertés constitutionelles qui sont garanties à notre pays.'

Łubieński to assist him in the task of restoring order.[1] A security guard of middle-class householders and their sons was hastily organized and armed with what weapons were to hand.[2] The situation seemed so serious that even General Chłopicki stirred himself, put on all his medals, a gesture familiar in Poland when a general aims at being impressive, and stamped down to the Bank of Poland to present himself for duty, announcing to his friends that he intended to put a stop to the folly.

In the meantime Constantine had devised a plan to call upon units of the Polish army stationed in the country districts, who were unaffected by the revolutionary movement, and with their aid to cordon off Warsaw, but the assumption of responsibility by the Administrative Council was bound to create confusion in the minds of the unit commanders. At 8.30 p.m. on 30 November Chłopicki reported that he had had a verbal inquiry from General Szembek commanding the 3rd Infantry Brigade of the 1st Infantry Division stationed at Sochaczew whether or not he ought to march on Warsaw. Chłopicki was authorized to bring this unit into the city.[3] At 2.30 a.m. on 1 December Szembek received an order from Constantine to march to Błonie where he would receive further orders.[4] On the morning of 1 December Szembek rode ahead to ask Constantine the reason for these two sets of instructions. Confusion was increased when Chłopicki was given permission to bring in more units, the whole of the 1st Infantry Division and the 8th Infantry Regiment, which were ordered to march on Warsaw.[5] On 2 December Constantine gave the order for the 1st Infantry

---

[1] K. A. Hoffman, *Wielki Tydzień Polaków*, pp. 63–4, reprints Węgrzecki's proclamation as proof that the propertied classes were supporting the revolution, but that was hardly its intention: '. . . Do not refuse me this essential aid. I address myself to you, Men of Property, Merchants, Master Craftsmen, Manufacturers— hasten to the ranks of the Security Guard! With arms in your hands none of the inhabitants of the capital will have doubts about the safety of their persons and property. Let the workmen and servants return to their work. . . .'
[2] T. W. Łubieński, *Henryk Łubieński i jego bracia*, p. 98, recalls this exciting moment of his childhood. 'I was too young to belong to this cohort, but I remember how jealously I watched my elder brother going off on this expedition, with some sort of sword strapped to his waist, and his pockets stuffed with rolls and butter with which our anxious mother had supplied him.'
[3] Pawłowski, *Źródła*, i, 10.   [4] *Ibid.*, i, 11.   [5] *Ibid.*, i, 13.

THE REVOLUTION OF 1830 127

Division to concentrate at Mokotów, south of Warsaw.[1] The issue of these two sets of orders was resolved by the action of the Polish troops themselves when they met a party of revolutionaries who rode out to General Szembek's men and informed them that an uprising had taken place in the city, imploring them not to fire on the insurgents. Szembek returned to his unit ready to carry out the orders of Constantine, but found that his troops had decided to join hands with the revolutionaries. Seeing no other solution Szembek chose the easy course and gave in to the wishes of the troops. This action settled the question for the men of the other formations marching towards the capital.[2] The army was to enter the city in support of the revolution, not, as the Administrative Council hoped, with the intention of restoring order. The danger grew that the Polish army, exalted with revolutionary ardour, would launch an attack upon Constantine's Russian troops and precipitate a war between the Kingdom and the Empire. An understanding with the grand duke was imperative.

Before an agreement could be reached with Constantine the Council's plans were to be complicated by the arrival of a small deputation on 1 December of members of the diet with a list of suggestions and observations. Though the composition of the deputation was mixed in its views, its opinions were more revolutionary than the Council would have wished.[3] It complained that the proclamation of 30 November had created a bad impression and that the Council obviously lacked revolutionary spirit. One of its members, Szaniecki, already thinking in terms of social transformation, singled out Prince Lubecki for attack as the leading spirit of a counter-revolution. The deputation insisted that the diet should be called, that the Council should co-opt new members and that supplies should be collected for the army. Once more the Council followed its policy of drift and compromise. Unpopular members of the Council were compelled to resign and their places were taken by Władysław Ostrowski, Gustaw Małachowski and the historian Lelewel, all

[1] *Ibid.*, i, 13-14. [2] *Ibid.*, i, 14.
[3] There are three accounts of this deputation which all differ. *Pamiętnik Jana Olrycha Szanieckiego*, pp. 57-8. L. Dembowski, *Moje wspomnienia*, ii, 40-1, and S. Barzykowski, *Historya powstania listopadowego*, i, 350.

of whom were popular with the general public. The reconstituted Council formed itself into an executive committee, which would give it the power to plead, if explanations had to be made in St. Petersburg, that no actual nominations, the prerogative of the Crown, had been made.

The Council was reckoning without the radicals of the city. Members of the diet and its committees had a constitutional right of access to the Council, but the radicals had first to gather their strength in the city before they could impress their will upon the Polish leaders. On the evening of 1 December a meeting was called in the town hall by the leading representatives of the Romantic movement in literature, of whom the two most important in the political sense were Ksawery Bronikowski and Maurycy Mochnacki. This meeting, attended by armed revolutionaries wild with excitement, was in no mood to tolerate the protestations of the town president, Węgrzecki, that the town hall might not be used for radical assemblies. The meeting decided to establish a revolutionary club, the Patriotic Society, of which Lelewel was elected president, though its real leaders were Mochnacki and his friends. The majority of the young radical leaders saw their purpose as the maintenance of the revolution's momentum to bring Poland to the point of war with Russia. There is little evidence that they wished to take control of the government and assume direction of the war. Mochnacki may have been the exception, because he claims that he desired to take the direction of affairs out of the hands of the traditional leaders, Czartoryski and his associates. He saw himself as the Romantic hero in real life, who would set himself at the head of a revolutionary commune and lead Poland to victory in her struggle for independence. It was the Council's fear of the radicals which caused it to secure its position by the establishment of security guards in all the towns of the Kingdom, composed of the propertied classes, and to be supervised by a Citizens' Council in each *wojewódzwo*.[1] It was hoped that the influence of the provinces would counterbalance the ardour of Warsaw.

Uncertain of the course which events would take in the capital, the Council sent on 2 December a second deputation

[1] Pawłowski, *Źródła*, i, 17-18.

to Constantine, composed of four of its members, Czartoryski and Lubecki on the one hand, and Władysław Ostrowski and Lelewel on the other, with the object of obtaining neutrality at least from the Russian troops. After a long and acrimonious conversation in which Ostrowski and Lelewel, to Czartoryski's obvious embarrassment, declared Poland's right to an extension of her frontiers in the east, Constantine eventually agreed to the compromise solution which Czartoryski and Lubecki wanted. He promised not to attack Warsaw without first giving twenty-four hours' notice and not to call troops into the Kingdom from Lithuania where he was also commander-in-chief. He undertook in addition to intercede with Nicholas I on behalf of the Poles.[1] Safe in the knowledge that from the Russian side there was no danger of attack, the delegation returned to Warsaw to find that not only had the Patriotic Society met again, but that it was at that moment placing its demands before the Council itself.

At its second meeting on 2 December the Society attracted a large crowd of curious onlookers. On the plea of Mochnacki a delegation was sent to the Council instructed to demand an immediate attack upon Russia and the issue of a summons to the Poles in Western Russia to rise in revolt. This was accompanied by the threat that if these demands were not accepted by the Council it would be forced to accept members of the Patriotic Society into its midst. The deputation marched to the Bank accompanied by a large crowd of spectators. 'Oh, God!' wrote Niemcewicz, 'Only those who had seen Robespierre, Danton, Marat and St. Just would not have been terrified by the frenzied countenances of these braggarts.'[2] The conservatives of the Council behaved in the spirit of their previous concessions. They first invited Mochnacki and Bronikowski with two of their followers to take part in their deliberations, in order for the moment to pacify the radicals, and on the following morning made a gesture which had the dual purpose of retaining for themselves the substance of power and conciliating

[1] For the text of the agreement, see M. Mochnacki, *Powstanie narodu polskiego w r. 1830 i 1831*, ii, 743–5. Lelewel's account of the interview appears in *Polska, dzieje i rzeczy jej*, vii (Poznań, 1859), 152–65, 'Rozmowa i umowa z W. K. Konstantym w Wierzbnie delegowanych Rady Administracyjnej'. (2 December 1830.)   [2] *Pamiętniki z 1830–1 r.*, p. 52.

K

revolutionary opinion. The Administrative Council was dissolved and in its place was set up the 'Temporary Government of the Kingdom of Poland', consisting of Czartoryski, Kochanowski, Niemcewicz, the senator Leon Dembowski and Władysław Ostrowski; Chłopicki was appointed to command the Polish forces. For the moderate revolutionaries nothing could have been more satisfactory. In this manner the Council shed not only Lubecki, whom in any case it could consult, but also Lelewel and the four radicals who had been forced upon it. To forestall the Patriotic Society, which was claiming to speak in the name of the nation in arms, the temporary government announced that the diet, as the representative body of the nation, would be summoned. Further action by the Patriotic Society would have the appearance of being prompted by a desire to override the constitution, the preservation of which the revolutionaries considered the aim of the rising. The ground was cut from under the feet of the extreme radicals at the price of calling in the well-to-do landlords. On the same day Constantine, probably feeling that his presence in the Kingdom was not only an embarrassment to the Council, but even provocative to revolutionary feeling, issued a proclamation permitting the Polish troops under his command to join their comrades in the city,[1] and himself correctly decided to withdraw with his Russians. For the moment there was no danger that war would break out and the Poles were left to find their own way out of the difficulties which the insurrection had created.

From the point of view of Mochnacki the advantages which the Patriotic Society had won on the previous day seemed lost. The dissolution of the Council convinced him that the radicals ought themselves to assume power. At the evening meeting of the Society on 3 December he set himself the task of rousing the mob against the government, but the conservatives had learned their lesson and realized that the mob could be led to almost any action which the fancy of the moment might suggest, provided that it was not directed against the revolution. There was no check on the persons who attended the Society's meetings, because that would have deprived it of its implied claim

[1] Pawłowski, *Źródła*, i, 23.

THE REVOLUTION OF 1830 131

to speak for the nation and have given the impression of organizing a faction. On this occasion the hall was filled with government officials, the friends, domestics and employees of the aristocrats, students from the Academic Guard who supported the revolution but feared Jacobinism, and anyone whom Lubecki and the conservatives could find to support them. Mochnacki, unaware of the composition of the audience brought his attack upon the conservatives to a climax with the declaration—'Gentlemen! Chłopicki is betraying the Nation!' There was an immediate outcry against Mochnacki. Bronikowski, fresh from a private interview with Lubecki, who had disingenuously convinced him of his own revolutionary ardour, tried to pacify the meeting with a statement that he for his part thought that the government was acting in a proper and revolutionary manner, but the conservatives in the hall doused the lights and drew their swords. The meeting closed in disorder.

Mochnacki was not prepared to accept this defeat. Early on the morning of 4 December he made his way to the other centre of authority in Warsaw, the Cadet School, from which the revolution had sprung. Finding the cadets in the street he urged them to renew their revolutionary rôle and murder Lubecki, in whom Mochnacki saw the prime mover of his discomfiture of the previous evening. The cadets were ready enough to deal with Lubecki, but by chance when they began their march they met Wysocki, who by comparing Chłopicki's apparent procrastinations with those of Fabius Cunctator succeeded in dissuading them from following Mochnacki.[1]

The demonstration of the rank and file of the conservatives against the Patriotic Society strengthened the temporary government. A fortuitous incident now pointed the way to an easy solution of the whole situation. Chłopicki, ever given to passionate rages, was seized with an attack of apoplexy during an exchange of opinion with General Krukowiecki, the commander of the 1st Infantry Division and one of the most irritating officers in the Polish army. This encounter gave the young conservatives the happy idea of spreading the rumour that Chłopicki's illness was produced by Mochnacki's onslaught on

[1] Harbut, *Noc listopadowa*, pp. 479–80.

him of the previous evening.¹ The news that 'the one hope of the nation' lay dangerously ill roused the Academic Guard, which took Chłopicki at his face value, to a fever pitch of fury. At 4 p.m. the Guard, of its own initiative, closed the meeting of the Patriotic Society and drew up a loyal address to Chłopicki. Mochnacki was now a hunted man and found refuge in the building of the Bank of Poland with Lubecki, whom he had been proposing to murder a few hours earlier.

Chłopicki's attack of apoplexy was of short duration. Feeling himself stronger with the closure of the Patriotic Society and able now to assess his popularity with the citizens of Warsaw he decided on 5 December, probably with the support of the generals who had now appeared in the city and certainly with the approval of the temporary government, to declare himself dictator.² Yet in taking this step Chłopicki revealed all the weakness of the Administrative Council. Popular personages had to be included in his government in order to silence the criticisms of the revolutionaries. Lelewel was given the ministry of education; Bonawentura Niemojowski, the proscribed constitutionalist from Kalisz, was appointed to the ministry of justice. It was to no purpose that conservatives opposed to the revolutionary movement were appointed to important ministries, or that on 8 December Tomasz Łubieński could write to his father: 'We have restored order among the disorderly mob of the city of Warsaw.'³ Little was to be obtained by giving Wysocki and his partner, Zaliwski, employment outside Warsaw, where they might no longer be dangerous to the government,⁴ or by extracting an apology from Mochnacki before he

---

[1] P. Popiel, *Pamiętnik*, p. 61.

[2] Mochnacki declared that this step was taken on the advice of Czartoryski and Niemcewicz, *Powstanie*, ii, 267–8, which Barzykowski, *Historya*, i, 402–5, denied. In his memoirs Niemcewicz records in an obscure passage that he met Chłopicki who said: 'Do you know what? I have decided to declare myself Dictator, because otherwise, what with these Mochnackis and Clubs, there will be no discipline, order or firmness anywhere.' *Pamiętniki*, p. 54. It was Niemcewicz who composed the proclamation of the dictatorship.

[3] *General Tomasz Pomian hr. Łubieński*, ii, 3. For a similar expression of relief, see Kajetan Garbiński's letter to Czartoryski of 12 February on the reorganization of Warsaw, A. Kraushar, *Miscellanea Archiwalne*, iii (Warsaw, 1913), 145–8, where Garbiński reported that the 'moments of terrorism have past'.

[4] Harbut, *Noc listopadowa*, pp. 480–1.

THE REVOLUTION OF 1830

too left the capital to try his luck in the provinces.[1] Chłopicki had given the impression that he was leading a national revolution. The ambiguities and contradictions of his position were the results of the policy of drift which the conservatives had followed from the outset. Instead of opposing the revolution openly, which would have drawn on them the accusation of lack of patriotism, they had found a temporary solution by placing themselves at its head and in the end were committed by public opinion to supporting the movement for which they had little love. They were conquered by the memories of the past which would permit Polish leaders only to think in terms of resistance. It was a situation in which Chłopicki could neither go forward nor go back. He was dictator only until the meeting of the diet, which was to assemble under the belief that he was prepared to lead an attack on the Russian Empire. On the Russian side there were hopes that he might yet find a peaceful solution. On 25 December 1830 Constantine wrote to Nicholas: 'Grand Dieu! Si cet homme pouvait devenir le second Monk de l'histoire!—quel beau rôle il jouerait!'[2]

---

[1] For Mochnacki's apology, first printed in *Polak Summienny*, see S. Szpotański, *Maurycy Mochnacki* (Cracow, 1910), pp. 221–2. A radical article which appeared in *Kurjer Polski* on 17 December 1830 over the initials of 'M.M.' demanding a settlement of the peasant question is almost certainly not Mochnacki's work and should not be taken as a proof that he demanded a bold social policy to provide a mass basis for the revolution. Mochnacki was too much of the *szlachta* for that.

[2] *Correspondance*, ii, 82.

CHAPTER IV

The Break with Russia and the War

THE question what action Chłopicki ought to have taken in December 1830 was hotly debated during the revolution and afterwards. The conservatives among the high nobility would undoubtedly have been satisfied with any solution which left undisturbed the semi-independence of the Congress Kingdom, a view which showed a clear understanding of the relative strengths of the Poles and the Russian Empire. There were others who insisted that no compromise could be expected and that it was better to seize the opportunity of marching into the former eastern provinces and to raise the standard of rebellion before Nicholas I could take effective counter-measures. Chłopicki turned down the self-appointed strategists' plans as unrealistic and argued that by obtaining concessions from the tsar the Poles might strengthen their position and by building up their military resources lay the foundations of success in the future.[1] The army in any case was not at that moment capable of taking the field. At the most only 25,000 men could have been assembled as a striking-force. If they had attacked Lithuania they would have been forced to hold their gains through the winter and have been in poor condition to meet a spring offensive by the Russians. An attack across the Niemen, moreover, would have left the Kingdom open to incursions in the south from the Russian cavalry divi-

[1] Chłopicki was evidently thinking of the model of the Prussian *landwehr*. A similar institution in Poland would have created a trained reserve which could rapidly be called to the colours when the chance arose. Cf. D. Chłapowski, *Szlakiem legionów* (*z Pamiętników Generała Dezyderego Chłapowskiego*) (Cracow, 1903), ii, 2. Cf. also *Lettre du général Chłapowski sur les événements militaires en Pologne et en Lithuanie* (Berlin, 1832), pp. 1–6.

sions stationed in Volhynia. Chłopicki has left no memoirs to justify his action, for they perished in the great fire of Cracow in 1850, but the best military opinion supported his caution.[1] Nevertheless, he did not neglect to take precautions. On 6 December he called all retired officers and men to the colours.[2] Two days later he appealed for volunteers.[3] Recruiting officers were appointed, one for the right bank of the Vistula and the other for the left.[4] All this created an atmosphere of bustle and confirmed the impression that Chłopicki was preparing for armed struggle, but unfortunately for the efficiency of the army and the course of the rising the quality of officers appointed was not always of the best.[5] Having set up the initial cadres Chłopicki then ordered new units to be brought up to strength by conscription of the peasantry. Internal security too was taken care of. A national guard was set up in Warsaw under the command of the senator Antoni Ostrowski, who devoted the rest of his life to playing the rôle of the Polish Lafayette, while in the countryside mobile guards were established as a local security force.

The fact that Chłopicki recognized the possibility of war caused some of the high aristocracy closely associated with the previous government to consider their own course of action. The senator Alexander Potocki, son of Stanisław Kostka Potocki, retired from Warsaw for the duration of the insurrection, though he sent his son to serve as an officer in the army. Similarly Tomasz Grabowski and his father, Franciszek, took no part in events. Ksawery Jabłonowski retired to his estates and Wincenty Krasiński, commander of the Royal Guard, fled to St. Petersburg where he arrived with only the clothes in

[1] Cf. H. Dembiński, *Rzut oka na ostatnie wypadki rewolucyi polskiej* (Paris, 1837) p. 12. Dembiński countered the argument that General Rosen's Lithuanian corps would have joined the Poles; though many of the officers would have come over, the rank and file were unwilling. This was a view expressed by the Russian commander, Field-Marshal Diebitsch in his letters to Nicholas I of 12 January and 19 January 1831, cf. *Russkaya Starina* (xli), 95–7, 103–5.
[2] Pawłowski, *Żródła*, i, 32–4.   [3] *Ibid.*, i, 42–3.   [4] *Ibid.*, i, pp. 38–9.
[5] Alfred Młocki records that on his arrival at his unit in the *województwo* of Cracow his commander complained that he dare not leave his men to take care of his personal affairs lest his officers, one of whom was a brothelkeeper, reduce the company to a shambles. 'Pamiętnik Alfreda Młockiego', *Zbiór pamiętników*, p. 300. This was an extreme example, but most of the newly appointed officers were without experience, owing their commissions to their *szlachta* descent.

which he stood. The magnate Stanisław Zamoyski, Czartoryski's brother-in-law, was summoned to St. Petersburg by Nesselrode; this order he obeyed, leaving the administration of his estates to his eldest son, Konstanty, who in accordance with Polish tradition raised a regiment at his own expense. The Zamoyski estates were thus saved from confiscation and at least a portion of the family honour was preserved. The timidity of the great landlords in 1830 had one important result, apart from lending colour to the radical suspicion that the aristocracy were only lukewarm in their enthusiasm for the national cause, in that the Senate was permanently weakened and compelled throughout the insurrection to play a rôle subordinate to that of the Chamber of Deputies.

While in Poland military preparations gave the impression that war was not far off, messages were being sent to St. Petersburg which indicated that this was not the Polish leaders' intention. The Administrative Council had reported on 4 December that its efforts were directed towards the maintenance of law and order.[1] The unconstitutional step of setting up the 'Temporary Government' was likewise explained as if it were but another measure with this end. A tactful appeal was made to Nicholas that he should regard the events of the rising in their true light and it was implied that everything depended upon his own careful handling of the situation.[2] Chłopicki's assumption of the dictatorship however was too serious to be explained away by letter. For the purpose of arranging a settlement a delegation, composed of Prince Lubecki and Count Jan Jezierski, a nonentity, but in close sympathy with Lubecki, was sent from Warsaw on 10 December, with instructions first to make contact with Constantine and secure his good offices before it went on to St. Petersburg.[3] Before Lubecki and Jezierski could arrive in St. Petersburg danger presented itself from another quarter. Colonel Hauke, an adjutant of the tsar

---

[1] *Dyaryusz sejmu*, i, 194–200.   [2] *Ibid.*, i, 200–1.
[3] Cf. Chłopicki's letter to Constantine, *ibid.*, i, 205–7. The appointment of Jezierski illustrates the processes of Polish politics; Władysław Ostrowski declined all part in the mission and the choice fell upon Jezierski because he was thought to be *persona grata* in St. Petersburg, having once been selected by the tsarina as a partner in the polonaise, T. Morawski, *Dzieje narodu polskiego* (Poznań, 1877), vi, 326.

and brother of Maurycy Hauke, the murdered vice-minister of war, appeared in Warsaw on 16 December, with a letter for Walenty Sobolewski, formally the presiding minister in the now defunct Administrative Council, informing him that extraordinary powers had been confirmed upon Constantine whose instructions were to be obeyed by all civil authorities.[1] He brought with him also a copy of orders to the commissioners of Augustów and Płock, who were to regard St. Petersburg as the capital of the Kingdom and prepare to receive the Lithuanian corps of General Rosen, which would occupy these *województwa* and receive the submission of the Polish army.[2] To avoid a premature outbreak of hostilities Chłopicki sent off a letter to Rosen, explaining that the situation was not what Nicholas I thought it was when he issued his orders and urging Rosen to refrain from crossing the frontier.[3] Rosen sensibly replied that he would refer the matter to the tsar.[4]

Chłopicki was successful in securing at least the neutrality of the Russian forces, but it was not as easy to obtain restraint on the Polish side. He had become dictator on the generally acceptable condition that he would hold office only until the diet met. The members of the Chamber of Deputies were for the most part substantial country gentry, who had not forgotten the excitements of eighteenth-century politics and who not without reason thought that yet another effort was to be made to restore Polish independence. If there had been party divisions in the Chamber the deputies would have been more open to persuasion and negotiation. Only one group existed with a definite political orientation, the deputies from the *województwo* of Kalisz, led by the Niemojowski brothers, Wincenty and Bonawentura, whose main concern was to affirm the principles of constitutional monarchy of Benjamin Constant and uphold the formalities of the law. This was not a political party in the modern sense and Chłopicki was obliged to deal rather with individuals, any of whom might at a given moment exercise some power of leadership. Chłopicki's first brush with the diet on 17 December, when he received its deputations, ought to have been sufficient

[1] *Dyaryusz sejmu*, i, 207. [2] *Ibid.*, i, 208–9.
[3] *Ibid.*, i, 213–4, letter of 16 December 1830.
[4] *Ibid.*, 214, Rosen's reply of 20 December 1830.

warning of what he might expect.¹ He explained bluntly that the connection with Russia ought to be maintained lest the army be destroyed altogether and that the army was bound by an oath of allegiance to Nicholas I; as far as Chłopicki was concerned, war for the lost provinces of historic Poland was out of the question. His speech was little to the taste of the deputations. Walenty Zwierkowski took up the question of the former eastern provinces, but Chłopicki shouted that he had come merely to state his opinion and not to argue. With that he left the room in a high temper and, as ever, it remained to Czartoryski to smooth the ruffled feelings of the deputations whom he bound to keep the interview a secret.

Chłopicki's tactical mistake in not seeking to influence the deputies before the diet met was revealed when the Chamber assembled on the evening of 18 December, ostensibly only to transact the formal business of electing its officers, an occasion on which members of the government did not normally appear. Chłopicki clearly expected to be able to win over the diet by a dramatic speech when debates began on 21 December.² Left to their own devices on 18 December and exalted by the mood of wild excitement in Warsaw, the deputies added new complications for the dictator. Wałchnowski, the senior deputy, presided in accordance with the rules and addressed the members with a revolutionary speech which was greeted with cries of 'Long live a free and independent Poland!' Ignoring the normal procedure, which excluded debates on the first day, Wałchnowski then permitted the deputies to begin a discussion of the revolution itself. Carried away by heady enthusiasm the Chamber unanimously resolved to recognize the rising as 'the act of the Nation'.³ Count Władysław Ostrowski, who was elected marshal or speaker of the Chamber, was in his opening speech only expressing the general consensus of opinion when he declared: 'May our deliberations, begun amid such noble scenes, be crowned with a most propitious end, and may the composition

---

¹ For contemporary accounts see Lelewel, *Pamiętnik*, p. 38, Barzykowski, *Historya*, i, 457–8, and Dembowski, *Moje Wspomnienia*, ii, 108–9.

² He had ordered copies of all the speeches of Alexander I to the diet to be produced, cf. *A.A.D. 456 (Sejm nadzwyczajny w r. 1830)*, letter of the secretary-general to the ministry of internal affairs, 13 December 1830, presumably to make certain that his oratory was in the best tradition.   ³ *Dyaryusz sejmu*, i, 6–7.

of the Chamber be augmented by our brother representatives from those Polish provinces which remain under foreign tyranny.'[1] The Chamber's resolution, accepted weakly by the Senate, appeared at first sight to make Chłopicki's attempt to secure a negotiated settlement with Russia impossible. Apart from the complications it added to Lubecki's mission in St. Petersburg and the affront it gave to Nicholas' personal dignity, it was a plain violation of Article I of the Final Act of the Congress of Vienna which bound the Kingdom in indissoluble personal union with Russia and clearly implied that the Poles of the Kingdom must accept the sovereignty of the tsar. Chłopicki refused point blank to continue as dictator and resigned his office without further ado. The diet however was not a little surprised by the public reaction to its resolution. At first it was met with approval, but when it was realized that it had occasioned Chłopicki's resignation the students began to murmur against the diet, while the army officers were of the opinion that Chłopicki must retain the office of dictator.[2] Feeling began to run so high in the city that Czartoryski feared another revolution. During the night he sent a personal letter to Chłopicki, pressing him to remain at his post, but the letter was returned to him with seals unbroken. At length at 11 a.m. on the morning of 19 December Czartroyski, Władysław Ostrowski and Leon Dembowski were admitted to Chłopicki's quarters. Lelewel too appeared to support with ingenuous comments Chłopicki's decision to resign,[3] but in the end Ostrowski prevailed upon Chłopicki to resume the dictatorship, undertaking himself to steer the motion defining his powers through the diet, the meeting of which was brought forward to 20 December.

Ostrowski was however not as good as his word. Chłopicki demanded that he be utterly irresponsible in his office, though assisted by a committee consisting of the president of the Senate,

[1] *Ibid.*, i, 8. The response to Ostrowski's appeal for voluntary contributions to the cause, to which he gave 30,000 złp, was less enthusiastic; only 15 deputies out of 115 made gifts, which totalled 168,000 złp, though this was enlarged by donations from members of the senate.   [2] Cf. Pawłowski, *Źródła*, i, nos. 95, 96, 97, pp. 94–6.
[3] J. Lelewel, *Pamiętnik*, pp. 35–7. The only effect of Lelewel's intervention was that Ostrowski, as marshal of the Chamber, did not call him to speak at the next session.

Czartoryski, who had assumed that office in the absence of Stanisław Zamoyski, with two senators to advise him, and the marshal and three deputies from the Chamber. The debate did not run according to plan; the deputy, Teofil Morawski, from the *województwo* of Kalisz, submitted a counter-motion which was almost a new constitution in itself,[1] which Ostrowski refused to place on the agenda, but the deputies were prepared to discuss the marshal's motion with relish. The charm of Chłopicki's name was still enough to produce a response in his favour for even the radical Szaniecki could cry out: 'Chłopicki shall be Dictator. He shall be the Washington of the Poles!' but the dictatorship was not to be without limitations. The committee to assist Chłopicki was wider than he wished, consisting of Czartoryski with five senators on the one hand and the marshal and eight deputies, one from each *województwo*, on the other; in this way vociferous elements were introduced who could claim to have a share in formulating policy. More important still was the resolution appointing a committee to draw up a manifesto outlining the grievances of the Nation, of which Lelewel was to be the guiding spirit.[2] The renewed dictatorship was circumscribed both by the committee of supervision and by the fact that the manifesto, as a declaration of national aspirations, would almost inevitably be regarded as an expression of policy. A further objection by Chłopicki could only have made the situation worse and he accepted the diet's decision in a speech which matched an earlier speech of Czartoryski in its vagueness. With that Czartoryski closed the diet *sine die*. His experience of what might be expected from the diet convinced him that if it were called again it ought not to exercise too much freedom in its discussions.[3]

Reinvested with dictatorial powers, Chłopicki changed the form of government once again. The Temporary Government was abolished and in its place was erected the 'Supreme National Council', a small oligarchical body consisting of Czartoryski, Ostrowski, Leon Dembowski, Prince Michał

---

[1] *Dyaryusz sejmu*, i, 19–20.   [2] *Ibid.*, i, 51.
[3] In a rough note of *c*. January 1831, *Muzeum Xiążąt Czartoryskich*, 5297, he recorded the need for strict control over debates, but he never took the pains to exert it himself.

Radziwiłł and the deputy Stanisław Barzykowski, with the task of supervising the public administration. Some effort was made in appointments to ministries to appease revolutionary feeling. Lelewel kept the ministry of public instruction and Bonawentura Niemojowski that of justice, but the important ministries were handed over to Chłopicki's supporters; General Izydor Krasiński remained at the ministry of war, while Jelski, one of Lubecki's men, took over finance and Tomasz Łubieński the key ministry of internal affairs. The situation was by now so serious that preparations for an armed conflict had to be pushed ahead. The really decisive step had occurred on 19 December when Czartoryski ordered the establishment of victualling committees in the *województwa* and districts.[1] This meant that the supply of the army was placed on a war footing. The regular regiments were hurriedly brought up to strength and by the beginning of January 1831 there were 56,161 men under arms, though still desperately short of ammunition and weapons. Chłopicki's ultimate aim was the traditional aspiration of an army of 100,000 men supported by 20,000 cavalry.[2] The policy of seeking a peaceful solution however was not abandoned. On the evening of 21 December Colonel Wyleżyński, the adjutant of General Krasiński who had sided with the tsar, was instructed to leave that night for St. Petersburg to inform Lubecki that there were no changes in his instructions and to describe to the tsar the exact circumstances in which Chłopicki found himself in Warsaw. That hopes of conciliation were not dead is revealed by the conduct of Chłopicki's entourage, for many officers, including Szembek who had held a key position in bringing over the army to the revolution, begged Wyleżyński to express to Nicholas their loyalty.[3]

Owing to the distance of St. Petersburg from Warsaw Nicholas was unable to obtain a clear picture of the events which were taking place in the Kingdom. When he received news of the rising on 7 December his first reaction was to order a formal partial mobilization in Russia. Only on 9 December did

[1] Pawłowski, *Źródła*, i, no. 94, pp. 90–3.   [2] *Ibid.*, i, no. 128, pp. 135–6.
[3] T. Wyleżyński, *Imperator Nikolai i Polsha v 1830 godu—Perevod s rukopisi Thaddea Vylezhinskavo*, ed. K. Voyensky (St. Petersburg, 1905), p. 9. This memoir was originally published in *Biblioteka Warszawska* (1903), but the British Museum copy of this series was destroyed during the war and I cite the Russian version.

Constantine's first two letters arrive. The tsar's incomplete appreciation of the situation is amply illustrated by his letter of 8 December informing Walenty Sobolewski of Constantine's extraordinary powers, but it was only on 17 December that he took the decisive step of issuing a manifesto to the Poles condemning the insurrection and ordering the Polish corps commanders to concentrate their forces at Płock, at the same time promising forgiveness to those who returned to their allegiance. The responsibility for shedding blood he placed firmly upon the Poles and appealed to them to comply with his orders.[1] His determination to resist pressure was shown by the issue of a manifesto to the Russian Empire on 24 December and by the declaration of a state of war in Lithuania, where the more energetic general, Khrapovitsky, replaced Rimsky-Korsakov, as military governor. Already on 13 December Field-Marshal Diebitsch, who had successfully commanded the Russian forces in the war with Turkey, was once more appointed to commander-in-chief of the field army. Even before the arrival of the Polish delegation in St. Petersburg Nicholas I had committed himself to a policy of refusing concessions and impressed upon the Poles that they themselves must find a way out of this difficult situation, but the very wording of the manifesto to the Poles had the effect only of increasing their will to resistance. From the outset the negotiations were to be bedevilled by the dignity of the Emperor of All the Russias and the self-esteem of the Polish nation.

When Lubecki and Jezierski left Warsaw on 10 December there was still no expressed intention of breaking with the tsar. Chłopicki entrusted them with a report for the tsar, which explained his intention of maintaining order in Warsaw and affirmed his loyalty to the throne.[2] The private instructions given to Lubecki were by no means so careful and have the appearance of being the maximum that could be hoped for; there is some likelihood that they were framed with a view to subsequent publication when awkward explanations might have to be made to the diet rather than for formal transmission to the tsar. Chłopicki's demand was nothing less than that consti-

---

[1] For the French text see *B. &. F.S.P.*, 17 (1829–30), pp. 1154–5.
[2] *Dyaryusz sejmu*, i, 202–4.

tutional privileges should be extended to the former eastern provinces and the summoning to Warsaw on 1 May 1831 of a general parliament of all Poland under the dominion of Russia, together with an amnesty and the exclusion of imperial troops from the Kingdom of Poland.[1] These instructions did not envisage the actual separation of Western Russia from the Empire, but there was little likelihood that a Russian emperor would consent to the surrender of the gains of the eighteenth century at the demand of a revolutionary movement in Warsaw, nor could indeed a case be made out why political disturbances in the Kingdom should have the effect of introducing political changes in the western *gubernii* which had not given active demonstration of discontent. In fact, Chłopicki's instructions were not and could not be translated into demands. Lubecki and Jezierski went to St. Petersburg cap in hand. When Lubecki arrived at Narva he was informed by the secretary of state, Grabowski, that he must appear in the capacity of minister of finance and Jezierski as a traveller. Lubecki's letter professing loyalty was published in the Russian press in order that there might be no doubt where the tsar stood in the dispute.[2]

On 26 December Nicholas I consented to grant Lubecki an audience, but from the outset adopted the attitude that Lubecki as a responsible minister, was in part to blame for the rising.[3] Lubecki bravely pointed to the malversation of municipal funds in Warsaw and the police spies of Constantine as a source of discontent, more or less in accordance with the memorandum

[1] Cf. *ibid.*, i, 204–5. 'The wishes of the Nation to serve as the basis for intended negotiations:
1. The sincere and complete execution in the Kingdom of the Constitutional Charter granted in the year 1815 as a result of treaties signed by his Imperial Majesty of blessed memory, Alexander.
2. The extension of this constitutional charter, in accordance with the said treaties to the provinces of Lithuania, Volhynia, Podolia and the Ukraine.
3. The calling of a general diet for 1 May 1831, to which shall be summoned not only deputies and representatives of the Kingdom, but also deputies and representatives of the above-mentioned provinces.
4. An undertaking not to introduce the Imperial army into the Kingdom.
5. A complete amnesty without exceptions for all political acts and opinions.

These magnanimous concessions, if His Royal and Imperial Majesty in his wisdom should consent to them, might be made public in the form of a royal edict and would cure all our ills.'

[2] *Ibid.*, 214–16 for Grabowski's letter of 22 December and Lubecki's reply of 23 December 1830. [3] *Correspondance*, ii, 90.

he had drawn up for his own use rather than in the spirit of Chłopicki's instructions.[1] It was Nicholas I who raised the question of demands upon Western Russia, to which Lubecki replied that these were aspirations rather than points upon which the Poles insisted.[2] As for the manifesto of 17 December, Lubecki declared that it would be without effect. ' "Une idée fixe domine la nation, elle craint qu'on ne veuille profiter de cette révolte pour lui ôter la Charte. La proclamation ne détruit pas cette crainte!" Sur cette réponse Sa Majesté se tourna vers le Comte Dibitsch et dit: "Donc, c'est la guerre Maréchal, vous partirez immédiatement." '[3]

On the same evening Nicholas received Jezierski, more affably than he treated Lubecki.[4] Jezierski was not a politician and to him Nicholas could put his position frankly. He disposed of the Polish view that the autocrat of Russia should contend with the constitutional king of Poland by declaring: 'Show me a means of settling the affair which would be worthy of a King of Poland who is at the same time the Emperor of Russia! I do not ask for more. My one desire is to get round the difficulties of the present situation through the Poles themselves and in conjunction with them alone.'[5] As for Polish claims on Western Russia, he refused, as he put it, to favour one state at the expense of another. Jezierski could offer no solution, but he was ordered to enter into conversations with General Benckendorf and presented to him a list of Polish grievances. Jezierski's list fell short of Chłopicki's demands. He appealed only for the observance of the terms of the constitution, the respect of personal liberty, freedom of the press and the immunity of private letters from scrutiny, as well as for a sympathetic treatment of petitions presented to the monarch.[6] To all this Nicholas replied in the form of a pencilled note in the margin of this letter that he had accepted the situation in Congress Poland as it had been left to him by Alexander I.[7] In a second meeting with Jezierski Nicholas informed him of the diet's decision to recognize the rising as the 'act of the Nation'. He professed himself amazed

[1] For Lubecki's memorandum on the causes of the rising, see *Korespondencya Lubeckiego*, iv, 406–13.
[2] *Lettres et papiers du chancelier Comte Nesselrode*, vii, 166.   [3] *Ibid.*, vii, 167.
[4] For Jezierski's account, see *Dyaryusz sejmu*, i, 217.   [5] *Ibid.*, i, 220.
[6] *Ibid.*, i, 225–9.   [7] *Ibid.*, i, 229.

that the Poles could seriously prepare for war and pointed to the economic and political dangers of hostilities. 'But should they win their independence, what would be their position without a port on the shores of the sea? What would happen to your industry without a market in Russia? You see the indignation that is appearing here against your insurgents. I curb it, because here I am master!'[1] Jezierski evidently pondered on this conversation and two days later reported to Benckendorf with a solution. His solution, which illustrates the low level of political understanding among the Poles, was that the tsar should declare that the Poles had committed a grievous error and that, to atone for the wrong they had done, the tsar should order the army to march into the Grand Duchy of Posen and Galicia and effect a conquest. 'Benckendorf fit de grands yeux et lui demanda s'il était fou.'[2]

Chłopicki's envoy, Wyleżyński, who arrived in St. Petersburg at 8 p.m. on the evening of 28 December, received much the same treatment as Jezierski. Diebitsch, who ordered him to write down an account of the events in Warsaw, professed himself unable to understand the reasons for the revolt. Benckendorf too found the rising difficult to comprehend and declared that it must have been the work of irresponsible elements. The Russian generals in Diebitsch's anteroom were shaking their heads over the behaviour of the Poles and declaiming against 'that villainous professor', by whom they meant Lelewel. The Russian willingness to see the revolution as the work of a politically immature minority was affirmed when Wyleżyński was summoned to an audience with Nicholas I on 30 December. The tsar expressed his indignation not against the Polish nation, but against the young rebels who had committed the senseless murders of 29 November and against Szembek who had allowed himself to be carried away by the enthusiasm of the moment and forgotten his duty as an officer.[3] Wyleżyński was ordered to return at once to Warsaw with despatches addressed to Walenty Sobolewski whom Nicholas still considered as head of the Polish administration; a verbal message was sent to Chłopicki that he should not be surprised if he received no formal

[1] *Ibid.*, p. 230. [2] *Correspondance*, ii, 91.
[3] T. Wyleżyński, *ibid.*, pp. 65–79, for an account of this audience.

recognition of his position. Jezierski on the other hand was detained in St. Petersburg for the moment. Evidently Nicholas wished to give Chłopicki time to make up his mind; the return of Jezierski, who was regarded in Poland as an official envoy would bring matters to a head and demand public decisions. An interval of a week between the arrival of Wyleżyński and the return of Jezierski would at least give Chłopicki a breathing space in which to make his preparations, if indeed he did intend to carry out the tsar's instructions to concentrate the army at Płock.

Wyleżyński arrived in Warsaw late on the night of 6 January 1831 and Jezierski on the 13th. Between them they brought, according to Barzykowski, four letters, of which two are reproduced in the *Dyaryusz sejmu*. The formal letter to Chłopicki was cautious in tone, but permitted a favourable interpretation:

I have received instructions to inform you that His Imperial Majesty and King received your letter of 10th ultimo and has observed with satisfaction in it the expression of the feelings by which you appear to be moved towards his person, and that he will believe them completely when you give incontrovertible proof of such by conforming, as exactly as possible, to his will expressed in the proclamation to the Polish Nation of 5/17 December.
Accept my assurances of deep respect,
Stefan Count Grabowski.[1]

The effect of the secretary of state's letter was reinforced by a message from Lubecki, who could have done no other, urging Chłopicki to find a peaceful solution of the crisis.[2] While the

[1] *Dyaryusz sejmu*, i, 216. This letter is dated 23 December 1830–4 January 1831 and was ostensibly brought by Jezierski. It is curious that the accounts of two members of the Supreme National Council, Dembowski and Barzykowski, differ on the question of when this letter was received. Barzykowski writes as if it were brought back by Wyleżyński, cf. *Historya*, ii, 99, which is accepted by another contemporary, T. Morawski, *Dzieje narodu polskiego*, vi, 324. Dembowski writes as if one letter from Grabowski was brought back by Wyleżyński, *Moje Wspomnienia*, ii, 123, and yet another by Jezierski. Dembowski mentions other incidents also as happening on 15 January, which Barzykowski ascribes to 7 January. Mochnacki, who was outside political circles offers no solution, *Powstanie*, ii, 595–6, while L. Mierosławski, *Histoire de la Révolution de Pologne* (Paris, 1836), i, 267, declared that Wyleżyński returned on 15 January. What the answer to this problem is I do not know, but it is quite clear that Chłopicki was left in no doubt of the tsar's intentions when Wyleżyński returned.

[2] *Dyaryusz sejmu*, i, 216–17, dated 5 January 1831.

THE BREAK WITH RUSSIA AND THE WAR 147

tsar adhered to the attitude of narrow legalism contained in the manifesto of 17 December, he had avoided giving any clear expression of his intentions and left the Polish leaders some degree of initiative, provided that they accepted the need for submission. From the Polish point of view it appeared that too much depended upon Nicholas' personal honour, in which there was no very great confidence. Chłopicki was given no legal recognition. No guarantee was made to uphold the decisions of the Administrative Council, Temporary Government or the Supreme National Council. On the other hand Russian troops had not yet clashed with the Poles or in any way violated the frontier between the Kingdom and Russia. In default of a better solution Nicholas had made certain that not he, but the Poles should take the responsibility for violating the terms of the 1815 settlement, which would then place the dispute outside the scope of international arbitration. In practice everything depended upon whether the Poles could pocket their pride or not.

At the beginning of January 1831 Chłopicki was in difficulties from which he could find no way out. In the eyes of the Polish patriots he was the symbol of martial glory, but his refusal to appear in the streets or make public show aroused suspicion. His one public appearance was outside Warsaw, a visit of inspection to the fortress of Modlin. Behind the scenes the leaders of the Chamber were discussing the outcome of events avidly. A host of newspapers kept alive the spirit of revolution, especially *Kurier Polski* over which the Kalisz constitutionalists gained control from 11 December onwards. Interest everywhere was centred upon the compilation and publication of the manifesto which the committee of the diet was drawing up. According to Lelewel, its chief architect, the final draft was ready on 2 January 1831. It was a statement of grievances and political aims, filled with the vague and high-flown phrases which were the stock-in-trade of Polish oratory.[1] The committee was at pains to make clear that it spoke not only for the Kingdom, but for the whole *Ojczyzna* or Fatherland. It complained that the Congress of Vienna had in fact not solved the Polish question; free commercial intercourse and representative institutions had

[1] *Dyaryusz sejmu*, i, 55–64.

not been obtained. Alexander I, it was added, had held out promises that the Congress Kingdom would be united with the former eastern territories, but these had not been implemented. A secondary motive of the rising had been to prevent the Polish army and Polish state funds from being devoted to a war against the risings in France and Belgium. The manifesto ended with a gesture of defiance:

> Yet if Providence has appointed this land for eternal subjection, if in this last fight Poland shall lay down her freedom amid the ashes of her towns and the corpses of her defenders, the enemy will extend his dominion over but yet another desert, and the true Pole will perish with joy in his heart that, if Heaven has not permitted him to save his own freedom and his Fatherland, he has at least in mortal combat protected the liberties of the peoples of Europe.[1]

Poles were always willing to harp on the theme that their country had been and would again be a bulwark against barbarism, which they identified with the Russian Empire and not with the Turks of whom they always had high hopes. The manifesto found a ready response outside Poland among radicals and progressives who thought of it as an expression of the demand everywhere for good government, freedom from arbitrary arrest and liberty of the press, and even among conservatives who feared the advance of Russia, but it did not aid Chłopicki in his immediate difficulties. For him it was arrant nonsense and he refused to authorize its publication. It was however quickly shown to him that his dictatorship could not restrain Polish exuberance. Jan Ledóchowski, a man with a genius for upsetting finely laid schemes and with a capacity for seizing the initiative in critical moments, took a copy of the manifesto and issued it to the press. On 3 January 1831 it appeared for all the world to read and reproduce. It could only be a question of time before it reached St. Petersburg. As if this were not enough, Chłopicki's position was further weakened by an irresponsible escapade which involved the Łubieński family who were closely associated with his régime. Henryk Łubieński assisted Józef Lubowidzki, vice-president of the Bank of Poland, to smuggle out of the country to the safety of Silesia his brother

[1] *Ibid.*, i, 63.

Mateusz Lubowidzki, the unpopular vice-president of Warsaw and police chief, who had been wounded in the Belvedere on 29 November and retained in protective custody ever since. A howl was raised against the entire Łubieński clan and Tomasz, who was in control of the ministry of internal affairs, was forced to resign. To quieten popular clamour Chłopicki was obliged to appoint on 6 January the constitutionalist Wincenty Niemojowski in his place, a man whose past prevented him from supporting compromise with Russia.

Evidence of the dictator's growing weakness was the appearance of a new journal, *Nowa Polska*, on 5 January, which was obviously directed by men who had been active in the proscribed Patriotic Society and which frankly made the claim, in opposition to the classicism of the Kalisz group which found expression in *Kurier Polski*, that romanticism had achieved a moral supremacy in Poland.[1] By asserting that the revolution of 29 November was the beginning of a renaissance produced by the romantics *Nowa Polska* appeared to suggest that the radicals spoke for the whole nation. None was more active in inventing principles for the revolution than J. B. Ostrowski, who argued that Poland ought to look to the great liberal powers, Britain and France, for example and succour. He declared that the year 1830 was the culmination of the victory of constitutional government: 'The French Revolution of 1830 is the final act, the closing of the great scene of the Middle Ages and the first moment, the first light of dawn of a new Europe.'[2] The events of 1791, 1807, 1815 and 1830 in Poland represented a logical progression towards liberty and freedom, which in its turn would 'bring on to the scene of history a nation twenty

---

[1] The editorial in the first number of 5 January makes clear the connection between radicalism and romanticism: 'This journal, *Nowa Polska* [i.e. 'New Poland'], is political and intellectual. It has already been mentioned that the Romantic School, by creating an intellectual revolution, evoked also a political one. Freedom, Truth, Faith, ever more openly crushed by a niggardly despotism, persecuted, denounced as criminal, found their defence, found their great field of action, and perhaps also their true meaning in artistic imagination, in beauty and in literature. Unable to speak of external, civil and political freedom, we spoke of the freedom of the spirit, of the freedom of art, of the imperative break with the past and with tradition. We proclaim that before us is a future, boundless, appalling, sublime and enchanting.'

[2] *Nowa Polska*, no. 20, 24 January 1831.

millions strong, a nation which may have a decisive influence upon Slavdom and Europe in its resurrection'.

The mood of the city found no echo with the dictator and Supreme National Council which met on 7 January to consider the report of Wyleżyński. Chłopicki begged the Council not to give up hope of finding a peaceful solution and suggested that an approach be made to Prussia to secure her intervention, but Władysław Ostrowski and Barzykowski insisted that no solution was possible. A vote was taken and all members of the Council agreed that there ought to be no submission, to which Chłopicki bitterly replied: 'You, gentlemen, see in war an existence for Poland, I only Poland's grave.'[1] Rather than take upon himself the responsibility of bringing Poland to the point of war he resolved that the diet be called to give a final decision, but even then he had evidently not entirely abandoned hope that he might bring the Poles to heel. On 11 January occurred one of the strangest incidents of the insurrection. It was reported to Chłopicki that Lelewel, commonly supposed to be the power behind all radical activity, was planning a *coup d'état* and intended to use as his instrument a sapper unit in which his brother, a serving officer, had some influence. It is not clear what actually happened, but it appears that a group of young conservatives, headed by Stanisław Rzewuski, who had been successful in instigating the Academic Guard to close the Patriotic Society in December, had spread yet another rumour, possibly with the intention of giving Chłopicki an excuse to make a proscription of the radicals. They were successful to the extent that Chłopicki ordered the arrest of Lelewel and of Bronikowski, J. B. Ostrowski and Franciszek Grzymala, who were thought to be the most prominent radical leaders in the city. Significantly enough Szembek, the general whom Nicholas most condemned for his part in the rising, was delegated to make the arrest, as if to atone for his past indiscretions. Chłopicki wished to try Lelewel by court-martial, but he could not find a military unit which would be prepared to carry out the execution, for even the Academic Guard which was most devoted to him refused all part in the episode, especially when it concerned a man who was regarded as being as symbolic of

[1] Barzykowski, *Historya*, ii, 104.

Polish achievement in historical studies as Chłopicki was in military affairs. Chłopicki lamented that 'it appears that I am a Dictator on paper only. I have unlimited authority entrusted to me which I cannot use'.[1] Under pressure from Wincenty Niemojowski he was forced to release Lelewel and the other prisoners and resign all intention of imposing his own will.

At the final consultation of the Supreme National Council on 14 January after Jezierski had returned, no one was found to uphold Chłopicki's view that war would be suicidal. The deputations of the diet whom he met on 16 January likewise received coldly his view that a further attempt at conciliation must be made. Here Chłopicki fell into furious argument with Count Ledóchowski, who declared that he was a coward and feared battle, and the meeting ended in confusion. All that Czartoryski could say of Chłopicki was: 'C'est le soldat le plus mal élevé que j'ai vu.' Though he secretly held the same view as Chłopicki that war would be disastrous he was not prepared to fly in the face of public opinion or exert a decisive influence in political discussions. In spite of the difference of opinion the deputations still wished to retain Chłopicki's services and on 17 January asked him under what conditions he would remain. Chłopicki, by now weak with anxiety, replied that Polish resources were insufficient to sustain the struggle and that annihilation must follow. 'I cannot take upon myself the responsibility of exposing our country to such a fate and in the present circumstances I could in good conscience retain the powers I have possessed up to this time only in so far as the discovery of means to save the country were left to me alone.'[2] The deputations replied that only the diet could alter his powers. Rather than carry out a policy of which he disapproved Chłopicki then resigned and surrendered the power of decision to the diet.[3]

When the diet had transacted its routine business on the

[1] Nicholas I clearly hoped that Chłopicki would use this incident to bring the rising to a close, cf. *Correspondance*, ii, 109. For an account of this episode see A. Kraushar, 'Zamach na dyktaturę Chłopickiego', *Przegląd historyczny* (1907). Mochnacki called the incident 'the farce of the counts', while Lelewel denied that he had had any subversive intentions, *Pamiętnik*, pp. 42–4.   [2] *Dyaryusz sejmu*, i, 79.

[3] L. Dembowski, *Moje wspomnienia*, ii, 138, wrote that delegations of officers came into Warsaw to restore him to the dictatorship if his resignation had been compelled by radical pressure, but were amazed to discover that he was acting of his own free will.

night of 19/20 January it took upon itself the task first of finding a commander-in-chief to fill Chłopicki's place. Secret discussions had already taken place behind the scenes between members of the Supreme National Council, the deputations and senior army officers. As a result four names were submitted to the diet, Prince Michał Radziwiłł, General Weyssenhoff, General Szembek and, in view of the doubt whether Weyssenhoff would accept the post, General Krukowiecki; of these candidates only Krukowiecki can be considered as having had the experience for the task, but when a vote was taken the choice of the diet fell upon Radziwiłł. Radziwiłł was a magnate of great wealth, who under the Duchy of Warsaw had equipped a regiment at his own expense and by accelerated promotion risen to the rank of divisional general, though he had never commanded a unit larger than a brigade; for eighteen years he had not been employed in the army.[1] Nevertheless, he fulfilled the requirements of many shades of opinion. He was a member of the high aristocracy and his brother, Antoni, was viceroy of the Grand Duchy of Posen; his name was therefore a guarantee of the eminent respectability of the Polish revolution and might be counted on to dispel fears that it was tainted with Jacobinism. At the same time, this very name, Radziwiłł, Lithuanian in its origin and historical associations, was likely to stir the imaginations of the Poles not only in the Kingdom but also in the former eastern provinces. There were however more immediate and practical reasons for his election. The senior officers were divided among themselves by professional jealousies and none would serve under an officer junior to himself. Radziwiłł was technically senior to all other candidates; he was besides a personal friend of Chłopicki and it was known that if he were appointed Chłopicki would join his staff and assume unofficial responsibility for the conduct of operations.[2] The election of Radziwiłł

[1] As he himself complained, cf. L. Dembowski, *ibid.*, ii, 146. Nicholas I thought his appointment yet another example of Polish folly; 'La nomination de Radzivil est le complément de toutes les sottises', cf. his letter to Diebitsch of 3 February 1831, *Russkaya Starina*, xli, 389–90.

[2] According to R. Sołtyk, *La Pologne, précis historique, politique et militaire de sa révolution* (Paris, 1833), i, 212–13, Chłopicki refused the pleas of two members of the Kalisz group, Morawski and Biernacki, to serve as commander-in-chief, but the Kalisz group threw its influence on the side of Radziwiłł, knowing that in fact Chłopicki would assist him.

was therefore not without advantages and there were no objections to granting him wide powers.¹ The commander-in-chief, appointed by the diet, was to be almost independent of the government, in accordance with the contemporary opinion that military affairs were a mystery not easily understood by civilians. The government for its part was required to supply all the men and materials he needed. The only limitation on his power was that he might appoint officers above the rank of colonel only from a list of candidates submitted by the government. With a Radziwiłł in command there seemed little danger that these wide powers would be abused, but it was not foreseen what might happen if there were a commander-in-chief with a policy of his own and the will to carry it out, as indeed was to be the case later.²

When once it had taken care of what it considered the most pressing need of the state the diet was able to turn its attention to the tsar's demand for unconditional surrender. It could not proceed directly to the election of a new government because in theory the government of the king was still operating. The Supreme National Council, set up by the will of the dictator, was not empowered to continue negotiations. Czartoryski and his friends had ample experience of what might happen in a Polish assembly in the heat of the moment, but though they were anxious to postpone until the last possible moment the outbreak of hostilities they lacked the moral courage to insist upon the secrecy of debates. The Additional Act of 1825, which excluded the public from all but the opening and closing sessions of the diet was quietly allowed to lapse and the galleries could be filled with young zealots who applauded or hissed in defiance of the marshal's warnings. Though in the senate there was only one member, Antoni Ostrowski, who favoured breaking off relations at once, and in the chamber at the most twenty deputies who could be classed as a party of action, the conservative rump was unlikely to run counter to the political code which Polish public opinion imposed upon its representatives. This situation was a great advantage to the deputies who

¹ For details see Pawłowski, *Źródła*, i, 201–3.
² Even Radziwiłł was not entirely satisfactory, failing to submit regular reports of his progress until the government protested, cf. Pawłowski, *ibid.*, i, 269–70.

wished for a complete break with Russia and they were aided by the atmosphere of excitement which was being created in the streets.

With the fall of Chłopicki the young radicals emerged once more to re-establish the Patriotic Society and influence public opinion, in spite of the opposition of the governor of Warsaw, Woyczyński. One lesson however had been learnt, that Jacobinism was unpopular. Mochnacki who afterwards uttered many sarcastic criticisms of the Society's members himself argued at this time that its aims were purely national and that it had no intention of overthrowing the social order.[1] The Society was to be a pressure group, whipping up excitement and exerting every moral compulsion it could find upon the members of the diet. For form's sake Lelewel was re-elected president and Roman Sołtyk vice-president, but the real direction of the Society remained as before with the exponents of literary romanticism. Through Sołtyk, a motion was submitted to the diet on 20 January for the exclusion of the Romanovs from the Polish throne and the dissolution of the oath of allegiance which bound the Poles of Western Russia to the tsar.[2] The marshal praised the intention of the motion, but decided that it must first be discussed in committee because it was an amendment to the constitution. The effect of Sołtyk's motion was reinforced by a series of addresses to the diet of which the most important was that of Poles from the former eastern provinces resident in Warsaw, appealing for an extension of the Polish frontiers to the east: 'Let us then announce to the world that our will and our cause is one and indivisible to the banks of the Dvina and the Dniepr, that we all form one, single Poland. . . .'[3] The campaign to influence debates in the diet reached its height on 25 January, the day set aside for rendering account of the negotiations in

---

[1] Cf. *Nowa Polska*, no. 18, 22 January 1831, reporting the reconstitution of the Patriotic Society: 'Maurycy Mochnacki, after a long persecution, was received with the greatest ovation, and, called upon to speak, set forth the needs and aims of the Society, assuring those who might be anxious that it had not taken on the character of the well-known French clubs. He argued that our revolution has nothing in common with the French Revolution, of which the aim was a change in the social order; we for our part are concerned with the vindication of independence; that it was a case of having to deal only with external dangers, that is dangers hampering or threatening our independence.'

[2] For the text, see *Dyaryusz sejmu*, i, 96–7.   [3] *Ibid.*, i, 171.

St. Petersburg and reading the documents connected with them. The aim of the Patriotic Society was to impress upon the diet the solidarity of public opinion in favour of a break with Russia. There was apparently some effort to bring out the working men of the Old City who had been so prominent in the events of 29 November. Mochnacki and Gurowski[1] both believed that by enlisting the aid of the people to override a diet elected under the old régime they could achieve their ends. 'I had always before my mind Pétion and the Commune of Paris who like a steam engine set in motion the vast wheels of the Convention.'[2] Some doubts have been expressed whether Mochnacki and the Society actually had relations with the working class, but it seems admissible to believe Mochnacki, for he himself provided the answer for his failure to obtain support: 'Our attempts to make contact with the mob also met with resistance. As for Zawisza and Kozłowski, the latter especially did what he could, but this was not enough. To win popularity among the people one must be of the people. One must not so much invite the people, as be invited by them.'[3] The demonstration did not reproduce the disorders of 29 November and was by all accounts an orderly affair. Mochnacki's aim was to bring as many spectators on to the streets as possible. For this purpose it was announced in *Nowa Polska* that a ceremony in honour of the Decembrist conspirators of 1825, Ryleyev, Bestuzhev-Riumin, Pestel, Muraviev-Apostol and Kakhovsky, would be held. From early morning five empty coffins were paraded in the streets and during a service in the Orthodox Church Gurowski addressed the crowd from the foot of the Zygmunt Column before the Castle. This activity and the apparent unanimity of sentiment greatly impressed the Chamber of Deputies which assembled at 10 a.m. It also impressed Radziwiłł who summoned Mochnacki to him and demanded an explanation, and, not being entirely satisfied, kept a battalion of riflemen under arms on the Saxon Square.

---

[1] Count Adam Gurowski, an old conspirator, come to Warsaw to fish in troubled waters, of whom Mochnacki wrote: '... he hated the diet as I did, only with this difference, that for him it was rather a question of personalities, whereas I was concerned with an institution which I considered harmful. Gurowski with all his heart wanted a revolutionary commune, a municipal power which might supervise the diet....' *Powstanie*, ii, 645. [2] *Ibid.*, ii, 650. [3] *Ibid.*, ii, 649.

On 25 January after a preliminary squabble in the Chamber over the expenses of the mission to St. Petersburg the two houses combined for a joint sitting to hear an account of the negotiations with Nicholas I. As the documents were read out it became ever more clear that there was no hope of substantial concessions from the tsar. Even so the debate which followed almost lost its thread in an acrimonious discussion of whether Jezierski had fulfilled his duty, but it was soon restored to its course by a speech of Lelewel explaining his personal conduct during the interview with Constantine in Wierzbno. Lelewel concluded with the words:

> In the first moments of the revolution there seemed no question of war breaking out against Nicholas. The idea was like this—'Let the King of Poland struggle with Tsar of Russia and the matter will find a solution.' Today through the clumsy handling of the affair the situation has completely changed. It will be necessary to declare what are the relations between the Nation and King Nicholas and that shall be decided by the diet.[1]

The marshal, Ostrowski, descending from the impartiality of his office, added fuel to the flames in a violent speech, declaring that without war they would never attain their ends; 'He (i.e. Nicholas) first broke the oath which was extorted from us by force. The only oath which can bind us now is that which the Pole for centuries took to the Piasts, the Jagiełłons, and the freely-elected kings!' Without considering the procedure of the diet or the consequences of his actions he placed on the immediate agenda the motion of Sołtyk for the deposition of the Romanovs. When he finished he gave permission to speak to his brother, Antoni, who not unnaturally supported him.[2] The deputy Wołowski too rose to his feet to declare: '. . . Let us finish the work so nobly begun. Let us today before Europe declare that Nicholas I has ceased to rule over us.' At these words Count Jan Ledóchowski, a cousin of the Ostrowskis,

---

[1] *Dyaryusz sejmu*, i, 240–1.
[2] Barzykowski, *Historya*, ii, 162, wrote that both brothers were acting under the influence of their sister, the Countess Potocka, who had been urging them to break with the tsar. During the sitting she is said to have sent a note to Władysław: 'I beg you, take advantage of this momentary emotion. Bring up the matter of the deposition. Otherwise I will not recognize you as my brother.'

THE BREAK WITH RUSSIA AND THE WAR 157

stood up and bawled at the top of his voice: 'Let us then cry "Down with Nicholas!" '[1] His cry was taken up immediately by the spectators in the galleries and by a few of the deputies. Within a few minutes the diet was overwhelmed. Jezierski was howled down when he tried to get the normal procedure of the diet observed. Czartoryski and even the marshal on reflection advised that the motion be referred to the committee, but there was no opposing the hotheads who demanded that after so clear a demonstration of unanimity the act of deposition be signed at once by all the senators and deputies present. Thus Nicholas I came to be deposed by the diet, without a formal vote being taken.[2] Acclamation had won the day. Czartoryski had not the courage to protest and when the senator Tomasz Łubieński wished to do so tugged at his arm, saying: 'What are you doing? Do you want to add civil war to all these misfortunes?'[3] When it came to his turn to sign the protocol, Czartoryski turned to the marshal and said: 'You have ruined Poland!' Privately he could object, but publicly he did not dare. As long as the Poles recognized Nicholas I as king of Poland they could have continued negotiations, but from the moment of deposition Nicholas I had a clear right in accordance with the Vienna settlement to deal with his rebellious subjects and order an army into the Kingdom to restore order. The dispute was removed from all possibility of international arbitration, as Palmerston was at this time warning the Polish envoy in London, Alexander Wielopolski.

Having deposed Nicholas in the tumultuous style of the eighteenth century the diet set to work. It soon became clear that the deputies intended to enjoy to the full the game of constitutional debate and discussion and to stand on their dignity as representatives of the nation. An address of the Patriotic Society setting forth the aims and purposes of the

[1] *Dyaryusz sejmu*, i, 243.
[2] This disorderly proceeding, carried through in the manner of an eighteenth-century dietine, was afterwards thought of as a remarkable instance of national solidarity. L. Dembowski, *Moje wspomnienia*, ii, 163, Barzykowski, *Historya*, ii, 164, and Lelewel, *Pamiętnik*, p. 72, all show that in cooler circumstances the debate would not have ended in the deposition of Nicholas.
[3] *General Tomasz Pomian hr. Łubieński*, ii, 28. This is a family tradition.

rising was contemptuously rejected by the Chamber.[1] This action called forth from Mochnacki an article in *Nowa Polska* which criticized the diet and declared that it could not represent the nation;[2] the diet's order that the editorial board should be prosecuted was enough to induce in Mochnacki a change of tone.[3] More important than asserting the dignity of the diet was the election of a new government. The Supreme National Council and the deputy ministers had discussed its form in a meeting on 19 January 1831. The Niemojowskis were opposed to continuing the dictatorship, but it was not easy to find a solution which satisfied all groups. The senator Leon Dembowski proposed a council of ministers responsible to the diet, while Barzykowski pressed for a viceroy exercising royal powers. It was obvious that whatever government was established Czartoryski would be its head, for he was the only prominent leader who was well known in Europe. On the other hand Poles disliked one-man rule, so that what eventually emerged was a proposal that a collegiate government should be set up, three persons exercising in committee the supreme functions of administration, but removed from the diet. This proposal was however modified in the diet when the form of the national government received final approval on 29 January.[4] Instead of three members the government was to consist of a president and four others, who were excluded from all administrative office

---

[1] *Dyaryusz sejmu*, i, 252. The text of the address may be found in S. Szpotański, *Maurycy Mochnacki* (Cracow, 1910), pp. 227–9. Polish radicalism found very little response in the provinces, cf. the Citizens' Council of the *województwo* of Lublin, which sent an address to the diet on 4 February 1831 condemning the factiousness of the Patriotic Society, *Dyaryusz sejmu*, ii, 89–90.

[2] 'Nowa własność języka polskiego', reprinted in M. Mochnacki, *Pisma Rozmaite*, pp. 4–8.

[3] Mochnacki found it necessary to reaffirm that he was not in sympathy with the methods of revolutionary France: 'There are countless types of terrorism. There is the terrorism of a party which in domestic discords, having overcome the weaker factions, justifies its principles by a systematic shedding of blood. Thus it was in France in the time of Danton. The guillotine struggled with and undermined social theories. People died under the law of the Maximum. You have no such terrorism in Poland and let us thank Heaven for it. The character of our revolution is completely different. It is not social, but directed against outside dangers, not internal, but external. We are concerned above all with independence and unity.' 'O terroryzmie nierozumu i obskurantyzmu polskiego', *Nowa Polska*, no. 26, 30 January 1831, reprinted in Mochnacki, *Pisma Rozmaite*, pp. 20–4.

[4] *Dyaryusz sejmu*, i, 365–8.

THE BREAK WITH RUSSIA AND THE WAR 159

and from sitting in the diet; if the commander-in-chief attended a meeting of the government, the member who had at the time of election received least votes was to absent himself in order that there might be a clear majority in disputed issues. The government was to be elected by the combined houses of the diet. It was empowered to control expenditure, provided that the budget was voted by the diet. It could enter into negotiations and conclude treaties, subject to their ratification by the diet, and it was empowered to appoint ministers and high officials, but not from the personnel of the ministries. This was the least satisfactory of all solutions. It permitted diversity of opinion within the government none of the members of which had the opportunity to explain policy in the diet. A similar lack of unity was to appear among the nominated ministers.

The personnel of the 'National Government' was elected on 30 January. As everyone expected Prince Adam Czartoryski was chosen president, though only on the second vote. The Poles were singularly unfortunate in having this man at the head of affairs. An aristocrat, he found the hurly-burly of revolutionary politics little to his taste; trained for diplomacy, he chose compromise and vagueness where only decisive action and frankness could succeed. He owed his pre-eminence in Poland not to his ability, but to his estates and the fact that he was head of the house of Czartoryski. His own nephew, Andrzej Zamoyski, could write: 'Prince Adam, the only man for the conference room, was in these circumstances quite incapable of being helpful owing to the purity of his character and his age; he did not stand aside for fear of deserting the cause, lest he surrender it into hands which might stain the name of the nation.'[1] The other four members of the government were not men likely to correct his weakness. Wincenty Niemojowski, popular on account of the treatment he had received from Alexander I and Nicholas I, deaf, dogmatic on all points of constitutional procedure, determined to uphold the letter of the law, and his friend, Teofil Morawski, also the Kalisz group, were more concerned to air their own views than seek unity of action. Stanis-

[1] A. Zamoyski, *Moje przeprawy—Pamiętnik o czasach powstania listopadowego, 1830–1831*, 2nd edn. (Cracow, 1911), i, 48.

ław Barzykowski, as a youngster an official of the Duchy of Warsaw, of peppery eloquence, probably owed his election to the belief that he would lend fire and enthusiasm to the government, though when he was removed from the exhilarating atmosphere of the Chamber he invariably sided with Czartoryski. The fifth member was Joachim Lelewel, the leading historian of his day, but more at home with numismatics and the formulation of patriotic addresses than with the serious problems which the revolt presented. Thought to be the father of all conspiracies and suspected by the conservatives of being the fountain head of radicalism, he bitterly resented losing his place in the diet to become a member of the government.[1] From the outset the five members refused to act as a unit, but divided among themselves the supervision of the functions of state. Czartoryski undertook to watch foreign affairs, Barzykowski war, Niemojowski internal affairs, Morawski finance and Lelewel education and religion. When it came to the appointment of ministers there were differences of opinion. Czartoryski and Barzykowski quarrelled with Niemojowski and Morawski, so that it was Lelewel who was asked to arbitrate. Czartoryski obtained the appointment of his man, Gustaw Małachowski, to the newly created ministry of foreign affairs, but the Kalisz group secured Bonawentura Niemojowski for internal affairs and Aloizy Biernacki for finance. War was given to General Izydor Krasiński who was recognized to be a nonentity, but was appointed because Tomasz Łubieński who was thought to have the necessary ability was unpopular. The ministry of justice fell to the senator Wiktor Rembieliński. The best that could be said for the responsible ministers was that they were in no way tainted with Jacobinism.[2]

Because Nicholas I had been deposed a new oath of allegiance was needed. After a long discussion the preamble and form of

---

[1] 'When it was repeated to Lelewel that he would be chosen for the government he warmly and bitterly complained against the condition which would temporarily remove him from the Chamber and said that he ought to esteem his rôle as a representative of the nation above all else and value it more highly than membership of the government.' J. Lelewel, *Pamiętnik*, p. 78.

[2] On 28 January Tomasz Łubieński could write to his father complaining that the clubs, instigated by Lelewel, were dominating politics, but on 31 January he wrote to his wife that he was on the whole satisfied with the government. *General Tomasz Pomian hr. Łubieński*, ii, 29, 38–9.

THE BREAK WITH RUSSIA AND THE WAR 161

the oath was finally accepted on 8 February.¹ Article I of the Law recognized constitituonal monarchy, with the right of succession in the family of the king elected for Poland. The right to elect the king was vested in the

> nation represented in the diet, but until the nation shall choose a King all public officials and all inhabitants of the country are required to take the oath in the following terms: 'I swear allegiance to the Fatherland and the Polish Nation represented in the Diet. I swear to recognize no authorities except those which the Diet has appointed or shall appoint in the future. I swear to support with all my power the cause of the national insurrection, for the purpose of achieving the existence, liberty and independence of the Polish Nation.'

There was however no extension of the franchise. There was no difference of opinion between the conservatives and the radicals on this problem. The revolution's aim was directed towards independence, not towards social change. In fact, the oath of allegiance to the diet strengthened an institution whose sittings Czartoryski and his friends would have preferred to adjourn; it was thought that the need to refer every and any measure to it would hamper the conduct of the war, but when the marshal, Ostrowski, attempted to raise the question of an adjournment the members of the diet refused to surrender their precious privileges. 'Such discussions have their place in the constitution of the Cortes, but our mandate is in accordance with our constitution. We cannot violate it. So it must be all of us or none.'² This was the opinion of Szaniecki. The Chamber of Deputies would consent neither to an adjournment nor the transaction of business by parliamentary committees. Ostrowski, in spite of pressure from Czartoryski, weakly submitted and withdrew his suggestion; the diet was to sit for the duration of the rising. In spite of the desire to play a rôle, not all members of the diet attended debates regularly. Up to the end of January over 100 out of a total of 128 members of the Chamber appeared, but numbers dropped during the month of February to 70–80. Until the end of the insurrection there was a steady decline in the number of members from the Kingdom who attended, an argument for the extension of constitutional representation

¹ *Dyaryusz sejmu*, i, 538–62.   ² *Dyaryusz sejmu*, i, 440.

to the former eastern provinces in order to make up the quorum of 65 for the Chamber of Deputies. As the numbers fell off the core of active members enjoyed a greater influence and promised to be a thorn in the side of the government, as Czartoryski was well aware. After the election of members of the government he made his final speech on 30 January before taking office.[1] He addressed himself to both the European governments and to the Poles. Having once been a minister of Alexander I, he skilfully drew attention to the fact that he had been in favour of the Russian connection, declaring that Alexander had done all he could for the Kingdom of Poland except join the former eastern provinces to it. This fact and the subsequent violation of the constitution had caused him to change his views. Having aroused in this way the sympathy of his audience he went on to give the diet a polite but unmistakable warning, that a condition of his accepting office was that he might be at liberty to resign at any moment and that he would not be obliged to assent to any proposal not in accordance with his convictions. He pleaded for unity among the members of the government and the co-operation of the diet. 'The new Government will not succeed in saving the Fatherland unless it is strong and powerful in your trust and the trust of the whole nation.' Only social stability could convince the foreign courts that Poland was worth support.

It is for us to assure the countries which are well disposed to us, that we will always be ready to listen to their advice and do that which appears to be in the interests of Europe. It is for us to convince her that our revolution is truly Polish, that is, has as its aim the existence and independence of our Fatherland, and not the overthrow of all social principles and the propagation of the hideous seeds of anarchy, from which morality and the policy and voice of all Europe demand salvation.... This is no time to think of institutions, of social improvements. The clash of arms removes the possibility of proper reflection and demands speedy action. Even freedom, that most precious treasure of Man, we must in these moments of threatening danger sacrifice for the time being to existence and independence. To save these things is our greatest need, our supreme law. Let all other considerations give way to this need for life!

[1] *Ibid.*, i, 385–9.

THE BREAK WITH RUSSIA AND THE WAR   163

Czartoryski was haunted by the chimera of Jacobinism and the memory of Polish political instability, but for the moment he was safe from serious attack from the left wing.

There was indeed no time for further deliberations on the forms of the Constitution. When Nicholas I heard the news of the deposition he gave orders for the Russian army to enter the Kingdom. Simultaneously a manifesto was issued to the Russian Empire calling upon all faithful subjects to support the war against the Poles. 'We are drawing the sword for the honour and integrity of our Empire.'[1] On the morning of 7 February the marshal, Ostrowski, announced that the Russian forces under the command of Field-Marshal Diebitsch had crossed the eastern frontier and that hostilities had begun. The diet voted that a state of war existed, though only in those parts of the country which were actually threatened by the enemy, which gives some indication of Polish confidence that the Russians could be held.[2] The government took the opportunity to include the city of Warsaw in this area, believing that martial law could be useful in restraining the radicalism it feared so much. At this moment however the radicals were unable to exert much influence. The majority of the population was too concerned with the advance of the Russians to tolerate factious opposition. A demonstration in honour of Jan Kiliński,[3] the revolutionary shoemaker who had led the lower classes of Warsaw in 1794, passed off without incident; even Stanisław Węgrzecki, the town president, who was an active opponent of the Patriotic Society, consented to attend, no doubt to lend a certain respectability to the occasion. The members of the Society themselves were not disposed to create difficulties. Most of them had been concerned only to bring relations with Russia to a breaking point. Beyond this they had little policy. The tone of their propaganda gives the impression that they wanted war not only because they might achieve much for their country, but

[1] *B. & F.S.P.*, 18 (1830–1), pp. 1331–2.
[2] Pawłowski, *Źródła*, 1, pp. 257–8.
[3] Shoemakers were regarded as the most revolutionary element among the lower classes in Warsaw. Chodorowski, leader of the shoemakers in 1830–1, attended this ceremony in honour of Kiliński. His presence gave rise to much apprehension among the propertied classes; Lelewel states this incident was responsible for including Warsaw in the area covered by the state of war, cf. *Pamiętnik*, p. 83.

because it would provide an opportunity for individual distinction. As *Nowa Polska* could declaim: 'War! War! Thus already our wishes turn into the crash of guns and the clash of arms.'[1] Having declared so insistently for war the Society was obliged to give some practical demonstration of its patriotism. On the proposal of Bronikowski the leading members decided to join the army. The ministry of war sent them to the independent corps of General Dwernicki where they might do less harm than in the main army. Mochnacki and Gurowski, however, did succeed in joining the main army, but they had little influence upon it. The rump of the radicals left in Warsaw offered the government no trouble. There was no danger that a Commune would seize power. The traditional leaders were left undisturbed for the moment to conduct the war as they pleased.[2]

The course of the war in its initial stages proved the correctness of Chłopicki's policy. The Russian army crossed into the Kingdom from its position of concentration in the district of Białystok. It consisted of 76 battalions of infantry, 98 squadrons of cavalry and 200 guns, in all some 79,000 men. The narrow tongue of Polish territory along the East Prussian frontier was quickly overrun by forces from Kaunas and Grodno. The movement of the Russian forces was hampered by a sudden rise in the temperature on 8 February; the snow disappeared and rain began to fall, so that the progress was extremely slow. It soon became obvious however that the main direction of the Russian advance was in a south-westerly direction towards the town of Węgrów, due east of Warsaw. The Polish forces for their part were concentrated east of the capital, with detachments on both flanks to protect them from sudden incursion. A small force, consisting of General Giełgud's infantry division, was based on the town of Zegrze on the Bug below its junction with the Narew to protect the north; the 1st Cavalry Division

---

[1] *No. 35* (8 February 1831).
[2] The number of persons who could be reckoned as active members of the Society was very small. After the insurrection the Russians drew up a list of 486 persons who were alleged to have been members, but some of the names are improbable, cf. Władysław Zamoyski and Franciszek Wężyk. This list must be considered rather more than the absolute total, cf. W. Smoleński, 'Towarzystwo Patriotyczne', *Przegląd Historyczny*, viii (1909), 91–105, where the Russian list is reprinted.

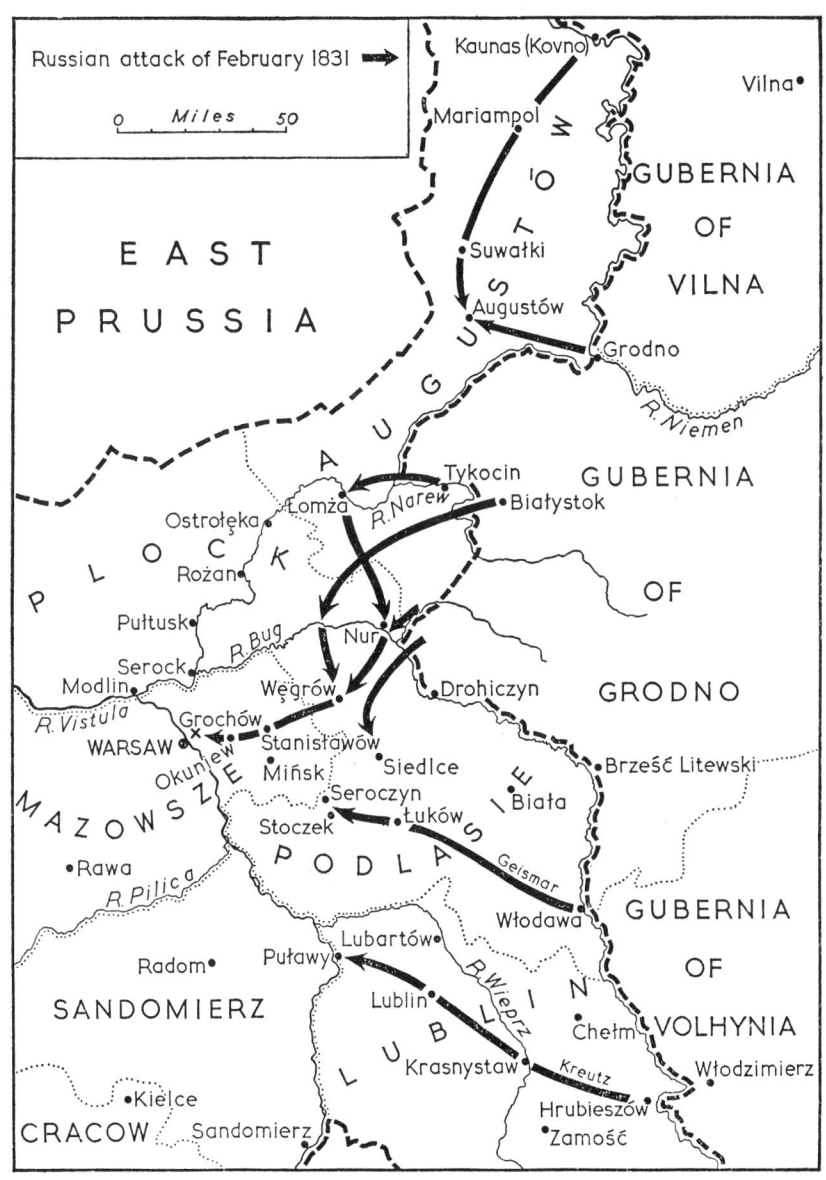

The Battle of Grochów: February, 1831

was stationed in the Narew Valley at Pułtusk, with advanced units at Kożan and Ostrołęka. In the south a small corps under General Dwernicki was detailed to fend off Russian troops marching from the upper reaches of the Bug. It was in fact Dwernicki who made contact with the enemy first. He crossed the Vistula from the left bank and marched south-east in the direction of Łuków. On 13 February he occupied the small town of Stoczek and on the next day launched a successful attack on the troops of General Geismar whom he forced to withdraw. This action had little significance, but it was the first encounter and gave encouragement to the main army which was becoming demoralized by the marching and countermarching which it was asked to perform; it was also the foundation of the military reputation of General Dwernicki. In the centre however the Russians continued to advance. The Polish army, though smaller in numbers than the Russians, began to obtain an advantage from being near to its base and from withdrawing on interior lines while Russian units tended to be slow in arriving on the field of battle. As the crisis approached the Polish command began to be divided by petty jealousies. The position of General Chłopicki was ambiguous; he had arrived to assist Radziwiłł, but had no formal authority. It was necessary on 22 February for Radziwiłł to issue an order that Chłopicki was in command of the forward troops and had the power to issue commands. During the three days 23–25 February fighting reached its intensity in the plain east of Praga. According to Polish estimates the losses inflicted on the Russians were greater than those sustained by the Poles; the Russians are said to have lost 9,400 men, while the Polish army lost 7,000. This encounter, which has been given the name of the battle of Grochów and which was thereafter counted as a Polish victory, produced at the time a state of panic in Warsaw. The generals Tomasz Łubieński and Szembek were of the opinion that negotiations ought to be started at once.[1] Deputations from the municipality of Warsaw and the National Guard came to the government and the diet to urge that the city should not be

---

[1] Łubieński in a letter to Berlin which was intercepted by Russian agents gave a depressing picture of the confusion in Warsaw. The tsar believed that if the Russians had been able to cross the Vistula the war would have been brought to an

subjected to destruction. Some of the deputies and senators were preparing to leave the city at once. The army streamed in disorder over the bridge from Praga and gangs of young officers presented themselves at the ministry of war to complain of the handling of operations by the general staff.[1] A council of war was called of the leading generals for the early hours of 26 February. Radziwiłł had resigned his command and Chłopicki had been wounded in the battle, but the government was determined to carry on the struggle. The one general who had distinguished himself in the battle, more by his personal valour than his tactical skill, General Skrzynecki, was appointed commander-in-chief. His rival, Krukowiecki, was removed from his command of the 1st Division lest Skrzynecki should be embarrassed by having an officer senior in the service to himself holding a subordinate post: Krukowiecki accepted the position of governor of Warsaw, telling the government that he ought to be given farms to support his new dignity.[2] Curiously enough Nicholas I seems to have thought that the appointment of a comparatively junior officer to supreme command was a sign that Jacobinism had won control,[3] but Skrzynecki was in fact very conservative in his views. He, and the same may be said for Krukowiecki, looked at the world from the point of view of professional soldiers; if their self-esteem were injured they might lend an ear to radical murmurings, but they were both concerned to uphold military discipline, provided that they themselves were not too closely bound by it. One thing Skrzynecki at least did was to appoint younger and abler men to his staff. Chrzanowski became chief of staff,

end quickly, *Correspondance*, ii, 134. Nicholas I let it be known that the battle had not been handled with sufficient vigour and wrote to Diebitsch: 'Pensez surtout à vos approvisionnements et ne vous exagérez pas la force de l'ennemi. Souvoroff savait battre les Polonais avec peu de monde.' Prince Shcherbatov, *General-Feldmarshal Knyaz Paskevich* (St. Petersburg, 1894), iv (Appendices), 12.

[1] Barzykowski, *Historya*, iii, 5–6.
[2] *Ibid.*, iii, 25. Krukowiecki's career is typical of that of many officers of petty *szlachta* origin. He had entered the Austrian army and fought in the war against the Turks in 1788–90. He was wounded at Belgrade. In 1792–4 he fought in the Austrian army against France and was twice wounded which gave him good excuse to resign his commission. In 1806 he entered the French army as a captain, the rank which he had held in the Austrian army. Under the Congress Kingdom he was a divisional general and Skrzynecki had been his adjutant.
[3] *Correspondance*, ii, 132.

an able man, with a conviction that indiscipline would bring disaster.[1] The new quartermaster-general, Ignacy Prądzyński, was able enough, full of plans and schemes, though with small regard to the physical effort demanded of the soldiers; unlike Chrzanowski, Prądzyński was an old conspirator and was too concerned to press his own point of view, even behind the back of Skrzynecki. New commanders were appointed also to the cavalry and infantry divisions and Izydor Krasiński gave way at the ministry of war to Franciszek Morawski, a general with connections with the Kalisz group and pretensions to being a poet in his own right. The general result of Skrzynecki's reorganization at the regimental level was to promote officers to posts for which they had little training or experience. This, coupled with the expansion of December and January, brought into responsible positions many subalterns and even newly commissioned officers. The barrack-square tradition of military discipline so carefully built up by the Grand Duke Constantine was irreparably weakened.

Skrzynecki believing firmly in the independence of the army from civil control, at once began to discover what the intentions of Diebitsch were, not by armed reconnaissance, but by direct negotiation. Colonel Mycielski was sent on three occasions to the Russian headquarters. It was characteristic of Skrzynecki that he revealed only two of these attempts to sound Diebitsch. Czartoryski was alarmed and demanded to know the reason for these negotiations, but Skrzynecki replied that he was attempting only to discover what he could of the dispositions and strength of the Russian army; in fact, he published part of the correspondence on 29 March when he issued his order of the day prior to the Polish counter-offensive, pleading that this was proof that the Poles had tried to reach agreement and that not they, but the Russians were responsible for further bloodshed.

[1] Wojciech Chrzanowski (1793–1861) had joined the army of Duchy, but was taken prisoner in 1812. He enlisted once more in the Polish army in 1815 and in 1828 was sent by Constantine to take part in the Russo-Turkish war. He was one of the few Polish officers who had practical experience of staff work in the field. He is better known as the envoy of Lord Palmerston sent on missions to Turkey after 1831, and as the *de facto* commander of the Piedmontese army at the battle of Novara in 1849; his Christian name is sometimes given as Albert or Alberto, which is strangely enough the equivalent of the Polish 'Wojciech'.

There is however some suspicion that Skrzynecki wished to find out whether the Russians would modify their terms after the losses before Grochów. Nicholas I however still stood firmly on the manifesto of 17 December 1830 demanding unconditional surrender and the concentration of the army before Płock.[1]

The position of the Polish forces was by no means desperate. Praga was still held, while the Russian army was in great difficulties in bringing up supplies. Roads were bad and food was short. There were many wounded and the cholera which had moved into Russia from Akstrakhan in 1830 was already beginning to have an effect in Poland. After reconnoitring the position at Praga Diebitsch decided that he was not strong enough for the moment to launch a direct assault upon Warsaw and elected to wait until he found a better opportunity. Nevertheless, he had won considerable advantage from his victory. He held almost half of the Kingdom, which meant that only the western half could be drawn upon by the Poles for supplies and men. In the south too the Russians had been able to make progress. On 8 February a small force under General Kreutz took the town of Lublin and crossed the Vistula with the object of dispersing the Polish troops assembling in the *województwo* of Sandomierz. Dwernicki, the victor of Stoczek, was ordered to cross once more to the left bank and assume command of the troops under General Sierawski. In all he had 8,500 men to deal with the 3,600 of Kreutz. Kreutz recrossed to the right bank on 24 February to evade attack and was pursued by Dwernicki. This was a temptation for the Polish command to resume activity in the south; Dwernicki's successes meant that he was a potential rival to the new commander-in-chief, who may not have been unwilling to assign him a task away from the main theatre of operations. Dwernicki was detailed to take 1,500 cavalry and 6 guns and attack the communications of the Russian army; a secondary task, if events turned in his favour, was to continue his march to the south-east in the direction of Volhynia and raise the standard of revolt in the three *gubernii*

[1] *Correspondance*, ii, 139. Colonel Mycielski undoubtedly gave the impression that he was seeking some guarantee that the Russians would grant something which did not involve unconditional surrender and would permit the Polish army to make its submission on honourable terms, cf. Diebitsch's letters of 5 and 10 March to Nicholas, *Russkaya Starina*, xlvi, 297–301, 513–17.

south of the Pripet marshes. For the moment this diversion succeeded. Diebitsch had no accurate information of the strength of Dwernicki's corps and sent 20,000 men under his chief of staff, Count Toll, to protect the southern flank of the main Russian army, which brought relief to the Polish army in Warsaw.

More alarming than the situation of the Polish army was the collapse of civilian morale in Warsaw. Symptomatic of the general fear was the action of Adam Gurowski, who had played so prominent a part in the demonstrations of 25 January. He arrived back in Warsaw after the battle of Grochów and reported to the ministry of foreign affairs that he thought he could best serve the Polish cause in Paris; Gustaw Małachowski lent him 3,000 *złp* and sped him on his way, glad to be rid of a dangerous radical. The members of the diet were equally frightened by the proximity of the Russian forces. The possibility that a quorum might not be found for the continuation of debates had been foreseen as the army withdrew. A law was passed on 12 February instructing the government to hold elections for vacant seats. On the same day it was ordained that deputies could not leave Warsaw without the written permission of the marshal, or overstay their leave without good reason.[1] The senate was authorized to carry on with a quorum of 19 members.[2] With the worsening of the military situation it was thought that the diet might be forced to leave Warsaw altogether. By a law of 19 February it was declared that the diet was in permanent session and could not be dissolved; on the authority of the combined chambers it could be adjourned to meet in another place, whether in the Kingdom or abroad. Article 3 laid down that the smallest quorum, if the Sejm met in Warsaw, was to be 11 senators and 33 deputies, but memory of the diet of Grodno of 1793 was still strong; all meetings held in the territory occupied by the emperor of Russia were declared illegal. In the event of a quorum not being found for the two chambers they were to meet jointly provided that a total of 33 members could be found.[3] By 26 February it was abundantly clear that many members wished to leave Warsaw. The chambers turned themselves into a secret committee to

[1] *Dyaryusz sejmu*, ii, 52–4.   [2] *Ibid.*, ii, 97.   [3] *Ibid.*, ii, 131.

discuss this delicate matter. It is not known whether there were in fact 65 members present to form the normal quorum on 26 February, for the secretary did not enter a list of those present in the *Dyaryusz sejmu*. It was decided in accordance with the law of 19 February that the two chambers should henceforth meet together, provided that a minimum quorum of 33 were found. It was left open to senators and deputies to choose whether or not they would stay in Warsaw, but laid down that unless there were at least 40 persons prepared to remain the others would not be allowed to depart.[1] Only 31 deputies and 10 senators actually signed the document expressing their determination to stay behind, though another five who were not present eventually signed the list. This group was composed very largely of persons who had taken an active part in debates, the so-called 'zealots' and deputies whose homes did not lie in enemy territory; only seven deputies appeared from the *województwa* of Lublin, Augustów and Podlasie. Thus the diet was reduced to the Small Quorum and on the morning of 28 February only a handful of senators and 48 deputies assembled to transact parliamentary business.

The first stage of the insurrection was now over. Within the space of a single month it had been proved that the Polish army could not march triumphantly into Western Russia and decide the fate of Poland on the battlefield. It was in fact remarkable that the Poles were able to continue the struggle at all. Their preparations had been hasty and the deposition of Nicholas I on 25 January had had the effect of throwing away any advantages which might have been obtained by dragging out the negotiations with Russia. The mood of the Polish public had shown a self-confidence which had been altogether unjustified, scarcely taking into account the relative strengths of the Kingdom and the Russian Empire. Defeat now induced a more sober feeling and revealed that war could not be fought lightheartedly without thought of the consequences.

[1] *Ibid.*, ii, 159.

CHAPTER V

The Failure of Agrarian Reform

THE defeat at Grochów had forced the Polish army back behind the Vistula and restricted it to so small an area that it seemed self-evident that desperate measures were demanded. The Poles thought that only if they gave proof of their power to survive could they expect foreign aid. It was consciousness of their weakness that turned Polish leaders' attention to the people, an untapped source of strength which Kościuszko had used in 1794 to great effect at Racławice. The same technique, a promise of economic emancipation, sprang immediately to mind as a method of securing the peasants' enthusiastic co-operation.

The revolution had been the work of the Warsaw intellectuals and army officers of *szlachta* origin, a local insurrection at the seat of administration unaccompanied by widespread disturbances in the countryside or provincial towns. The peasants had not risen to force their claims upon the authorities. The revolutionary government was indeed anxious that order should be maintained in the countryside and as a means to this end instructed the clergy to educate the peasants in the aims of the insurrection.[1] The ministry of religion and public instruction was careful to warn priests that information should be couched in the most general terms and that social questions should be avoided.[2] To issue an order from Warsaw was one thing, to have it carried out another. In the summer of 1831 Prince Sapieha, returning from Zamość to Warsaw encountered pea-

---

[1] Cf. *A.A.D. 451ᵃ* (*Powstanie narodu polskiego*), letter of the ministry of internal affairs to the ministry of religion and public instruction, 11 December 1830.

[2] *A.A.D. 603* (*Ogólne rozporządzenia do duchowieństwa w czasie ostatniego rokoszu*), temporary government's letter to the ministry of religion, 16 December 1830.

THE FAILURE OF AGRARIAN REFORM 173

sants bringing in supplies for the army: 'I got into conversation with the peasants leading these wagons. They knew that there was a war, because a number of recruits and supplies was being collected, but they did not know what the war was about, or who was fighting with whom.'[1] In January the ministry of internal affairs reported that in Mazowsze, the immediate area of Warsaw, the peasants had not heard of Chłopicki's decision of 18 December to exempt them from the purveyance tax in token of their being asked to provide recruits for the army.[2] Not all the peasants however remained in ignorance of events in Warsaw and not a few of them interpreted talk of freedom to mean that labour services would no longer be enforced, but the sporadic instances of refusal did not seriously alarm the ministry of internal affairs, which congratulated itself in its report to the government that obedience had been enforced.[3] In the spring however peasant insubordination became more formidable. Chłopicki's policy of falling back on the line of the Vistula with a view to being able to continue the struggle behind a strong defensive position in the event of severe defeat was militarily correct, but it meant that after Grochów the whole weight of the Polish effort was thrown on the *województwa* on the left bank of the river, where the peasants had been most severely hit by the crop failure of the previous year and where the landowners had in the past been least considerate of the interests of the people. Here taxes and supplies had to be collected with more than the usual thoroughness. At the same time the peasants were required to serve in the local security forces. Because there was no reduction of labour services, which would have meant a threat to production on demesne lands, the amount of time which the peasants could devote to their own holdings was reduced. An added cause of discontent was the requisitioning of the government which made serious inroads on the stocks of the landlords, who found it difficult to fulfil the traditional obligation of assisting the peasants in their distress.

The *województwo* of Sandomierz is always illustrative of the

[1] Leon Sapieha, *Wspomnienia* (Lvov, 1912), p. 143.
[2] *A.A.D. 451a*, Report of 15 January 1831.
[3] *A.A.D. 553* (*Zdawanie rządowi rapportów ogólnych z działań policyjnych*), Report of police activity, 14 January 1831.

worst social and economic conditions of this period. In his report of 14 March 1831[1] the commissioner stated that only one quarter of the normal crop of grain had been harvested and potatoes had failed.

There are absolutely no stocks of corn among the peasants of the *województwo*, for the husbandman in these parts, being only the tenant of a small patch of land given him by the landlord, in years of good harvest hardly enjoys the certainty that he will succeed in feeding himself from his holding, while in years of harvest failure he reckons entirely upon the assistance of the landlord. Supplies of corn, potatoes and vegetables are not to be found on the manors at the present time, for they must be used to assist the peasants. This has occurred among those who are hastening to meet the extraordinary needs of arming the nation.[2]

Some manors were not even in a position to assist the peasants. There were large numbers of cattle, but these were draught animals, a last means of subsistence which could not be taken from the peasants. To add to the miseries of the area the Russians were making incursions from the right bank of the Vistula.

By contrast social conditions in the *województwo* of Płock were very different from those in the provinces on the left bank of the river. Here there were large numbers of petty *szlachta* who were technically citizens and could voice grievances for themselves. Passive resistance caused the district commissioner of Ostrołęka as early as December 1830 to call for troops to carry out the orders of the government.

The greatest efforts of both myself and the citizens who compose the district committee in fulfilling the orders of the government and in particular in the supply of cavalrymen, in sending men to Modlin,

---

[1] *A.A.D. 515 (Zaopatrzenie mieszkańców w żywność i jarych obsiewów w r. 1831 w województwie sandomierskiem)*, Report of 14 March 1831. The commissioner had been recently appointed and depressing reports could not reflect upon his own administration, whereas in the *województwo* of Kalisz, where Gabriel Niemojowski, brother of Wincenty and Bonawentura, was commissioner, conditions were usually presented in a favourable light.

[2] Lubecki before the rising had intended to use this situation to promote his schemes of industrialization; by a scheme of public works he hoped to be able to relieve peasant distress, cf. *Korespondencya Lubeckiego*, iii, 388, Letter to Grabowski, 28 October 1830.

THE FAILURE OF AGRARIAN REFORM 175

and in obtaining food and forage, are paralized by the unheard-of slackness of the village mayors and the landed gentry, especially of the lesser *szlachta* and other inhabitants. The employment of distrainers from the Security Guard brings no result because they are moved by self-interest in the matter.[1]

The people of Lipno actually tore down the Polish eagles which patriots displayed on their houses.[2] A courier had shown his lack of enthusiasm for the national cause by throwing official correspondence down a well. The government was in consequence forced to admit the principle that the petty *szlachta* should enjoy some tax reliefs, just as the peasants under Chłopicki's order had been exempted from purveyance, and conceded that *szlachta* with holdings assessed at less than 10 *groszy* according to the rules of 1789 should be classed as peasants.[3] If the *województwa* of Augustów and Podlasie, together with parts of Płock, had not been overrun by the Russians in early February it is likely that the Polish government would have had even more trouble in the north-eastern regions of the Kingdom.

The peasants in some districts objected strongly to service in the local security forces. Disturbances occurred among the native Lithuanians around Augustów in December 1830, especially at Wołkowyszki near the East Prussian frontier, southeast of Kaunas, where high-handed conduct by local commanders and language difficulties created some confusion. Riots occurred in the *województwo* of Kalisz, where the peasant levies were expected to provide their own food on training days. Unit commanders had the same story to tell from Sandomierz and the *województwo* of Cracow. In the end it became apparent that the system of local security was too elaborate, leading both to peasant disturbances and to a fall in agricultural production. With the approach of spring the government released from service all but the cadres of the mobile guard.[4]

[1] *A.A.D. 451ᵃ*, district commissioner's report of 24 December 1830.
[2] *Ibid.*, commissioner of the *województwo* to the ministry of internal affairs, 6 December 1830.
[3] This was the local recommendation, cf. *A.A.D. 454* (*Żywienie wojska polskiego*), committee for the supply of food to the ministry of internal affairs, 11 January 1831.
[4] Pawłowski, *Źródła*, ii, 46–7.

In the spring and summer however there were more cases of peasant recalcitrance and refusal of services, especially in the *województwo* of Mazowsze where garbled reports of the intentions of the revolution had filtered through to the peasants. Sapalski, the administrator of the estates of Count Alexander Potocki, experienced great difficulties and appealed to the government for troops to enforce order: 'How will the landowner be in a position to carry out the orders of the government if he does not obtain effective aid to keep insubordinate peasants in the bonds of obedience and order?' Possibly there was something amiss with the methods of Sapalski because he reported identical troubles in Count Potocki's properties in the *województwo* of Sandomierz: 'The peasants through an ill-conceived interest in freedom think that they are free from all obligations to the government and their lords.'[1] Efforts to stop desertion of peasants from the army in Mazowsze do not seem to have been very effective. A number of villages in the rural districts near Warsaw were notorious for harbouring runaways. The governor of Warsaw, Krukowiecki, in May 1831 complained to the ministry of internal affairs: 'Some regimental commanders are making representations to me that, having newly conscripted and inexperienced young soldiers, they are suffering frequent losses from desertion. As a circumstance facilitating this offence they cite the fact that proprietors of villages and other landowners are harbouring them and giving them refuge on their farms for the purpose of using them as agricultural labour.'[2]

The payment of taxes was never a popular civic duty in Congress Poland. In normal times it would have been difficult to collect them when the population, both peasants and *szlachta*, were impoverished by harvest failure. The war situation brought back the conditions which had existed under the Duchy of Warsaw. Polish produce and raw materials which normally went abroad were diverted to home needs. Trade and industry stagnated and everywhere there was a shortage of ready money. From the *województwo* of Sandomierz in the first quarter of 1831 only 302,435 *złp* 19 *gr* were received in direct and indirect taxes, rents from government properties and

---

[1] *A.A.D. 507 (Deserterze i marauderze z wojska narodowego)*, letter to the ministry of internal affairs, 30 June 1831. [2] *A.A.D. 507*, letter of 14 May 1831.

THE FAILURE OF AGRARIAN REFORM 177

miscellaneous sources compared with 1,338,435 złp 23 gr for the corresponding quarter of the previous year.[1] In this case the citizens' council asked for the use of troops for distraint of taxes because the local security forces were useless, being composed of peasants. The pressing need for money, especially after the battle of Ostrołęka, the second crisis of the war, caused the authorities everywhere to use ruthless methods. There were in the small towns instances of flight to avoid taxation.[2] The government's demands were made in the name of a cause which few had the basic education to appreciate. When in the summer the government tried to stir patriotic feeling in the provincial towns by establishing municipal councils a sorry state of affairs came to light. No less than seven towns in the *województwo* of Sandomierz had their elections annulled either because the councillors included illiterates or because there were not enough literates to form a council. The comparatively large religious centre of Częstochowa had 454 persons on the electoral roll of whom 251 were illiterates; when the elections were held on 20 July 1831 only 299 persons bothered to attend.[3] Similar indifference may be found in the town of Płock. An examination of the Polish countryside in 1831 leaves the impression that the mass of the population lacked both the means and the spirit to make any substantial contribution to the success of the national movement. Enthusiasm for the revolution was confined to the educated classes of the community. The mass of the population adopted an attitude of passivity, rendering only that aid which was unavoidable.

In isolated instances however the people showed open and armed hostility to the revolution. The most serious of all peasant disturbances in 1831 occurred in the *województwo* of Cracow,

[1] *A.A.D. 461 (Rady obywatelskie)*, citizens' council to the ministry of internal affairs, 30 April 1831.
[2] Cf. *A.A.D. 463ᵇ (Formowanie siły zbrojnej w Królestwie Polskiem)*, where the burgomaster of Kurzelów reported on 26 April to the district commissioner that 'up to 12 inhabitants have completely abandoned their homes. They are paying no contributions and this is not because of insolence, but because of their lack of means and poverty. Besides this, many inhabitants have not sown their fields for want of corn and in the whole town hardly twenty persons may be found who have even very small supplies of food, while others eat but once a day.'
[3] *A.A.D. 545 (Rady Municypalne po miastach w województwie kaliskiem)*, commissioner's report of 17 June 1831, which contains a complete list of voters.

in the district of Olkusz, where it was contiguous with the Prussian Silesian frontier. The possibility of evading punishment by flight into Silesia undoubtedly encouraged a bold spirit; the border regions of Silesia to a considerable depth were inhabited by Polish peasants and it was not as if the peasants of Congress Poland were fleeing to a completely foreign country. Over 800 desertions are mentioned from the *województwo* of Cracow alone. Here holdings were small and often labour services were exacted in the form of work in mines and foundries, the beginnings of the great Upper Silesian industry. In the early months of 1831 the peasants are said to have declared: 'We will march against the Muscovite, but first we will cut down the *szlachta* because they are the cause of our misery.'[1] These were sentiments which foretold the jacquerie of 1846 just over the Austrian frontier in Galicia. In May 1831 the frontier area was in a state of unrest. Deserters hiding in the woods near Siewierz in the subdistrict of Lelów decided to attack the village of Toporowice on the night of 18/19 May to prevent officials from confiscating peasant property. The commissioner of the *województwo* underestimated the strength of peasant hostility and thought that the clergy would have enough influence to restore order and point out to the villagers 'that they are guilty of disobedience and contravention of the social principles and religion which they profess'.[2] When it turned out that some thousand peasants were involved all the local security forces had to be mobilized to disperse the rioters. Thirty-five persons were arrested and the eight chief offenders tried at Kielce. As usual, it was the more prosperous peasants who had been the ringleaders, while the poorer peasants remained aloof. In this particular case, the troubles had been caused by the policy of the local landlords who had made a practice of rearranging holdings to suit their own convenience.

The government was faced with twin problems, in the first place how to obtain supplies for the army and the city of Warsaw, and, secondly, how to maintain the level of grain production in the face of the shortages caused by the harvest

---

[1] M. Meloch, *Sprawa włościańska w powstaniu listopadowym*, 2nd edn. (Warsaw, 1948), p. 174, quoting *A.A.D. 274* which I have not seen.

[2] *A.A.D. 464*, for his report to the ministry of internal affairs, 21 May 1831.

THE FAILURE OF AGRARIAN REFORM 179

failure of 1830.¹ The two aspects were closely related. If the countryside were denuded of grain there would be little possibility of carrying the struggle into the winter. On the other hand the current needs of the army were pressing. The government was not assisted in finding a solution by the obstruction of landlords everywhere. To assure stocks for the spring sowing and the central magazines the ministry of internal affairs in February 1831 issued a questionnaire to all the *województwa*, demanding an answer to three questions: Have the peasants enough corn and will it suffice until next harvest? Have they enough corn for spring sowings? What quantities of cattle exist?² By the end of the month only Kalisz and Sandomierz had replied; Podlasie, Lublin and Augustów were in the hands of the Russians. On 23 March only 40 days' supplies were left in Warsaw. Instead of drafting a provisional plan the ministry of internal affairs dallied and waited for information. Only on 10 April did the government agree to a grant of 1,000,000 *złp* to relieve peasant distress, and of that sum only a very small part was taken up for the purpose by the provincial authorities.³ There was evidently some objection to the government's method of payment. The citizens' council of Mazowsze declared that it was 'not at all satisfied with the plan communicated to it by the Ministry of Internal Affairs, dated 13 April of this year . . . because the very instruction to take spring corn lying in store on estates is an act of force, being in fact a requisition and rightly hated in our day, in the same way as the undermining of the currency with treasury bills at the rate of 80 in the 100, when properly they stand at 73, is a violation of property rights'.⁴

On 26 January, the day after the deposition of Nicholas I, the governor of Warsaw, General Wojczyński, had urged the need for at least two months' reserve supply of food for the city and at the request of the Supreme National Council the

¹ The same difficulty existed in the areas occupied by the Russian army, cf. *Correspondance*, ii, 133.
² *A.A.D. 511* (*Zaopatrzenie mieszkańców w żywność i zapewnienie jarych obsiewów w r. 1831 w Królestwie Polskiem*), Rescript of 17 February 1831.
³ The landlords of Płock declared that the aid had come too late, cf. *A.A.D. 511*, citizens' council's letter to ministry, 19 April 1831. Cf. similar objections of the *województwo* of Cracow, *A.A.D. 514*, letters of 15 April and 10 May 1831.
⁴ *A.A.D. 518*, citizens' council of Mazowsze to the national government, 16 April 1831.

ministry of internal affairs drew up a plan to achieve this aim.[1] It was proposed to collect as much rye, the staple foodstuff of the population, as possible. The ministry estimated that the population of Warsaw at the end of January was 134,000, but that it might rise to 220,000 if the city were subjected to a siege. In practice, however, the plan was seen to contain a number of miscalculations. Unprecedented bulk purchases in a period of shortage sent prices up to abnormally high levels, except for meat, which may reflect increased slaughtering in the face of the lack of foodstuffs for cattle. The *korzec* of rye rose in Warsaw from 17 *złp* in January to 30 *złp* 20 *gr* in August, while wheat rose from 21 *złp* to 44 *złp* over the same period; similar rises were recorded for other grains. In the rescript of 19 February 1831,[2] issued to the *województwa* of Mazowsze, Płock and Sandomierz, the ministry of internal affairs fixed its purchase prices at the January levels; the maximum price for rye was to be 17–20 *złp* and for wheat 20–26 *złp*. It was only to be expected that the victualling officers would meet with difficulties. Parębski, an agent in the *województwo* of Płock, reported that 'market prices immediately jumped out of all proportion through the towns and hamlets and when I went into the countryside to the landowners it was impossible to buy anything, because speculators, especially those who sell at third hand and not without profit to agents from Warsaw, are all the time raising the price of corn excessively. In the markets the purchase of corn cannot be advantageous to the government, because the grain brought to market by the peasants is for the most part neither as reasonably priced nor in as good condition as that which may be found in the barn of a landowner with a fair-sized property.... Even the landowners are refusing to sell, in the hope of a more advantageous sale of their produce, which already stands at a rather high price at the moment.'[3] In Mazowsze merchants were holding supplies in the hope of being allowed to export to Prussia, which the government had

---

[1] *A.A.D. 487ª (Magazyny reserwowe w Warszawie)*. The ministry's estimates of 30 January are given as follows: Rye: 25,000 *korce* at 500,000 *złp*, Wheat: 15,000 *korce* at 375,000 *złp*, Pease: 3,000 *korce* at 60,000 *złp*, Oats: 10,000 *korce* at 100,000 *złp*, Barley: 5,000 *korce* at 30,000 *złp*, 10,000 centnars of Hay at 75,000 *złp*, 5,000 centnars of Straw at 10,000 *złp*, and 2,000 head of cattle at 300,000 *złp*.

[2] *A.A.D. 487ª*.   [3] *A.A.D. 487ª*, Parębski's report of 22 March 1831.

THE FAILURE OF AGRARIAN REFORM 181

forbidden,[1] while from Sandomierz the citizens' council reported that many burgomasters were using their official position to indulge in speculation. The outcome of this unsatisfactory state of affairs was that the ministry of internal affairs had to abandon its original plan and take supplies wherever they could be found. The best solution seemed to be to purchase the large stocks of wheat which had accumulated at Włocławek on the Prussian frontier owing to the ban on exports. It was arranged for the shipment of 30,069 *korce* of wheat, 525 of rye and 95 of pease up the Vistula to be afforded the protection of the army. The acquisition of these supplies eased the situation in Warsaw, but they fell very far short of the aims of the ministry. Never during the whole course of the war were there enough stocks in Warsaw and such as there were suffered occasional raiding to meet immediate military needs.[2] While the Polish army remained in control of the west bank of the Vistula there was always the hope that fresh supplies could be obtained, but quite clearly a dangerous situation would arise if the Russians crossed the river and attacked Warsaw from the west. In that event the Polish army would be forced to draw upon supplies from the east bank where the Russian army had been in occupation. From the point of view of supply Polish survival depended upon the ability to defend the line of the Vistula. In fact, the Russians did eventually succeed in making their crossing, but until they did it was possible to believe that the struggle could be carried on.

It was in this depressing situation that the Polish politicians

[1] *Ibid.*, the ministry's report to the government of 4 April.
[2] The position up to July was as follows:

Stocks held in Warsaw (in korce)

	Aim	22 Feb.	21 Mar.	20 Apr.	27 May	June	8 July
Wheat	15,000	222	2,743	24,014	19,006	—	22,108
Rye	25,000	235	1,527	2,032	1,092	—	3,397
Barley	5,000	158	1,914	760	—	—	1,585
Oats	10,000	492	644	—	100	—	317
Pease	3,000	30	91	191	100	—	794

These figures are based upon the monthly reports to the ministry of internal affairs, contained in *A.A.D. 487ᵃ*. I have seen no figures for June.

turned their attention to the lot of the peasants. It was admitted that Poland could not for ever remain a serf state, but few had a clear appreciation of the problem. No member of the national government was prepared to press for decisive action. The Kalisz element took its stand upon narrow constitutionalism and was unlikely to propose a social transformation in the middle of a desperate war. Lelewel was without power in the government and made no serious effort. His contribution to the discussion was an article in *Nowa Polska* of 18 March 1831 in which he proposed hereditary leases.[1] Czartoryski's views may be obtained indirectly from a memorial which he drew up later in the war concerning the attitude to be adopted towards the former eastern provinces; his appreciation is entitled 'Thoughts on the insurrection in the annexed provinces', of 12 May 1831.[2] While he urged that the ancient privileges of these regions should be observed, he proposed that the *szlachta* of the east should make concessions to the peasants and draw them into participation in the revolution:

> The revolt of these provinces can bring us to these desired objects only when it is universal, when the whole people shall rise. The peoples of these provinces, held by the Russians in an animal passivity, have almost no idea at all of the Fatherland, though they cannot like the Muscovites, because they are oppressed by the soul tax and by recruiting, because in the last reign they experienced especial hardships, and because in their misery any change at the present time they reckon as a hope of improvement. They have borne up to the present the yoke of slavery peacefully, as the ox driven under it in the plough bears it. To stir such a people therefore it is necessary to give them, clearly and immediately, material advan-

---

[1] 'Nadanie własności włościanom', reprinted in *Polska, dzieje i rzeczy jej*, vii, 177–84. He attacked Lubecki's policy towards the crown lands, but was not much more radical than the rest left-wing leaders. 'The abolition of labour services and the introduction of rents is called the grant of property rights. The landowner was compelled to agree to this in Prussia by a despotic government, a measure which has been called a brutal extortion from the landed proprietors of a portion of their land to give it thus to the peasants. This has been called the grant of property rights and this definition has come to us from the Duchy of Posen. I would have thought it better to call this donation of property rights a "perpetual hereditary lease".'

[2] 'Myśli o powstaniu prowincji zabranych', *Muzeum Xiążąt Czartoryskich*, 5298 (Papiery publiczne, 1831), ii, 7–31.

THE FAILURE OF AGRARIAN REFORM 183

tages coupled with emancipation. Then only will their revolt be sincere and effective. Indeed, advantages which might with a favourable turn of the insurrection have an influence upon the peasants are obviously as follows: Ownership of movable property, freedom of movement from village to village after the completion of certain formalities, equality before the law, freedom to engage in trade, freedom to acquire land by hereditary right, the freedom of choice between labour services and rent, the leasing of land from the lord, the reduction of the number of years military service, and the removal of oppression. Those who distinguish themselves in the fight for independence may expect great advantages promised by the vote of the Diet and the patriotism of individual landowners in the Kingdom.

In other words, Czartoryski advocated the extension of the purely civil rights obtained under the Duchy of Warsaw to the *gubernii* of Western Russia, which he knew would not be without advantage to the landlords themselves.

Some of the benefits enumerated here will be assured to the peasants by the Government, others will be granted by the landowners themselves. They will be the result of their own patriotic generosity, which will ultimately appear equally profitable to themselves as the experience of the Kingdom shows. The landlords, by retaining property rights over the land, will not lose by their voluntary emancipation of the peasants. Estates have benefited here in this way . . .

Among the official papers of the insurrection is a letter of the ministry of internal affairs to the Supreme National Council of 5 January 1831, which is marked 'Urgent'.[1] The letter enumerates measures which might assist in winning over the peasants for the rebellion and is the first example of official awareness of the problem. It suggested the reduction of salt prices, an amnesty for petty offences, the exemption of wives of soldiers serving with the army from labour services for the period of the war, security of tenure for all soldiers recalled to the colours and a system of rewards for gallantry in the field for N.C.O.s and men. The final paragraph is the most important:

Para. 6: To promise that the Nation will consider means of assuring, gradually at least, property rights to the peasants. However, in

[1] *A.A.D. 451ᵃ* (*Powstanie narodu polskiego*).

keeping this promise to consider measures of the kind which the Prussian government arbitrarily employed to the detriment of the rights of third parties and prejudicial to the rights of property, different methods, it would appear, will be devised; with the aid of propitious and equitably assessed compensations the Nation will find itself in a position to discharge the obligation thus undertaken and thus make so important a contribution towards coming into line with the rest of European civilization [*and here is added in another hand*] for which the most suitable inducement and example might be the grant of property rights to the peasants of government estates. These suggestions the Minitsry of Internal Affairs and Police submits for the illustrious consideration of the Supreme National Council and awaits a speedy decision, with the observation that all exemptions or concessions to which the Council shall agree ought to be announced not only through official publications, but that in all the communes the clergy also ought to give the people this news from the pulpit.

The Supreme National Council immediately turned down all discussion of tenures; while it agreed to a reduction in the price of salt and to concessions for wives of serving soldiers, with regard to paragraph 6 of the ministry's letter the Council declared that 'in so important a matter touching the whole country, in the council's opinion, only a National Parliament itself can decide'.[1] There for the moment the matter was allowed to rest.

Outside official circles there was at first little pressure for reform. Maurycy Mochnacki and Adam Gurowski at the opening of the war had joined the main army and were struck by the lack of interest which the people at large showed towards the insurrection. From Pułtusk they sent to the newspaper, *Nowa Polska*, an article entitled 'Why do the masses not rise?' which was printed on 14 February.[2] They reported that 'the enemy has entered the country, he mixes with the people and says that "he will act not against the Nation, but against a handful of malefactors". The Muscovites buy food from the natives and behave reasonably. They declare that they have orders to

---

[1] *A.A.D. 451ᵃ*, letter of 6 January.
[2] Reprinted in Mochnacki's *Pisma rozmaite*, pp. 58–64.

THE FAILURE OF AGRARIAN REFORM 185

march to Warsaw and that not a hair of anyone's head will be touched, provided that no one hinders their progress. The policy of Moscow is very astute. Diebitsch must have noticed that our war will not be a national one.' To put matters right they were prepared to use desperate words, even at the cost of being called Jacobins, terrorists and demagogues. 'A social revolution is needed. It is necessary to use those means which a social revolution procures to save our dying Fatherland.' They advocated calling upon the Polish people and urged that the movement should be extended to Volhynia, Podolia and the Ukraine, and, thence, a familiar Polish will-o'-the-wisp, to the Turks, Persians and peoples of the Caucasus, but how this international revolution was to be set in motion they did not state. All they suggested was the admission of the peasants to political privileges. The economic question they did not touch upon.[1] The generally accepted point of view in Poland was that rewards might be granted to soldiers who distinguished themselves in battle. A system of rewards, pensions for the wounded ranging from 50 to 300 złp according to rank, provided at public expense, and grants from crown lands to the value of 10,000,000 złp, half for officers and half for other ranks, as an endowment for those who won the Silver Cross, was voted without discussion in the diet on 19 February 1831.[2] Books were opened to record the voluntary offerings of landlords who wished to reward returning soldiers or their widows and orphans. This was the limit of Polish solicitude for the common people before the battle of Grochów.

For J. O. Szaniecki, the radical whose petition for tenurial reform had been so contemptuously rejected in the diet of 1830, the military reverse was an opportunity to revive his plans for a transformation of Polish society. He now submitted to the marshal an eight-point resolution calling for the abolition of labour services, the grant of property rights to the peasants, though with compensation from a state fund, the extension of constitutional rights to the Jews and finally for an appeal to

[1] S. Szpotański, *Maurycy Mochnacki*, pp. 87-8, claims that Mochnacki demanded in this article the grant of property rights to the peasants, but of that I find no evidence.
[2] *Dyaryusz sejmu*, ii, 131-3.

the entire population to defend Poland from Russian invasion.¹ In practice Szaniecki was ready to accept any concession to the peasantry which would stir them from their passivity. On his own estates he had done what he could to improve their lot, but it must be admitted that he was mainly concerned with the question of liquidating landed debt. He thought that from a free peasantry a free labour force would develop which could be employed in industrial enterprise. The recognition of the peasants' individual rights would open the way to separation and consolidation of strips and thus allow manorial lands to be converted into unitary farms. By increasing the value of his land Szaniecki argued the proprietor could extricate himself from the consequences of the lean years under the Duchy of Warsaw, or by surrendering a portion obtain the cancellation of mortgage deeds. There were other landlords with similar ideas. Roman Sołtyk was attempting to develop his estates on these lines. Men of this type were willing to grant their peasants emancipation, but insisted that the principle of compensation to the landlords must be observed.²

¹ *Pamiętnik Jana Olrycha Szanieckiego*, pp. 59–60, gives the text of his proposal:
'1. To abolish every serf due or labour service performed by the peasants.
2. To abolish all feudal monopolies, i.e. the so-called *Jura Banaria*, in town and country.
3. To announce that all hereditary leases and rights *in perpetuum* may be bought out.
4. To recognize all holdings of peasants as their absolute property.
5. To fix a general tax for the partial amortization of this debt, which must be reckoned as a national obligation for compensating the owners of estates.
6. To grant to the Jewish community civic rights.
7. To call upon the whole body of the population to defend these rights and freedoms, which henceforth shall be common.
8. To assign to all Russian soldiers, or soldiers of other nations, who fight for our cause, a reward in land or in money.'
² This point of view was put with some force in *Nowa Polska*, no. 77 (22 March 1831), by an anonymous writer, possibly Roman Sołtyk himself. 'I am today in favour of the purchase of property rights, except where the land, being national property can be distributed for nothing. To take away from a landowner land which he possesses, which he has acquired, of which the ownership and the use is the most holy and inviolable right, to enforce the surrender of it, whether by statute or by an act of confiscation, I have always considered and consider now a source of confusion, a source of harmful internal disruption. Speculations on the social order, on the mutual relations of citizens, on rights, on public morality and good faith have increased, have acquired great importance. I consider the arbitrary transfer of property a crime, a declaration of war upon the social order. I am the irreconcilable enemy of such a mad, such a ruinous principle. . . . I do not like

THE FAILURE OF AGRARIAN REFORM

The diet, which at the beginning of the war had declared that reform ought to wait until the end of hostilities,[1] was now ready to listen to any proposals which the government cared to put before it. The government for its part dared not leave the initiative to Szaniecki and on 3 March the minister of finance laid his proposals before the diet. Szaniecki had hoped for a measure which would embrace all the peasantry, but the government, fearing social disruption in the midst of war and with its characteristic policy of going half-way to meeting external pressure, confined its proposals to the crown lands and refused to consider the question of private estates at all. The government thus began from the proposal of the ministry of internal affairs of 5 January. The government estates amounted to about 15 per cent of all landed properties in the Kingdom, though in some areas they formed an unusually large element in the agrarian structure; in the *województwo* of Augustów they were 36.9 per cent of all available lands. Of the 22,365 villages given by Rodecki for 1827 5,373 belonged to the state, from which must be deducted villages which passed out of the government's possession under Lubecki's scheme of sale; these sales amounted up to 27 June 1831 to 16,086,973 *złp* 19 *gr* and affected 150 properties, though it is not clear how many villages this included. Though the bill of the minister of finance was limited in its scope, it was none the less important for the *szlachta* who feared that it would be taken as a model if ever the state attempted to enforce a solution on private estates and was as hotly debated as if it did in fact affect private lands.[2]

The wording of the government's bill gives the impression that it was hastily prepared.[3] It was not an attempt to apply concessions obtained by crimes. I do not like improvements brought about by domestic commotions, by interference with the principles of law and property. The gradual voluntary redemption of property destined for donation and the complete emancipation of the peasants do not frighten anyone at all.'

[1] *Dyaryusz sejmu*, i, 159.

[2] The principle was admitted on all sides that the state had no right to deal with private lands, cf. the minister of finance's statement of 28 March: 'The dues of peasants on private estates are based upon freely negotiated agreements, whether verbal or in writing. The legislator cannot violate existing agreements or limit the freedom of the contracting parties.' *Ibid.*, ii, 319. This view was subscribed to by the president of the Senate, Nakwaski, *ibid.*, ii, 352, and by others who were quite well disposed towards the peasants, cf. Rembowski, *ibid.*, ii, 356, and Szaniecki, *ibid.*, ii, 371.   [3] The text is given in *Dyaryusz sejmu*, ii, 314 n.

drastic remedies, but a recognition that labour services were degrading and that the peasants, in spite of the introduction of the *Code Napoléon* had, on government lands at least, some hereditary claims which the legislation of 1825 had not invalidated. Labour services were to be converted into rents by the year 1841, provided that the peasants submitted to the rearrangement of their fields; the details were left to the ministry of finance to work out. The government was obviously attempting to compromise between the view that immediate action was needed and the case for postponing so complicated a matter to the end of the war, but the bill was transformed in the committee stage and what amounted to a new bill was submitted to the Small Quorum of the diet on 26 March 1831.[1] No record of the discussions in committee have remained, but the modifications to the government's bill show the influence of both radicals and conservatives. A propaganda point was made in the preamble by attacking Lubecki's administration of these lands and a sop was thrown to the private landlords by the statement that the mass of the peasantry was not ready for the new system, but that the bill would set an example on government lands and enable the *szlachta* to convince their own peasants of the need for a change, which would bring about a new spirit of enterprise in the countryside. There was even a suggestion that demesnes might at the government's discretion be leased to returning soldiers with the privilege of purchasing their freeholds. In place of the ministry's vague clause which in effect postponed an evaluation of the rent to be paid, the committee recommended that the capital value of the holdings be reckoned at twenty times the annual income to the treasury, which the peasants might pay off in order to acquire outright ownership. Until the freehold had been acquired a peasant might not divide his holding. So long as this had not been done the peasant was to pay a moderate rent, but his title to the soil was to be entered in the Land Registry, which would go some way to protecting him from the chicanery of leaseholders of crown lands. If the law had ever been put in force in this form a curious result would have followed; the peasant would have been required to pay a quit-rent throughout the period in

[1] For the Polish text see *Dyaryusz sejmu*, ii, 315–17.

THE FAILURE OF AGRARIAN REFORM 189

which he was paying off the capital value of the holding, for it was not foreseen that the quit-rent would be reduced in proportion to the capital payments, with the result that he would have been obliged to pay a full rent when he was almost the absolute owner of his land. In other words, the landlord, in this case the state, was to have his cake and eat it too. Another concession to the landlord was that his right of distilling and selling vodka was to remain unchanged and thus a social evil was to be perpetuated. Perhaps the most serious criticism was that the bill took no account of regional variations or of different types of land, but sought to enforce a single solution for the whole country.

The bill was not however to remain in this form. In all, ten sittings were devoted to it between 28 March and 14 April, which gives some indication of the importance attached to it and of the capacity of members for dragging out the debate. The opening discussion showed clearly that even in the Small Quorum there were serious misgivings. The senator Lewiński thought that the Small Quorum had insufficient authority to debate so important a matter; the details of the Prussian scheme of emancipation ought first to be considered and efforts made to spread out the process of emancipation over a period of years, with due allowance for regional problems, and indeed for its adaptation to the former eastern provinces.[1] Another senator, Bniński, feared that it might have the effect of denuding private estates of peasants who might wish to transfer to state properties. No less alarming for the conservatives was Klimontowicz's view that the measure, embracing only the government peasants, did not go far enough. The marshal however ruled that the bill must be discussed in detail first and then a vote be taken on the whole measure in its emended form. On 30 March under pressure from the conservative Ignacy Dembowski it was conceded that absent senators and deputies should be recalled to Warsaw, although there was then no appreciable improvement in the military situation.[2] The conservatives were thus secured against the danger of a *fait accompli* because a final

---
[1] *Ibid.*, ii, 344–8.
[2] The break-out from Warsaw actually took place on that very night, 30-31 March 1831.

decision would have to be taken when the diet met in full again. It was unlikely that the members who had scuttled out of Warsaw when the Russians approached would allow a radical measure to pass, but for the moment the radicals of the Small Quorum could have their say until the conservative rump returned.

No rigid divisions were shown in the discussion which followed. Some fears were expressed lest a sudden transformation to a money economy cause hardship for the peasants who would not have the means to pay rents. The deputy, Mazurkiewicz, thought that it was useless to give the peasants property rights until they had the education to enable them to make full use of their new social standing, while Klimontowicz insisted that the peasants could never become good farmers and citizens until they had the incentive of ownership. In the press Słubicki expressed doubts concerning the economics of the bill and questioned whether, if demesnes were leased out, peasants could be found to take the holdings.[1] For Słubicki there was also the problem of the landless rural workers who performed labour services for richer peasants and who might as a result of the bill lose their livelihood. The concern of the conservatives for the peasants was actively combated by the political economists. The councillor of state, Brodzki, pleaded that the bill was to the advantage of all parties; the landlord would be able to dispose of a fixed sum instead of being forced to accept unwilling labour services, while the peasant, freed from his burdens, would be able to take paid employment on the demesnes and earn the money with which to pay the rents. When one deputy expressed concern that the money relationship might place the peasant at the mercy of market conditions and bring him hardship in time of economic fluctuation, Szaniecki hotly set forth his economic doctrine:

> ... If anyone does not wish to pay the rent, he can transfer himself to a private estate, he can become a ploughman ... I am not for fixing a price on labour. It is not a loaf or meat, which can have a price put on it. Supply and demand fix it. In districts where there are few hands, it will have a high rate. Where there are many, it will have a low one... He who will not be in a position to pay the rent, let

[1] *Polak Sumienny*, no. 116, p. 82 (21 April 1831).

THE FAILURE OF AGRARIAN REFORM

him not take it on. This discussion about compulsion is to no purpose. If the peasant is to enjoy freedom of choice, so equally ought the landlord. If he does not want labour services, but only money, no one can compel him to receive labour services. I conclude that this matter is made sufficiently clear and that it should be possible to get on with composing the draft. [2]

Szaniecki's iron-fisted economics however did not appeal to the diet and the problem of a free choice between services and rent was solved by a compromise; the labour services were to be abolished and a rent set in their place, but the method of payment of the rent was to be left open, whether in money, kind or services.[3]

Up to this stage in the debates the deputies and senators had been thinking in terms of rents (*oczynszowanie*) and not so much of the purchase of freeholds (*uwłaszczenie*), two concepts which were to be commonplaces of Polish politics until 1863–4. Szaniecki, within the limits of his doctrines, however, was determined to open the way to the peasants to secure their freeholds as opposed to security of tenure only. It was a personal triumph for him when he succeeded in persuading the diet to recognize the principle that the annual income derived from a holding by the treasury, after it had paid its expenses, should be assessed on equitable terms and multiplied twenty times to represent the capital value of the land, which the peasants should pay in instalments in order to purchase their freeholds. The objection that the peasants might not find the opportunity to earn money was met by the sentence obliging the government to devise schemes of employment. After some quibbling a relatively simple scheme of purchase was agreed. Some government estates had already been mortgaged to the Land Credit Society and no scheme of emancipation could be considered which might add fresh burdens for the state.[4] The Small Quorum therefore agreed that the peasants should be allowed to pay $6\frac{1}{4}$ per cent per annum, the Land Credit Society's rate, on the total estimated value of their farms, so that they would

[2] *Dyaryusz sejmu*, ii, 454–5.   [3] *Ibid.*, ii, 460.
[4] According to Brodzki 5,151,450 morgs were the extent of the government lands. The net value to the state of the *włoka* (30 morgs) was 616 *złp*, if the 20-year purchase scheme were admitted. The average debt for the *włoka* covered by the Land Credit Society was 349 *złp*. *Ibid.*, ii, 497.

have purchased their freeholds in 28 years. Within the government estates the principle of emancipation with land, though with compensation to the landlord, was recognized, a slight improvement on the Prussian scheme of 1823 which permitted surrender of land by the peasants.

The main provisions of the scheme were embodied in Articles 3 and 4. The succeeding articles dealt with subsidiary, but no less important matters. Peasants were to be liable to distraint when they did not make their payments. Reciprocal rights of village and manor to pasturing, gathering wood and cutting hay were to cease from the moment of the new survey, if they were not based upon written agreements, a clause which would have enabled the landlord to exert intolerable pressure on the peasants. Holdings were to be properly registered to avoid protracted lawsuits. Under Article 11, proposed by Bonawentura Niemojowski, but never actually passed by the Small Quorum, a central committee of the diet and local committees of the landlords and government officials were to supervise the operation of the law; no peasants were to be admitted to this work. The dangerous clause in the committee's version, which authorized the parcelization of the demesnes was dropped, possibly for fear of the precedent it would create. Altogether the administrative clauses were vague enough to have permitted interpretations favourable to the landlord and unfavourable to the peasants if ever the bill had become law.[1]

The senators and deputies who had been recalled to Warsaw joined with the Small Quorum for a combined sitting of the diet on 18 April, comfortable in the knowledge that the Polish army had begun its offensive eastwards with two minor successes at Dembe Wielkie and Iganie. News had reached Warsaw that the Lithuanian *szlachta* had risen against the Russians. If the opponents of reform in the Small Quorum had had any doubts of the attitude of the majority to the plan of peasant emancipation these were soon dispelled. Barzykowski wrote that the newly arrived deputies were smarting under the threat that they would lose their seats in the diet if they refused to return and that one way of obtaining a cheap revenge upon the Small

---

[1] The text of the bill as it stood at the end of the Small Quorum's discussions may be found in Appendix B.

THE FAILURE OF AGRARIAN REFORM

Quorum was the unceremonious rejection of reform. The immediate business was to receive an account of the diet's activity in their absence. The Small Quorum was severely criticized on two grounds, first, that so important a matter as peasant emancipation could not be discussed by a mere fraction of the diet, and, second, that the Small Quorum ought to have occupied itself with more immediate matters. This argument not unnaturally aroused annoyance among those members who had stayed in Warsaw. As the deputy Ziemięcki put it: 'The honourable member, Jasieński, would not have said that on 26 February. Today when God blesses us, when the enemy has been repulsed, he considers such a matter less important!'[1] Bonawentura Niemojowski bitterly complained that 'suggestions with the object of nullifying all the work transacted in the Small Quorum remind me of the lamentable *Liberum Veto*'.[2] An indication of the irritation of deputies came from Count Jan Jezierski in a brush with Ledóchowski; he shouted at the marshal, Ostrowski, who refused him permission to speak: 'It is necessary to be a cousin of the honourable Marshal in order to get a hearing!'

The question was put whether the two chambers should meet separately or jointly. The diet decided by 88 votes to 23 that discussions should henceforth be held in the Senate and Chamber separately. On the following day the Chamber of Deputies dismissed the emancipation bill for ever. Two other matters were before the Chamber, the bill for providing relief for the peasants, and the question of parliamentary representation for Lithuania, the former being only a matter of confirming the government's action in authorizing a credit of 1,000,000 *złp* to the *województwa*, and that too late, and the latter of no immediate importance because it would be some weeks before Lithuanian deputies could arrive to take their seats, but the emancipation bill, though it touched only government estates, was removed from the agenda and never taken up again during the whole period of the insurrection. Success for the moment in the field enabled the diet to escape much public criticism, but in retrospect the narrow attitude of self-interest displayed in 1831 was to appear to Polish radicals as one of the main causes of the revolution's failure.

[1] *Ibid.*, ii, 606.   [2] *Ibid.*, ii, 612.

CHAPTER VI

The Rising in the former Eastern Provinces and the Battle of Ostrołęka

AT the beginning of April the Polish army, now reorganized after the defeat at Grochów in February, was able to achieve a minor success. Skrzynecki had kept his plans for a counter-attack a secret from all except the senior commanders and the head of the government, Prince Czartoryski. On 30 March 1831 the Polish army assembled, ostensibly for a ceremonial muster. Compared with the Russian force it was still small, 49,000 infantry, 19,000 cavalry and 144 guns; in the main army under Skrzynecki there were about 52,000 troops. Nevertheless the dispersal of the Russian army gave the Poles some advantages. The Russian forward troops, the 6th Corps, which had been detailed to watch Polish movements, were stretched out along the line of the road from the village of Wawer to Mińsk Mazowiecki. This meant that in fact only a small force was stationed opposite Warsaw, consisting of 6 battalions of infantry, 6 squadrons of cavalry and 10 guns, with a few Cossack hundreds. In the north the 1st Corps stood at Stanisławów and in the south were the Guards at Stoczek, Constantine's Guards at Zelechów, and the 3rd Reserve Corps at Garwolin. The Poles were in a position to attack the 6th Corps in the centre before the other formations could come to its assistance.

Skrzynecki took every precaution to prevent the Russians from obtaining information of his intentions. Straw was laid down on the bridge over the Vistula on the evening of 30 March to deaden the noise of the soldiers' boots as they marched across it. The Polish troops crossed in the night, on the following morning took the Russian advanced guards by surprise at Wawer and Dembe Wielkie, and on 1 April captured Mińsk Mazowiecki. Yet Skrzynecki's success was an embarrassment.

Czartoryski pressed for further advances to lend strength to his diplomacy, but it was dangerous to push the Polish advance too far. Prądzyński with 7,000 men attacked the Russians at Iganie, west of Siedlce, killing and wounding 5,000 and taking 1,500 prisoners, but this engagement did not turn in favour of the Poles. Colonel Bem,[1] the commander of the artillery ran short of ammunition, while Skrzynecki cautiously kept back his troops and did not press his advantage. On 12 April Skrzynecki stood south-west of Mińsk Mazowiecki uncertain of what step he ought to take next. For Field-Marshal Diebitsch this was the crisis of the war. The 6th Corps had been dispersed, food was short, and, although he had some 65,000 men, it was not easy to concentrate them. It is estimated that the Russians had fourteen days' reserve of food, which would have been sufficient if they had crossed the Vistula and obtained supplies from Danzig, but now they were farther than ever from the river and hardly capable of undertaking a full-scale assault.[2] It was therefore in the Russian interest to withdraw slightly and allow the Poles to take the initiative in the hope that they would make a false move. At the same time the Russian lines of communication were threatened both in Lithuania proper and in the south.

In the *gubernii* of the South, Kiev, Podolia and Volhynia, the Polish element was not strong. It is doubtful whether in any of them there were much more than 50,000 male *szlachta* capable of taking the field.[3] The success of the rising depended upon the ability of the Polish leaders to call out every available noble and enlist the support of large sections of the Ruthenian population.

[1] Józef Bem (1794–1850), who in 1826 had resigned his commission after a stormy career in the army of the Congress Kingdom, subsequently obtained the rank of brigadier-general in 1831. In emigration he was attached to the Czartoryski interest. In 1833 he was engaged in the effort to assemble a Polish legion for Dom Pedro and in 1848, after an abortive effort to persuade the Galician Poles to convert the national guard at Lvov into a regular army, took command of the Hungarian forces in the Siebenburgen. Forced to leave Hungary, he fled to Turkey where he embraced Islam and assumed the name of Murat Pasha. He died in Aleppo in 1850.

[2] The difficulty of the Russians in concentrating enough men for a direct assault prompted Nicholas I to suggest a change of tactics in his memorandum of 19 April to Diebitsch, see below, p. 210.

[3] I have discovered detailed figures only for the *gubernia* of Podolia and those not for 1831, W. Marczyński, *Statystyczne, topograficzne i historyczne opisanie gubernii podolskiey* (Vilna, 1820–3), iii: out of a total population of 1,143,269 there were 93,064 persons of *szlachta* status of whom 46,580 were males of all ages.

To raise the *szlachta* was not easy, because the majority of the nobles were extremely poor. Exemption from taxation granted to the petty *szlachta* by the Russian government discouraged them from supporting the Polish cause. The great landowners were often absentees. The core of Polish strength consisted of the well-to-do families of the medium *szlachta*. The problem also arose of their relations with the peasants. There was little evidence of Ukrainian nationalism in the southern *gubernii*; the home of that movement was Lvov in Galicia and it was still in 1830–1 confined to a few Uniate priests. In the Russian Ukraine the priests had everything to gain from the Orthodox tsar and nothing from a revived Republic. The peasants were on the whole neutral. Where one family had held estates for several centuries there were traditional feelings of loyalty, but the peasants were equally impressed by their duty to the tsar. In these circumstances the priests held the balance.[1] The Jews, though they were forbidden by the Ukaz of 1827 from taking residence in almost all the *gubernii* which had not formerly been part of the Polish Republic, looked upon the tsar as their protector. Perhaps the only factor in favour of the Poles was the survival of archaic conceptions; the Ukraine had not been invaded by Napoleon and was still shielded from modern influences. Peasants in many districts still identified themselves closely with their immediate lord and the name of a Czartoryski or a Potocki still counted for something among the simple people of the south-east.

The news of the rising in Warsaw had reached the southern group of provinces about 18 December 1830 and found the *szlachta* completely unprepared. Lubecki's journey to St. Petersburg puzzled the Polish leaders and they decided to await further information before committing themselves. Nevertheless, skeleton organizations were set up almost immediately,

[1] The Poles tried to enlist prisoners of war born in the area of the former Republic, but they disliked breaking their oath to the tsar. 700 recruits were obtained from among them at Zamość when Leon Sapieha, addressing each man, threatened to take away their boots on the grounds that they would no longer need them; rather than go barefooted they agreed to join the Polish army, cf. L. Sapieha, *Wspomnienia*, p. 140. General Umiński complained that this type of soldier compared Polish officers very unfavourably with the better trained Russians and frequently deserted, taking with him valuable information to the Russian staff, Pawłowski, *Źródła*, iii, 29. Umiński to Skrzynecki, 17 May 1831.

THE RISING IN THE EAST 197

though they were confined to individual localities and not subject to any central direction. Count Olizar, a Volhynian leader, made little progress at first and was unable to obtain the support of Eustachy Sanguszko, the greatest of the resident Volhynian magnates; Sanguszko, who had been one of the first to desert Napoleon in 1813, welcomed an insurrection, but on second thoughts tendered his apologies and refused co-operation. Olizar handed over command to his lieutenant, Prażmowski, and went north to discover what aid he could obtain in Polesie, where Stanisław Worcell, a future revolutionary leader in exile, had some influence. In Podolia there were two Polish organizations, one in Upper Podolia called the 'Junta', and the other in Lower Podolia, led by the families of the Sobańskis and the Jełowieckis. In the *gubernia* of Kiev, Wincenty Tyszkiewicz, a prominent landlord, was elected to command the local rising. Tyszkiewicz wished to co-ordinate the insurrection in Kiev and Podolia and on 22 March succeeded in getting his leadership recognized in both *gubernii*. Nevertheless, in the absence of definite news from Warsaw he was unable to decide upon an exact date for the rising. Deniszko, an emissary who had been sent to Warsaw to make contact with Chłopicki, found that the authorities in these early stages had no plans for a revolt in the east, hoping that concessions from the tsar would make open hostilities unnecessary. Deniszko arrived back in the south-east at the end of March without firm orders, but almost simultaneously Tyszkiewicz received information that Dwernicki was at Zamość with his corps and intended to march towards Volhynia. The confusion was increased by the appearance in the area at the end of February of a certain Major Chrościechowski, commissioned by Radziwiłł to make contact with the insurgent leaders.[1] Though he had no definite orders and certainly no powers, he interpreted his mission in the widest possible terms. While Dwernicki was waiting at Zamość for the roads to dry and make military movement possible Chrościechowski arrived at his headquarters and gave him an altogether too rosy impression of the state of preparedness in the east.

[1] See B. Pawłowski's article on Chrościechowski in *Polski Słownik Biograficzny*. It is characteristic of the Poles in this period that many should have blamed Chrościechowski for the entire failure in the south-east.

Under his influence Dwernicki issued a circular to the insurgents ordering them to be ready to meet him with as many supplies as possible, for his corps was desperately short of all materials. The local leaders however were not ready to receive him. Tyszkiewicz wished for more time to make his preparations and arrange for a simultaneous rising, but Dwernicki, without accurate information of the situation, began his advance to the Bug on 3 April.

The authorities in Warsaw expected much from this incursion, but it was clear from the smallness of Dwernicki's force that the success of the expedition depended upon the resources of the local *szlachta* and not upon the aid of the Polish army. A small corps under General Chrzanowski, until then chief of staff, was sent forward to Zamość to fill the vacuum left by Dwernicki's departure and, if Dwernicki succeeded in his task, to keep the way to the Ukraine open. There was a strong suspicion that Skrzynecki's main anxiety was not the conduct of operations, but the presence of radicals from the Patriotic Society in Dwernicki's force. On 15 March an adjutant of the commander-in-chief appeared in Zamość, none other than Captain Piotr Wysocki, with orders to take stock of Dwernicki's corps, but with the secret task of using his influence with the radicals to prevent the extension of revolutionary propaganda to the south-east, which it was thought might disturb the propertied classes. Skrzynecki seems to have realized that Wysocki was loyal and would restrain the more reckless spirits. In fact, he did nothing which might have detracted from the authority of Dwernicki with whom he parted on the best of terms.[1] At the same time a number of high-born officers, Leon Sapieha, Roman Sanguszko, a Rzewuski and a Małachowski, were appointed adjutants to the commander-in-chief and sent to Chrzanowski's corps with instructions to use their influence, if Dwernicki succeeded, to prevent the alienation of the substantial gentry by the radicals of his corps.[2]

On 11 April Dwernicki crossed the Bug and on the following

---

[1] J. Dwernicki, *Pamiętniki* (Lvov, 1870), pp. 60-2.
[2] All these young men belonged to families with influence in the south-east. General Prądzyński explained to them that their task was to combat radicalism, cf. L. Sapieha, *Wspomnienia*, pp. 130-1.

day issued an appeal to the *szlachta* to rise in support of the revolution.¹ But everywhere the *szlachta* were unprepared. Worcełł called a rising in the Kowel region of Polesie. A nobleman, Stecki, attacked and took the town of Włodzimierz (Vladimir). In Central Volhynia, however, Olizar's lieutenant, Prażmowski, was unable to assemble enough followers to take effective action. All this was insufficient to assist Dwernicki who was marching dangerously near the Austrian frontier and had little room to manœuvre. The Russian general, Rüdiger, followed him closely with a large force, cautiously at first because he had no information of Dwernicki's strength. On 18 April the two forces clashed at Boromel, which revealed the true strength of the Poles. Dwernicki was unable to risk another battle and Rüdiger was encouraged to press home his advantage. On 27 April Dwernicki was forced over the Galician frontier where the Austrian army disarmed the Polish troops, imprisoning Dwernicki, but allowing the officers and men to pass through Galicia to the Kingdom. Dwernicki's excursion had not only failed miserably, but had also brought about the premature collapse of the insurrection in the south-east.²

The insurgent government's agent, Chróściechowski, had returned from Dwernicki's headquarters in Northern Podolia and in his anxiety to do his best for him issued on 24 April a circular calling for an immediate rising. On the following day under pressure from the local leaders he was induced to cancel his appeal, but the damage was done.³ Some of the *szlachta* were under the impression that they were to rise at once. Others thought that they had to wait. One of the Sobańskis in Lower Podolia, who was under danger of arrest by the local Russian authorities, wished to rise within three days, but Tyszkiewicz in the *gubernia* of Kiev, to whom the Sobańskis had sworn obedience, demanded a delay of ten days. The Northern Podolians

¹ J. Dwernicki, *Pamiętniki*, pp. 83–5.
² The skirmish at Boromel has often been represented as a 'fine cavalry victory' and from the very beginning Dwernicki's officers had a very high opinion of their own achievements, cf. Sapieha, *Wspomnienia*, p. 139. Since many radicals were serving in the force it was an article of faith on the left wing to see Boromel as a victory.
³ Różycki at Zhytomir received both letters on the same day, cf. K. Różycki, *Powstanie na Wołyniu* (Bourges, 1832), p. 5. Instead of obtaining 450 men from his district he found only 130 when he called the rising.

and the Volhynians, however, were already compromised and crossed the frontier with Dwernicki in order to make their way back to the Kingdom; Różycki at Zhytomir actually succeeded in fighting his way through the Russian cordon to join the Polish forces at Zamość.

By this time the Russians had no illusions of what was afoot farther east. When Tyszkiewicz called a meeting of the *szlachta* leaders in the *gubernia* of Kiev the majority decided that the time was not ripe for rebellion. Tyszkiewicz resigned his command and issued an independent summons for a rising in support of the Southern Podolians. On 7 May the Jełowickis at Haysyn rose and were joined by the Sobańskis from Olhopol. The force they assembled was disappointing. Altogether they were able to collect only 990 cavalry and 50 infantry. The septuagenarian general, Kołyszko, was elected commander of the force and as much as 600,000 *złp* were raised to purchase supplies. The first act of the insurgents was to call upon the *szlachta* to rise on pain of forfeiting noble privileges. The peasants were offered freedom and security of tenure, though always with the proviso that such grants should be in accordance with the decisions of the diet in Warsaw. No formal document was drawn up laying down the conditions of emancipation, nor did the peasants show more than lukewarm support for the rising. Alexander Jełowicki, politically the most active of the insurgent leaders in this area, recorded that no reliance could be placed upon the peasantry, who were under the influence of the local priests.[1] The main hope of the insurgents was that they would be able to enlist mass support on estates which had traditional feelings of loyalty to the Polish lords.

[1] 'At the entrance to every village the peasants greeted us with bread and salt. The priests usually hid themselves from us, because there were few places where the lord was on good terms with the pope, for almost everywhere mutual hatred divided them completely.... So when it came to the insurrection we were deprived of every influence that the priests have with the people, who see in them their teachers and the holders of the keys to heaven... Where the priest was on good terms with the lord there he blessed the rising and where it failed the priest defended the lord against the government, sometimes even on his oath, but where the lord had ill-treated the priest he was a spy and afterwards a plain informer. This was bad. Let us improve ourselves. Let the pride of the lord cease among us. Without this the old glory of Poland will never be heard of.' A Jełowicki, *Moje Wspomnienia*, 3rd edn. (Cracow, 1891), p. 251. Cf. also F. Wrotnowski, *Powstanie na Wołyniu, Podolu i Ukrainie w r. 1831* (Paris, 1837–8), i, 191.

One of their first actions was to march to the great Czartoryski estate at Granów, where they hoped that the French administrator, de l'Arbre, would have made preparations to equip the force. Before the collapse of the Republic Granów had supplied a regiment to the Polish army. De l'Arbre however replied coldly that he had no interest in the struggle and would not support it. The insurgents wished to punish him, but feared the impression that the punishment of a popular administrator might have upon the peasants. Alexander Jełowicki therefore had recourse to a deception. In a speech to the peasants of the estate he confirmed the rumour which was circulating in the district that Adam Czartoryski was now king of Poland and declared that it was the peasants' duty to rise in support of their liege lord.[1] A similar deception was practised by Erasmus Dobrowolski, an official on the Czartoryski estate at Międzyboż.[2] These attempts to move the peasants were entirely without success.

On 13 May the Southern Podolians linked up with the insurgents from the *gubernia* of Kiev, which brought their strength to 1,500 men.[3] On 14 May the decision was taken to march to Dashov, the property of Włodzimierz Potocki, whose relations with his peasantry were excellent, and who, it was hoped, would be able to enlist mass support. Thence it was intended to march to Byelaya Tserkov to settle accounts with the Countess Branicka, the Russian widow of the Branicki who had been one of the authors of the Confederation of Targowica, and confiscate the 3,000,000 roubles which she was rumoured to have in her chests. The Russians understood the Poles well enough to know that this would be one of their first tasks. A Russian detachment attacked the Poles at Dashov on 14 May and threw them into confusion. One the following day only

[1] A. Jełowicki, *Moje Wspomnienia*, p. 253.
[2] 'I summoned ten retainers and lied to them, that the Prince was king of Poland and demanded their aid.' They agreed to join the rising but the lesser *szlachta* were by no means as eager. 'I also gave the tenant *szlachta* six roubles each, but for shame I must here record that some were so base that they took the money, but when it came to mounting on a horse there was not a sign of them.' 'Powstanie powiatu latyczowskiego na Podolu—Pamiętnik Erazma Dobrowolskiego', *Pamiętniki polskie zebrane przez K. Bronikowskiego*, 2nd edn. (Przemyśl, 1883–4), ii, 225–6.
[3] F. Wrotnowski, *Powstanie na Wołyniu, Podolu i Ukrainie*, ii, 96, estimated that in the whole area not more than 3,000 took the field.

two or three hundred men were left out of the original 1,500, though only forty men had been killed by the Russians. After this encounter there was no chance that the Polish cause in the south-east would prosper. The insurgents made their way westwards and three days after their final engagement on 23 May they crossed the Galician frontier. Thus ended the rising in the Ukraine, though the government in Warsaw continued to hope for miracles.[1]

The rising in Lithuania revealed features similar to those of the insurrection in the Ukraine, but it was far more important in the struggle of 1831. Lithuania lay across the Russian lines of communication with St. Petersburg and Moscow. At the same time the Poles had a rather more solid basis of support among the people. Numerically, the *szlachta* were weak,[2] but there was a strong Roman Catholic element, especially in the former Duchy of Samogitia, which on the whole favoured the Poles. Samogitia, in 1831 administered within the *gubernia* of Vilna, was more prosperous than the rest of Lithuania. Its three districts, Telsze, Szawle and Rosienie, had access to the sea at Polanga, and the peasants, native Lithuanians by speech and Roman Catholic by religion, had been among the most prosperous in the former Republic. They had then held their land on three-year contracts on private estates and had complete possession of all their movable property and chattels, while on the *starostwa*, or government lands, and ecclesiastical properties had owned their buildings and paid rents, which were uniformly low, under hereditary contracts. The Russian system of taxation by 'souls' had not been conducive to the retention of large numbers of peasants on estates, while the 1812 campaign had seriously impoverished the countryside. The Russian landowners set the Poles an example in the eviction of peasants, so that there seemed to be an unfavourable

---

[1] It is remarkable that Chróściechowski received instructions for a second mission to the Ukraine, when he returned to Warsaw to render an account of his activities, cf. F. Wrotnowski, *ibid.*, i, 313, where a letter of General Prądzyński, dated 13 May 1831, authorizing him to foment another rebellion, is printed.

[2] Detailed figures are lacking, but statistics for the *gubernia* of Grodno are given in J. E. Lachnicki, *Statystyka gubernii litewsko-grodzieńskiey* (Vilna, 1817): out of a total population of 536,163, the *szlachta* numbered 22,576 and the Christian bourgeoisie 9,045.

THE RISING IN THE EAST 203

contrast between the conditions prevailing under the Republic and those under Russian occupation. Freedom in 1831 was identified with the abolition of labour services, which the peasants had indeed refused to pay during the crisis of 1812.[1] By contrast with Samogitia the rest of Lithuania was by no means as prosperous under the Republic and there were fewer nostalgic yearnings for the past; moreover, in the eastern districts of the former Grand Duchy the hold of the Roman Catholic Church was weaker, which meant an absence of the religious bond which gave Samogitia its community of spirit. It was in the west that the main strength of the Polish nobility lay. One cause of Polish weakness was the uncertain attitude of the *szlachta* themselves to the cause of national independence. The *szlachta* in Lithuania may be divided into three groups as elsewhere. The aristocrats generally preferred not to become involved in the rising; in the crisis of 1812 many of them had favoured the Russian connection. The petty gentry did not wish to lose their tax exemptions. Once again it was the medium landowners who were the most ardent supporters of union with the Kingdom of Poland.[2]

The Russian authorities were fully aware of the dangers in Lithuania. The garrison of Vilna was strengthened almost as soon as the rising broke out in Warsaw and a number of prominent Poles was taken into protective custody. The civil governor of Mińsk for example, Wincenty Giecewicz, a Pole, was replaced by a Russian and the *gubernia* placed under military control. Unfortunately for the Russians the reserve army, which was being mobilized under the command of Prince Piotr Tolstoy, was not yet ready to move forward and occupy Lithuania to secure the rear of the field army which was to operate in Poland proper. In consequence the local security forces were responsible for holding the area in the early stages

---

[1] At the time of the Confederation of Bar, Prince Alexander Sapieha, the lord of Skudy, had ordered that rents on his estates were not to be increased, but his son, Franciszek, cancelled this order. The original instruction of Prince Alexander was said to have been in the possession of the peasants still in 1831. For details of Samogitia see 'O stanie włościan w powiecie telszewskim na Żmudzi przed rokiem 1794', *Zbiór pamiętników o powstaniu Litwy*, pp. 130–42.

[2] Cf. 'Pamiętnik Onufrego Jacewicza', *Zbiór pamiętników o powstaniu Litwy*, pp. 87–8.

of the rising. It was probably hoped that the presence of a large Russian army in the Kingdom would act as a deterrent in Lithuania. Nevertheless, the *szlachta* rose in revolt at the end of March 1831 and the beginning of April.

The news of the insurrection in Warsaw reached Lithuania through East Prussia. The peasants were alarmed by the intention of the Russians to carry out a levy of recruits and there was a premature outbreak of disturbance in the district of Telsze. A local nobleman and a peasant leader, Giedrym, organized a riot, but the Russian police easily restored order. The *szlachta* however knew that the Russian commission of inquiry into this affair would discover a network of intrigue in the district and that this would lead to military occupation. Moreover, the peasants were prepared to rise independently of the *szlachta* and might, if the situation got out of hand, turn against the local Polish proprietors as well as the Russians. The leaders of the districts of Samogitia consequently sent a request to the central committee, which had been set up in Vilna, for permission to revolt. Ezechiel Staniewicz, the marshal of the nobility in the district of Rosienie, on the pretext of selling grain, journeyed to Libau to buy powder and arms, intending to declare a revolt on his return, but was delayed by sickness. Rumours were current that he had been arrested. On 17 March 1831 a meeting of Polish leaders took place at Cytowiany, north of Rosienie on the road to Szawle, to consider an insurrection. Only a dozen persons were present at this meeting, but these were enough to plunge Lithuania into revolt. It was decided to name 26 March for the rising, the day before the Russians were to carry out the levy of recruits when discontent would be at its height. A small force of *szlachta*, manor servants and peasants armed with scythes was assembled. An attack was made on the town of Rosienie and the garrison of sixty old soldiers easily overpowered. There followed quickly outbreaks in the other districts of Samogitia. At Telsze a *coup* was carried out on 28 March and the Act of Confederation signed on the next day. Staniewicz, returning to Rosienie, organized an insurrection at Szawle. Outside Samogitia the district of Wiłkomierz joined the insurrection almost at once. The Russian colonel, Bartholomej, recaptured Rosienie by bringing up 1,000 men and four guns from Kaunas, but though the insurgents were forced to evacuate the town they soon recaptured it on 10 April when Bartholomej, short of ammunition, was forced to cross the Prussian frontier. This success was won by the union of the forces of the district of Rosienie with those of Szawle, but once it had been achieved the Szawle group went home. In the meantime the forces at Telsze had not been inactive. On the night of 30/31 March the administrator of Dorbiany, with a force of a few hundred peasants liberally plied with drink, made an attack on the port of Polanga, through which it was hoped supplies would come from abroad, but was repulsed by 200 hussars of the frontier guard. This private effort was followed by an attempt by the forces from Telsze on 2 April which likewise failed, but on 5 April the town fell to a third attempt. The Russians however soon recaptured the port on 8 April. If the insurgents of Samogitia were left for the moment in possession of their districts, this was almost entirely due to the absence of Russian soldiers to impede them.

Outside Samogitia in the district of Oszmiana, south-east of Vilna, there was a different story to tell. Here the rising was delayed because of the doubts of the marshal of the nobility, Józef Tyszkiewicz, who saw no hope in the project, but delegates from Vilna, after threatening to hang him, decided that they themselves would declare the rising. On the morning of 6 April a score of conspirators called upon the people of Oszmiana to revolt. The garrison was easily overpowered, but Khrapovitsky, the military governor of Vilna, reacted quickly and sent a battalion of infantry with a regiment of cossacks to clear the town. The insurgents decided to evacuate it, but the commander of their rearguard against orders chose to offer resistance. The Russian detachment commander deployed his guns and launched an assault. About 350 Poles were killed in the fight and churches and religious institutions looted. The 'Massacre of Oszmiana' made a deep impression on the Poles and a feeling of extreme bitterness was infused into the struggle.

Other Lithuanian districts, at the news of the rebellion in Samogitia, automatically rose in revolt, though with varying degrees of success. In the district of Upita, which lay on the borders of the ancient Duchy of Samogitia, the marshal of the *szlachta*, Count Karol Załuski, was convinced like Tyszkiewicz at Oszmiana, that the rising was without hope, but for honour's sake assumed the leadership of the insurgents. At Vilna a rising could not take place owing to the presence of the Russian garrison. Similarly in the district of Brasław there was no chance of success owing to its proximity to the Russian stronghold at Dünaborg. The Brasław conspirators therefore crossed into the *gubernia* of Minsk to join forces with the insurgents of the district of Dzisno. Another district of the *gubernia* of Minsk, Wilejka, rose with the assistance of a party from Oszmiana. Everywhere the insurrections were local in their vision as well as in their operation. Nevertheless the Lithuanian insurgents seriously embarrassed the Russians. The highway from Dünaborg to Kaunas was cut and only the road through Minsk, Orsha and Smolensk to Moscow was relatively safe. However, so long as the Russians held Vilna they could build up their forces and make their preparations for clearing the area.

From the Polish point of view it seemed necessary to launch an attack on Vilna at the earliest moment, but the *szlachta* and their peasant levies disliked serving outside their own districts. When at length it was decided that the marshal of Upita, Count Załuski, should be appointed commander-in-chief and attack Vilna, an approach was made to the district of Telsze to obtain reinforcements. Jacewicz, the local commander at Telsze, declared that he was convinced that a unified command was necessary, but he did not believe that Załuski was the man for the task and accordingly refused all aid. Załuski therefore was forced to reiy upon the non-Samogitian districts for his attack. His plan was simple enough. The insurgents at Kaunas were to provide a screen against attack from the south, while the remaining districts were to concentrate their forces at Vilna for an assault. Załuski hoped to muster 10,000 to 20,000 men for the task, but when he moved on Vilna on 17 April he found that he had at his command only 3,500 of whom 2,000 were armed with scythes and obsolete weapons. After reconnoitring the positions Załuski was compelled to call off his attack, which was indeed as well, for Vilna taken would have had to have been defended. This the Poles could not have done, especially when they lacked artillery.

THE RISING IN THE EAST

When the insurrection broke out in the individual districts the insurgents all set up local governments for the civil administration of the area. In Telsze there was a government consisting of no less than ten departments. The first act of the governments was to declare that the purpose of the insurrection was to give complete freedom to all classes of the community. The peasants were to enjoy, like the peasants of the Kingdom, equality before the law and eventually to be emancipated from economic bondage. Nevertheless, to avoid disruption of the economy labour services were to be retained.[1] For the *szlachta* a *juristitium* was declared. Conscription both of the *szlachta* and the peasants was the general rule. The Jews were required to pay a heavy tax for exemption. In fact, the Jews refused to co-operate because their leaders in Vilna had issued instructions that they should assist the Russians. When the peasants found there was to be no change in the social order they began to lose faith in the *szlachta*. The local levies were never as numerous as the insurgents hoped and the peasants melted away when ordered to serve outside the locality, leaving only the *szlachta* to carry on the struggle. In the district of Telsze may be detected signs of a native Lithuanian *jacquerie*. On the large estates or *hrabstwa* between Telsze and the port of Polanga the peasants had been severely oppressed by the administrators of the absentee landlords whose lands covered about eight-tenths of the area. In

---

[1] 'La froide raison fit taire pour le moment le cri de l'humanité; on se contenta de faire une promesse d'affranchisement dans des termes assez vagues pour pouvoir électriser le peuple, assez clairs pour donner ombrage aux propriétaires qui tenaient fort à leurs privilèges d'absolutisme.' M. Pietkiewicz, *La Lithuanie et sa dernière insurrection* (Brussels, 1832), pp. 205–6. 'Indeed there was no true son of the fatherland among us who would have thought that after the liberation of the country the peasant would still remain a serf. But to grant to the people freedom and the property rights due to them immediately, to put this into practice at once, this did not enter the minds of the *szlachta*. It was not easy to carry out. We armed against an enemy, who was present among us, and saw that the people were willing for the struggle. Reliance was placed on the purity of our intentions. We avoided not the principle, but the countless difficult questions which must straight away have been brought up by it.' 'Pamiętnik Onufrego Jacewicza', *Zbiór pamiętników o powstaniu Litwy w r. 1831*, p. 97. Giecewicz, the leader of the rising in the district of Wilejka, gave his instructions 'to watch carefully that the peasants are not insubordinate and perform their work in accordance with the old duties.' Cf. para. 3 of his order of 6/18 April 1831, reprinted in S. Dangel, *Rok 1831 w Mińszczyźnie* (Warsaw, 1925), p. 27.

April disorders broke out.¹ The peasants shot some of the *szlachta* and the leading farmers in the villages and put others in chains. They elected their own officers to command the local levies and uttered threats to march on Telsze to execute members of the insurgent government. The date of this outbreak is not known, but it is possible that it was the cause of Jacewicz's refusal to join Załuski for the attack on Vilna. Though Jacewicz was slow to give aid to Załuski he dealt with the peasants quickly enough. The *szlachta* levies broke up the revolt and once more threw a cordon round Polanga, but never again did Jacewicz obtain large-scale support from the peasants and some of his units fell from 800 to 200 men or less.²

At the end of April Russian forces began to march into Samogitia from Dünaborg, Vilna and Kaunas. Załuski was unable to halt the advance in the north and was forced to evacuate Poniewież. In the middle of this crisis two emissaries arrived back from Warsaw to report that arms and ammunition would be brought to Polanga on English ships. They urged him to make an immediate expedition to capture the port, but Załuski, perhaps because he had not received aid from Jacewicz for the attack on Vilna, declared that this was the responsibility of the Samogitian districts. Załuski had his eyes on Poniewież in his own district of Upita, which the Russians captured but did not garrison. On 30 April he took the opportunity to slip back into the town where he found a sorry state of affairs. The leading families had left. The Russian troops had brought cholera with them. There was an outbreak of revolutionary violence when the younger members of the *szlachta* tried to carry out a pogrom of the Jews. 'The youth, its pride wounded, and the unruly mob were not however restored to order before evening. In the streets there was open talk of forming patriotic clubs, setting up a national tribunal and taking similar steps to deal with treachery. It was agreed that there was a need for terrorism against those who were lukewarm towards the rising and against the aristocrats.'³ Violence of this kind was a feature

[1] The places affected were Kule, Plungiany and Salanty. Jacewicz blamed the outbreak on 'evil persons, themselves *szlachta*, with no standards of conduct, no property and no character, taking the side of the people....' 'Pamiętnik', *Zbiór Pamiętników*, p. 98. [2] *Ibid.*, pp. 24–8.
[3] 'Pamiętnik obywatela powiatu upitskiego', *ibid.*, pp. 192–3.

of the Lithuanian rising. In moments of excitement the Poles committed excesses against the communities of Old Believers settled in Lithuania, who retaliated by attacking and burning the manors of the *szlachta*.[1]

Załuski could not stay long in Poniewież because more Russian troops were approaching. Accordingly, he withdrew to the district of Rosienie, but the marshal, Staniewicz, was in no mood to receive him, for the two emissaries from Warsaw had pleaded their cause to him for an attack on Polanga and though he had declared that it was the duty of Telsze to carry out this task had lent some 350 of his own men. Załuski was by no means a welcome visitor. As Staniewicz said, by withdrawing into the district of Rosienie Załuski was attracting the attention of the Russian forces and that at a moment when some of Rosienie's best men were absent. He bluntly told Załuski to break up his force into small groups and carry on guerrilla warfare, which Załuski did. In the meantime the Polish forces at Telsze were engaged in attacking Polanga. Jacewicz had not wished to make the attempt, but was compelled by the local *szlachta*. He made two assaults, one on 9 and the other on 13 May. In the end he had to withdraw because Count Pahlen, the Russian military governor of the Baltic provinces, was advancing to clear the Lithuanian coast. Jacewicz fled to Rosienie where he and Staniewicz were obliged to break up their forces into small groups to carry on guerrilla warfare. By the middle of May the Russians had broken the rising everywhere in Lithuania. Nowhere could the insurgents stand against the cannon which were deployed against them. This rather than the dubious collection of gendarmes and customs officials stiffened by some cossacks and a few regular infantry, which composed the forces at the Russian officers' disposal, was responsible for the Polish defeat. In the first days of June as the rising was petering out the Russian reserve army, which had been mobilized to meet the emergency of the Polish revolution, was beginning to move forward into Lithuania. The Russians were well equipped to meet the next threat, the invasion of Lithuania by regular Polish troops from the Kingdom.

On 13 May Skrzynecki at last decided to take active measures

[1] M. Pietkiewicz, *La Lithuanie et sa dernière insurrection*, p. 135.

P

against the Russian army in the Kingdom. It was obvious that he could not launch a direct assault against Diebitsch, but the Russian corps of guards lay in a semi-isolated position north of the Bug under the command of the Grand Duke Michael. If the Poles could annihilate this group they would make a great contribution towards keeping the Russian army immobile. At least, this was the argument which the quartermaster-general Prądzyński put forward, but the plan when it was put into operation had the effect only of resolving Russian hesitation. After the Polish breakout from Warsaw and the withdrawal of the Russians, Nicholas I had written to Diebitsch on 19 April arguing that a direct assault on the Vistula was impracticable owing to the difficulty of gathering supplies to sustain it, especially in view of the outbreak of revolt in Lithuania. For this reason the army ought to move from its central position northwards to the *województwo* of Płock where it might draw upon food and supplies gathered in West and East Prussia. When supplies had been gathered the army could cross the Vistula at Płock and fight a decisive battle west of Warsaw, probably at Sochaczew.[1] Diebitsch hesitated to put this plan into operation, but was forced to comply when the main Polish army began to move across the projected Russian line of march.

Leaving a small corps under General Umiński to protect the Polish army's movement against a sudden incursion from the east of Warsaw, Skrzynecki on 12/13 May had set out with the bulk of his forces northwards, crossing the Bug above Modlin at Sierock and thence marching north-east in the direction of the Russian guards. They withdrew before the Polish advance and the units holding the Narew valley retreated in the direction of Augustów. On the left flank General Giełgud's infantry division was able to advance up the right bank of the Narew to take Łomża. On the right flank General Tomasz Łubieński's corps pushed along the north bank of the Bug as far as its junction with the Nurzec at Nur, while Skrzynecki in the centre pursued the guards as far as the frontier at Tykocin, a small town east of Białystok. It was at this point that Skrzynecki,

[1] For the text of Nicholas I's letter see Shcherbatov, *General-Feldmarshal Knyaz Paskevich*, iv (Appendices), 12–15.

THE RISING IN THE EAST

The Battle of Ostrołęka: May, 1831

yielding to pressure of public opinion, sent forward on 18 May a cadre of instructors, some 700 strong, under General Chłapowski, to reinforce the insurgents in Lithuania, far too small a force to influence the success of the rising.[1] When the Russian guards did not oblige Skrzynecki by offering battle his position between the Bug and the Narew became extremely dangerous. Once more he was faced with the problem which had perplexed him before Siedlce in April. With inferior forces he could not push too far ahead without leaving his rear open to attack. Diebitsch for his part, standing at Siedlce with the Russian main army, was not left in doubt for long of the Polish plan. When Skrzynecki took Tykocin on 21 May he ordered Łubieński to move forward and destroy the bridge over the Bug at Drohiczyn, north-east of Siedlce, but Diebitsch had forestalled this move. The advance-guard of the Russian army had already crossed the Bug north of Drohiczyn at Granne, while a small demonstration was being made against Umiński's corps covering Warsaw. Łubieński's corps was withdrawn in the face of Diebitsch's thrust and the main army fell back on the town of Ostrołęka in order to pass to the left bank of the Narew, a repetition of Chłopicki's tactics in February before Warsaw but the Russians were not to be foiled again. On 26 May, using their artillery to great advantage, they threw the Poles out of Ostrołęka and captured the bridge over the river intact. In the late afternoon they began to attack the Poles on the left bank and a complete disaster for the Polish army was averted only by resolute counter-attacks led in true Polish style by General Skrzynecki in person. This was enough to halt the Russians and force them to withdraw, leaving only a few battalions to hold the bridgehead. The Russians are said to have suffered the loss of 5,868 against the Polish 6,418, but the Russian advantage was obvious because Diebitsch's army was intact while the Poles were streaming back towards Warsaw in disorder. Though

[1] This was one of the few occasions when Lelewel influenced the course of the rising. On 9 May he took the Lithuanian emissary and his former pupil at Vilna, Feliks Wrotnowski, to the general headquarters at Jędrzejów, where Skrzynecki put him off with a few pious expressions of concern, but Prądzyński advised him to enlist the support of Czartoryski for aid to the Lithuanians, cf. Lelewel, *Pamiętnik*, pp. 102–3. Czartoryski was already pressing for action in Lithuania and Lelewel's intervention may have served to decide the issue.

THE RISING IN THE ESST 213

Nicholas I had recalled Field-Marshal Paskevich from Georgia, possibly with the intention of giving him command of the field army in Poland, Diebitsch had made amends for his lack of vigour by winning a resounding victory. Nicholas soon returned to his complaints when the success at Ostrołęka was not exploited,[1] but the question whether Diebitsch ought to be replaced, if it had been raised at all, was resolved when Diebitsch fell a victim to the cholera epidemic on 10 June and died within a few hours.[2]

General Skrzynecki thought that Diebitsch would press home his attacks and was at first in despair, writing to Czartoryski that the war had been lost; 'Nous avons livré la plus honteuse bataille. Finis Poloniae! Nothing remains but to get an agreement with the enemy and the Government must open negotiations at once.'[3] On the following day however he recovered his spirits and announced his intention of carrying on the war, for the army might yet be reorganized. One difficult decision had already been forced upon the Polish command because General Giełgud's infantry division had been cut off at Łomża and could not be expected to break through the entire Russian army to rejoin the main body of the Polish forces. There was one alternative which seemed to make the best of a bad situation and that was to send Giełgud forward to Lithuania to sustain the revolt there. Pressed by his friend, the cavalry general, Henryk Dembiński,[4] he issued orders to Giełgud to

[1] Cf. his letter to Diebitsch, Shcherbatov, *Knyaz Paskevich*, iv (Appendices), p. 20.

[2] Rumour had it that Diebitsch died of poison administered by the tsar's adjutant, Orlov, or was at least told by him that he would be relieved of his command, but of this there is no proof. On 7 June Nicholas wrote to Diebitsch: 'Activité, prudence et vigueur et que le Ciel vous soit en aide, un grand pas est fait, sachez en profiter et prouvez vous êtes encore le *starii Zabalkansky*.' Shilder, *Imperator Nikolai Pervii*, ii, 483 n. (The appeal to the 'Old Zabalkansky' was a reference to the energy which Diebitsch had shown in the Balkan campaign which had earned him the title of *Zabalkansky*.) There is no good reason to suppose that Diebitsch did not die of the cholera, which was extremely rapid in its effect; Constantine died in a few hours on 27 June, cf. his wife's pathetic letter to Nicholas, *Correspondance*, ii, 243.

[3] L. Gadon, *Książę Adam Czartoryski podczas powstania listopadowego*, edn. of 1900 (Cracow), p. 85.

[4] Dembiński's rapid promotion from captain to general had given some cause for jealousy. Henry Dembiński (1791–1864) was a landlord with property in the *województwo* of Cracow and in the Free City itself. His sister was the mother of the Marquis Alexander Wielopolski. In 1832, after his expulsion from the Free City at

march northwards to assist the Lithuanian insurgents. When these orders arrived through Dembiński's adjutant Giełgud was astonished. He is reported to have said: 'I would have preferred to break through the whole army of Diebitsch to Warsaw at the point of the bayonet.' This he threatened to do unless Dembiński who had volunteered to join him arrived with his cavalry unit within a quarter of an hour.[1] Dembiński however arrived with his cavalry bringing the instructions that Skrzynecki had given him full authority to act as he saw fit in Lithuania. Against his will and against his better judgment Giełgud marched northwards with $14\frac{1}{2}$ battalions of infantry, seven squadrons of cavalry and 26 guns. Together with the partisan detachment of Zaliwski which it picked up in the *województwo* of Augustów, Giełgud's force numbered 12,000 men. This number was far too few to revive the insurrection in the north or offer a challenge to the Russian Reserve Army which was moving south. This Skrzynecki knew well and warned Chłapowski on 1 July, but this very letter revealed how little he knew of the situation in Lithuania: 'You are to make haste to take Vilna. It is necessary to extend the rising and organize an army. You ought to take Polanga and Libau as well as try to capture Dünaborg and Bobruisk.'[2] The instructions of the government of the same date were no less wide. Chłapowski was to induce the landowners to win over the peasants with a policy of concessions, win over the Jews, respect all religions, ensure that the rights of property were respected, raise taxes and above all secure an outlet to the sea.[3] All this Chłapowski was expected to do with 700 men and his Lithuanian levies, supported by Giełgud who was marching to meet him.

Giełgud had no difficulty in entering Lithuania in spite of the slowness of his march which was hampered by a baggage

the demand of the powers, he allied himself with Czartoryski and in 1833 went to Egypt to negotiate with Mehemet Ali for the formation of a Polish legion. In 1835–7 he was active in promoting the formation of a legion in Spain. His chance came in 1848 when he became commander in Northern Hungary on behalf of the Hungarian revolution.

[1] Pawłowski, *Źródła*, iii, 177–8 n., the account of Captain Kowalski, an eyewitness of the episode.
[2] Pawłowski, *ibid.*, iii, 285. [3] Pawłowski, *ibid.*, iii, 286–8.

train crammed with loot from Łomża which Dembiński unsuccessfully tried to get abandoned.[1] Equally troublesome was the preoccupation of his officers with factious discussion and intrigue. An added difficulty was the presence of Dembiński, who had arrived with verbal instructions from Skrzynecki and assumed the attitude of one whose duty it was to supervise Giełgud's conduct of operations, a situation which was not made any the easier when Chłapowski, who had been unable to do more than collect scattered bands of insurgents, joined the expeditionary force at Kejdany; Chłapowski was recognized by Skrzynecki and the government as the commander in Lithuania, which complicated relations with Giełgud, because the Lithuanians soon discovered a dislike of him and pressed Chłapowski to adopt an attitude of independence.[2] Chłapowski, influenced by the Lithuanians, wanted Giełgud to march on Vilna, while Dembiński, more concerned by the shortage of ammunition, advised the capture of the port, Polanga, but neither course had much to recommend it and Giełgud hesitated between the two. While he was making up his mind he set up a temporary government of Lithuania on 12 June which further increased his unpopularity. His uncle, Józef Tyszkiewicz, was appointed president, Gabriel Ogiński vice-president and Jan Giełgud, the general's brother, minister of internal affairs. Count Załuski was passed over. This was too much for the Lithuanian insurgents who had been accustomed to administer their own affairs and conduct their own operations. For them Giełgud was as bad as the Russians and intrigues against him gathered strength.[3]

[1] H. Dembiński, *Mémoires sur la campagne de Lithuanie* (Strasbourg, 1832), p. 44.

[2] 'Pamiętniki Michała Jackowskiego', *Pamiętniki polskie zebrane przez K. Bronikowskiego*, i, 359–60.

[3] 'The clauses of this act, voted arbitrarily without the knowledge of the Lithuanians, without any acquaintance with local needs and above all against the principles which up to that time had been observed in order to appeal to all inhabitants, could not have obtained general approval. Giełgud ruled more absolutely than the Muscovites had done. Reckoning the whole of the insurgent body to be recruits he embodied them into the army. To this or that citizen he gave badges of rank according to his caprice, as if he were rewarding them for their devotion. He changed the district governments and their members as he pleased. He treated the patriots coming to him in a high-handed manner. The hopes of personal freedom, the one inducement which had any effect upon the peasants he weakened. The last means of preserving our national rights in those circumstances,

When on 15 June Giełgud gave in to Chłapowski and marched on Vilna the Russians were well prepared to receive him. Vilna had been reinforced and now had a garrison of 24,000 men with 40 guns. The Poles lost 2,000 men and the artillery expended its ammunition in a preliminary encounter on 19 June. The Polish cause in Lithuania was lost. Giełgud might have divided his forces and carried on partisan warfare, but that was not easy when the majority of his soldiers were peasants from the Kingdom. Instead he chose now to march to the port of Polanga to obtain arms and ammunition. The Russians were not quick to follow him. They waited until they had amassed 49,000 men and 180 guns before they set out in pursuit on 26 June. As Giełgud marched westwards the discipline of his force began to break down. Russian forces barred his way to Polanga and to Kaunas. He could not risk a battle and on 9 July decided to split his force into three groups in order to deceive the Russians of the exact direction of his line of march, but there was no way out. At a council of war Giełgud put the question to his officers whether they would submit to the Russians or withdraw over the Prussian frontier. The officers chose to be interned in Prussia as a gesture of defiance against Russian domination and Giełgud drew up a proclamation to this effect.[1] For Dembiński's cavalry the situation was not so difficult. They had advanced to Poniewież and still had room to manœuvre. Dembiński took a chance and made a dash for Warsaw, in which he succeeded with great honour to himself; he had begun the war as a captain and had become a candidate for the post of commander-in-chief. For Giełgud the future was not so bright. On 13–15 July his troops crossed over into the strip of Prussian territory north of the Niemen. As the troops withdrew into Prussia discipline finally broke. On 13 July one of Giełgud's officers drew his pistol and

the general trust in persons called to office, he destroyed. In a word, he behaved not like one sent to help, but rather like a conquering invader of Lithuania.' 'Pamiętnik obywatela upitskiego', *Zbiór pamiętników*, p. 203. Cf. also M. Pietkiewicz, *La Lithuanie et sa dernière insurrection*, pp. 176–81. Chłapowski recorded that the Lithuanian *szlachta* scrambled over one another in their desire for nomination as officers. 'Tous étaient pressés comme si avant la mort ils avaient voulu régler leur comptes.' *Lettre . . . sur les événements militaires en Pologne et en Lithuanie*, p. 41. There were apparently more officers than men in the insurgent units, cf. *ibid.*, p. 44.

[1] For the text see M. Pietkiewicz, *ibid.*, p. 312.

shot Gielgud dead. There were cries for Chłapowski to lead the army back against the Russians, but Chłapowski was nowhere to be found.¹ In this sordid confusion the rising in Lithuania came to an end.

The revolt in the former eastern provinces was not merely a failure in itself, but it also created complications for the Poles in the Kingdom. The attitude of Nicholas I was that the insurgents in Western Russia were guilty of high treason. Under the Ukaz of 22 March–3 April 1831 Russian local commanders were instructed to put down the revolt with the utmost severity.² All members of the *szlachta* who had taken an active part in the rebellion were to be tried by field general court-martial and the sentences on them to be carried out on the spot, while their property was to be confiscated and the income from it to be devoted to the veterans' funds; their male children were to make a formal declaration of their loyalty, but children of persons who claimed noble status, though without any formal evidence to prove their claims, were to be taken as recruits for the military cantons. Persons of non-noble status who were captured in arms were to be enlisted and sent to the Siberian line battalions and their children likewise to be handed over to the military cantons. Some indulgence however was given to persons of the lower classes who had been forced to join the rebellion by the landed proprietors under pressure of threats; in this case complete forgiveness was granted. When the news of this order arrived in Warsaw the Poles without exception were horrified by its severity. On 26 April the government, in response to the general outcry, submitted to the diet a motion to extend the protection of the Polish state to the former eastern provinces, which was passed with modifications by the combined chambers on 5 May 1831. Article I of this law laid down that 'every part of the former Kingdom of Poland, duchies and lands once joined with it and annexed to Russia, which revolts and joins the rising

---

¹ It was then remembered that Chłapowski was actually the brother-in-law of the Grand Duke Constantine and the suspicion of treachery was attached to him also, cf. 'Pamiętniki Michała Jackowskiego', *Pamiętniki polskie*, i, 379. Chłapowski, as a Prussian subject, was held in prison by the authorities, and after his release turned his face against all thoughts of an armed uprising.

² The Polish text reprinted from *Gazeta Warszawska*, no. 110, 24 April 1831, is in *Dyaryusz sejmu*, iii, 117–19 n.

of the Kingdom, joins it under exactly the same conditions as it enjoyed before the partitions and is restored to its rights . . .' The eastern provinces were likewise assured part in the representative institutions of the Kingdom and a voice in the making of treaties. Article II threatened to judge all persons who hindered the insurrection in the east with trial by court martial.[1] The logical consequence of this law was the extension of the representative system of the Kingdom to include the eastern provinces on 19 May.[2] Little was in fact achieved by these gestures, except to show that the Polish insurrection in fact did not take its stand upon the Vienna treaties. They brought not one tittle of aid to the eastern insurrection, but rather complicated the politics of the Kingdom itself; the deputies who were elected to the diet from the former eastern provinces had lost their all in the rising and clamoured in Warsaw for resistance to the very end, demanding of the deputies the same unstinting self-sacrifice which they themselves had shown. During the actual debates on 2 May there was a clear difference of opinion within the government when Bonawentura Niemojowski, the minister of internal affairs, opposed the amalgamation of the former eastern provinces on the basis of the relationship to Poland which existed before the partitions as preserving the old distinction between the *Korona* and the Grand Duchy of Lithuania. The ministry of foreign affairs, through the councillor of state, Wielopolski, pleaded that this was the only possible basis of reunion and moreover showed that the Poles of the Congress Kingdom would respect local rights. The curious result of all this was that, though the government's version was accepted, the minister of foreign affairs, Gustaw Małachowski, resigned and was replaced by a follower of Skrzynecki, Andrzej Horodyski, which gave the general staff some pretensions to a voice in Polish diplomacy. Equality of sacrifice demanded that Bonawentura Niemojowski should resign as well, to be replaced by Gliszczyński, a member of the Kalisz clique; freed from the cares of departmental duties Bonawentura found ample scope for his talents in the diet, where allied with the eastern deputies he became the leader of the party of no-surrender.

Undoubtedly the insurrection in Western Russia made a

[1] *Dyaryusz sejmu*, iii, 317. [2] *Ibid.*, iii, 567–9.

valuable contribution to the relative success of the Polish army from the breakout from Warsaw at the beginning of April up to the battle of Ostrołęka, tying down Russian troops and hindering the smooth passage of supplies, but it was unorganized from the beginning and too weak to survive against a systematic pacification., The response of the mass of the people was unenthusiastic and held out no hopes that Poland could ever again be extended to the eastern frontiers of 1772 unless the effort were backed with overwhelming military force; but the upper classes of these regions were to remain Polish in outlook and their aspirations were to find their place in every Polish political programme, complicating relations with Russia and perpetuating the antagonisms of the two nations.

CHAPTER VII

The Last Phase of the Insurrection

THE tactical successes of Dembe Wielkie and Iganie in the first half of April which drove the Russians back from Praga to Siedlce brought stability to the National Government and the urgency of reform which seemed self-evident after Grochów in February was forgotten. When the Polish army was again defeated at Ostrołęka in May the situation was too desperate to resurrect projects of reform. The question which confronted the government was one of survival until the severity of the winter brought military operations to a standstill. What marked the last phase of the insurrection was the complete breakdown of discipline within the *szlachta* caste. In retrospect a bold recognition of failure and an approach to Nicholas was the policy which the National Government ought to have followed, but that was a course which no Polish leader remembering the dishonour of Targowica could take. Likewise, though direct negotiation might have saved Congress Poland, for emotional reasons the insurgents of the former eastern provinces could not be deserted and left to the mercy of the Russian government. In these circumstances it is hardly surprising, the Polish *szlachta* being what they were, that the insurrection dissolved into a series of petty squabbles. The Russians could hardly have failed to win the war, but their task was made easier by the Poles themselves. Hostilities were brought to a close in October 1831 without another battle of the magnitude of Ostrołęka being fought. The story of the rising's collapse is instructive only of the self-deception and weakness of which the *szlachta* were capable.

As far as Czartoryski was concerned the chief source of self-deception was the belief that Congress Poland could achieve the status of an independent state and assume normal diplomatic relations with the powers which had been party to the Vienna treaties. It is however difficult to speak of a Polish foreign policy during the revolution of 1830–1, though this is not to say that there was not much Polish diplomatic activity or that the Polish question did not interest foreign ministers, because it was a complication to the involved negotiations over the Belgian question and prevented Russia from speaking with full authority. The Polish government could only plead for assistance. It could not speak from strength or even base its arguments upon its rights under international law. By the deposition of Nicholas I and the incorporation of the eastern provinces into the Kingdom of Poland it had violated the fundamental principles of the Vienna treaties. The sole aid which sympathetic powers might have given was to insist upon the preservation of national institutions in Poland, whatever the nature of the struggle or its outcome, and upon the observance of the legal and political distinction between the Congress Kingdom and the Russian Empire, but the precise form of independence was the concern of the tsar alone. Polish diplomats in their hearts knew all this and were in fact more concerned to play upon the self-interest of the powers, or, where the chance arose, on their difficulties. In France the government of Louis Philippe had its hands full in the Netherlands and in Italy, and was as anxious as the Polish to prove its respectability, even though it had counter-armed against Russia in the late autumn of 1830. The French foreign minister, Sebastiani, however, was aware of the sentimental support for Poland in France and to silence the opposition consented to discuss the Polish question with the insurgent government's representatives, whether Konstanty Wołowski, Leon Sapieha or Teodor Morawski, who were present in Paris during the early stages of the rising, or the semi-official mission of General Kniaziewicz and Ludwik Plater, which arrived at the beginning of March 1831. Sebastiani held out vague promises that something would be done for Poland when the situation cleared, which the Poles hoped meant diplomatic intervention to secure a peaceful solution. At the beginning of July 1831 Sebastiani made proposals to Britain, Austria and Prussia for joint intervention in the Polish question, knowing full well that it would be refused. The fact however that he made this approach gave him a good weapon against the new Chamber of Deputies which was then being elected and of whose temper in the new parliament he would be uncertain. When the powers refused his proposals he could plead that France was unable to act alone, the implication of the vagueness of Louis Philippe's reference to Poland in his speech from the throne of 23 July. There was still hope for the Poles if the Belgian crisis were solved and the basic cause of Anglo-French antagonism disappeared, which accounts for the mission to Brussels of Count Roman Załuski, who had originally been assigned to Sweden, with the object of pressing the Belgian groups to accept the London Proposals, which in fact did happen on 9 July. All hope that the Belgian question would be solved promptly vanished when the Dutch invaded the Southern Netherlands on 2 August. The French Parliament supported the intervention of Casimir Périer and though the extreme left continued to press for aid to Poland it was clear that the Belgian crisis was of greater importance to the deputies.[1]

No more could there be hope of British aid. The Whig government was too concerned with the reform crisis at home and events in the Netherlands abroad to occupy itself with what for Britain was the periphery of Europe. Leon Sapieha, Alexander Wielopolski, Alexander Walewski, who was Napoleon's natural son and later, under Napoleon III, foreign minister of France, and Julian Niemcewicz appeared to plead the Polish cause, but there was little to be obtained. At least Palmerston and Grey were honest enough to state openly that British intervention was unlikely, in contrast with Sebastiani who always implied that he thought he had a moral duty towards Poland. Wielopolski was advised in January by Palmerston that little was to be hoped for,[2] though Wielopolski convinced himself that this was only diplomatic form. His successor, Walewski, was even told by Grey that it was in the interest of Britain that Russia should solve her problem in Poland in order to be able to intervene with greater force in the Netherlands dispute.

[1] J. Dutkiewicz, *Francja a Polska w 1831 r*. (Łódź, 1950), is the most recent study of Franco-Polish relations during the rising.
[2] H. Lisicki, *Aleksander Wielopolski, 1803–1877*, (Cracow, 1878–9) iv, 344–6, 354.

THE INSURRECTION: LAST PHASE 223

The Austrian government for its part was anxious to avoid trouble in Galicia, and Metternich was ready to listen to Polish representations as a means of giving the government in Warsaw to suppose that something might be obtained from Austria and thus causing it to restrain hotheads in Austrian Poland; at the same time care was taken to avoid giving the impression to Russia that a flirtation was being conducted with the revolutionary government. The first emissary, Count Jelski, was not allowed to reach Vienna, but held near Brno for conversations with General Clam-Martinitz, while Andrzej Zamoyski was obliged to grow a beard and smuggle himself into Vienna on 30 March 1831, but it was only on 16 April that he obtained an interview with Metternich, who had been ordered by Francis I to sound him. Metternich was prepared to hold him in Vienna with the vague hope that Austria might lend Poland her good offices, but his initial advice offered nothing: 'Posez les armes. Les Polonais n'avaient pas besoin de cette nouvelle guerre pour faire dire qu'ils sont bons soldats, pas plus que les Italiens de leur dernière émeute, pour qu'on repète, qu'ils sont des poltrons.'[1] In the summer the Austrian government began to establish a cordon on the Galician frontier, on the plea that the cholera epidemic required extraordinary precautions; Zamoyski slipped over the Austrian frontier again in July, but once more Austria had nothing to offer.[2]

The Prussian government was not prepared to offer the slightest encouragement to the Poles. From the outset Prussia showed great hostility towards the insurrection. Poznanian Poles were warned against taking part in the rising under the threat of confiscation of their property, or, where they had no property, of three years compulsory military service. The Poznanian *landwehr*, composed mainly of peasants, was called up and evacuated from the Duchy, while the Königsberg, Stettin, Poznań and Breslau regular corps were drawn up on the frontier to isolate the revolution from western Europe and prevent the shipment of arms. In fact, only some 2,000 Poznanian

[1] A. Zamoyski, *Moje przeprawy*, i, 85.
[2] Reference should be made to J. Dutkiewicz, *Austrja wobec powstania listopadowego* (Cracow, 1933), for details of the Austrian attitude. It should be noted that though Austria interned Dwernicki the majority of the soldiers in his corps were allowed to make their return to the Kingdom.

Poles made their way into the Kingdom.[1] As for the other powers, Sweden refused to consider Polish representations, the Porte turned down the mission of Wołowski, while the Papacy relied too much upon the Austrians in Italy to encourage a Polish revolution.

The slight encouragement which the Poles received nevertheless kept up the hope of the Czartoryski group in the government. The Poles, traditionally fond of fabricating miraculous diplomatic combinations, persisted in the belief that something might turn up. Czartoryski hoped that in London and Paris liberal feeling might assert itself on behalf of Poland, while in Berlin and Vienna he strove to prove the ultra-conservative and monarchical character of the revolution, disclaiming all connection with Jacobinism and Carbonarism and holding out the possibility that the Poles would accept a Prussian prince or an Austrian archduke, preferably the Archduke Charles, as king of Poland.[2] An appreciation of Polish chances drawn up at some time after the battle of Ostrołęka shows that even then he was very far from considering that all was lost.[3] He was well aware that the army lacked food and money and could not hold out indefinitely; he thought that an expedition to the Ukraine might be necessary to gather food for the winter. If food were not obtained Poland would have to enter into some agreement with the tsar. In this case there were three solutions. In the first instance, Poland ought to be extended to the Dvina and the Dniepr under a monarch not of the Russian royal family, but appointed by the European powers. If these terms could not be obtained a Russian prince might be accepted, but Poland was to be granted some degree of independence. If all else failed and a European conference insisted upon the sovereignty of the tsar,

[1] For the Poznanian contribution see A. Wojtkowski, 'Udział Wielkopolski w powstaniu listopadowyem', *Kwartalnik Historyczny*, xliv (1930).
[2] Skrzynecki added his weight to Czartoryski's diplomacy in two letters of 3 May 1831 to the Archduke Charles, cf. T. Schiemann, *Geschichte Russlands unter Kaiser Nikolaus I* (Berlin, 1913), iii, 444–9, making it clear that 'la Nation Polonaise, s'est soulevée, non pour former une Révolution de Jacobins, ni pour courir après des illusions de l'Utopie, mais plutôt pour reconquérir son ancienne indépendance et reprendre sa place parmi les autres nations...', p. 446.
[3] *Muzeum Xiążąt Czartoryskich*, 5298, pp. 265–87 (n.d.). 'Uwagi następujące nastręczają się przeciw mającej się wnieść opinji—warunki układów z nieprzyjacielem na wszelki wypadek.'

Poland ought to accept on condition that she was completely independent of the Russian empire and her frontiers extended in the east, that no Russian army was to be quartered in the Kingdom, that constitutional representation was granted to the new provinces and the whole settlement guaranteed by the European powers

Skrzynecki, the commander-in-chief, was no less capable of building castles in the air. He was an avid reader of foreign newspapers and well versed in European politics. Either he or a member of his staff drew up a draft solution for the ills of Europe.[1] Poland was to have a British prince as king and Prussia to be compensated by the acquisition of Hanover. Galicia was to be ceded to Poland and Austria given Bosnia-Herzegovina. Russia in return for the cession of the former eastern provinces was to be compensated in the Balkans and the Southern Caucasus. Prussia and Poland were then to contract an alliance, forming a *Mitteleuropa* capable of withstanding attack from east and west; it was conceded that in the event of no British prince being found to become king of Poland a Hohenzollern might do as well.[2]

There was nothing in the situation in Poland to encourage these rosy dreams. The disaster at Ostrołęka was even more serious than the defeat at Grochów in February. The Russians once more held most of the Kingdom on the right bank of the Vistula, so that, unless the Polish army was able to advance again, the Polish government would have to rely upon the districts on the left bank of the river. One of the complaints against the government under Alexander I and Nicholas I was that a budget had never been submitted to the diet, but the National Government in 1831 was not able to remedy this error. On 1 February the government had been granted a credit of 67,223,873 *złp* 13 *gr* to enable it to meet its commitments in the first quarter of the year. For the second quarter its demands had not been so great and only 24,786,535 *złp* 22 *gr* had been

---

[1] *Muzeum Xiążąt Czartoryskich*, 3940, pp. 23 *seq*. "Myśli względem ustalenia pokoju na północy Europy, zapewnienia tronów od rewolucji i pomnożenia dobrego bytu ludów."

[2] This was a period of plans and projects, cf. *Myśli wojskowe*, Pawłowski, *Źródła*, iii, 182–9, which proposed a reorganization of Poland through a series of Jacobin clubs, a solution hardly to the taste of Skrzynecki.

Q

voted on 9 March. On 8 June a further credit of 14,000,000 *złp* was granted and on 15 July another credit was demanded. It was one thing to authorize expenditure and another to lay hands on the money. Normal receipts from customs had ceased. Landowners in the first flush of enthusiasm had made voluntary contributions to the war effort and were now finding that they were unable to pay their ordinary taxes. The prohibition on the export of grain to Danzig for the period of the emergency meant that the income of the *szlachta* had been curtailed.

The government in desperation tried every means at its disposal. It was too late to think of constitutional niceties. Aloizy Biernacki, a man close to the Kalisz group, who had acted as minister of finance, was forced to give way to the more capable Leon Dembowski, who was well known for his sympathy with Czartoryski. Some hope was entertained that money could be raised from a loan, but when a loan of 60,000,000 *złp* was launched only 88,000 *złp* were subscribed by the public. There was nothing to be obtained from abroad. In the summer Niemcewicz was sent to London where one financier held out the possibility of a loan at a very high rate of interest, but nothing was promised before the winter, when presumably the stability of the Polish government would be assured. All that the government could do was to scrape together everything it could from the limited area which it controlled. In times of distress the Poles had always turned to the Jews, a source of income which public opinion demanded should be tapped to the full. The Jews were unsuitable for military service on account of their poor physique, for which reason they had been exempted from conscription. In peace-time their contribution to secure this exemption was only 700,000 *złp*, but in 1831 there was talk of raising as much as 24,000,000 *złp* from this source. At length it was agreed to raise a sum of 3,500,000 *złp*, although a committee of the diet recommended only 2,800,000. As far as the *szlachta* were concerned, it was hoped that the subsidy (*ofiara*) might be raised from its normal level of about 16,000,000 *złp*, but the *szlachta* were determined that the clergy also should pay their share. Increases were voted, 12 per cent from the *szlachta* and 22.5 per cent from the clergy. The hearth tax for one whole year was to be collected from the city of Warsaw. Persons holding lands as security for debts and tenants of landed properties were to be taxed at the rate of 5 per cent on their incomes. New taxes were to be collected in two instalments, in July and October. In addition the subsidy for the year 1832 was to be collected in October and December if the loan of 60,000,000 *złp* were not realized. The need for money was so great that the government, forgetting the condemnations of Lubecki's policy, confirmed outstanding agreements for the sale of state lands in order to obtain money from the speculators who had undertaken to buy them before November 1832 but had not entered into possession.[1]

The realization that money would be hard to find led the government to measures of a different type, the collection of supplies in kind. The army could not wait to be fed and the diet, in spite of the general feeling that requisition was a violation of the rights of property, agreed on 3 June to empower the government to collect large quantities of agricultural produce simply by giving the landowners a certificate. Sums due to landowners were to be treated as a debt to be repaid in four years at 6 per cent interest. The exemption which Chłopicki had granted from the purveyance tax normally imposed upon the peasants was cancelled and the government empowered to collect sums due in kind. Church silver and valuables in the possession of landowners and merchants might also be taken by the authorities to enable money to be minted. Most serious of all, for it affected the whole economy of the country, power was granted to requisition horses and plough oxen.

The mass of the people too were to be called upon to serve in person. In the old days it had been the custom to call a *levée-en-masse* (*pospolite ruszenie*) to meet extraordinary dangers. A proclamation was issued to the people, calling upon all Christians between the ages of 16 and 50 to take up arms in defence of the country, which Czartoryski coupled on 1 July 1831 with a personal appeal for all classes to rally in a final effort to save the revolution. The response was lukewarm. Nowhere was to be seen the fighting spirit which had been shown by the peasants in the Kościuszko rising of 1794. In one instance at least the authorities met with solid opposition. This occurred in the town

[1] *Dyaryusz sejmu*, v, 57–63, 107–55.

of Sandomierz on the Vistula, in an area which had suffered most from the crop failure of 1830 and Russian incursions from the *województwo* of Lublin. The local commander, Jan Ledóchowski on leave of absence from the diet, ordered the peasants to be gathered together in the cathedral and arranged for a military unit to be present while they took the oath. As was usual when the *szlachta* dealt with the peasants, a popular priest was ordered to deliver a patriotic sermon, but when the peasants were called upon to swear the oath there was no response. Ledóchowski ordered that they should be assembled outside and that the soldiers should mix with them to try to persuade them to take up arms. The peasants listened politely, but the majority refused to change their attitude: One peasant expressed their grievances frankly:

> We do not like the Russians and we do not want to have them here among us. We should be glad if they did not set foot here and if they for ever kept away, but will it be better for us peasants if we drive them out or destroy them? . . . As we have been up to now, so we shall be afterwards. Our misery will not change. Even now in time of war the manor drives out to field services the wives and children of households from which the farmers have gone to join the army or the levy. He who complains gets in answer the severe command to keep quiet. If those farmers, from whose houses someone has been recruited to the army, were exempted from services at least for the time of the war, and, if when the farmer fell in battle, the family were given some reduction of services, then we would all have gone to the levy, but then! to such demands we have always obtained and always do obtain a refusal. Indeed, it will be better for the lords when they defeat the Russians. So let them fight them. We certainly will not stop them and we shall be glad if they crush them all. Many peasants have gone to the army gladly and still go, even from our parishes. We of course do not stop them. Let them go! But I and many more of us will not go and we will not take the oath.[1]

So dangerous was the situation that the officers were obliged to order the soldiers moving among the peasants to reform their ranks lest they should be infected with the same spirit. In this case only one-third of the peasants consented to swear the oath. Other isolated incidents of refusal did occur, but in the main

[1] 'Pamiętnik Henryka Bogdańskiego', *Zbiór pamiętników do historyi powstania polskiego roku 1830–31*, pp. 138–9.

THE INSURRECTION: LAST PHASE 229

the peasants enrolled in the *levée* and disappeared as soon as the Russian army advanced, when they were safe from *szlachta* victimization. These were the realities of the summer of 1831 in the provinces. In Warsaw and the army a different spirit prevailed. Skrzynecki had ridden back to Warsaw determined that he at least should not be held responsible for the disaster at Ostrołęka. General Krukowiecki, the governor of Warsaw, had made it plain that he had no very high opinion of Skrzynecki's ability. On 26 May he had objected to the weakening of Warsaw's defences, from which Skrzynecki had withdrawn a number of units for service with the main army; Krukowiecki criticized him for 'leaving in this manner the protection of Praga and the supervision of prisoners working on the fortifications to Almighty Providence which is very pious, but not a military method of safeguarding the capital'.[1] After the defeat at Ostrołęka Krukowiecki set forth for the government his criticisms of Skrzynecki's conduct of operations; he stated bluntly that Skrzynecki was personally brave, but as a general incompetent.[2] Skrzynecki for his part decided to use Krukowiecki's letter of 26 May as an excuse for his removal from his post of governor of Warsaw. The government was anxious to maintain an appearance of unity and strength and consented to Skrzynecki's request. Czartoryski was himself little concerned for Krukowiecki, but feared that his humiliation might cause him to join the radicals or encourage the factions in the city; he urged Skrzynecki to make an example of no one else: '... il me paraît inutile de continuer. Je crois que les arrêts et surtout le jugement de Gén. Kruk. ne servit qu'une pâture pour les badeaux de la ville, pour les garetiers et le Club. Je suis convaincu que le départ et l'éloignement du Général produira un beaucoup meilleur effet, que son jugement....'[3] Czartoryski was later to appeal for the re-employment of General Umiński, whom Skrzynecki with the agreement of the government had removed from active command during the Ostrołęka campaign for alleged insubordination: 'He is in despair because of his unemployment and despair can lead to evil. We have many

[1] Pawłowski, *Źródła*, iii, 116, Krukowiecki to the commander-in-chief.
[2] *Ibid.*, iii, 130, Krukowiecki to the National Government, 28 May 1831.
[3] *Muzeum Xiążąt Czartoryskich*, 3934, letter of Czartoryski to Skrzynecki of 29 May 1831.

acid elements at the moment which ought to be neutralized. The number of our malcontents may be increased when we perhaps are to be shut up in so small an area. . . .'[1] Skrzynecki had yet another enemy, his quartermaster-general, Prądzyński, who was beginning to be more vocal in his criticisms. It was perhaps unfortunate that the Russian army did not press home its advantage after Ostrołęka, for military activity might have calmed the disputes among the Poles.

The breathing space which the Poles obtained was used not only for rallying their forces, but also for another round of political dispute. Skrzynecki made an attempt to divert attention from himself to the National Government. In one way his position was strong. Polish pride would not admit to the outside world that a reverse had been suffered in battle, nor did the government wish to give the impression that the insurrection was on the point of collapse. The diet, in order to create a mood of confidence, voted that a deputation be sent to the commander in-chief to thank him for his efforts. The deputy chosen to bear this message was Count Ledóchowski, a man almost certain to fish in troubled waters. At Skrzynecki's headquarters he listened to a stream of complaints, that the government made the worst possible impression abroad, that Lelewel—the leading radical in Poland—was sitting in it as its fifth member, and that the conduct of operations was hampered by the inflexibility of the government which was unable to supply the army with its needs. Ledóchowski, who loved nothing better than to be in the limelight, chose to take these complaints at their face value and returned to the diet determined to bring Skrzynecki's views before the Chamber of Deputies. On 4 June he raised the whole question of the reform of the government in the Chamber, claiming that a government consisting of five persons was weak, that it was unable to control the abuses of freedom of the press, and that Joachim Lelewel, the president of the Patriotic Society, could hardly inspire confidence in foreign governments; Lelewel had actually dared to write in an article in the newspaper, *Gazeta Polska*, that the revolution was not only for independence, but also for social reform. Ledóchowski declared that Lelewel's opinions were anti-national and against the diet and for this

[1] *Ibid.*, 3934, letter of Czartyski to Skrorzynecki, 29 July 1831.

reason demanded an immediate debate upon the question of a change of government. The deputy Rembowski said all that ought to have been said: '. . . If these communications had been made from the banks of the Dniepr and the Dvina I would have said that the commander-in-chief is badly informed of the situation, but, when they have followed the battle at Ostrołęka, I must confess that they give rise to the saddest thoughts. In this manner distrust of the National Government is being excited. . . .'[1]
There was however nothing more to the taste of the deputies than a debate upon the organic nature of the state. In response to the wishes of the Chamber a debate was arranged for 9 June 1831 which gave such an opportunity for eloquence that it lasted three days and was accompanied by heated discussion in the Warsaw Press. On theoretical questions at least definite orientations appeared. The Kalisz group rallied to the defence of the existing government. The Patriotic Society had seen so little purpose in its continued activity that on 2 June it had decided to wind up its affairs and had been revived only after Lelewel had made one of his rare appearances at its meetings to deliver a spirited protest against its dissolution,[2] but now it obtained a new lease of life and threw its influence on the side of the National Government for fear of return to one-man rule. Indeed, in the committee stage the deputies decided that power ought to be entrusted to one person.[3] In the diet, however, in spite of Ledóchowski's plea that a government of five members was bound to be divided, and Świdziński's attack upon Lelewel, there was considerable support for the government as it existed. The motion for a change in the form of the government was rejected by 42 votes to 35. 'The Kalisz group immediately began to celebrate its triumph by liberal libations to Bacchus', as Wężyk bitterly complained.[4]

The government had survived what was in effect a motion of no confidence, but a majority of seven was not an indication

[1] *Dyaryusz sejmu*, iv, 218.
[2] 'Protestacya prezesa Towarzystwa Patriotycznego przeciw jego rozwiązaniu', in J. Lelewel, *Polska, dzieje i rzeczy jej*, xx (Poznań, 1864), 80–2.
[3] Of 19 members of the committee, 13 were for a change in the organization of the Government, while of the 22 who discussed the future form of the government 19 favoured entrusting it to one person, *Dyaryusz sejmu*, iv, 269–70, the opening speech of Ledóchowski, 9 June 1831.
[4] *Powstanie królestwa polskiego w roku 1830 i 1831* (Cracow, 1895) p. 128.

of overwhelming support. Barzykowski's view was that there was no other course but to strengthen the government and that by instituting a change in its form and composition. Wincenty Niemojowski, persisting in the view that the diet, the highest authority of the nation, had pronounced against change, refused to admit Barzykowski's suggestion. Barzykowski himself wished to resign, but was prevented by Czartoryski who declined to continue as president without his support. Barzykowski, believing that without Czartoryski at the head of affairs the insurrection would cease to command respect abroad, consented to remain in the government. The collegiate government however was still very far from finding a solution to the opposition of the commander-in-chief, who continued to express his opinion that stronger measures were needed. Some idea of the factious nature of his opposition can be obtained from the fact that on the last day of the debates on the motion to change the form of government Lelewel, the alleged cause of much of Skrzynecki's criticisms, met his adjutant, Tytus Działyński, who argued that Czartoryski's presence at the head of the state was a drawback, because he was not *persona grata* in St. Petersburg and for this reason other European cabinets would not enter into relations with him.[1] On 14 June the government presented to Skrzynecki its appreciation of the situation in an effort to secure his co-operation.[2] It declared that public opinion abroad favoured the Polish cause, but nothing could be expected of the governments unless a military success were achieved; the commander-in-chief alone could decide how best this might be obtained. Three questions were put to Skrzynecki: Could a military success be achieved? How long could the country continue the war with its own resources? What diplomatic action ought to be taken? Skrzynecki was not disposed to answer these representations in detail. In a personal letter to Czartoryski he expressed amazement that he could have signed such a letter and could only conclude that he had acted under pressure: '*Non sic tractantur amici et non sic tractatur vir probus.* . . . To all this I will reply to Your Highness, as my pious old father used to say: "Christ suffered more!"'[3] Czartoryski as ever tried to

[1] Lelewel, *Pamiętnik*, p. 142.   [2] Pawłowski, *Źródła*, iii, 207–10.
[3] *Ibid.*, iii, 221, letter of Skrzynecki to Czartoryski, 18 June 1831.

smooth Skrzynecki's ruffled feelings,[1] but obtained no positive answer to his representations.

The immunity of the commander-in-chief himself from public criticism was to be short-lived. General Jankowski had been sent south in the direction of Lublin to carry out a reconnaissance in force against the Russian general, Rüdiger, whom he met on the line of the river Wieprz at Łysobyki on 19 June. Jankowski divided his force into three groups and closed in on the Russians, but only one of the groups actually engaged the enemy owing to a failure to synchronize the attack. On the same day Jankowski was ordered to retire in the direction of Warsaw, because news had been received that the Russians had moved forward and occupied the town of Płock on the 18th. News of Jankowski's incompetent handling of the engagement and the fact that the Russians were left in possession of the field of battle aroused a storm of indignation in Warsaw. On 25 June the combined chambers passed a resolution demanding investigation of the affair and the punishment of guilty generals.[2] In deference Skrzynecki appointed a committee of inquiry, but this was not enough to appease growing discontent in Warsaw. The temper of the petty *szlachta* in Warsaw was rising. A demonstration against Jankowski and his fellow officers was organized on 29 June. Demands were made for their immediate punishment. Czartoryski, true to his role of preserving at least the appearance of unity, drove in his carriage to the disturbance and addressed the crowd from the foot of the Zygmunt Column. Gradually he succeeded in soothing the tempers of the rioters, promising that the conduct of Jankowski's expedition would be investigated as soon as possible. He did not, as the radicals alleged at the time and afterwards, promise that punishments would be exacted within twenty-four hours,[3] but the news

[1] *Ibid.*, iii, 228–9.
[2] *Dyaryusz sejmu*, v, 72–84. The minister of war attempted to argue that the matter concerned only the commander-in-chief, but the diet was not disposed to agree and insisted upon an inquiry.
[3] Alexander Jełowicki, the insurgent leader from Podolia, saw Czartoryski for the first time in his life on this occasion, and was therefore probably paying great attention to what he said; he states that Czartoryski made no promise to ensure that punishment was carried out on Jankowski within 24 hours, which indeed would seem unlikely and not in harmony with Czartoryski's character, cf. *Moje wspomnienia*, p. 316.

quickly spread through the city that this was what he had said. Jankowski, General Bukowski and several other officers connected with the expedition, were arrested and confined in the Castle pending inquiry. Their presence in custody was a source of continued irritation and when on 8 August Jankowski was, with his fellows, acquitted by the military court the young radicals and junior officers in the city were convinced that treachery was afoot. They had believed that Jankowski was in the pay of the Russians; his acquittal invited the suspicion that there was treachery in high places.

The new Russian commander-in-chief, Count Paskevich, arrived at Pułtusk from St. Petersburg through Prussian territory on 25 June, commissioned to bring the war to an end. While the Prussian government was extremely cautious of permitting anything which might be interpreted as active intervention in the war and had actually turned down Diebitsch's proposal of May 1831 that the Russian army should be allowed to enter Prussian territory and cross the Vistula by the bridge at Toruń,[1] it was nevertheless prepared to give considerable unofficial aid. Russian agents, Peucker and Tengoborsky, were actively engaged in collecting stores at Toruń with the approval of Field-Marshal Gneisenau, the Prussian commander.[2] Supplies were not however easy to collect, the theme of Paskevich's endless complaints to Nicholas. It could however be only a question of time before the Russians crossed the river and advanced on Warsaw from the west. Clear indication of their intention was given when the Russian main army established itself at Płock on 8 July. For his part Nicholas I was confident that the army would succeed and that there was no longer any point in Polish resistance. Yet another offer of an amnesty was made on 29 July when the crossing of the Vistula had been effected.[3] The Poles however were not disposed to accept amnesties as long as their army kept the field.

[1] Cf. F. Martens, *Recueil des traités et conventions conclus par la Russie*, viii, 173.
[2] In common with most Prussian militarists Gneisenau believed in friendly relations with Russia, cf. his letter to the Russian minister of war, Chernishev, 19 July 1831, in which he promised to render Paskevich every assistance to bring 'la guerre scandaleuse' to an end, recalling that Prussia owed her existence to Russian exertions in 1812–13, Shilder, *Imperator Nikolai Pervii*, ii, 581.
[3] *B. & F.S.P.*, 18 (1830–1), p. 1333.

THE INSURRECTION: LAST PHASE 235

The efforts of Skrzynecki to meet the military danger were singularly ineffective. On 19 June 1831 he had protested to the Prussian government against the aid which t was giving to the Russians,[1] and on 14 July the Polish government issued its manifesto of protest,[2] but it was only on 17 July that Skrzynecki ordered the Polish army to move forward although Russian reconnaissance units had been active on the left bank of the Vistula for some time. On 21 July the main body of the Russian troops crossed the river and methodically built up its supplies. Instead of fighting on the Vistula Skrzynecki took up a position on the line of the river Bzura which runs through Łęczyca, Łowicz and Sochaczew and empties into the Vistula opposite Wyszogród. He feared to advance to the Russian bridgehead near the Prussian frontier lest Warsaw be left open to attack from Russian troops operating immediately east of the city. By taking up an intermediary position on the Bzura from which he could protect Warsaw he gave Paskevich ample room for manœuvre. It was obvious that he had placed himself in a position where he had to face a direct attack from Paskevich and that the issue of the battle would decide the fate of the insurrection.

For all his caution in dealing with the Russians Skrzynecki at least defended himself against the pressure of the Polish government with zeal. On 5 July he had replied, somewhat tardily, to the government's representations of 14 June,[3] but he offered no solution except that the army would fight to the last. His vacillations at length drove the Kalisz group to take action. On 12 July Wincenty Niemojowski and Teofil Morawski began to canvass support in the diet. At a meeting with Bonawentura Niemojowski and two deputies from the eastern regions, Olizar, the Volhynian leader, and Jełowicki from Podolia, they discussed the removal of Skrzynecki, but were unable to decide upon a successor.[4] As the situation grew more serious the civilian leaders decided that interference with Skrzynecki's conduct of operations could not long be postponed. On 23 July Bonawentura Niemojowski carried a motion at a secret session of the diet that the government should call a council of war at

[1] Angeberg, *Recueil*, pp. 825–6.   [2] *Ibid.*, pp. 837–9.
[3] Pawłowski, *Źródła*, iii, 293–9.   [4] A. Jełowicki, *Moje wspomnienia*, p. 325.

which a committee of the diet itself should be present.¹ Skrzynecki readily agreed to this suggestion, but insisted that the council of war should be confidential. No doubt he knew that his quartermaster-general, Prądzyński, was intriguing behind his back; he had actually submitted a memorandum to the delegation elected to confer with Skrzynecki. He stated bluntly that Skrzynecki was incompetent to command the army; 'Our situation has greatly deteriorated. If there is still an opportunity of salvation—this will never be under the supreme command of Skrzynecki who will only make good a promise to dig a grave for the army.'² That a quartermaster-general should criticize a commander-in-chief in this way could hardly have failed to impress the civilian members of the council of war. Skrzynecki however had an answer for Prądzyński. When the council of war met on 27 July it was a fiasco. Bonawentura Niemojowski was ill and could not attend. Skrzynecki outlined the military situation, but forbade the military members to voice their opinions so that Prądzyński dared not open his mouth. On the following day Skrzynecki, having won in the council of war, dismissed Prądzyński and appointed in his place the inoffensive General Kołaczkowski.³ The delegation of the diet, sworn to treat the council of war as confidential, could not even raise the matter in the chamber. The sole satisfaction that they obtained was that Skrzynecki ordered the whole Polish army to concentrate on the Bzura at Sochaczew, though even in this he showed some reluctance and had to be held to his promise by Czartoryski. Skrzynecki bitterly lamented that 'it now remains for me to shed the last drop of blood. I shall be obedient to the general will'. On 1 August the advance guards of Paskevich reached Łowicz. On 2 August Skrzynecki himself appeared at Sochaczew and called a council of war of his officers. He called four

---

¹ *Dyaryusz sejmu*, vi, 37–9. The discussion did not pass by without some show of animosity. Chobrzyński, the deputy for Ostrołęka, declared that 'when the enemy occupied the *województwo* of Płock no one considered this a great ill . . . Only when he has approached the *województwa* of Mazowsze and Kalisz . . .' Here he was cut short by shouts of protest, *ibid.*, vi, 44. Gustaw Małachowski accused Niemojowski of taking his revenge on the commander-in-chief for the debates on the need to change the government of 9–11 June 1831, *ibid.*, vi, 59.
² Pawłowski, *Źródła*, iv, 53.
³ Ignacy Prądzyński, *Pamiętniki*, ed. B. Gembarzewski (Cracow, 1909), iii, 231–8.

more councils of war, but other than that the army should contain the Russians on the line of the Bzura no decision of importance was taken. The Polish army had to wait for the Russian attack.

It was not to be wondered that a mood of profound depression had fallen on Warsaw. Then suddenly the morale of the city was raised by the appearance of General Dembiński with his detachment from Lithuania. He brought but few troops with him, but his arrival was greeted with elation. In one way this was more than the government could have hoped for. Dembiński was a symbol of victory, but he was also a severe disciplinarian and a well-known enemy of radicalism. Without delay he was appointed governor of Warsaw and immediately set himself to deal with the dangerous cliques in the city who might in a crisis renew the disorders of 29/30 November 1830. He found no less than 700 unemployed officers in the city who were drawing rations; one of the unfortunate features of the insurrection was the claims of the *szlachta* to serve as officers, of whom there were more than the number of soldiers justified. Dembiński ordered them out of Warsaw,[1] but he discovered that the government feared to give him full powers in the city lest it draw unpopularity upon itself.

All unity in the government itself was beginning to disappear. At a meeting on 4 August Lelewel at last roused himself to condemn the aristocratic policy of Czartoryski. Disappointed in his hopes of support from the European powers Czartoryski decided to appeal to the self-interest of Francis I. He proposed that the Kingdom of Poland should be placed under the protection of Austria, with the implication that a Hapsburg prince might occupy the throne. He wished to assure the emperor that, because the National Government was suspected of revolutionary aims, each of its members was willing to resign if this should be demanded. Lelewel had not taken a prominent part in the business of government and had acquiesced in most of its decisions, but he understood and sympathized with the aspirations of the lesser *szlachta*. To hand Congress Poland over to yet another monarch and leave the Poles of the former eastern provinces in the lurch was more than he could stomach. He refused

[1] H. Dembiński, *Pamiętniki o powstaniu w Polsce r. 1830–31* (Cracow, 1875), ii, 13.

to sign the despatch to the Austrian emperor. For Czartoryski Lelewel was the personification of the radicalism which he feared so much and which for eight months he had tried to neutralize. For once he descended from his aristocratic dignity and fiercely attacked Lelewel. When he had finished his tirade he stormed out of the government offices and refused to attend the evening sitting.[1] His departure threw the other members of the government into confusion. For once Wincenty Niemojowski found himself in command of the situation. It was impossible to consider continuing without Czartoryski who was the one person of European reputation in the government. To smooth over the differences of the two men he suggested that they should both set out their views in writing.[2] Both consented to this solution. Czartoryski once more recorded his belief that the only course was the maintenance of social order lest the Poles be divided in their struggle for independence. Political divisions would give the neighbouring powers the impression that Poland was as unstable as ever. Only the detachment of Austria from Russia and Prussia would induce France and England to intervene on Poland's behalf. 'As far as the Patriotic Society is concerned, I am of the opinion that . . . at the present critical moment it is becoming exceedingly harmful to our national revolution, because its particular purpose is social upheaval and in this way divides and alarms less steady minds; it excites distrust and aversion in neighbouring governments, whose favour would be so necessary to us. . . .'[3] Lelewel's answer was that the revolution had broken out because of deep dissatisfaction with Russian rule and that it was by its very nature social. The task of the

---

[1] According to Barzykowski Lelewel accused Czartoryski of betraying the revolution. The incident reveals the limited philosophy of both Lelewel and of Czartoryski. Lelewel is alleged to have said: 'Yes, the reason for all our misfortunes and failures has been and is still that the Diet and the Government is not revolutionary enough! They are not republicans, only monarchists. Yes, yes, you are betraying us. . . .' To which Czartoryski, inwardly convinced that Lelewel was plotting the ruin of Poland, replied: 'Is it I, or is it you who are betraying us? Gentlemen, you decide, you give us your verdict.' *Historya Powstania Listopadowego*, iv, 433. A. Śliwiński, *Joachim Lelewel* (Warsaw, 1932), pp. 343–7, casts doubt on Barzykowski's account, but it is clear that the divisions of the Poles which became acute in emigration after 1831 had already appeared.

[2] S. Barzykowski, *Historya*, iv, 433–5.

[3] The full text of Czartoryski's statement may be found in L. Gadon, *Książę Czartoryski podczas powstania listopadowego*, pp. 119–21.

government was to give direction to the nation's revolutionary aims and there could be no question of handing the Kingdom of Poland to Austria. The cabinets of Europe ought to be informed that Polish law must be re-established in the former eastern provinces, that all Polish provinces should be embraced by one constitution and that the lot of the peasant population must be improved. These sentiments were good-hearted in their muddled way, but of no significance at a moment when the Russians were advancing on Warsaw.[1] All that Czartoryski could do was to issue a last appeal to Skrzynecki on 8 August and urge him to a last desperate effort to snatch victory from disaster.[2]

On 9 August the combined chambers of the diet, alarmed by the inactivity of Skrzynecki, decided at a secret session to send a delegation to Skrzynecki's headquarters with unlimited authority both to investigate the military situation and, if necessary, remove Skrzynecki from his command and appoint a successor. The delegation arrived at the village of Bolimów on 10 August to begin its deliberations. Having read the minutes of the war councils of 3, 4, 6 and 7 August the delegation called upon all the generals and unit commanders to give their opinions. No less than seventy general and field officers were consulted. The knowledge that these discussions were taking place could not be kept a secret from the army and the junior officers themselves took up the question of the commander-in-chief's strategy and tactics. So far from instilling an aggressive spirit into the high command, the delegation of the diet succeeded only in bringing about a breakdown of discipline. Prince Leon Sapieha was so enraged by the presence of the delegation that he refused to converse with his brother-in-law, Czartoryski.[3]

Skrzynecki was asked by the delegation if he intended to

[1] For Barzykowski's version of Lelewel's statement see *Historya*, iv, 436–8.
[2] Pawłowski, *Źródła*, iv, 107–8. 'La nécessité de ne pas venir s'il est possible au dernier acte de notre existence, je veux dire au siège, ou plutôt au blocus de Varsovie, m'ôte le sommeil et me remets la plume dans la main. Pour faire agir les puissances et faire taire les factieux, il faut un succès, il faut battre et refouler Paskiewicz avant que d'autres corps ennemis ne nous viennent sous les bras. C'est indispensable, la sûreté de l'état et la vôtre en dépend.'
[3] Leon Sapieha, *Wspomnienia*, pp. 158–9.

relieve the pressure on Warsaw, but he countered this question by asking why the capital was not provided with stores and food to withstand a siege. Wincenty Niemojowski replied that the shortage was due to the concentration of troops in the area around the city. After some wrangling between Skrzynecki and Niemojowski the opinion of the other officers was asked. Their answers were diverse because they were asked not one, but three questions; whether the morale of the army was good, whether an offensive ought to be undertaken and whether there ought to be a new commander-in-chief. Only about one-third of the officers present were in favour of the removal of Skrzynecki, but even they were unable to propose a successor. It appears from the answers that the morale of the army was on the whole good, but that the junior officers, the young noblemen who had been commissioned at the beginning of the war, were a discontented element. If Chrzanowski is to be believed some of the soldiers of the regular regiments were inclined to insubordination, but in the new regiments discipline was good. Chrzanowski was himself in favour of opening negotiations with Paskevich.[1] The diversity of opinions was such that the delegation could not complete its work on 10 August and was compelled to continue its debates on the following morning. At length a vote was taken and it was agreed to remove Skrzynecki from his command by seven votes to one against, with one abstention. The majority of the delegates were in favour of the appointment of General Dembiński as acting commander-in-chief.

Dembiński, called out from Warsaw, received his nomination with extreme displeasure. He was comparatively junior, having begun the war as a captain. He was a personal friend of Skrzynecki whose outlook he shared and like all the generals he objected to the interference of inexperienced civilians in military matters. The bitterness which Skrzynecki himself felt is shown by his remark at dinner in the general headquarters: 'Moi, je suis tranquille à présent. Je connais le caractère du général-en-chef que vous venez de choisir. Il ne se laisserait mener pas plus que moi. Il ferait un 18 brumaire!'[2] Dembiński kept his silence having no intention of carrying out a *coup*. The limit of his opposition was shown on 12 August when Czartory-

[1] *Dyaryusz sejmu*, vi, 340–1. [2] H. Dembiński, *Pamiętniki o powstaniu w Polsce*, ii, 59.

ski informed him that he must accept Tomasz Łubieńisk as his chief of staff and Prądzyński as his quartermaster-general and that his powers would not be the same as those granted on 24 January to Radziwiłł, but would be subject to modification. Dembiński declared he must have complete freedom to choose his own staff and would accept only powers which were substantially the same as those of Skrzynecki; the sole revision he would accept was that armistices might be concluded only for periods up to five days' duration when he was in close enough contact with the government to obtain its views. Not one order did he give to the army until the delegation had left headquarters. When the delegation did leave, Skrzynecki agreed to present Dembiński to the troops. As the two generals rode past the regiments there were cries of 'Long live Skrzynecki!' Only after a speech in praise of Dembiński could Skrzynecki obtain the troops' acceptance of the new commander, and even then Skrzynecki's name was coupled with that of Dembiński in the ovation which the soldiers gave. In spite of its good intentions the delegation had succeeded only in reducing one of Poland's best armies to a state of indiscipline.[1]

This was not the end of the matter. An acting commander-in-chief only had been appointed and it was clear that Dembiński intended to carry out the same policy as Skrzynecki. Fearing hostile criticism from the radicals and unemployed officers of the city, and knowing that the diet, reduced in numbers, of whom a large proportion were deputies from the eastern provinces, was in favour of fighting to the last, the government was willing to accept any commander-in-chief who could avert a siege of the capital. On 13 August the diet considered the report of the delegation to Bolimów and consented to surrender its power of appointing the commander-in-chief to the five members of the government.[2] A decision was urgent. On 14 August Dembiński took the decision to abandon his positions and fall back on Warsaw. The city was full of rumours. Everywhere excitement was reaching a fever pitch. The town president, Garbiński, warned Czartoryski that there was danger of an outbreak of

[1] This matter was the subject of Wężyk's minority report, *Dyaryusz sejmu*, vi, 270–2, and his *Powstanie Królestwa Polskiego*, pp. 277–9.
[2] *Dyaryusz sejmu*, vi, 404–32.

revolutionary violence, though he could not put his finger on intrigues. Czartoryski seems to have had no hope of avoiding disorder and began to remove his papers from his office. Dembowski who visited him there on the morning of 14 August found that only the furniture was left. Everything else had been removed.[1] The government however could not find an officer willing to accept the responsibility of supreme command. It nominated the aged general Małachowski. It nominated Prądzyński. Both refused. Both were ordered to take over the command, but the reply came back that neither Małachowski, nor Prądzyński, nor Tomasz Łubieński, whom Małachowski had suggested as a substitute for himself, would accept responsibility.[2] Confusion was now added to confusion. While the generals and the government searched for a commander-in-chief the radicals of Warsaw emerged once more to bring pressure on the government.

A meeting of the Patriotic Society was called for 5 p.m. on the evening of 15 August to discuss what representations ought to be made. The Patriotic Society had regained some of the fire which it had lost at the beginning of the war when its most enthusiastic members had gone off to join the army. Once more it was claiming to speak for the nation. In July a ruling was passed that every citizen had a right to vote at its meetings. As the army fell back before the Russians it began to attract not only the literary men but all the discontented elements in the city, the unemployed officers, the young boys who had flocked to join the army or who had escaped with Dembiński from Lithuania, and indeed many of the officers of the National Guard. At first they attended its meetings out of curiosity to observe the strange spectacle of Jacobinism in Poland, or because there was no other place in the city where they could express

---

[1] *Moje wspomnienia*, ii, 347–8.

[2] Pawłowski, *Źródła*, iv, nos. 1211, 1212, 1214, 1215, 1217, 1218, pp. 123–27 (14–15 August 1831). The members of the Kalisz group were in favour of Prądzyński, while Czartoryski and Barzykowski wanted to retain Dembiński. The decision rested with Lelewel. According to Barzykowski, *Historya*, v, 58–60, Lelewel decided by throwing two balls of paper across the room, one marked 'Dembiński' and the other 'Prądzyński'. The one marked 'Prądzyński' went farther than the other and Lelewel thus light-heartedly decided in favour of the Kalisz group's candidate.

THE INSURRECTION: LAST PHASE 243

their dissatisfaction,[1] but when Dembiński ordered the withdrawal from the Bzura there seemed every ground for suspecting betrayal of the national cause. There is no evidence that Lelewel, or any of the discontented leaders like General Krukowiecki, instigated the meeting of 15 August. The initiative came from the leaders of the society itself. When the meeting began at 5 p.m. Father Puławski complained that Skrzynecki's influence was still powerful in the army, but neither he nor any other speaker proposed to overthrow or attack the government. It was decided simply to repeat the tactics of December 1830 and to send a deputation to the government to present the Society's demands for offensive action. As the deputation made its way to the government building it was followed by a large crowd.[2] Radical writers customarily speak of the 'people' (*lud*) as being present, but there seems little doubt that the crowd was composed almost entirely of *szlachta*, unemployed officers, officers of the National Guard and other idle and curious persons. The people of Warsaw, the artisans and the craftsmen, watched the procession with interest, but took no part in the events of the evening.[3] The crowd which gathered seems to have been only about 3,000, very much smaller than the 30,000 which had gathered on the night of 29/30 November 1830.

The deputation was admitted to the salon of the government at the moment when it was discussing the thorny question of appointing a new commander-in-chief. The crowd remained outside to await the result of the interview. Removed from the heated atmosphere of the mass meeting the leaders of the Society addressed the government in moderate terms. Czartoryski assured the vice-president Czyński that the government was at that very moment considering the problem which was the reason for the Society's representations. Niemojowski took Puławski aside and explained to him the nature of the situation.

[1] The Patriotic Society terrified the less resolute members of the diet. Jełowicki, however, seems to have thought it was in ordinary circumstances innocuous enough, cf. *Moje wspomnienia*, pp, 344–5.
[2] Feeling had run very high at the meeting and at first everyone had wanted to go to the government offices, but Czyński managed to quieten the crowd: 'Citoyens, c'est un devoir religieux pour nous d'obéir à la volonté souveraine du peuple, mais il est de sa dignité et de la nôtre de mettre le plus grand ordre dans son accomplissement.' J. Czyński, *La nuit du 15 août 1831 à Varsovie* (Paris, 1832), p. 43. A delegation was therefore elected. [3] Barzykowski, *Historya*, v, 106.

In the end, in spite of a heated exchange between Barzykowski and the delegate, Boski, the leaders of the Society accepted the government's explanations. When Boski went outside and began to harangue the crowd Czyński and Puławski themselves went out and expressed their conviction that the government was acting in a patriotic manner. The leaders, having urged the crowd to go home, themselves departed, but while the crowd was dispersing there were cries from the restless sections that they ought to carry out vengeance on General Jankowski and the other Polish officers kept in protective custody in the Castle, as well as upon the Russian spies and agents there. Instantly the crowd began to stream down the Krakowskie Przedmieście to the Castle. Antoni Ostrowski, the commander of the National Guard, hurried to the scene, but seeing many of his own officers among the rioters hastened off to Praga to be as far away from the disturbance as possible.[1] The mob broke into the Castle and dragged out the prisoners. Jankowski, Bukowski and other Polish officers were hanged. Some Russian officers were killed and a Russian woman disembowelled and her entrails lifted high in the air for the crowd to see and applaud. When the crowd had had its fill of pleasure at the Castle a section went off to the prison at the Wola gates to mete out similar justice to Russian spies and, for good measure, hanged a few Jews convicted of smuggling.

For Czartoryski this was the end of the government. He went to the Zamoyski palace where he borrowed a uniform and rode to the safety of general headquarters. As he rode off in the darkness he was seen by some demonstrators who fired on him. Like everyone else General Krukowiecki was taken by surprise. Having no military command he was taking tea in civilian clothes when he received the first news of the riot. He hurried home, dressed in his uniform and presented himself for duty at the government offices.[2] There he found Wincenty Niemojowski

[1] The defence of Ostrowski's conduct in *Krótki rys politycznego biegu życia Antoniego Ostrowskiego* (Paris, 1839), p. 11, is hollow; Ostrowski prides himself on showing the presence of mind not to give in to persons who were pressing him to use force to disperse the mob 'among whom were seen deputies, many officials and women and not a few children.'

[2] *Z pamiętników Krukowieckiego Gubernatora i prezesa Rządu Narodowego w powstaniu 1831 r.*, 2nd ed. (Cracow, 1906), pp. 18–19, 28.

THE INSURRECTION: LAST PHASE 245

in despair. The only troops in Warsaw were the young Lithuanians whom Dembiński had brought back, who declared that they had come to fight the Russians and not the Poles and who refused point-blank to restore order. Krukowiecki was popular for his dispute with Skrzynecki and was one of the few persons in Warsaw who could have calmed the mob.[1] Niemojowski offered him the governorship of the city if he could succeed in suppressing the riot, and he hurried off to the Castle, without any troops at his disposal and relying upon his popularity alone to restore order. Cajoling and humouring the crowd he eventually succeeded in inducing the rioters to go home. It is difficult to see anything in this episode other than a demonstration of mob violence at its worst. It was not, as radical apologists would have liked to prove,[2] a last attempt of the people to save the revolution. There was no plan to it and no attempt to follow up the events of the night with further violence. It was however enough to send Czartoryski off in panic to the army and finally destroy the National Government.

Dembiński went to bed at 12 p.m. on 15 August and was roused shortly afterwards by his staff with the news that Adam Czartoryski had arrived in the camp, a refugee from revolution in Warsaw. He placed a guard on Czartoryski and Skrzynecki and sent a detachment to the capital under General Szneide to restore order. On the next day he himself went to Warsaw at 5 p.m. not knowing whether he was still commander-in-chief.[3] He was quite uncertain of what action he ought to take, but he would have liked to have followed the advice of Chrzanowski who exclaimed: 'Put an end to this. I do not wish to be hanged. I prefer to go into captivity and hand myself over to the enemy rather than be a witness and a victim of such licence.'[4] Instruc-

[1] It was afterwards said that Krukowiecki was the man who had instigated the riot in the hope that he would be able to obtain supreme power, but there is no evidence of anything more than casual contacts on his part with the radicals of the city. He had evidently grumbled to Mochnacki and his friends that if he had power he would get rid of Czartoryski, Skrzynecki and the Niemojowskis, put the old conspirator Zaliwski in charge of the Security Guard, give Zwierkowski the National Guard and instal young revolutionaries in important offices, cf. M. Mochnacki, *Dzieła* (Poznań, 1863), i (*Listy M. Mochnackiego i brata jego Kamila*), Maurycy's letter to his mother of 14 January 1832, p. 2.
[2] Cf. J. Czyński, *ibid.*, p. 71.
[3] H. Dembiński, *Pamiętniki o powstaniu w Polsce*, ii, 110–17.   [4] *Ibid.*, ii, 119.

tions were given to arrest the leaders of the Patriotic Society, but Dembiński could not bring himself to close the diet and declare himself dictator. Władysław Ostrowski, the marshal, at first was inclined to support in a *coup*, but drew back at the last moment.[1] Dembiński's nephew, Alexander Wielopolski, was sent to canvass support among the members of the diet. While Dembiński waited for a reply he thought of every possible solution. He wanted to arrest Lelewel, but consulted Ludwik Nabielak, one of the conspirators of 29 November 1830 who had taken part in the attack on the Belvedere. Nabielak advised him that Lelewel had been without influence upon the events of the night and that his arrest was without point.[2] Krukowiecki, suspected by everyone as the man next to Lelewel who had been chiefly responsible for the disturbances, disclaimed all knowledge of the affair.[3] Dembiński was thus confronted with a situation in which he did not know whom to blame. He hesitated too long. Wielopolski returned with a report that a majority of the members of the diet was against another dictatorship. At 10 a.m. on 17 August the leaders in the government building began to murmur 'Let's go to the diet. The matter will be settled there.'[4] In the absence of wide support Dembiński was obliged to abandon all attempts to play the part of a Cromwell as his entourage urged him.

The diet now decided that the time had come to change the form of government. After much quibbling it was agreed to appoint a president with six responsible ministers; the president was to have the power to nominate the commander-in-chief and was authorized to do everything else short of concluding treaties and declaring war. When it came to the selection of the president, Bonawentura Niemojowski obtained a majority in the committee stage, but General Krukowiecki, the one man whom the members of the diet thought capable of maintaining order and discipline was chosen. Krukowiecki had indeed his

[1] *Ibid.*, ii, 127.
[2] Lelewel was as much taken by surprise as anyone by the disturbances, cf. *Korespondencya Joachima Lelewela z Karolem Sienkiewiczem* (Poznań, 1872), pp. 92–3.
[3] H. Dembiński, *ibid.*, ii, 121 n. Dembiński to Krukowiecki: 'Général, j'espère que vous avez fait arrêter les coupables après le renfort de troupes que j'ai mises hier à votre disposition.' Krukowiecki: 'Les coupables, général? On ne les connait pas. C'est tout le monde et personne.' [4] *Ibid.*, ii, 153.

THE INSURRECTION: LAST PHASE 247

own way of dealing with Polish radicalism. Zaliwski, Wysocki's partner of 29 November, was given the command of the Security Guard and promptly despatched from the city with his men to hold the woods outside Warsaw. Hopes of office were held out to Maurycy Mochnacki, who obligingly issued a series of articles in praise of strong government and demanding unity of purpose in the face of the enemy's attack,[1] but, as soon as he discovered that Krukowiecki in fact did not intend to give him a post in the government, changed his golden opinions of the new president and on 30 August resigned the post of councillor of state which had been granted him, but to which no duties were attached, accusing Krukowiecki of being led astray by the Kalisz faction. Chrzanowski, well known for his stern discipline and dislike of radicalism was made governor of Warsaw; a number of persons were put on trial for their part in the events of 15/16 August, but there could be no proscription of the radicals, for the leaders who had been arrested on 16 August could scarcely have been convicted of leading the riot. All that Krukowiecki could do was to watch against further disturbances. Never once were the troops sent into the city by Dembiński to restore order released for service with the army; they were retained to watch the unruly population of Warsaw.[2] Little trouble was experienced with the left wing. More trouble was given by those senators and deputies who thought that they had a right to advancement and who were so anxious to obtain a high rank that they could besiege Krukowiecki's office even at this late stage.[3]

The main problem before Krukowiecki was that of the forthcoming Russian attack. He, like Skrzynecki whom he had criticized, could find no solution. His objections to Skrzynecki

[1] Cf. *Pisma Rozmaite*, pp. 65–104, where his articles in Dziennik Powszechny Krajowy 17–22 August 1831 are reprinted.
[2] Cf. Kazimierz Małachowski's complaint in his description of events printed in W. Zwierkowski, *Korpus 2-gi Polski w 1831 roku* (Paris, 1844), pp. 20–1. Małachowski wrote that Nabielak, one of the civilians engaged in the attack on the Belvedere on 29 November, was made an adjutant and shipped out of the way with the 2nd Corps in its foray into Podlasie. Matuszewicz's group of Lithuanian partisans with its elected officers, which had found its way to Warsaw with Dembiński, was likewise removed from the city.
[3] K. Forster, *Powstanie narodu polskiego*, iii, 86. Roman Sołtyk for example pestered Krukowiecki to make him a general.

had been personal, for which reason he sent orders to Dembiński that Skrzynecki should be removed from the army, but that was no way out of his difficulties. The most important decision to be taken was whether or not the army was to defend Warsaw. All that Krukowiecki could do was to call another council of war on 19 August.

There was not enough food in Warsaw to maintain the army for more than two weeks. Krukowiecki's suggestion was that the army should give battle, but this solution depended upon the willingness of Paskevich to undertake an assault. Dembiński was in favour of abandoning the city and moving to the right bank of the Vistula; if necessary, the troops could be withdrawn to Volhynia, Podolia and the Ukraine where supplies were thought to be available. Dembiński had no love for radical Warsaw and his feelings were shared by the foreign volunteer, General Ramorino: 'La ville est devenue un cloaque par les menées du Club. Il faut évacuer ce cloaque.'[1] A third solution was offered by Łubieński and Umiński; a force was to be left to hold the city against Paskevich while a detachment was to be sent to the right bank of the Vistula to gather supplies, which were to be brought back before Paskevich could launch his attack. Krukowiecki was unwilling to take personal responsibility for the decision and the matter was put to the vote. It was the third solution which the generals chose. Dembiński was unconvinced of its efficacy and was relieved of his command. The aged Kazimierz Małachowski was appointed acting commander-in-chief in his place.[2] Łubieński was sent north to the *województwo* of Płock with a small corps, while General Ramorino with 18,000 men marched off in the direction of Podlasie.

General Krukowiecki was fast losing faith in the ability of the army to hold out against the Russians, but like Dembiński

---

[1] H. Dembiński, *Pamiętniki*, ii, 174. Girolamo Ramorino had served in the French army at Waterloo. In 1834 he was to lead Mazzini's invasion of Savoy. He took part in the campaigns of 1848–9 in Italy and was executed by La Marmora in May 1849 for his share in the Genoese insurrection against Piedmont.

[2] Kazimierz Małachowski (1765–1845) was one of the oldest officers in the army. He had served from 1784 to 1818 and was a survivor of the San Domingo expedition. He himself considered that he was too old to command an army. He had never in his life led a larger unit than a regiment before 1830.

THE INSURRECTION: LAST PHASE 249

he did not feel strong enough to resist the diet. His colleagues, men like Bonawentura Niemojowski, still believed that something could be saved, but as the Russians cautiously advanced upon Warsaw Krukowiecki received disquietening news from the troops on the right bank. Łubieński reported that there were still some supplies in the region of Płock in spite of the ravages of war, but that his strength was insufficient to deal with the cossacks who were active in the district. Ramorino was not making good progress in Podlasie. His troops were beginning to desert, especially from the 11th Infantry Regiment which had been raised in Sandomierz, and his officers were unable to put down looting. At length on 6 September Krukowiecki ordered Ramorino to return to Warsaw, but by then it was too late to alter the situation before the city. Paskevich was prepared to launch his assault.

On 3 September the Polish government received word from the Russian general, Witt, acting on behalf of Paskevich, that he wished to conduct talks with the Poles. On the following day General Prądzyński was nominated to meet the Russian negotiator, General Dannenberg.[1] Dannenberg advised the Poles to submit, indicating that they could expect fairly generous terms, but the council of ministers to whom Prądzyński reported all this was not in favour of accepting the Russian offer. Bonawentura Niemojowski at the head of the party of no surrender was able to override Krukowiecki, believing even at this stage that the Poles could insist upon the restoration of the former eastern provinces. Very much against his convictions Krukowiecki signed a letter to Paskevich to this effect.[2] On 4 September he wrote to Czartoryski, then serving as a private soldier in Ramorino's corps:

Mon prince, nous sommes destinés à périr, car il est impossible de faire arriver à la raison les messieurs du gouvernement et ceux de la Diète. Le bon Dieu nous a présenté une planche de salut et nous la repoussons. Le parti de Kalisz et celui de la société patriotique vont

[1] I. Prądzyński, *Pamiętniki*, iii, 443–9, and iv, 262–6. Piotr Wysocki was sent with Prądzyński, presumably to show that all persons connected with the original rising would where possible be handed over. Wysocki could not speak or understand French and took no part in the conversations, cf. Barzykowski, *Historya*, v, 245.
[2] I. Prądzyński, *Pamiętnik historyczny i wojskowy o wojnie polsko-rosyjskiej w r. 1831* (Cracow, 1894), p. 251.

à qui mieux mieux pour repousser les conditions que le général Dannenberg nous a communiqué par ordre de Maréchal Paskevich. L'on veut à toute force avoir la Pologne dans ses anciennes limites quand nous manquons de tous les moyens pour y forcer l'Empereur.[1]

No sooner did Paskevich receive Krukowiecki's refusal than he gave the order for the advance to be renewed. He had 78,594 men and 390 guns and therefore little to fear from the 33,000 men and 90 guns which had been left to hold Warsaw under Małachowski.

On 6 August the Russians arrived on the outskirts of Warsaw and took without much trouble the strong-point of Wola. The council of ministers was at last convinced that Warsaw must fall and was not willing to ask for terms. Prądzyński was once more selected as the Polish envoy and was received on the morning of 7 August by Paskevich in the presence of the Grand Duke Michael, the tsar's brother, and the chief of staff, Count Toll. There was an angry exchange of words in which Paskevich professed not to understand why the Poles should now ask for terms when they had previously refused Dannenberg's offer to open negotiations, but when he had cooled down he demanded that the Poles should first recognize Nicholas I as king of Poland. Prądzyński had been authorized by Krukowiecki to take this step, though he knew that formal approval had not been given by the diet, and accordingly he complied with Paskevich's demand.[2] He realized that if he refused Paskevich would at once order the assault to be renewed. His passage through the Russian lines had convinced him that nothing could stop the Russian army which had been liberally plied with vodka and was confident of its ability to take the city; he could not take upon himself the responsibility of letting the drunken Russian soldiers loose on the capital. When Prądzyński gave his assurance that recognition of Nicholas I as king of Poland would be

[1] K. Forster, *Powstanie narodu polskiego*, iii, no. iv, pp. 178–81. Yet even Czartoryski was subject to day-dreams. He suspected that Paskevich's offer was prompted by weakness and wrote back to Krukowiecki that perhaps the Grand Duke Michael might be accepted as king, but that if Krukowiecki were obliged to accept Nicholas I, then Poland was to be distinct from Russia, have its own diplomatic service, army and militia, not to be occupied by Russian troops and should have the former eastern provinces joined to it. *Ibid.*, p. 181. Czartoryski's letter is also printed in L. Gadon, *Książę Adam Czartoryski*, pp. 152–3.

[2] I. Prądzyński, *Pamiętnik historyczny*, pp. 260–1.

THE INSURRECTION: LAST PHASE 251

approved, Paskevich ordered him to ask Krukowiecki to come to his headquarters. Though Krukowiecki still had no authority from the diet he reported at once to Paskevich and found him in no mood to mince words. Paskevich bluntly called the Poles rebels, while Krukowiecki replied equally hotly that while the Polish army still had its arms in its hands Paskevich was to treat him as an equal. Paskevich shouted that the assault was to be begun again, but the Grand Duke Michael and Prądzyński managed to soothe their respective commanders. At length it was agreed that hostilities should be suspended until 1 p.m. by which time Krukowiecki was to obtain the authority of the diet for negotiating a surrender. The council of ministers agreed that surrender was unavoidable, but the two members of the Kalisz group, Bonawentura Niemojowski and Morawski resigned rather than take the responsibility for this decision, taking up their places in the diet to resist it to the last.

The diet met at 10 a.m. to hear the statement of Prądzyński. He warned the diet that Warsaw could no longer be defended after the loss of Wola and that the army could not evacuate the city with all its equipment in less than two or three days. To fight in Warsaw would be to submit the city to complete destruction. 'If the Chambers decide upon the rejection of negotiations a storm will follow which cannot be unsuccessful for the Russians. Warsaw will be taken by storm with a drunken soldiery, because they always lead their men to the attack in that condition. Without question they will destroy Warsaw. Perhaps bands of looters from the Warsaw rabble will join them.'[1] The conditions which Prądzyński set forth were the return of the Kingdom of Poland to its allegiance to Nicholas I, under its existing political institutions, and the grant of an amnesty to all Poles. The deputies from the former eastern provinces at once protested that they were not embraced by these conditions. Bonawentura Niemojowski refused to believe that the army was incapable of resisting the Russians and asked for a council of generals to give its opinion. Even at this stage the Kalisz group could insist on the niceties of parliamentary procedure. When Pradzyński attempted to reply Niemojowski

[1] *Dyaryusz sejmu*, vi, 550.

demanded that he should be forbidden to speak because he was not a member of the diet. In this he was upheld by the marshal, Ostrowski, who threatened to resign if the rules of the diet were not observed. The discussion dragged on. The deputies could not bring themselves to the point of admitting that surrender was necessary. The memory of the diet of Grodno in 1793 was too strong. There was talk of leaving Warsaw and establishing a seat of government in another place. Jełowicki urged that the army should hold out until the arrival of Ramorino from Podlasie. In fact the discussion went on for so long that Krukowiecki was obliged to obtain an extension of the cease-fire for one hour. Paskevich evidently realized what was happening. At 2 p.m. 300 guns of the Russian army opened fire simultaneously as a reminder to the diet of the penalties of indecision. The diet hurriedly gave authority for negotiations and Prądzyński, having received verbal assurance that Krukowiecki would be given formal authority, left the chamber to fix the terms of surrender.[1]

The diet did not complete the formal business of voting authority to Krukowiecki in a hurry. Bonawentura Niemojowski urged it to sit to the last and deliberate quietly. Two bills were on the agenda, one for an address to the army, the other for an address to the citizens of Warsaw. Roman Sołtyk arrived from the battle where he had been commanding a battery of artillery and reported that the situation was well under control. The senators and deputies plucked up courage and voted the two addresses unanimously. When they adjourned at 4 p.m. they had recovered from the first impressions of the bombardment, but they had not voted the formal authority for Krukowiecki to recognize Nicholas I as king of Poland and fix the terms of surrender. Prądzyński, under the belief that it would be a matter of minutes only before Krukowiecki received authorization, returned to the government building and then went through the Russian lines to agree upon terms. He was

[1] The *Dyaryusz sejmu* does not record what was said to Prądzyński but it is obvious from the remark of Bonawentura Niemojowski that he did receive authority: 'Because General Prądzyński has already left with the impression that the combined Chambers grant the authority to conduct negotiations to the President of the Government, reserving to the Diet the ratification of agreements, we can deliberate at our leisure and not take any sudden decision.' *Dyaryusz sejmu*, vi, 561.

met by the Grand Duke Michael acting on behalf of Paskevich and arranged with him that Nicholas I should be recognized by the Poles and that their oath of allegiance would be renewed; that the Polish army would evacuate Warsaw which was to be treated as a friendly city and that there would be a general amnesty included in the final settlement, at least for political offences committed since November 1830. When Prądzyński returned he found that Krukowiecki had still not obtained the authority of the diet. Prądzyński presented himself again to the marshal, this time with the resignation of Krukowiecki, and at last obtained a written authority. Once more he returned to the Grand Duke Michael for the final confirmation of the terms, but again on return to Warsaw found that the situation was not clear. The marshal, Ostrowski, had gone to confer with Krukowiecki and asked for a copy of the terms. Krukowiecki had no copy; he merely stated that surrender was unconditional and that the Polish forces had been ordered to withdraw to Praga. Ostrowski took Krukowiecki at his word when he fiercely offered his resignation; an impromptu meeting was called of the diet from those who had followed the marshal to the government building. Bonawentura Niemojowski was elected president on the spot. When Count Berg arrived to negotiate with Krukowiecki he found that he had gone to Praga and that a new government was in existence. He protested that he was empowered to deal with Krukowiecki for whom a summons was sent. When Krukowiecki arrived he told Berg that he was no longer in office and bitterly upbraided Ostrowski for his interference, but he would not sign the act of surrender. He attempted to go back to Praga, but General Umiński had given orders that Krukowiecki was to be shot if he set foot on the right bank of the river. It was left to General Małachowski to negotiate a military convention with Count Berg under which the Poles agreed to evacuate Warsaw by 6 a.m. on the morning of 8 August.

Paskevich's forces entered Warsaw, but the insurrection was not at an end. Bonawentura Niemojowski formed a makeshift government, but the army no longer had its heart in the struggle. On 9 September the military leaders voted on the appointment of a new commander-in-chief. Their choice was

General Rybiński who was known to be in favour of negotiations, unlike the other candidate, Bem, who wished to carry on the war. Some attempt was made to reassemble the Polish army at Modlin which might have caused the Russians some embarrassment, but General Ramorino was forced over the Galician frontier on 16/17 September. As far as the Poles in the main army were concerned the comedy of evasion and refusal to take responsibility for surrender was repeated over and over again. The Russians for their part had nothing to lose by conducting negotiations.[1] Russian generals were sent forward to meet Polish plenipotentiaries, but it was not easy to bring the Poles to surrender. On 19 September Rybiński who was determined to conduct affairs in his own way refused to guarantee the safety of Bonawentura Niemojowski's government and on 23 September called a council of war to discuss the conditions which General Morawski had been offered by Count Berg. Bonawentura Niemojowski got wind of this meeting to be held at Słupno and arrived in time to conduct a last argument with Rybiński upon the superiority of the civil over the military authorities. Rybiński refused to listen to him and secured the approval of almost all his officers for acceptance of the Russian terms. Niemojowski however persisted to the last. A meeting of the diet was called at Płock and General Umiński, who was in favour of fighting, was appointed commander-in-chief. General Morawski who had been sent to tell Berg of the army's acceptance of his terms threw up his mission in horror when he heard of the new turn of events and took advantage of the amnesty offered by Nicholas I while he had the chance. The army however refused to accept Umiński and declared once more in favour of Rybiński. A new envoy, this time General Milberg, had to be sent off in search of Count Berg. Berg had returned to the Russian headquarters, but Milberg managed to come to a gentleman's agreement with General Dellinghaus. In the meantime Rybiński had escorted Bonawentura Niemojowski out of the country; from that moment Rybiński was the sole

---

[1] The most important documents of the last stage in the negotiations may be found in *Mémoires officielles sur la Pologne; Précis des negotiations entre le Maréchal Paskiewitch et le Commandant en Chef de l'Armée Polonaise après l'évacuation de Varsovie, par un témoin oculaire* (Leipzig, Paris, 1832).

THE INSURRECTION: LAST PHASE 255

Polish authority in Poland. Bonawentura Niemojowski issued a manifesto on 26 September condemning the unconstitutional action of the commander-in-chief,[1] which the Polish representatives in Paris did not see fit to publish on the grounds that it might disparage the honour of the Polish army. On 26 September Berg offered Rybiński's force terms and on 28 September a final council of war was called to make a decision. It was attended by an unusually large number of officers. From the beginning it was clear that almost all of them wanted to accept the Russian terms and that none of them wished to take the responsibility for complying with them. It was proposed that a secret vote should be taken, which would have solved that particular difficulty, but there were some officers, notably General Pac, who insisted that it should be open. Pac made an appeal to the officers not to agree to surrender. *Szlachta* honour was deeply involved and rather than face the accusation of being traitors to the national cause the officers of the council voted against the proposal to accept the Russian offer. The generals who voted for capitulation resigned immediately and were joined by many officers who had voted against surrender. Rybiński however had to make a show of defiance. On 4 October the Polish army crossed into Prussian territory. General Rybiński issued his order of the day.[2] At the same time a manifesto to Europe was drawn up condemning Russia and announcing the irrevocable hostility of the Polish nation to Russian rule.[3] The gesture had been made. It was then open to the Polish officers to decide whether or not they would remain in exile or return to the Kingdom.

[1] B. Niemojowski, *O ostatnich wypadkach rewolucyi polskiey w odpowiedzi na biografią Jenerała Rybińskiego* (Paris, 1833), (G), pp. 50–1.
[2] Angeberg, *Recueil*, p. 873.   [3] *Ibid.*, 873–5.

CHAPTER VIII

After the Rising

WHEN Rybiński's army passed into Prussia the last remaining Polish fortresses, Modlin and Zamość, were obliged to surrender. On 18 October 1831 Nicholas I was able to issue a manifesto to the Russian Empire announcing the end of hostilities, which he followed on 1 November with a partial amnesty for the Poles of the Kingdom. Thus came to an end the November Revolution. At least, the Polish forces no longer kept the field, but the battles and political disputes were to be topics of hot discussion in the future gatherings of the *szlachta*. Some of the Poles came out of it all with enhanced reputations. It became a point of honour to think of the dull-witted Piotr Wysocki as a national hero. Some of the more able Polish officers, though they had started the war in junior ranks, were to be considered commanders capable of leading large armies. Chrzanowski for Piedmont, Dembiński and Bem for the Hungarian Revolution of 1848-9. General Sowiński, who died a hero's death in the ditches before Warsaw, remained a symbol of the Polish will to resistance. Yet when the brave deeds are praised and heroism acknowledged it must be recognized that the Polish revolution had cut a very poor figure. In the space of ten months there had been no less than six governments, the Administrative Council, the Temporary Government, the dictatorship with its Supreme National Council, the National Government of five members, and the one-man government of General Krukowiecki replaced in its turn by that of Bonawentura Niemojowski; General Rybiński insisted that there were seven governments because he claimed that as the last independent authority to exist in Poland he embodied in himself the only legal government of the country. The revolution was almost as prolific of commanders-in-chief, Radziwiłł propped up by Chłopicki, Skrzynecki, Dembiński, Małachowski and Rybiński; if Bonawentura Niemojowski had had his way, Rybiński would have been replaced by Umiński. With this fluidity at the top it could not be wondered that there was indiscipline at the bottom, whether it took the form of the aimless riot of 15/16 August in Warsaw or the constant debating that went on in the army after the conference at Bolimów, matched only by the petty carpings of the Lithuanian insurgents. In all, the revolution presents the picture of timid statesmanship, of cardboard men playing in the diet what they imagined was the rôle of the senators of Ancient Rome, of play-acting radicals and swaggering junior officers who realized only when it was too late what had happened to their country. In a revolution brought about by a handful of youths and in a war declared on 25 January in a mood of reckless bravado the Polish leaders awaited deliverance at the hands of the signatory powers of the Vienna treaties and waited in vain. There had been tragi-comedies like this before in Polish history. No doubt the confederations of the eighteenth century and especially the Confederation of Bar exhibited many of these features, but the failure of 1831 was altogether different in its consequences. In 1772 and 1793 there were still portions of independent Poland in which Poles might work for the reconstruction of their country, while in 1795 a state of war prevailed in Europe from which anything might emerge and which did produce the Duchy of Warsaw, miraculously preserved in part as the Kingdom of Poland in 1815. In 1831 even a semi-independent Poland no longer existed, for the free city of Cracow, ruled by its municipal oligarchs in close collaboration with the foreign Residents, was never truly independent. In 1831 moreover there was no general European war to deliver Poland, though the Poles kept their spirits alive with expectations and rumours of wars for several years. 1831 therefore saw the division of the Polish political class into the *szlachta* who chose to go into emigration and the *szlachta* who remained at home. The *szlachta* in emigration were to be a permanent factor in Polish politics until they were finally discredited in 1863–4.

In the first place it must be understood that the Poles who

refused to reconcile themselves to the rule of Nicholas I were not the entire *élite* of the Polish nation, nor yet of that portion of it which had been ruled by the tsar. Among the *émigrés* were to be found the three great Romantic poets, Mickiewicz, Słowacki and Krasiński, the composer Chopin and the historian Lelewel, but this is only to say that the arts flourished beyond the reach of the censorship imposed at home. To Paris went Prince Adam Czartoryski, Niemcewicz, Bonawentura Niemojowski and several prominent leaders of the rising, but this does not mean that the country was denuded of political talent. In Poland where one-tenth at least of the population considered itself born to politics there would always be an embarrassing abundance of leaders. The truth is that the *émigrés* were articulate when the Poles at home were compelled to silence. When General Jakub Lewiński sat down in 1867 to write his memoirs of the part which he had played as deputy chief of staff under Tomasz Łubieński he gave as his reason that there had been many pamphlets dealing with the revolution and the policy which the Poles ought to have adopted, all of them written by *émigrés* or foreigners who accepted the *émigrés*' point of view, and that it was time that a man who had stayed behind explained his own position.[1] The Poles in emigration might maintain that they represented the *élite* of the nation, whether to impress upon their sympathizers the importance of their own views, or to justify to themselves their own choice of exile, but no claim gave greater annoyance to their countrymen at home. The historian will not obtain much insight into Polish politics in the period 1832–64 if he takes the emigration's estimate of its own worth at its face value.

There had been risings neither in Poznania nor in Galicia and in consequence no emigration from those regions. The Poles who left Poland came from the Kingdom or the former eastern provinces. Nicholas I continued after 1831 to draw a distinction between the Russian Empire and the Kingdom. From the amnesty which he granted the Kingdom on 1 November 1831[2] the conspirators who had taken part in the events which had

---

[1] *Pamiętniki z 1831 roku*, edited K. Kozłowski (Poznań, 1895), pp. 1–2. In 1861 General Lewiński was influential among the prosperous merchants of Warsaw who rejected revolutionary tactics.   [2] *B. & F.S.P., 18, (1830–1)*, pp. 1335–7.

led up to the outbreak of 29/30 November 1830 were excluded and with them the authors of the acts of violence on 15/16 August 1831. Similarly, an exception was made of the members of the National Government who had not made their submission by 13 September 1831 and those members of the diet who had suggested or supported by their speeches the act of deposition on 25 January 1831. Those members of the diet who had signed the act were permanently excluded from holding public office, but not required to suffer any other disabilities. In the same way the officers of the various corps which had crossed the frontiers to escape from the Russian armies were excluded from the amnesty, but subsequently allowed to return home if they were willing to acknowledge their guilt and were even restored to their sequestrated properties; this privilege was however extended only to those officers who were not citizens of the Russian Empire.[1] A great number of officers had indeed submitted before and after the collapse. The official Russian estimate was that about 1,000 remained behind.[2] The private soldiers returned almost to a man. The actual size of the emigration to the West will never be known exactly, but it was never in the first instance as high as 10,000. One *émigré* estimate puts it at 5,050 in 1834, of whom 4,500 were resident in France, 500 in England and 50 in Belgium.[3] According to K. A. Hoffman there were 5,074 in 1837 and 5,182 in 1838 settled in France.[4] Another authority puts the entire emigration at 7,000 in 1837, of whom 4,982 lived in France.[5] Numerically therefore the emigration was very small in relation to the whole body of the *szlachta*, or even to the *szlachta* of the Congress Kingdom, who alone amounted to some 300,000 in 1827, 62,000 of them heads of families. The names of the members of the Senate and the Chamber of Deputies who went into exile are known. There were after 1831 only eight senators and forty-five deputies who had taken up residence abroad, but of these two senators and twenty-five deputies belonged to the former eastern provinces which had been granted representation in the diet in 1831. Thus

[1] *Zbiór przepisów administracyjnych—wydział skarbu*, iii (Sequestration and Confiscation), no. 2, 16-28 February 1832, and *ibid.*, iii, no. 6, 30 May-11 June 1832.
[2] *Kronika Emigracji Polskiej*, i (1834), 80.   [3] *Ibid.*, ii (1834), 307.
[4] *Vademecum Polskie* (Paris, 1839), p. 66.
[5] *Kalendarz pielgrzymstwa polskiego na rok 1838* (Paris, 1838), p. 53.

six senators and twenty deputies from the Kingdom of Poland chose exile; at the outbreak of the revolution in 1830 there were altogether forty-eight senators, excluding the bishops, and 128 seats in the Chamber of Deputies. As far as the Kingdom of Poland was concerned the courts issued decrees of confiscation against 2,339 persons of whom 1,146 were condemned to death in their absence. Because confiscation of property is an indication of emigration from Poland, it may be supposed, if a round figure of 5,000 is taken as being approximately correct for the 1831 emigration, that about half of the *émigrés* came from the Congress Kingdom and half from the Polish areas of Western Russia, where the Ukaz of 3 April 1931 had made rebels liable for summary trial and execution. The *émigrés* were thus largely provincial *szlachta*, though none the less willing to pose as nobles of the Western European type; their sympathizers were not to know that they had in their own country fewer worldly goods than a substantial farmer in the West and often less education. Only a very few of the *émigrés* could lay claim to more than moderate education and ability. Politics in exile revolved around a few prominent names, Czartoryski at the Hotel Lambert in Paris, Lelewel after 1834 in Brussels, General Dwernicki, Jan Ledóchowski, Stanisław Worcell and some of the lesser lights of the Patriotic Society. The majority of the *émigrés* were too much concerned with making a living to devote themselves entirely to politics. They were certainly not in a position to dictate a policy to the Polish leaders in Poznania or Galicia. In Congress Poland the conservative rump of the substantial *szlachta* remained behind and it was only to be a few years before a new generation of radicals appeared even there. In the long run it was always the home country which was to determine policies. Leaders at home would listen to *émigré* advice and pay close attention to discussions in exile. Emigration was even attractive for the freedom it offered, but no Polish politician was ever ready to hand over the leadership of the national cause to an *émigré* theorizing at a distance in France about the needs of a country with which he had lost touch.

The Russian settlement of the Congress Kingdom was much less severe than the Poles expected. At some time after the Russian victory Nicholas I drew up a memorandum defining his attitude towards Polish affairs.¹ He drew the simple lesson from events that the constitution of 1815, the separate army and the economic advantages granted in 1822 had not succeeded in allaying the hostility of the Poles towards Russia, which was as strong as it had been in 1812, and that Russian interests must in future take precedence. The tsar in a revulsion of feeling was almost prepared to establish the Russian frontier on the line of the Narew and the Vistula and dispose of the rest of the Congress Kingdom where he might, but on reflection this turned out to be hardly within the realm of practical politics. Clearly the Congress Kingdom had to be retained, but every effort was made to secure the co-operation of Austria and Prussia in producing stability in the Polish areas. The revolution of 1830 had aroused patriotic ardour in Poznania and, more especially, in Galicia which had been in the doldrums since 1772. Some 2,000 Poznanians had enlisted in the Polish army, while in Galicia funds had been collected to support the national cause and the enthusiasm which greeted the Polish troops forced over the frontier acted as a stimulus to conspiratorial activity. In Poznania the administration was taken over by Edward Flottwell who was responsible for a policy of germanization which was halted only on the accession of Frederick William IV in 1841, while in Galicia police supervision became more strict. The common interest of the three powers in keeping the Poles under control found expression at Münchengrätz in 1833 where Austria and Russia agreed to co-operate in extraditing Polish political offenders who had crossed into one another's territory or, where extradition was not applied, to prompt trial and punishment of revolutionaries.² This agreement was followed by an almost identical convention between Russia and Prussia, concluded at Berlin on 16 October 1833.³ In 1835 the Russian security system in the Polish areas was completed by a secret understanding with Austria and Prussia for the regulation of the free city of Cracow, which had been a centre for Polish agents in 1831 and after the collapse of the rising a base for the

[1] F. Martens, *Recueil des Traités et conventions conclus par la Russie*, viii, 177–81. This version differs slightly from that printed in N. K. Shilder, *Imperator Nikolai Pervii*, ii, 582–4.
[2] Martens, *ibid.*, iv, 454–60, 19 September 1833.   [3] *Ibid.*, viii, 188–93.

revolutionary movement; in this case it was agreed that when the opportunity arose the City should be incorporated into the Austrian Empire, but in the meantime other powers should not be allowed to have any influence in its administration or even to appoint ambassadors or consuls.[1]

Throughout the rising Nicholas I had declared his good will towards those Poles of the Congress Kingdom who would acknowledge him as king of Poland. Though the Vienna treaties of 1815 were vague, he could not afford to give the impression that he was anxious to ignore the stipulations with regard to Poland; his attitude was that he had certain obligations towards the Kingdom, but that he was entitled to deal with his rebellious subjects in Western Russia as he wished. On 26 February 1832 he signed the Organic Statute for the Kingdom which was promulgated in Warsaw on 15 March.[2] It proclaimed its purpose to be not very different from the constitution of 1815. The Kingdom, though united to Russia for ever, was to have its own distinct administration, system of law and budget. Freedom of religious observance and from arbitrary arrest was assured. Local assemblies of the *szlachta* in the administrative sub-districts were promised and with them councils of the *województwa*, but the central diet, which had had the effrontery to depose Nicholas I was abolished and with it the separate army. The supreme body remained the Council of State, while the Administrative Council, a committee of the Council of State was to control as before the general policy of the government; in 1841 however the functions of the Council of State were assumed by the specially created 9th and 10th departments of the Russian Senate, which meant that the Poles were to have no say in the framing of laws. In place of the five commissions there were to be three: finance, justice and internal affairs, which included in its functions the supervision of the police, religion and education. Because there was to be no army the ministry of war was abolished. The three new commissions were to be administered by directors-general. Laws were to be promulgated directly by the tsar in the form of Ukazy or as edicts of the viceroy. There was in this nothing which on the face of it could not be justified as being within the rights obtained

[1] *Ibid.*, iv, 472–4, 14 October 1835.   [2] *B. & F.S.P.*, 19 (1831–2), pp. 962–70.

by the tsar in 1815 over his Polish subjects. In practice, in spite of the statute's professed intention of obtaining the opinion of the *szlachta* in local assemblies, these were never called under Nicholas I and the government was very much more closely connected with St. Petersburg. The viceroy was Count Paskevich, created Prince of Warsaw in token of his victory. At the head of the important commission of internal affairs stood Strogonov, a Russian who had been employed in the Polish Chancery in St. Petersburg. Another Russian, Furhman, took over the direction of finance. Only the new director of justice was a Pole, General Kossecki, a man closely identified with the Russian interest before 1830; presumably the Russians thought that the legal settlement of the Kingdom's affairs would arouse antagonism and that it was better for the odium to be borne by a Pole. Because Paskevich was also commander-in-chief of the Russian army of occupation the general staff came to assume a disproportionate influence in the administration and frequently voiced opinions in other than military affairs. The Church for its part came into line with the new system after the issue of the Encyclical *Cum Primum* of 9 June 1832, which ordered obedience to the secular power, and the bishops, though they had some misgivings, can hardly be said to have rallied the opposition to the Russian connection.[1] Until 1861, when a combination of diplomatic convenience, domestic discords within the Congress Kingdom and the need to bring Poland into line with internal reforms in the Russian Empire brought Alexander Wielopolski into the government, Russians controlled the central administration, though the minor officials were for the most part Poles. The conservative *szlachta* learned to accept foreign domination and supervision and grew accustomed to direction from above.

The Russians did not however expect the Poles of the Congress Kingdom to assume an attitude of sullen non-co-operation. Paskevich from the beginning strove to attract members of the aristocracy and substantial *szlachta* to his salon in Warsaw where friendly warnings might be issued and information exchanged.

---

[1] For the complicated questions of church affairs see M. Żywczyński, *Geneza i następstwa Encykliki Cum Primum z 9 vi 1832—Watykan i sprawa polska w latach 1830–1837* (Warsaw, 1935).

The pro-Russian party which had taken no part in the insurrection returned to the capital to be forced, rather against its will, to act in minor official capacities. General Wincenty Krasiński, Rożniecki, the senator Alexander Potocki, Count Jan Jezierski and General Rautenstrauch all earned great unpopularity for their submissiveness to the viceroy. Of greater interest was the attitude of the Łubieński clan and their friends who had been closely connected with Lubecki before the rising. The Łubieńskis had disapproved of the rising from the beginning, but, when once the war appeared inevitable, had thrown themselves into the organization of the army with enthusiasm. General Tomasz Łubieński had become chief of staff of the army and his brother, Henryk, had been particularly active in arranging for the casting of cannon. With the collapse of the rising they chose to remain behind to do what they could for their country. Very much to his surprise Tomasz Łubieński, after being lectured like a naughty schoolboy in St. Petersburg by Nicholas I himself, was allowed to return to Warsaw and was accorded at the same time the rank of general in the Russian army, unlike some of the other military leaders, Krukowiecki, Prądzyński and Morawski, who were obliged to take up residence in Russia where they would be out of harm's way. The Łubieńskis were set free to do what they could towards the economic reconstruction of the Kingdom through the medium of the institutions which Lubecki had created, the Land Credit Society and the Bank of Poland. The restoration of the finances and economy of the Kingdom was an uphill task and it was not until 1840 that a favourable balance of trade was again achieved with Russia.[1] This was very largely due to the pressure of Russian manufacturers who represented to the tsar that the commercial arrangement of 1822 was an unwarranted concession to rebels. By the Ukaz of 12/24 November 1831 this customs treaty was annulled and the Poles of the Kingdom obliged to compete in the Russian market on an equal footing with other countries.[2] Thus the favourable balances achieved

---

[1] For details of Polish trade in the 1830's see M. Zavelejsky, *Statistika Tsartsva Pol'skavo*, St. Petersburg, 1842, 'Tablitsa pokazivayushchaya torgovi balans Tsarstva Pol'skavo s 1819 po 1840'.

[2] *Polnoe sobranie zakonov* (*2nd series*), vi (Pt ii), no. 4941, pp. 202–6.

with Russia in 1826-8 were replaced by trade deficits and economic expansion for the moment retarded.

Hard times and the absence of active political life in Warsaw, coupled with a feeling that too close a connection with the new government might be considered disloyalty to the national ideal, served to confine the *szlachta* to their estates. Deprived of their usual round of activity and subject to some slight supervision by the viceroy, the landed gentry began to turn to the administration of their properties and seek to give realization to the ideas of agricultural improvement which had been current but never seriously taken up in the 1820's. None were more active in this respect than the Zamoyski family, who, though Władysław, the former *aide-de-camp* of Constantine, had gone into emigration to become the most active lieutenant of Prince Adam Czartoryski in Paris, rejected, as indeed they had rejected before, all idea of an armed uprising and turned to the reorganization of their estates. Władysław's brother, Andrzej Zamoyski, gradually built up for himself such a reputation as an agricultural expert that he attracted *szlachta* from all over the kingdom to his farms to inspect his methods. By the 1850's he was to be almost the uncrowned king of the Polish gentry in the Congress Kingdom, but his followers were not to be men who spoke of revolution and independence. The substantial *szlachta* accepted the Russian occupation and began to talk of ploughs, potatoes, beetroot and distilling as if they were their whole existence. In this they were accepting the standards of conduct which were in fashion in the Grand Duchy of Posen.

One factor in keeping the *szlachta* of Congress Poland within the confines of legal action was the appalling muddle of sequestration and confiscation which followed the collapse of the rising. At the time of the Russian army's advance to the Vistula the Pole Franciszek Dąbrowski presented himself at Paskevich's headquarters in the uniform of a retired lieutenant-general of the Russian forces and was appointed head of the 'Government of the Liberated Polish Provinces', with instructions to carry out the sequestration of well-known insurgents' property, but almost at once complications arose. The meaning of sequestration was ill-understood by the Russian commanders who believed that these lands had become the exclusive property of the state. Most Polish estates were encumbered with debts. No sooner had General Hurko, the Russian commander at Lublin, taken over the Puławy estates of Prince Czartoryski than creditors began to besiege him with demands for the payment of outstanding debts. It was discovered that the Princess Sapieha, Czartoryski's mother-in-law, had claims amounting to 325,000 *złp*. Throughout Poland the same situation arose. Likewise the claims of the Land Credit Society had to be satisfied. Moreover, in the absence of any formal decision by the courts the Russian authorities had little idea at the beginning which estates were liable for sequestration and confiscation. It was only in April 1835 that the government was able to draw up its first accurate list of persons whose property was to be taken over by the state. This confusion held out hope for some persons only partially implicated in the events of 1830–1, among them the Marquis Wielopolski, that they would save their lands. Creditors likewise had every reason to court the government in order to obtain their due. According to Kaczkowski, the historian of this problem, the total value of estates held by the government in 1834 was 37,011,318 *złp* 9 *gr*, of which 21,149,951 *złp* 23 *gr*, represented the claims of third parties which were not liable for confiscation.[1] If the figures supplied to Lubecki in 1823 for the total value of estates in the Kingdom, 799,006,048 *złp* 2 *gr*, represent their value in the 1830's, it would seem that only a very small proportion of Polish landed assets were affected. The gains of the government were indeed more of a liability than an asset because the costs of administration were greater than the income derived from them. When Nicholas I made his first visit to Warsaw after the rebellion in October 1835, besides indicating his continued displeasure with the Poles, he took the opportunity of distributing estates among seventeen Russian generals who were to satisfy the claims of third parties upon them and within six years make arrangements for their peasants to be able to proceed to absolute ownership of their holdings.[2] Not all recipients of these and subsequent grants were able to administer them with success and some estates became such a liability that in 1846 permission

[1] J. Kaczkowski, *Konfiskaty na ziemiach polskich pod zaborem rosyjskim po powstaniach roku 1831 i 1863* (Warsaw, 1918), pp. 174–7. [2] *Dziennik Praw Królestwa Polskiego*, xvii, 323–67.

AFTER THE RISING

had to be given for these lands to be handed back to the state if the landlord so requested.[1] On the whole the agrarian structure of the Kingdom was very much less severely affected by confiscation than that of Western Russia. The former eastern provinces of the Republic were subjected to a long period of inquiry and investigation. The writers who have collected materials relative to the confiscations after 1831 from all the snippets of information in newspapers and elsewhere have been unable to arrive at any definite conclusions.[2] In the Russian Empire land values were assessed in accordance with the number of male serfs on each estate; each serf was reckoned to be worth 175 silver roubles. Out of 2,889 sentences of confiscation only 355 cases are reported in which property is actually listed, but these accounted for no less than 180,734 serfs and in cash, 1,066,914 roubles, 1,074,376 złp and 13,591 ducates, which converted into Polish złote would amount to some 220,000,000, an incomparably greater sum than the losses sustained in the Kingdom. The Polish element in the east was still further weakened by the Russian government's decision to transport families of petty szlachta to the military frontier districts in Siberia and the Caucasus, though it should be remembered that not all these families spoke Polish. Whether or not the figure quoted by some Polish writers for these deportations, 45,000 families in all, is correct I do not know. Polish influence was also diminished by a systematic campaign for promoting conversion from the Uniate to the Russian Orthodox Church. Obstacles were put in the way of mixed marriages and the gentry's right of presentation to livings, a process which culminated in February 1839 with the petition of the Uniate bishops of Lithuania, Orsha and Brest and their clergy for admission into the Russian Orthodox Church, which Nicholas I promptly granted.[3] It is quite clear that if anyone lost as a result of the war it was above all the gentry of the former eastern provinces.

[1] Ibid., xxxvii, 372 seq.
[2] The first attempt to assess the losses of the Polish landlords was that of L. Lubliner, Les confiscations des biens des Polonais sous le règne de L'Empereur Nicholas Ier (Brussels-Leipzig), 1861.
[3] E. Likowski, Dzieje kościoła unickiego na Litwie i Rusi w XVIII i XIX wieku, 2nd ed. (Warsaw, 1906), ii, 44–5, argued on the basis of Józef Siemiaszko's plan of 1827, ibid., pp. 280–97, that this was Russian policy even before the rising of 1830.

The Russian authorities in the Congress Kingdom did little to court the common people, unlike the Prussian administration in Poznania which in 1830 began to encourage the peasants to think of the government as their defenders against the exploitation of the *szlachta*.[1] Perhaps the Russians were too sure that the peasantry were neutral. In the disturbances of 1833, when Zaliwski, Piotr Wysocki's principal lieutenant in November 1831, organized an incursion of small bands of *émigrés* into the Kingdom, the peasants co-operated with the authorities in tracking down the insurgents. Likewise, in 1834, when a law was put into force for a conscription in the Kingdom according to the ratio of 2.5 to every 1,000 of the population, a measure designed to re-enlist the trained soldiers of the former Polish army who had melted away into the countryside, the peasants assisted the recruiting officers in finding the men they wanted.

In the autumn of 1831 the Kingdom was confronted with a serious economic crisis following the pacification and the Russian forces could be supplied only if agricultural production were restored to normal. On 13 October 1831 an order was issued that the peasants, who everywhere had ceased to perform labour services, must resume their obligations to work on the manor lands.[2] At least one member of the temporary administration, Feodor Engiel, seems to have realized that the Russians could have taken advantage of the situation to carry out some improvement of the peasants' conditions and thus cement their loyalty to the throne. In January 1832 Nicholas I himself informed Paskevich that he intended to give the peasants his special consideration. Unfortunately Engiel was withdrawn from Poland in the spring of 1832 after the promulgation of the organic statute and the matter referred to the council of state where the decision was taken to let the matter rest.[3] Nothing was done to alter the system of agrarian relationships introduced by the *Code Napoléon* until 1846 when the Galician massacres compelled Nicholas I to make concessions to the peasants in the Kingdom lest the peasant *jacquerie* spread over the Austrian

[1] Cf. W. Jakóbczyk, 'Z dziejów pruskiej propagandy w Poznańskiem', *Roczniki Historyczne*, xix (1950), 178 *seq.*
[2] *Dziennik Praw Królestwa Polskiego*, xiii, 227–34.
[3] For details of this episode, see H. Grynwaser, *Kwestia agrarna i ruch włoscian w królestwie polskim w pierwszej połowie XIX wieku* (*Pisma*, ii) 77–89.

frontier. Thus in 1846 fixity of tenure was granted to all peasant farmers with holdings over three morgs, but for fifteen years the old order prevailed, and that was a period in which the *szlachta* landowners were increasingly anxious to carry out evictions.

The long experience of failure made the propertied classes at home more cautious than ever before. The one element of Polish nationalism which the partitioning powers could not control was the emigration in the west. The *émigrés* could hardly have been expected to accept their exile as permanent or cease to strive for their country's independence. Diversity of opinion had appeared in the Congress Kingdom during the insurrection, but there was little evidence of the formation of hard and fast political groups. The prevailing feeling among the Poles while the Russian army was seeking to overrun the Kingdom was that the military effort took priority over all other questions. Certain definite orientations had existed. Czartoryski had throughout emphasized the need for discipline and unity in order to create the impression that the Poles were worthy of self-government. He had believed that the powers hostile to Russia might intervene to assist the Poles and that for this reason nothing should be done which might discourage them or put difficulties in the way of diplomatic intervention. Nothing had indeed occurred to upset his view that in the future the powers might at a favourable moment again take up the Polish question. In the circumstances of defeat his position was not to be challenged by the conservative constitutionalists of the Kalisz group. There was no longer a constitution to be observed or interpreted so that everything that had formed the stock-in-trade of the Niemojowskis had disappeared. Indeed, the Niemojowski brothers had themselves departed from the scene by 1835. Wincenty, who had fallen into the hands of a cossack troop in the autumn of 1831, was condemned to death in 1834; this sentence was commuted to a term of imprisonment, but he did not survive the journey to Siberia. Bonawentura made his way to Paris, but himself died on 15 June 1835. The rest of their followers were not men of such energy and readily accorded the leadership of the conservative section among the emigration to Prince Czartoryski. On the other hand there were the critics of the government. Joachim Lelewel, though himself a member of the

National Government, had had his republicanism confirmed by all that he had seen and heard in 1830–1. Beyond the government had been the ill-assorted radicals of the Patriotic Society, ever pressing for resolute action, but uncertain at vital moments what form that action ought to take, objecting to the narrow conservatism of Czartoryski, but unable to formulate a distinct radical doctrine. These differences were to harden in emigration and to take a more concrete form as definite political organizations, rivals among themselves for the ear of both the emigration and their countrymen at home. During the war of 1830–1 the majority of the insurgents had shown little appreciation of political doctrine. The meetings of the Patriotic Society had been a curiosity and often attended only for the interest they offered as the spectacle of a Polish radicalism which had made its last previous appearance in 1794. In emigration the exiles were slow to give their allegiance to any one side. Though the left and the right were soon to be at loggerheads, there existed a centre group without definite opinions, anxious only to find a common ground for action and taking its stand upon the doctrine of Polish independence and constitutional government. In the end, however, the centre was to lose to left and right and disappear as a distinct organization.

At the beginning therefore there was no sharp split. It was hoped that the *émigrés* would maintain a common front and present themselves as a united body to the rest of the world. On 6 November 1831 a Polish national committee with Bonawentura Niemojowski at its head was set up in Paris, but Lelewel was soon to object to its conservatism and, on 8 December, to set up his own national committee with the aid of Walenty Zwierkowski, the former deputy to the diet, Adam Gurowski, Krępowiecki, both members of the Patriotic Society, and the publicist, Leonard Chodźko, already resident in France from before the war. Lelewel's national republicanism was little to the taste of Gurowski and Krępowiecki, who on 17 March 1832 founded the 'Polish Democratic Society' with such members of the old Patriotic Society as they could find. The thought that the emigration might dissolve into several dissident groups worried the majority of the exiles and General Dwernicki, now released from internment in Austria, used his own personal prestige to form the 'Committee of the Polish Emigration' on 31 August 1832, which attracted most of the moderates to it. On 21 January 1833 the Czartoryski group, centred at the Hotel Lambert in Paris, came into line and established the secret 'Association of National Unity', which filled the gap left by the collapse of the Polish national committee set up in October 1831. It would be unwise to suppose that these were hard and fast alignments. All four groups tried to find common ground and extreme divisions were to appear only very gradually.

For Czartoryski there was but one policy to follow, that the Poles in exile should preserve their unity. Czartoryski thought that in the Hotel Lambert he might establish a *de facto* government and indeed, under the guidance of his nephew, Władysław Zamoyski, did create something which had the appearance of a presidential palace. The conservatives believed that a Polish army might be created after the manner of the legions during the revolutionary and Napoleonic wars. There was hardly a leading commander of the war of 1830–1 who in exile did not throw in his lot with Czartoryski. It is sometimes said that the Poles were the general staff of the European revolutionary movement, but it should be remembered that the Polish general staff did not consist of men who approved of social revolutions.[1] Bem, whom Czartoryski sent to Portugal to establish a Polish legion there, was a confirmed conservative. Henryk Dembiński, who went to Egypt to sound Mehemet Ali, was the man who had restored order in Warsaw on 16 August 1831 and well known for his right-wing views. Wojciech Chrzanowski, who was to be employed by Palmerston in fact-finding missions in the Turkish Empire, which he thought of as reconnaissance tasks to discover whether the Porte would enlist Poles against the possibility of war with Russia, had exactly the same views as Dembiński. Skrzynecki, who threw in his lot with Czartoryski after the Russians had secured his dismissal from the new Belgian army, was no radical. The policy of forming legions in

[1] According to Prince Shcherbatov, *General Feld-Marshal Knyaz Paskevich*, v (Appendices), 58–60, there were 2,339 persons whose property was liable for confiscation, of whom 13 were generals, 4 adjutants and 1,036 staff officers and regimental officers.

exile suited the tastes of the right-wing soldiers because the vociferous radicals might be controlled within the bonds of military discipline and isolated from European Jacobinism. On the other hand, the legions that were to be created would remain on the periphery of Europe, in Portugal, Spain, the French colonies, Egypt and Turkey. The majority of the Polish *émigrés* thought that their task was to fight the partitioning powers and that for this purpose they ought to remain as near to the scene of future operations as possible.

It was natural that the Hotel Lambert should look to the propertied classes at home, but even Czartoryski's brother-in-law, Leon Sapieha, who settled in Galicia after the loss of his estates in the Kingdom and Western Russia and became one of the most influential leaders in Austrian Poland, was slow to take directions from Paris. The high aristocracy had always been a little suspicious of the Czartoryski clan and the appearance in exile of propaganda urging that Adam Czartoryski was the best candidate for the Polish throne, the 'king *de facto*', to which the almost regal etiquette of the Hotel Lambert seemed to point approval, served to some extent to revive eighteenth-century prejudices. Czartoryski had to proceed towards the landed gentry at home with as much caution as he dealt with the western European powers. His policy was from the beginning essentially one of waiting for an opportunity and the avoidance of hasty measures. To wait was the one thing which the majority of the *émigrés* had no wish to do. The early 1830's were like the years immediately before 1848, a period when a general European upheaval was expected. The passage of the exiles through Germany in 1831 on their journey to France had convinced them that everywhere they had the sympathy of the peoples of Europe. So far from thinking of themselves as the remnants of a defeated army, they saw themselves on the crest of a revolutionary wave which would sweep triumphantly across Europe. Their exile would be only of short duration and within a few years they would be back in Poland taking the struggle to the line of the Dvina and the Dniepr, a conviction which at the outset caused them to deplore political divisions among themselves.

At first the Lelewel group and the radicals generally thought that they should ally themselves with the European Revolution.

They had close connections with international Carbonarism in Paris and looked upon every revolutionary outbreak as their cause also. Because the Polish *szlachta* were traditionally a soldier caste and had practical experience of war in 1830–1 they thought that the emigration could play a valuable role in the European revolution. At this stage Lelewel was willing to make appeals to everyone under the sun. A flood of manifestos were issued from Paris, and it was an appeal to the Russian people that they should consider themselves as brothers of the Poles which led to the protest of the Russian ambassador in Paris and the suppression of the Lelewelist national committee, together with the expulsion of Lelewel from France in the summer of 1833. The internationalism of the early years of emigration brought many disappointments. The Polish exiles in Besançon and Dijon under the leadership of Karol Stolzman undertook to assist the conspiracy to raise the standard of rebellion at Frankfurt in April 1833, but when five hundred Poles set out for Germany through Switzerland they heard too late that the revolutionary movement had failed and found that the French authorities, glad to be rid of them, had closed the frontier against their return. In Switzerland they formed a soldiers' commune, significantly called the 'Sacred Band', but pressure from the reactionary cantons and the partitioning powers led to a forced exodus in December 1833 which left only one hundred Poles in the canton of Berne. This group in its turn supplied seventy-five men to the expedition of Mazzini against Savoy of 31 January–1 February 1834, the failure of which the Poles put down to the mismanagement of its commander, Ramorino, of whom they already had had bitter experience in Poland.[1] In April 1834 it was evident that the French government, by its suppression of troubles in Lyons and Paris, had a firm grip on the situation and that the revolutionary movement in France had temporarily lost its momentum. The failure in Germany of 1833 showed clearly that there were no grounds for thinking that the revolutionary explosion would necessarily occur there. The Polish left began to turn its attention to Mazzini's doctrine that every nation had a role to fulfil which

---

[1] For details of this episode see W. Prechner, 'Wyprawa do Sabaudji w roku 1834', *Przegląd historyczny*, xxiv (1924), 97–119.

it would be national apostasy to refuse. If each nation had a mission, then it followed that no one nation might concede priority to another in the revolutionary struggle and that though the peoples of Europe might live in fraternity one with another they nevertheless ought to fight each for their own cause within their own national field of action and not submit to the Carbonarist doctrine that the revolution should be universal and therefore centrally directed. 'Young Poland', founded in 1834 and inspired by Lelewel, undertook to play its part in the federal revolution in collaboration with Young Europe and carry the struggle to the homeland.

Even before this swing of Polish opinion in emigration Zaliwski by his expedition of 1833 to Galicia and Russian Poland had shown that he placed the national above the international revolution. Maurycy Mochnacki had declared against the policy of joining any and every outbreak and urged his compatriots to think only of their task in Poland.[1] He condemned the group which saw salvation in a general war and the democrats and radicals who believed in the peoples of Europe. He was willing to accept help, but wrote in his celebrated *Circular from Auxerre* in 1834: 'Let us believe in nothing but ourselves alone.'[2] For that reason he urged the Poles to unite and get in touch with their countrymen at home. Lelewel likewise could write: 'It is my conception that the Polish nation cannot resurrect itself except on the spot and by its own forces . . . not counting on any help.'[3] One by-product of this new development was that the left wing of the emigration was able to organize in July 1834 a condemnation of Prince Czartoryski and his policy of setting up legions, which was signed ultimately by 2,840 *émigrés*, well over half of the Poles in exile.[4] Cosmopolitanism was rejected and attention turned again to Poland. Once more the lesser *szlachta* saw themselves as inheriting the cause of Poland.

---

[1] 'O characterze polskiej emigracji' (1 July 1832), printed in his *Pisma rozmaite*, pp. 112–20.

[2] 'Pismo okólne officerów, podofficerów i żołnierzy z zakładu Auxerre—Do rodaków w emigracji', *ibid.*, p. 466.

[3] *Listy emigracyjne Joachima Lelewela*, ed. H. Więckowska (Cracow, 1948), i (1831–5), no. 172, p. 240, 27 January 1834.

[4] Cf. *Akt z roku 1834 przeciw Adamowi Czartoryskiemu wyobrazicielowi systemu polskiej aristokracji* (Poitiers, 1839).

It was obvious that if Poland were to be able to achieve her independence by her own efforts the old methods, which had failed even when an organized army could be put into the field, would no longer be sufficient. The whole people of Poland had to be mobilized to fight against partition and it was known that the people had shown little interest in and even hostility towards Zaliwski's expedition of 1833.[1] To rouse the people, a programme of economic and social emancipation, which would show that the national movement had broken with the narrow conservatism of the diet of 1830–1 and had the welfare of the masses at heart, had to be worked out. Lelewel's contribution had the object of restoring the dignity of the peasant, and of showing that in the past he had enjoyed complete freedom. For Lelewel the peasants were the element in Polish society which represented equality, whereas the aristocracy stood only for inequality.[2] He favoured the complete abolition of labour services and rejected their conversion into rents as but another form of exploitation.[3] What he proposed meant emancipation without compensation being paid to the landlords by the peasants, a policy hardly likely to win over the landed *szlachta* at home, whether in Galicia or in Russian Poland, who believed that they had claims upon the peasant lands. The landlords hoped at the best to convert their peasants into tenants, and at the worst to obtain compensation, to be paid by the peasants, for whom redemption payments would act as a compulsion to work on the demesnes in order to obtain ready money. The very nature of the left wing's revolutionary tactics was bound to divide the propertied from the unpropertied *szlachta*. The Polish Democratic Society was for its part from the outset cautious and slow in its approach to the problem. Like Lelewel, the democrats had no intention of standing on the 1815 frontiers; if the people were to be called on at all, then they had to be roused throughout the length and breadth of pre-1772 Poland and the appeal issued to them to be based upon the principle of liberty, equality and fraternity. Heltman, the chief theorist of the

[1] Cf. K. Borkowski, *Pamiętnik historyczny o wyprawie partyzanckiej do Polski w roku 1833*, printed in *Biblioteka pisarzy polskich*, vii (Leipzig, 1862), 37–8, 49.
[2] *Stracone obywatelstwo stanu kmiecego w Polsce*, 2nd ed. (1847), p. 4.
[3] 'Myśli skreslone z powodu pisma Kubrakiewicza' (1833), in his *Lotniki piśmiennictwa tułaczki polskiej* (Brussels, 1859), pp. 55–6.

Society after Gurowski and Krępowiecki had left it, was himself steeped in the literature of the French Revolution of 1789 and had come to the conclusion that the people was essentially good and would see the justice of the national cause if only the revolutionaries offered them freedom and property. Because the means to national independence was to be the exploitation of the peasants' acquisitive instincts it followed that the Polish revolution must reject socialism. On this Heltman was quite clear: 'In a socialist system society is everything and individuals simply its tools. Therefore everything is a devouring unity. Individual, independent life is destroyed.'[1] History he saw as the eternal struggle of individualism against collectivism and for this reason would have nothing to do with the only genuine peasant organization in exile, 'The Polish People', a small group of disgruntled peasant soldiers settled in Portsmouth and Jersey, who were the exponents of a primitive agrarian socialism. For Heltman surrender to socialism would be to abandon the traditions of the West: 'The Greeks and the Romans, fighting continually with oriental socialism, eventually conquered.'[2] He did not however suggest that mankind should be submitted to the reign of unbridled individualism. In private property he saw no harm, provided that it did not exist in too great concentrations and here he obviously had his eye on the great estates of the Polish aristocracy, always a source of discontent for the petty *szlachta*. The Society's programme obviously meant that the peasants must be accorded property rights. The Society's manifesto of 1836[3] stated that the principle of emancipation without compensation being paid by the peasants must be adhered to and the people brought within the framework of the political community. Cautious though the manifesto was, avoiding closer definition of its principles, it aroused great interest in Poland by its appeal to the Polish *szlachta* to surrender their social primacy. Its great fault was that it could conceive only of the people. Very few of the *émigrés* had much knowledge of the

---

[1] Zasady demokracji polskiej', printed in *Demokracya polska na emigracyi— wyjątki z pism Wiktora Heltmana, Biblioteka pisarzy polskich*, xxxv (Leipzig, 1866), 22.
[2] *Ibid.*, p. 23.
[3] There is an English translation, *Manifesto of the Polish Democratic Society* (London, 1837).

peasants or saw that the donation of property rights on the basis of existing tenures left unsolved the problem of dwarf holdings and of the labourers with no land at all. The idealization too of a people brutalized by the serf system and lacking the education to analyse political programmes was in itself dangerous. To the peasants there seemed little difference between a *szlachta* revolutionary and a *szlachta* landlord.

The manifesto of 1836 was addressed to the *szlachta* through whom the society would have in the first instance to work. The first efforts to make contacts inside Poland received a cold douche from the poet, Seweryn Goszczyński, a man of considerable prestige for the part he played in the attack on the Belvedere palace and who had been at the centre of Galician conspiracies after 1831. In a letter of December 1838 he informed the Society that care should be taken in Galicia not to annoy the landed proprietors. 'Do not expect to find help and support except among the *szlachta* landlords. They alone still have the means to safeguard you from the police, to shield you from spies, the power to assist you in your journeys and supply similar needs. Neither the towns nor still less the peasants, nor even the poor *szlachta* will take their place.'[1] It appeared that the country had settled down after the turmoil of 1830–1. The policy of the Democratic Society was determined to no small extent by this letter, for it had few funds of its own and was utterly dependent on the landed gentry for assistance. The Democrats saw as their immediate task the conversion of the educated classes to their ideas and wished to bring at first only a very few persons into the conspiracy for fear of attracting the attention of the police if mass propaganda were employed. As late as 1843 the exponent of this policy in the Society, Malinowski, wrote: 'It is better to do nothing than to make mistakes.'[2] Thus at home and abroad it appeared that the left and right had accepted the need for caution. Yet to form any association was dangerous in Poland and there were always extremists who called for action. The young men at home were not prepared to accept lying down the servitude which the partitions imposed

[1] For the text of this letter see Z. Wasilewski, *Z życia poety romantycznego—Seweryn Goszczyński w Galicji* (Lvov, 1910), pp. i, 11–39. I quote from pp. 131–2.
[2] *Kilka rad ku oswobodzeniu Polski* (Paris 1843), pp. 71–2.

upon them. It was they and not the *émigrés* who had in the first place to suffer the restraints and frustrations of government by aliens. In Poznania especially they were to lead the Democratic Society by the nose and bring Poland to the point of revolution again in 1846.[1]

The failure of 1831 did not break the spirit of the Polish *szlachta*, least of all of the young generation. It turned the attention of the left wing to an insurrection throughout the area of the former Republic in order to mobilize the entire strength of the nation in the struggle for freedom, but the policy of declaring at the beginning of a fresh revolution the complete emancipation of the peasantry and the donation of property rights compelled the propertied classes to reconsider their own position. It was from them that the sacrifices to achieve independence were demanded. There was a general realization that emancipation would be achieved in time. If it came during a national insurrection there was every likelihood that it would take a radical turn, whereas in Poznania and in the free city of Cracow where the liquidation of economic serfdom had been carried out in peaceful conditions the solution had not been unduly unfavourable to the landlords. For this reason the landlords of Congress Poland, Western Russia and Galicia viewed with suspicion the aims of the left wing and preferred to accept foreign domination in the hope that the terms of emancipation would not impose severe hardships upon themselves. A loyal nobility had more to obtain than a disloyal one. It would have been considered treachery to the national cause to demand anything less than the pre-1772 frontiers, but the conservatives could represent that the first need of Poland was to prepare the economic and cultural bases of future independence. The left wing's championship of the cause of the people was to compel the propertied classes to plead for the indefinite postponement of revolutionary adventures. The fissure between left and right, which had existed in only an elementary form during the November Revolution, became clearer after 1832. A profound ocial question had appeared which divided the educated

---

[1] I offer some suggestions for an interpretation of the aims and consequences of the revolution of 1846 in my article 'Polish Left-Wing Political Tactics, 1831–46', *Slavonic Review*, xxxiii, No. 80 (1954), pp. 120–39.

classes and contributed a new weakness to the cause of national independence.

A second cause of weakness was the diverse ethnic composition of the former Republic. The left wing could represent that their aim was economic justice, which was not an ignoble programme so long as the people of non-Polish stock remained unconscious of modern revolutionary nationalism, but as literacy became more prevalent in the eastern regions the claims of the Polish nationalists served as a stimulus to yearnings of the Ruthenians, Lithuanians and White Russians for nationhood. In the middle of the nineteenth century the nationalism of the peoples of the east was not strong, but already in the 1830's there were ominous developments in the Ruthenian districts of Galicia, especially in the Uniate circles at Lvov, where Ukrainian nationalism appeared as an independent political force in 1848. The achievement of the Polish left wing was that it forced the Austrian and Russian governments themselves to find a solution of the social question. When once the economic plank had disappeared from the programme of the left wing, there remained nothing but the desire to obtain the historic boundaries of pre-1772 Poland. This aim could easily be represented as the wish to perpetuate Polish landlordism in ethnically non-Polish regions.

In 1815 the Russian Empire had secured a defensible frontier in the west by its occupation of Congress Poland and at the same time won the goodwill of its Polish subjects. The revolution of 1830, though there had been many misunderstandings and irritations, was not the culminating point in fifteen years of oppression, but an accidental and fortuitous event, which led in its turn to war because the temper of Polish public opinion would not permit conciliation with Nicholas I upon his own terms. In the military sense Russia won the war, but she lost what Alexander I had won for her in 1815, the loyal co-operation of the Poles. Henceforth the western frontier of Russia was secured by treating the Polish areas as occupied enemy territory. Russian public opinion became sceptical of the value of conciliating the Polish *szlachta*, while the Poles could never afterwards cease to think of Russia except as the national enemy. This deep-rooted enmity had international complications. The Polish question could always be raised by powers hostile to Russia when they wished to add to her difficulties, a move which usually excited manifestations of pro-Polish sentiment in Western Europe. In the West liberals thought of the Polish cause as part of the universal quest for good government, while conservatives saw an independent Poland as a buffer state against Russia. The result of this widespread sympathy was often to encourage Polish leaders to believe that their position was stronger than it really was and that they could on occasions be obstinate in their dealings with Russia. Though disappointment and failure in 1864 forced the Polish subjects of Russia to adopt different tactics and accept foreign domination, as it was accepted in Galicia and Poznania after 1848, the bitter enmity remained. The Revolution of November 1830 ensured that the Polish question would continue to attract attention in the world and revealed that the settlement of 1815 was not accepted by the Poles any more than the partitions of the eighteenth century. What outside observers did not always see was the economic and social background of the struggle for national independence. After 1832 the Polish question was as much a struggle to determine who should rule at home as it was to free Poland of the foreigner.

APPENDICES

APPENDIX A
The Polish Aristocracy: Czartoryski,

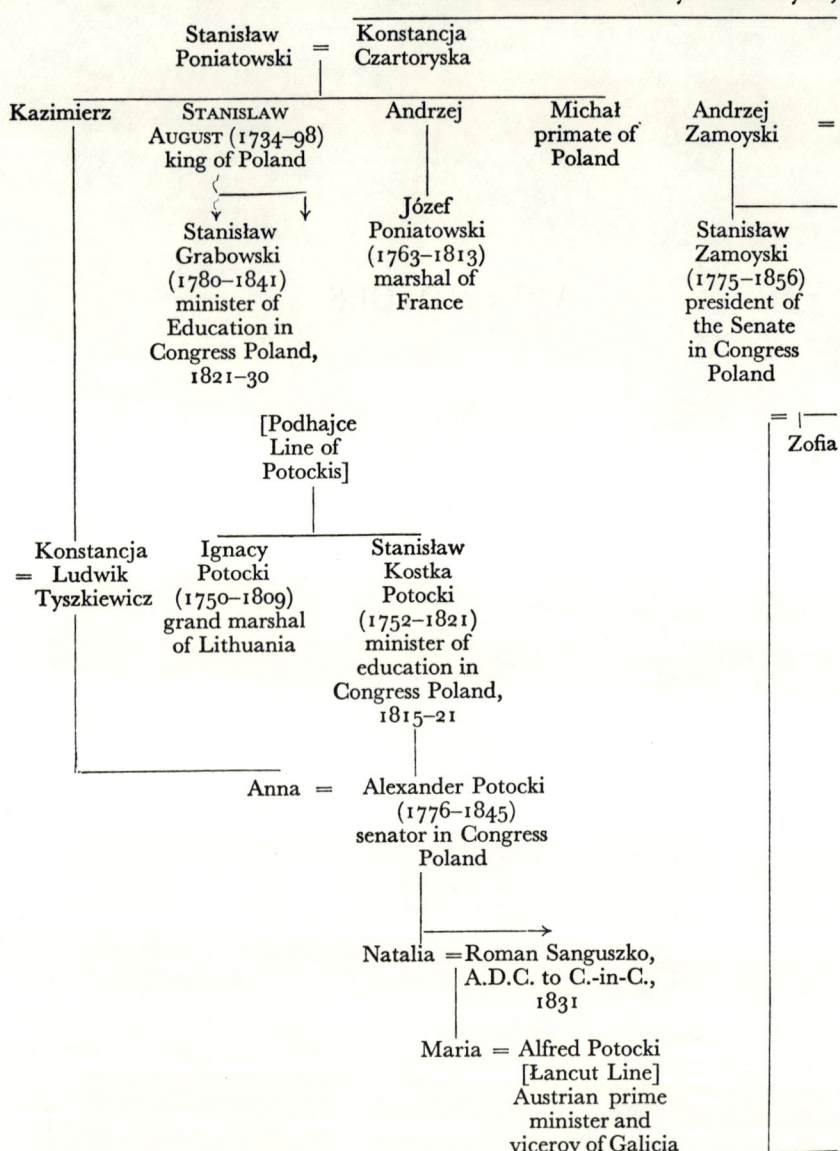

APPENDIX A
Zamoyski, Sapieha, Sanguszko

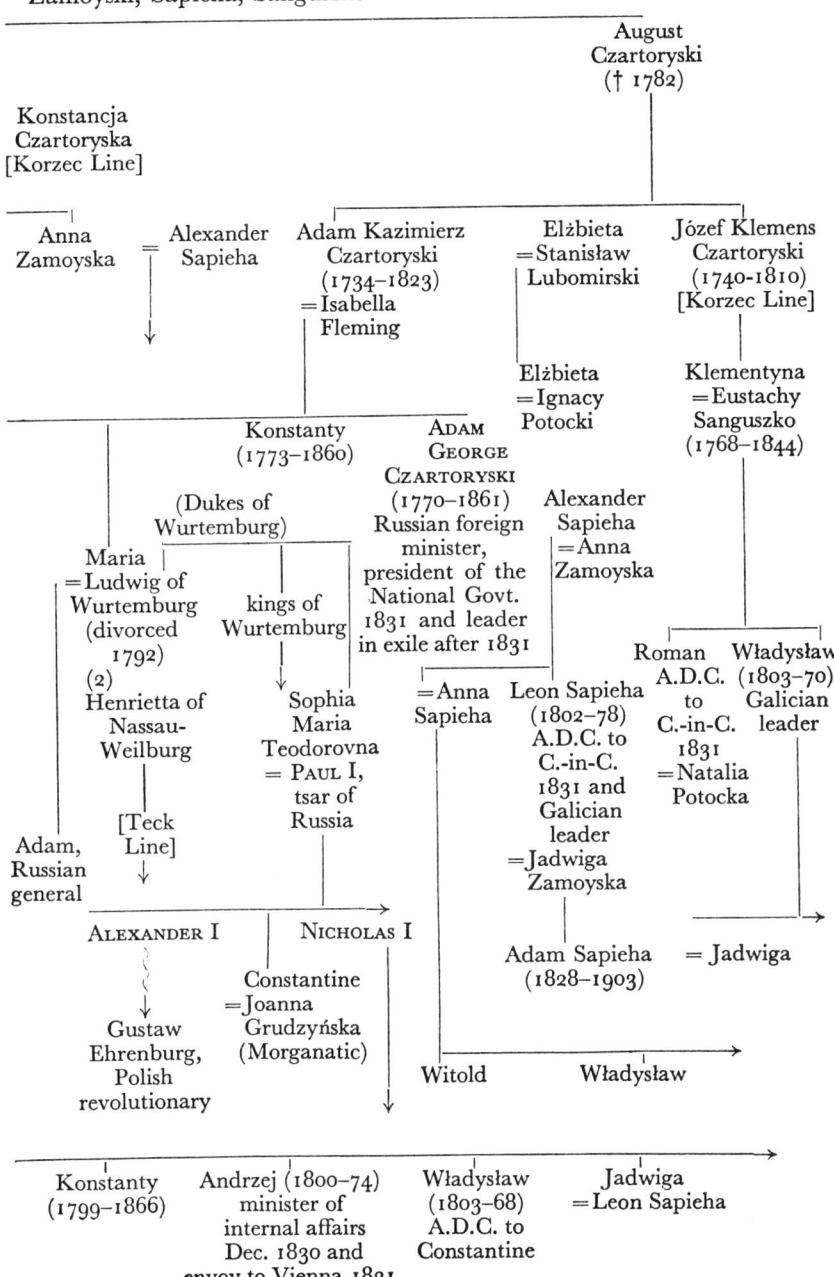

APPENDIX B

The form of the Bill for reform on the State Lands at the end of the debates in the Diet

The Senate and the Chamber of Deputies, in the conviction that the conditions of the peasants who perform personal services under any manner of title on the estates which constitute the landed property of the state, or who remain either under the administration or under the care of the public authorities, are prejudicial to the growth of rural economy and to the well-being of these peasants; and being of the opinion that the affirmation of the hitherto doubtful and contested property rights of the peasants will strengthen their attachment to their native hearths, as well as confirm in them a public feeling and a spirit of rural enterprise; and, furthermore, being of the opinion that respect for the rights of property does not permit the said law to extend to private estates, though the ease of acquiring property rights on government estates will encourage other landlords to make agreements with their peasants based upon principles according with justice and the interests of the common weal; and, finally, that without violation to the rights of any person whomsoever there will be attained the aim of granting property rights to that section of the Nation which constitutes its real material strength, on the suggestion of the National Government and the Committees of the Diet, have decided and decide as follows:

1. All peasants of estates constituting the landed property of the state, or remaining under the administration or care of the Government, are recognized as the hereditary holders of the lands and buildings, such as they now possess, with the reservation however of the rights of third parties and with the limitations contained in the following articles.

2. That the grant of this property right may be combined with an orderliness in the agrarian economy, the aforesaid peasants have to agree to the rearrangement of their lands, both from the point of view of its location, where that may happen to be necessary, and not less from the point of view of the individual separation and unification of holdings, with however just compensation with regard to the quantity and quality of the lands which are at present in the legal possession of each peasant.

APPENDIX B 285

3. From the lands so arranged and given in hereditary right to the peasants by the said law there has to be reckoned the net income according to principles which are to be determined in a spirit of improving the conditions of the peasants, and in a spirit of fixing rather than increasing the revenue received up to the present time. The Government will devise measures for those peasants to earn a livelihood who, not being in a position to satisfy these requirements in money, may ask to pay in labour instead. There shall also be forbidden any revision of rents established earlier, while, wherever an overcharge in relation to the present principles may appear, there these charges may be subject to a diminution.

4. The income reckoned as above, multiplied twenty times, shall constitute the estimated capital value of each holding, which capital, considered as the value of the property acquired, it shall be permitted to the holder to pay off each year in cash, according to the rate of interest prescribed for the Land Credit Society, either *in toto* or *in parte*, provided that the residue of the capital shall at least be terminated with one nought. If such properties are mortgaged to the Land Credit Society, then the Government shall be obliged to use the above payments to pay off the said Society.

5. So long as the proprietor of the holding does not pay off the capital value, he shall be subjected to administrative distraint for the payment of the rate of interest, with the omission of the money fines which have applied up to the present.

6. Rights of cutting wood, pasturing and other rights enjoyed up to the present time by the peasants on demesne lands, and the reciprocal rights of the manor on peasant lands, after the promulgation of this law of separating holdings and of their regulation, shall cease in so far as they are not based upon written evidence. The rights over the manufacture and sale of liquor are reserved exclusively to those proprietors who have enjoyed them up to the present time.

7. The period for the execution of the said law is fixed for the ten years following its promulgation. So long as the regulation of any property, described in Articles 2 and 3, is not completed, the conditions of the peasants with regard to their rights and duties shall remain the same as they are at the present time.

8. Above all, immediately after the promulgation of the said law, all estates constituting the landed property of the Government, or under the administration, care or ultimate titular ownership of the Government, which up to that time have not been entered in the Land Registry, are to be regulated in the shortest possible time, while

on such estates liable for regulation, or already regulated by the Land Credit Society, is to be entered a reservation of the property rights in favour of the peasants granted to them by the said law. The regulation of the particular land titles of each individual holding in the Land Registries of the sub-districts will take place from the time of the fulfilment of the rules contained in Articles 2 and 3.

9. So long as the holder of the land does not pay off the capital, which he owes for such land to the public treasury, the division of this land into smaller portions cannot take place without the Government's approval.

10. The disposal of the capital derived from the redemption of these lands, in so far as it may not have been disposed of under Article 4 of the said law, belongs to the Diet.

(11. *For the purpose of assuring the execution of the said law a peasant committee shall be appointed, composed of 3 senators and 6 members of the Chamber of Deputies, chosen by the Chamber, which shall direct the entire work of regulating peasant conditions. The Government from its side shall appoint to this committee 3 members. In the* województwa, *the Citizens' Councils shall each choose 6 resident citizens, enjoying political rights, while the Government from its side shall appoint also 3 members for each palatine committee. The cost of the regulation shall be borne, half by the public treasury and half by the peasants, provided that on no account the costs exceed two per cent of the capital value.*)

12. The earliest and most ceremonial announcement of this law for the Government estates, as well as the execution of it, is entrusted to the National Government.

(*Dyaryusz sejmu*, ii, 402–3, 410, 440–1, 496, 515, 533, 547 and 549, 562–3, 572, 596, 597.)

Bibliography

I. Manuscript sources
II. Printed sources
III. Histories
IV. Memoirs
V. Contemporary political and economic literature
VI. Secondary works
    (*a*) General
    (*b*) Biographies
    (*c*) Economic
    (*d*) Works dealing specifically with the November Revolution
VII. Bibliographical

I. Manuscript Sources

The study of Polish history has become more difficult since the war of 1939–45 owing to the destruction of important manuscript collections in Poland, but there is still much material for the study of the Revolution of November 1830. The shortness of my stay in Poland prevented me from making use of all the available archive material. Some but not all of the material I collected is included in this book.

The central depository of Polish official manuscripts is the *Archiwum Akt Dawnych, Główne Archiwum Państwowe w Warszawie*. During the last war many documents in it were destroyed, but some were housed outside the city and escaped destruction. I found useful material in the *Akta Władz Centralnych, 1830–1*, especially Folios 451[a]–605, which are the records of the Ministry of Internal Affairs and Police. Where I use this material I cite it by the abbreviation of A.A.D. and identify the document by its date. Another important collection of documents is housed in the *Muzeum Xiążąt Czartoryskich* (The Museum of the Czartoryski Princes) in Cracow. Folios 3934–6 (The Correspondence of Skrzynecki) and 5295–9, 5301–2, and 5310–12 are especially valuable.

II. Printed Sources

The bulk of the material for the history of the Revolution of November 1830 is to be found in printed collections, which permit a reasonably accurate picture to be obtained of the main political events of the insurrection. It should however be remembered that many secondary works include valuable documents in the form of appendices. Similarly, the principal Polish periodicals print historical documents from time to time. I list below the principal printed collections.

D'Angeberg, Comte (pseudonym of J. L. Chodźko). *Recueil des traités, conventions et actes diplomatiques concernant la Pologne, 1762–1862*. Paris, 1862.

Dziennik Praw Księstwa Warszawskiego. 4 vols., 1807–13. (Bulletin of the laws of the Duchy of Warsaw.)

Dziennik Praw Królestwa Polskiego, 1815–71. (Bulletin of the laws of the Kingdom of Poland.) A continuation of the above.

Handelsman, M. (ed.), *Instrukcye i depesze rezydentów francuskich w Warszawie, 1807–1813*. 2 vols., Cracow, 1914. (Instructions and despatches of the French Residents in Warsaw, 1807–13.)

Kieniewicz, S., *Przemiany społeczne i gospodarcze w Królestwie Polskim (1815–1830)*. Warsaw, 1951. (Social and economic transformation in the Kingdom of Poland, 1815–30.) A useful collection of documents.

Kraushar, A., *Miscellanea Archiwalne III,—Memorabilia z czasów powstania listopadowego, 1830–1831*. Warsaw-Cracow, 1913. (A miscellany of documents—Notes from the period of the November Revolution, 1830–1.)

Łubieński, R. (ed.), *General Tomasz Pomian hr. Lubieński*. 2 vols., Warsaw, 1899. The letters of Tomasz Łubieński to his father, the former Minister of Justice of the Duchy of Warsaw.

Lutostański, K., *Recueil des actes diplomatiques, traités et documents concernant la Pologne*, T.1er (*Les Partages de Pologne et la lutte pour indépendance*). Paris-Lausanne, 1918.

Martens, F. de, *Recueil des traités conclus par la Russie avec les puissances étrangères*. 15 vols., St. Petersburg, 1874–1909. Each document is preceded by a short essay which often quotes otherwise inaccessible archives.

Pawłowski, B. (ed.), *Źródła do dziejów wojny polsko-rosyjskiej, 1830–1831*. 4 vols., Warsaw, 1931. (Sources for the history of the Polish-Russian War of 1830–1.) Mainly military documents.

BIBLIOGRAPHY

Pomarański, St. (ed.), *Dyaryusz senatu z roku 1830–1 (Collectanea ex archivo collegii historici*, serja 2 z. ii, pp. 431–629). (Proceedings of the Senate, 1830–1.)

Polnoe sobranie zakonov Rossiskoi Imperii. (The Complete Collection of the Laws of the Russian Empire.)
1st series (1649–1825), St. Petersburg, 1830.
2nd series (1825–1881), St. Petersburg, 1830–84.

Rocznik Towarzystwa Historyczno-Literackiego w Paryżu, 1870–2. 'Protokoły posiedzeń rady administracyjnej, wydziału wykonawczego tejże rady i rządu tymczasowego w Warszawie od 30 listopada do 5 grudnia 1830.' Poznań, 1872. (Protocols of the sessions of the Administrative Council, its executive department and of the Temporary Government in Warsaw from 30 November to 3 December 1830.)

Rostworowski, M. (ed.), *Materyały do dziejów komisyi rządzącej z r. 1807*, I—*Dziennik czynności komisyi rządzącej*. Cracow, 1918. (Materials for the History of the Governing Commission, 1807, I, The Records of the Governing Commission's activity.)

— *Dyaryusz sejmu z r. 1830–1831.* 6 vols., Cracow, 1907–12. (Proceedings of the Diet, 1830–1.)

Sbornik Imperatorskavo Russkavo Istoricheskavo Obshchestva, CXXXI, CXXXII. *Correspondance de l'Empereur Nicholas Ier et du Grand Duc Constantin*, T.I (1825–9), T.II, (1830–1). St. Petersburg, 1910–11.

Shilder, N. K. (ed.), 'Voina s polskimi myatezhnikami 1831 goda—V perepiske Imperatora Nikolaya I-go s grafom Dibich-Zabalkanskim', *Russkaya Starina*, xli (1884), xliii (1884), xlvi (1885), xlvii (1885), and xlix (1886). (The war with the Polish rebels of 1831—From the correspondence of the Emperor Nicholas I with Count Diebitsch-Zabalkansky.)

Smolka, S. (ed.), *Korespondencya X. Lubeckiego z ministrami sekretarzami stanu Ignacym Sobolewskim i Stefanem Grabowskim.* 4 vols., Cracow, 1909. (The correspondence of Prince Lubecki with the secretaries of state, Ignacy Sobolewski and Stefan Grabowski.)

III. HISTORIES

Barzykowski, S. (1792–1872), *Historya powstania listopadowego.* 5 vols., Poznań, 1883–4. (The history of the November Revolution.) Barzykowski was a member of the National Government of 1831.

Hoffman, K. A., *Wielki tydzień Polaków, czyli opis pamiętnych wypadków w Warszawie . . . 29 listopada do 5 grudnia 1830 r.* Warsaw, 1830. (The Great Week of the Poles—a description of the events in Warsaw from 29 November to 5 December 1830.)

— *Rzut oka na stan polityczny królestwa polskiego pod panowaniem rossyjskiem . . . 1815–1830*. Warsaw, 1831. (A glance at the political condition of the Kingdom of Poland under Russian rule, 1815–30.)
Mierosławski, L. (1814–78), *Powstanie narodu polskiego w roku 1830 i 1831*. 2 vols., Paris, 1845–6. (The rising of the Polish nation, 1830–1.)
Mochnacki, M. (1804–34), *Powstanie narodu polskiego w r. 1830 i 1831*. 2 vols., Paris, 1834. (The rising of the Polish Nation, 1830–1.) An eye-witness account up to the beginning of the war in 1831.
Morawski, Teodor (1797–1879), *Dzieje narodu polskiego*. 2nd ed., 7 vols., Poznań, 1875. (The history of the Polish nation.)
Pietkiewicz, M., *La Lithuanie et sa dernière insurrection*. Brussels, 1832.
Skarbek, F. (1792–1866), *Dzieje Xięstwa Warszawskiego*. 2 vols., Poznań, 1860. (The history of the Duchy of Warsaw.)
— *Dzieje polskie*. 2nd ed., 3 parts, Poznań, 1876–7. (Polish History). Includes *Dzieje Xięstwa Warszawskiego*, with a continuation to cover the Congress Kingdom.
Smitt, F. von, *Geschichte des polnischen Aufstandes und Krieges in den Jahren 1830 und 1831*. 2 vols., Berlin, 1839.
Spazier, R. O., *Geschichte des Aufstandes des polnischen Volkes in den Jahren 1830 und 1831*. 3 vols., Altenburg, 1832. There are Polish and French translations.
Wężyk, F. (1785–1862), *Powstanie królestwa polskiego w r. 1830 i 1831*. Cracow, 1895. (The Rising of the Kingdom of Poland, 1830–1.) Written in the 1830's.
Wrotnowski, F., *Powstanie na Wołyniu, Podolu i Ukrainie w r. 1831*. 2 vols., Paris, 1837–8. (The Rising in Volhynia, Podolia and the Ukraine in 1831.)
Zaliwski, J. (1797–1855), *Rewolucyja polska 29 listopada 1830 r*. Paris, 1833. (The Polish Revolution of 29 November 1830.)

IV. Memoirs

Bronikowski, K. (1795–1852), *Pamiętniki polskie zebrane przez . . .* 2nd ed., Przemyśl, 1883–4. (Polish memoirs collected by . . .)
— 'Sprostowanie niektórych szczegółów tyczących się klubu patriotycznego w Warszawie' (An explanation of certain details concerning the Patriotic Club in Warsaw), *Kronika emigracji polskiej*, iii (1835), 307–17.
Chłapowski, Dezydery (1788–1879), *Pamiętniki*. 2 parts, Poznań, 1899. (Memoirs.)

BIBLIOGRAPHY

— *Szlakiem legionów*. 2 vols., Cracow, 1903. (In the path of the Legions.) An abbreviation of his *Pamiętniki*.

Czyński, J. (1801–67), *Dzien piętnasty sierpnia i sąd na członków Towarzystwa Patriotycznego*. Warsaw, 1831. (The Fifteenth of August and the Trial of the Members of the Patriotic Society.) There is a French translation: *La nuit du 15 aout 1831 à Varsovie*. Paris, 1832.

Deczyński, K. (1800–38), 'Opis życia wieśniaka polskiego' in *Żywot chłopa polskiego na początku xix stulecia*. Ed. M. Handelsman. Warsaw, 1909. (The description of a Polish countryman's life.)

Dembiński, H. (1791–1864), *Mémoires sur la campagne de Lithuanie*. Strasbourg, 1832.

— *Quelques mots sur les derniers événements de la Pologne*. Paris, 1833.

— *Pamiętnik* . . . Poznań, 1860. (A memoir.)

— *Pamiętniki o powstaniu w Polsce r. 1830–1*. 2 vols., Cracow, 1875. (Memoirs of the rising in Poland, 1830–1.)

Dembowski. L. (1789–1878), *Moje wspomnienia*. 2 vols., St. Petersburg, 1898. (My recollections.)

Dwernicki, J. (1779–1857), *Pamiętniki* . . . Lvov, 1870. (Memoirs.)

Fałkowski, J. (1815–92), *Upadek powstania polskiego w roku 1831*. Poznań, 1881. (The collapse of the Polish Rising, 1831.)

Forster, K. (1800–79), *Z pamiętników Krukowieckiego*. 2nd ed., Cracow, 1906. (From the memoirs of Krukowiecki.)

Goszczyński, S. (1801–76), *Noc belwederska*, in *Dzieła zbiorowe Seweryna Goszczyńskiego*, vol. iv. Lvov, 1911. (The Night of the Belvedere.) A memoir of the attack on the Belvedere Palace, first published in 1870.

Harro-Harring, P., *Poland under Russian Dominion*. London, 1831.

Jełowicki, A. (1804–77), *Moje wspomnienia*. 3rd ed., Cracow, 1891. (My recollections.) First published in 1839.

Kołaczkowski, K., *Wspomnienia* . . . 5 vols., Cracow, 1898–1901. (Recollections.)

Koźmian, K. (1771–1856), *Pamiętniki*, vol. iii. Cracow, 1865. (Memoirs.)

Janowski, J. N., *Notatki autobiograficzne*, 1803–53, ed. M. Tyrowicz. Breslau, 1950. (Autobiographcal notes, 1803–53.)

Lelewel, J. (1786–1861), *Pamiętnik z roku 1830–31*, ed. J. Iwaszkiewicz. Warsaw, 1924. (A memoir of 1830–1.)

— 'Rozmowa i umowa z W. Ks. Konstantym w Wierzbnie delegowanych Rady Administracyjnej', in his *Polska, dzieje i rzeczy jej*. (Poznań, 1859), vii, 152–65. (The conversation and agreement of the delegates of the Administrative Council with the Grand Duke Constantine in Wierzbno.)

Lewiński, J. (1792–1867), *Pamiętniki z roku 1830–1*, ed. K. Kozłowski, Poznań, 1895. (Memoirs of 1830–1.)

U*

Lipiński, T. (1797–1856), *Zapiski z lat 1825–1831*, ed. K. Bartoszewicz. Cracow, 1895. (Notes from the years 1825–31.)

Młocki, A. (1804–79), *Księga wspomnień*. Paris, 1884. (A volume of recollections.)

Niemcewicz, J. U. (1757–1841), *Pamiętniki z roku 1830–1831*, ed. M. A. Kurpiel. Cracow, 1909. (Memoirs of 1830–1.)

Niemojowski, B. (1787–1835), *O ostatnich wypadkach rewolycyi polskiey w odpowiedzi na biografią jenerała Macieja Rybińskiego*. Paris, 1833. (On the final events of the Polish revolution in answer to the biography of General Maciej Rybiński.)

Olizar, Narcyz, *Mémoires du Comte Narcis Olizar, sénateur polonais*. Leipzig, 1845.

Popiel, P., *Pamiętniki 1807–1892*. Cracow, 1927. (Memoirs, 1807–92.)

Prądzyński, I. (1792–1850), *Pamiętnik historyczny i wojskowy o wojnie polsko-rosyjskiej w r. 1831*. Cracow, 1894. (A historical and military memoir of the Polish-Russian War of 1831.) Drawn up at the request of Nicholas I.

— *Pamiętniki*, ed. B. Gembarzewski. 4 vols., Cracow, 1909. (Memoirs.) Vol. iv contains documents.

Różycki, K. (1798–1870), *Powstanie na Wołyniu, czyli pamiętnik półku jazdy wołyńskiej uformowanego w czasie wojny ... 1831 roku*. Bourges 1832. (The rising in Volhynia—A memoir of the Volhynian cavalry regiment raised during the war of 1831.)

— *Uwagi nad wyprawą Jenerała Dwiernickiego na Ruś*. Brussels, 1837. (Observations on the expedition of General Dwernicki into Ruthenia.)

Sapieha, L. (1803–78), *Wspomnienia (z lat od 1803 do 1863)*, ed. B. Pawłowski. Lvov, 1912. (Recollections from the years 1803–63.)

Skarbek, F. (1792–1866), *Pamiętniki*. Poznań, 1878. (Memoirs.)

Szaniecki, J. O., *Pamiętnik*, ed. M. Handelsman. Warsaw, 1912. (A memoir.)

Wrotnowski, F. (ed.), *Zbiór pamiętników o powstaniu Litwy w r. 1831*. Paris, 1835. (A collection of memoirs of the rising of Lithuania in 1831.)

Wylezyński, T., 'Szesnaście dni z mojego życia, cyzli relacya z podróży do Petersburgu podczas rewolucyi polskiej z r. 1830–1', *Biblioteka warszawska* (1903), ii, 221–43, 478–592. (Sixteen days of my life—an account of a journey to St. Petersburg during the Polish revolution of 1830–1.) There is a Russian translation: *Imperator Nikolai i Polsha v 1830 godu* (The Emperor Nicholas and Poland), ed. K. Voyensky. St. Petersburg, 1905.

Wysocki, P. (1797–1875), *Pamiętnik o powstaniu 29 listopada r. 1830*. 2 vols., Paris, 1867. (A memoir of the rising of 29 November 1830.)
Zamoyski, A. (1800–74), *Moje przeprawy—pamiętnik . . . o czasach powstania listopadowego*, ed. A. Kraushar. Cracow, 1911. (My experiences—a memoir of the days of the November Rising.)
Zamoyski, W., *Jenerał Zamoyski (1803–68)*. 5 vols., Poznań, 1910–14. (General Zamoyski, 1803–68.) Biographical notes.
Zbiór pamiętników do historyi powstania polskiego w roku 1830–1831. Lvov, 1882. (A collection of memoirs illustrating the Polish rising of 1830–1.)

V. CONTEMPORARY POLITICAL AND ECONOMIC LITERATURE

Chłapowski, D., *O rolnictwie*. Poznań, 1835. (Concerning agriculture.)
Gawarecki, W. H., *Wiadomość o mieście Płocku*. Warsaw, 1821. (Information of the town of Płock.)
— *Opis topograficzno-historyczny ziemi dobrzyńskiey*. Płock, 1825. (A topographical and historical description of the land of Dobrzyń.)
— *Wiadomość historyczna miasta Pułtusku*. Warsaw, 1826. (Historical information of the town of Pułtusk.)
Gołębiowski, L., *Opisanie historyczno-statystyczne miasta Warszawy*. 2nd ed., Warsaw, 1827. (A historical and statistical description of the town of Warsaw.)
Grevenitz, F. A. F. von, *Der Bauer in Polen—Monografie mit Andeutungen für die Gesetzgebung*. Berlin, 1818.
Holsche, A. C. von, *Geographie und Statistik von West-, Süd- und Neuöstpreussen*. 3 vols., Berlin, 1800–7.
Jacob, W., *Report on the Trade in Foreign Corn and on the agriculture of the North of Europe*. 2nd ed., London, 1826. A British Parliamentary report.
— 'Notices respecting the Commerce of the Black Sea and the Sea of Azoff', in *Tracts relating to the Corn Trade and Corn Laws*. London, 1828.
Kołłątaj, H., *Listy Anonima i Prawo Polityczne Narodu Polskiego*, ed. B. Leśnodorski and H. Wereszycka. 2 vols., Warsaw, 1954. (Letters of an Anonymous Writer and the Political Law of the Polish Nation.)
Krompolc, K., *Sposób urządzenia włościan w dobrach Konińskowoli dziedzycznych J.O. Xięcia J. Imci A. Czartoryskiego*. Warsaw, 1816. (The manner of regulating peasants on the estate of Końskowola, the property of His Highness Prince A. Czartoryski.)

Krzyżtopor, A. (pseudonym of Count Tomasz Potocki), *O urządzeniu stosunków rolniczych w Polsce.* 2nd ed., Poznań, 1859. (Concerning the regulation of agrarian relationships in Poland.)

Lachnicki, J. E., *Statystyka gubernii litewsko-grodzieńskiej.* Vilna, 1817. (Statistics of the Government of Grodno in Lithuania.)

Marczyński, W., *Statystyczne, topograficzne i historyczne opisanie gubernii podolskiej.* 3 vols., Vilna, 1820–3. (A statistical, topographical and historical description of the Government of Podolia.)

Michalski, J., *Regulacya stosunków włościan.* Lvov, 1845. (The regulation of peasant conditions.)

Rodecki, F., *Obraz jeograficzno-statystyczny królestwa polskiego.* Warsaw, 1830. (A geographical and statistical picture of the Kingdom of Poland.)

Skorzewski, F., *Uwagi nad polepszeniem stanu włościan.* Bydgoszcz, 1814. (Observations on improving the condition of the peasants.)

Słowaczyński, J., *Polska w kształcie dykcyonarza historyczno-statystyczno-jeograficznego opisana.* Paris, 1833–8. (Poland described in the form of a historical, statistical and geographical dictionary.)

— *Statistique générale de la Pologne.* 4 vols. (5 parts), Paris, 1838–9.

Sobieszczański, F. M., *Rys historyczno-statystyczny wzrostu i stanu miasta Warszawy do 1847 roku.* Warsaw, 1848. (A historical and statistical outline of the growth and condition of Warsaw to the year 1847.)

Sołtykowicz, J., *O przyczynach wewnętrznych i naybliższych tudież zewnętrznych i dalszych nędzy naszych włościan.* Cracow, 1815. (On the reasons ... for the misery of our peasants.)

Surowiecki, W., *O upadku przemysłu i miast w Polszcze.* Warsaw, 1810. (On the collapse of industry and towns in Poland.)

— *Uwagi względem poddanych w Polszcze y projekt do ich uwolnienia.* Warsaw, 1807. (Observations on the serfs in Poland and a plan for their liberation.)

Wolski, L., 'Statystyka ruchu ludności królestwa polskiego od roku 1816 do 1856 włącznie' (Statistics of the movement of population in the Kingdom of Poland from 1816 to 1856 inclusive), in *Kalendarz wydany przez Obserwatorium Astronomiczne Warszawy na rok zwyczajny 1858* (Warsaw, 1858), pp. 97–126.

Zavelejsky, M., *Statistika Tsarstva Pol'skavo.* St. Petersburg, 1842. (Russian.) (Statistics of the Kingdom of Poland.)

VI. Secondary Works
(a) General

Askenazy, S., *Rosya-Polska, 1815–1830.* Lvov, 1907. (Russia and

BIBLIOGRAPHY

Poland, 1815–30.) This work is an adaptation of Askenazy's chapters in the *Cambridge Modern History*, vol. x, chapters xiii and xiv. The English version is misleading in places, and the Polish does not deal with the 1830 revolution.

— *Dwa stulecia, xviii i xix.* 2 vols., Warsaw, 1901–10. (Two centuries, the Eighteenth and Nineteenth.) A collection of essays.

Wczasy historyczny. 3 vols., Warsaw, 1902–10. (A historical miscellany.)

Bartoszewicz, K., *Utworzenie królestwa kongresowego.* Warsaw, 1916. (The creation of the Congress Kingdom.)

Baumgarten, L., *Dekabryści a Polska.* Warsaw, 1952. (The Decembrists and Poland.)

Bieliński, J., *Królewski uniwersytet warszawski 1816–1831.* 4 vols., Warsaw, 1907–13. (The Royal University of Warsaw, 1816–31.)

— *Uniwersytet wileński, 1579–1831.* 3 vols., Cracow, 1899–1900. (The University of Vilna, 1579–1831.)

Bieniarzowna, J., *Rzeczpospolita krakowska, 1815–1846.* Cracow, 1948. (The Republic of Cracow, 1815–46.)

Bojasiński, J., *Rządy tymczasowe w królestwie polskiem, maj-grudzień 1815.* Warsaw, 1902. (The Temporary Government in the Kingdom of Poland, May–December 1815.)

Feldman, J., *Dzieje polskiej myśli politycznej w okresie porozbiorowej*, vol. i. Cracow, 1913. (The history of Polish political concepts in the post-partition period.)

Gąsiorowska, N., *Wolność druku w królestwie kongresowym, 1813–1830.* Warsaw, 1916. (Freedom of the Press in the Congress Kingdom, 1813–30.)

Grynwaser, H., *Demokracja szlachecka 1795–1831.* Warsaw, 1918. (Szlachta democracy, 1795–1831.) A brilliant essay, reprinted in his *Pisma*, vol. i, Breslau, 1951.

Handelsman, M., *Studia historyczne.* Warsaw, 1911. (Historical studies.)

— 2nd series, *Pod znakiem Napoleona* (Under the banner of Napoleon). Warsaw, 1913.

— 3rd series, *Pomiędzy Prusami a Rosją* (Between Prussia and Russia). Warsaw, 1922.

Iwaskiewicz, J., *Litwa w roku 1812.* Warsaw, 1912. (Lithuania in 1812.)

Konic, H., *Dzieje prawa małżeńskiego w królestwie polskiem 1818–1836.* Cracow, 1903. (The history of Marriage Law in the Kingdom of Poland, 1818–36.)

Kozłowski, W. M., *Autonomia królestwa polskiego 1815–1831*. Warsaw, 1907. (The autonomy of the Kingdom of Poland, 1815–31.)

Kraushar, A., *Miscellanea historyczne*. Lvov, 1904–20. (Historical miscellany.) Reprints of Kraushar's articles.

— *Echa przeszłości*. Warsaw, 1917. (Echoes of the Past.)

Limanowski, B., *Historia demokracji polskiej w epoce porozbiorowej*. Zurich, 1901. (The history of Polish Democracy in the post-partition period.)

Łubieński, T. W., *Henry Łubieński i jego bracia*. Cracow, 1886. (H. Łubieński and his brothers.)

Manteuffel, T., *Centralne władze oświatowe na terenie b. królestwa kongresowego (1807–1915)*. Warsaw, 1929. (The central educational authorities in the area of the former Kingdom of Poland.)

Manteuflowa, M., *J. K. Szaniawski—Ideologia i działalność 1815–1830*. Warsaw, 1936. (J. K. Szaniawski—His ideology and activity, 1815–30.)

Marchlewski, J. B., *Der Physiokratismus in Polen*. Zürich, 1897. (Translated as *Fizyokratyzm w Polsce*, Warsaw, 1898.)

— *Stosunki społeczno-ekonomiczne pod panowaniem pruskiem*. Lvov-Warsaw, 1903.

Moszyński, J., *Geneza powstania listopadowego*. Cracow, 1909. (The genesis of the November Revolution.) Printed as the introductory volume to I. Prądzyński, *Pamiętniki*, Cracow, 1909.

Przelaskowski, R., *Sejm warszawski roku 1825*. Warsaw, 1929. (The Warsaw Diet of 1825.)

Rembowski, A., *Z życia konstytucyjnego księstwa warszawskiego*. Cracow, 1900. (From the constitutional life of the Duchy of Warsaw.)

Rodkiewicz, J. A., *Pierwsza politechnika polska, 1825–1831*. Warsaw, 1904. (The first Polish polytechnic, 1825–31.)

Rolle, M., *Ateny wołyńskie*. 2nd ed., Lvov, 1923. (The Athens of Volhynia.) Deals with education and culture at Krzemieniec in Volhynia.

Smoleński, W., *Rządy pruskie na ziemiach polskich, 1793–1807*. Warsaw, 1886. (Prussian rule in the Polish territories, 1793–1807.) Reprinted in his *Pisma historyczne*, Cracow, 1901, vol. iii.

Wawrzkowicz, E., *Anglia a sprawa polska, 1813–1815*. Warsaw, 1919. (England and the Polish Question, 1813–15).

Więckowska, H., *Opozycja liberalna w królestwie kongresowym, 1815–1830*. Warsaw, 1923. (Liberal opposition in the Congress Kingdom, 1815–30.)

Willaume, J., *Polityka Prus wobec Księstwa Warszawskiego*. Łódź, 1952. (Prussian policy towards the Duchy of Warsaw.)

Żywczyński, M., *Geneza i następstwa Encykliki 'Cum Primum' z 9 vi 1832—Watykan i sprawa polska w latach 1830–1837*. Warsaw, 1935. (The origin and consequences of the Encyclical *Cum Primum* of 9 June 1832—The Vatican and the Polish Question, 1832–7.)

(b) *Biographies*

Askenazy, S., *Łukasiński*. 2 vols., Warsaw, 1908.

Gadon, L., *Książę Adam Czartoryski podczas powstania listopadowego*. New edition, Cracow, 1900. (Prince Adam Czartoryski during the November Revolution.)

Gollenhofer, J., *Polityczna strona działalności Maurycego Mochnackiego*. Cracow, 1910. (The political side of Maurycy Mochnacki's activity.)

Handelsman, M., *Adam Czartoryski*. 3 vols., Warsaw, 1948–50.

Limanowski, B., *Stanisław Worcell*. Cracow, 1910.

Lisicki, H., *Aleksander Wielopolski, 1803–1877*. 4 vols., Cracow, 1878–9. Vol. iv is a history of the Congress Kingdom.

— *Le marquis Wielopolski, sa vie et sa temps*. Vienna-Cracow, 1880. A French translation of the above, more important for the period 1861–4.

Mencel, T., *Feliks Łubieński, minister sprawiedliwości Księstwa Warszawskiego, 1758–1848*. Warsaw, 1952. (Feliks Łubieński, minister of justice in the Duchy of Warsaw, 1758–1848.)

Romanov, Grand Duke Nikolai Mikhailovich, *Imperator Aleksander I*. 2 vols., St. Petersburg, 1912. (The Emperor Alexander I.) Contains many documents.

Shcherbatov, Prince, *General Feldmarshal Knyaz Paskevich*. 7 vols., St. Petersburg, 1888–1904.

— *Le Feld Maréchal Prince Paskevich, sa vie politique et militaire*. St. Petersburg, 1888–99.

Two versions of the same work. The Russian version is liberally provided with documents, which however relate mainly to the post-1832 period in Congress Poland.

Shilder, N. K., *Imperator Aleksander Pervii*. 4 vols., St. Petersburg, 1897–8. (The Emperor Alexander I.)

— *Imperator Nikolai Pervii*. 2 vols., St. Petersburg, 1903. (The Emperor Nicholas I.)

Two rather official biographies, which have the merit of appendices of valuable documents.

Skałkowski, A. M., *Aleksander Wielopolski w świetle archiwów rodzinnych (1803–1877)*. 3 vols., Poznań, 1947. (Alexander Wielopolski in the light of his family archives.)

Sliwiński, A., *Joachim Lelewel, Zarys biograficzny lat 1786–1831*. 2nd ed., Warsaw, 1932. (Joachim Lelewel, a biographical sketch of the years 1786–1831.)
Szpotański, S., *Mochnacki*. Cracow, 1910.
Zdzitowiecki, J., *Xiążę Minister Franciszek Xawery Drucki-Lubecki, 1778–1846*. Warsaw, 1946.

(c) *Economic*

Ajzen, M., *Polityka gospodarcza Lubeckiego, 1821–1830*. Warsaw, 1932. (The economic policy of Lubecki, 1821–30.)
Bloch, J., *Finanse Rosji xix wieku*. 3 vols., Warsaw, 1883. (The finances of Russia in the nineteenth century.) Vol. iii deals with the Kingdom of Poland.
Borowski, W., *Kredyt rolniczy w Polsce*. Warsaw, 1927. (Agricultural credit in Poland.)
Czermiński, F., *O towarzystwie kreditowem w królestwie polskiem*, part i. Warsaw, 1866. (On the Land Credit Society in the Kingdom of Poland.)
Gąsiorowska, N., *Polska w przełomie życia gospodarczego, 1764–1830*. New edition, Warsaw, 1947. (Poland in economic transition, 1764–1830.) An excellent survey.
— *Gornictwo i hutnictwo w królestwie polskim, 1815–1830*. Warsaw, 1923. (Mines and foundries in the Kingdom of Poland, 1815–30.)
— 'Rekwizycje w księstwie warszawskim okupowanym przez Rosję w roku 1813–15' (Requisitions in the Duchy of Warsaw under Russian occupation, 1813–15), in *Likwidacja skutków wojny w dziedzinie stosunków prawnych*. Warsaw, vol. ii, 1917.
Grynwaser, H., *Kwestja agrarna i ruch włościan w królestwie polskiem w I-ej połowie xix wieku*. Warsaw, 1935. (The agrarian question and the peasant movement in the Kingdom of Poland in the first half of the nineteenth century.) Reprinted in his *Pisma*, ii, Breslau, 1951.
— 'Przywódcy i burzyciele włościan. Szkice z dziejów skarbowych w królestwie polskiem 1815–1830', *Przegląd współczesny*, 1936–7. Reprinted in his *Pisma*, ii, Breslau, 1951. (Leaders and instigators of the peasants. Essays in the history of the Treasury in the Kingdom of Poland, 1815–30.)
Jasiukowicz, S., *Der landschaftliche Kreditverein im Königreich Polen*. Munich, 1911.
Kaczkowski, J., *Konfiskaty na ziemiach polskich pod zaborem rosyjskiem po powstaniach roku 1831 i 1863*. Warsaw, 1918. (Confiscations in

BIBLIOGRAPHY

the Polish territories under the occupation of Russia after the risings of 1831 and 1863.)

Kirkor-Kiedroniowa, Z., *Włościanie i ich sprawa w dobie organizacyjnej i konstytucyjnej królestwa polskiego*. Cracow, 1912. (The peasants and their problems at the time of the constitutional organization of the Kingdom of Poland.)

Kniat, M., *Dzieje uwłaszczenia włościan w wielkim księstwie poznańskim*. 2 vols., Poznań, 1939-48. (The history of the emancipation [i.e. with land] of the peasants in the Grand Duchy of Posen.) Dr. Kniat died in a concentration camp before completing the second volume.

Lubliner, L., *Les confiscations des biens des Polonais sous le règne de l'Empereur Nicholas Ier*. Brussels-Leipzig, 1861.

Mościcki, H., *Sprawa włościańska na Litwie w pierwszej ćwierci xix wieku*. An offprint from *Biblioteka warszawska*, 1908.

Radziszewski, H., *Skarb i organizacja władz skarbowych w królestwie polskiem*, vol. i (1815-30). Warsaw, 1907. (The Treasury and the organization of the financial administration in the Kingdom of Poland.)

— *Bank Polski*. Warsaw, 1910. (The Bank of Poland.)

Rynkowska, A., *Działalność gospodarcza władz Królestwa Polskiego na terenie Łodzi przemysłowej w latach 1821-1831*. Łódź, 1951. (The economic activity of the Government of the Kingdom of Poland in the industrial region of Łódź, 1821-31.)

Siegel, S., *Ceny w Warszawie w latach 1701-1815*. Lvov, 1936. (Prices in Warsaw, 1701-1815.)

— *Ceny w Warszawie w latach 1816-1914*. Poznań, 1949. (Prices in Warsaw, 1816-1914.)

Smolka, S., *Polityka Lubeckiego przed powstaniem listopadowem*. 2 vols., Cracow, 1907. (The Policy of Lubecki before the November Rising.)

Strzeszewski, C., *Kryzys rolniczy na ziemiach księstwa warszawskiego i królestwa kongresowego, 1807-1830*. Lublin, 1934. (The agrarian crisis in the territories of the Duchy of Warsaw and the Congress Kingdom, 1807-30.)

— *Handel zagraniczny królestwa kongresowego, 1815-1830*. Lublin, 1937. (The foreign trade of the Congress Kingdom, 1815-30.)

Zembrzuski, S., *Polityka celna królestwa kongresowego, 1815-1830 r.* Warsaw, 1930. (The tariff policy of the Congress Kingdom, 1815-30.)

(d) Works dealing specifically with the November Revolution

Dangel, S., *Rok 1831 w Mińszczyźnie*. Warsaw, 1925. (The year 1831 in the region of Minsk.)

Dutkiewicz, J., *Austrja wobec powstania listopadowego*. Cracow, 1933. (Austria's attitude to the November Rising.)

— *Francja a Polska w 1830*. Łódź, 1950. (France and Poland, 1830–1.)

Eile, H., *Rok 1830*. Warsaw, 1930. (The year 1830.)

— *Powstanie listopadowe—Finanse i administracja wojska*. Warsaw, 1930. (The November Rising—The finance and administration of the army.)

Gadon, L., *Przeście Polaków przez Niemcy po upadku powstania listopadowego*. Poznań, 1889. (The crossing of the Poles through Germany after the collapse of the November Rising.)

— *Emigracya Polska—Pierwsze lata po upadku powstania listopadowego*. 3 vols., Cracow, 1901–2. (The Polish Emigration—The first years after the collapse of the November Rising.)

Harbut, J. S., *Noc Listopadowa w świetle i cieniach procesu przed najwyższym sądem kryminalnym*. Warsaw, 1926. (The November Night in the lights and shades of the trial before the Supreme Criminal Court.)

Meloch, M., *Sprawa włościańska w powstaniu listopadowym*. Warsaw, 1939. (The peasant question during the November Rising.)

Oppman, E., *Warsawskie 'Towarzystwo Patriotyczne' 1830–1*. Warsaw, 1937. (The Warsaw 'Patriotic Society', 1830–1.)

Schiper, I., *Żydzi królestwa polskiego w dobie powstania listopadowego*. Warsaw, 1932. (The Jews of the Kingdom of Poland during the November Rising.)

Sierpiński, R., *Tło gospodarcze i istota klasowa powstania listopadowego 1830 r.* Minsk, 1934. (The economic background and class character of the November Rising of 1830.) The work of a Marxist exile in the U.S.S.R.

Sokołowski, A., *Wyprawa Dwernickiego na Wołyn*. Cracow, 1918. (The expedition of Dwernicki to Volhynia.)

Tokarz, W., *Sprzysiężenie Wysockiego i noc listopadowa*. Warsaw, 1925. (Wysocki's conspiracy and the November night.)

— *Wojna polsko-rosyjska 1830–1*. Warsaw, 1930. (The Polish-Russian War of 1830–1.) The standard history of the military campaign.

VII. BIBLIOGRAPHICAL

Historical bibliographies for Poland are not altogether satisfactory, but the student will soon discover the difficulties. The following are standard works:

Estreicher, K., *Bibliografia Polska*. Cracow, 1870–80. —Dopełnienia, 1873, 1881, 1882.
— *Bibliografia polska xix stulecia, 1881–1900*. Cracow, 1906–16.
Finkel, L., *Bibliografia historyi polskiej*. Cracow, 1891–1906. Extends only to 1815.
Hirschberg, A., *Bibliografia powstania narodu polskiego z r. 1830–1831*. Lvov, 1882. Now out of date.
Maliszewski, E., *Bibliografia pamiętników polskich i Polski dotyczących (Druki i rękopisy)*. Warsaw, 1928. Still a handy means of reference.

For current writings the excellent *Przewodnik Bibliograficzny— Urzędowy wykaz druków wydanych w Rzeczypospolitej Polskiej*, which appears weekly, is indispensable.

An effort is now being made to end the bibliographical confusion which exists for the nineteenth century. The first volume of a new project, *Bibliografia historii polskiej, 1815–1914*, entitled *Tom Wstępny*, edited by H. Bachulska with W. and B. Konarska, has been advertised, but I have not yet seen it.

The Polish equivalent of the *Dictionary of National Biography* is *Polski Słownik Biograficzny*, which was begun in Cracow, and has now reached *Gemma, Jan*. Genealogies and some obituaries of persons of noble descent are contained in T. Żychliński's series, *Złota księga szlachty polskiej*, 31 vols., Poznań, 1879–1908. Place names and details of individual localities, down to the level of villages and estates, may be found in *Słownik geograficzny królestwa polskiego i innych krajów słowiańskich*, Warsaw, 1880–95; this work covers almost all the areas ever embraced by the Polish state.

Important articles appear in the principal Polish periodical publications, some of which issue summaries in English, French and Russian. *Kwartalnik Historyczny* (Historical Quarterly) is published in Warsaw by the Polish Academy of Sciences (Polska Akademia Nauk —Instytut Historii); *Przegląd Historyczny* (Historical Review) is the organ of the Warsaw Historical Association (Towarzystwo Miłośników Historii w Warszawie). *Przegląd Zachodni*, published by the Instytut Zachodni (The Western Institute) in Poznań, deals with the specific problems of western Poland. *Roczniki historyczne (Annales Historiques)* is another Poznań publication, but is wider in its scope than *Przegląd Zachodni*. *Rocznik dziejów społecznych i gospodarczych (Annales d'histoire sociale et économique)* is also issued in Poznań. *Przegląd Nauk Historycznych i Społecznych* (Review of Historical and Social Sciences) reflects the industrial background of its place of publication, Łódź. Breslau (Wrocław), which is now the home of the Polish university formerly at Lvov, has its own historical association (Wrocławskie Towarzystwo Miłośników Historii), which publishes *Sobótka*, a periodical dealing in the main with Polish Silesia, but often containing important articles on topics of general application. *Zapiski Towarzystwa Naukowego w Toruniu* covers from Toruń the history of Polish Pomerania in its widest sense. Legal history is the theme of *Czasopismo prawno-historyczne* (*Annales d'histoire du droit*), published first in Poznań in 1948, but since 1953 in Warsaw by the Legal Studies Section of the Polish Academy of Sciences; the monthly *Państwo i Prawo* (The State and Law), the organ of the Association of Polish Lawyers, is mainly devoted to contemporary problems, but does occasionally have articles of historical interest.

Index

Administrative Council, organization, 48; attempt to deal with the crisis (1831), 124; new members co-opted, 127–8; admission of radicals, 129; dissolved, 130
Agrarian reform, 66–9, 71–3, 181–93; *see also* Joseph II, Prussian Policy, Szaniecki
Alexander I, emperor of Russia, 41, 43; retention of Napoleonic organization in the Kingdom of Poland, 48, 96–7, 98; meeting with Czartoryski (1823) at Wołosowce, nr. Latychov, 109; death, 114
Amnesty of 1831, 256, 258–9
Aristocracy, *see* Szlachta
Army, 'army of 100,000 men', 17, 20; reorganization before 1791, 28–9; Napoleonic influence, 39–41; Grand Duke Constantine, 48–9; issue of contradictory orders to (1830), 126–7; support of Chłopicki, 139, 151n; deputations to ministry of war, 166–7; breakdown of discipline, 239; demoralization, 253–4

Bank of Poland, 92–3
Barzykowski, Stanisław, member of the National Government, 141, 150, 158, 160, 232
Bayonne Debts, 81, 83–4
Benckendorf, General Alexander, interview with Jezierski, 144–5
Berg, General Theodor, 253–4
Biernacki, Aloizy, minister of finance, 1831, 160; resignation, 226
Bolimów conference, 239–40
Boromel, battle of, 199
Bourgeoisie, *see* Middle Class
Branicka, Countess Alexandra, 201
Branicki, Franciszek Ksawery, hetman, 19–20, 29
Bronikowski, Ksawery, 128–9, 164

Cadet school, 115–16
Chłapowski, General Dezydery, 134n, 212; Skrzynecki's instructions to, 214; in Lithuania, 215–17
Chłopicki, General Józef, 116, 125n; calls army into Warsaw, 126–7, 130–1; declares himself dictator, 132; refuses to accept diet's approval of the rising, 138–9; letter from secretary of state, 146; unable to control revolutionary spirit, 148–50; hostility to war policy, 150; resignation from dictatorship, 151; undertaking to guide Radziwiłł, 152–3; wounded at Grochów, 167
Cholera epidemic, 169, 213, 223
Chopin, Frédéric, 104
Chróściechowski, Major Bazyli, commissioned by Radziwiłł to act as agent, 197; causes confusion by premature summons in the Ukraine, 199–200
Chrzanowski, General Wojciech, chief of staff, 166–7; independent command, 198; advice at Bolimów, 240; urged Dembiński to restore discipline, 245; Governor of Warsaw, 247; activity in emigration, 271
Code Napoléon, economic effects of introduction, 69–71; retained by Alexander I, 72
Confederations, 9; *see also* Targowica
Conspiracies of 1820's, 106
Constantine Pavlovich, grand duke of Russia, 48, 112, 115; refusal to use Russian troops (1831), 123–5, 126–7, 129, 133; death, 213n
Constitutions: of 1791, 27; of 1807, 42; of 1815, 45–8; Additional Article of 1825, 98–9, 153; of 1831, 158–61; *see also* Organic Statute
Cracow, free city of, 45, 257, 261

INDEX

Cracow, *województwo* of (i.e. part of the Kingdom of Poland), conditions in 1831, 177–8
Crown lands, 68, 81; sale of, 93–4; government's proposals for, (1831), 187–8
Czartoryski, family of, 11–12
Czartoryski, Prince Adam Kazimierz, 19, 36
Czartoryski, Prince Adam George (Jerzy), 43, 45, 71, 109, 114; action in November 1830, 124, 129, 139–40, 141, 151, 157; elected head of the insurgent government, 159; speech of 30 January 1831, 162; views on the peasant question, 182–3, 220–3, 224; attitude to Krukowiecki and Umiński, 229–30; pressure on Skrzynecki to undertake offensive action, 232; pacifies street demonstration, 233–4; quarrel with Lelewel, 237–8; flight from Warsaw, 244; diplomatic solution of the Polish Question, 269, 271–2; condemned by majority of *émigrés*, 274
Czartoryski, Prince August, 12
Czyński, Jan, 243–4

Dąbrowski, General Jan, 37; commander of Polish legion in Italy, 38–9
Dashov, skirmish at (1831), 201
Debt question, 79–80; Duchy of Warsaw, 81, 183; Kingdom of Poland, 84–5, 91–2
Decembrists, 113–14, 155
Dekert, Jan, burgomaster of Warsaw, 25
Dembe Wielkie, Polish victory at, 192, 194–5
Dembiński, General Henryk, 135n, 213; escape from Lithuania to Warsaw, 216; arrival in Warsaw and appointment as governor, 237; appointed acting commander-in-chief, 240–1; failure to carry out *coup d'état*, 245–6; relieved of command, 248; activities in emigration, 256, 271
Dembowski, Leon, senator, 140, 158; minister of finance, 226
Deniszko, Ukrainian Polish envoy to Warsaw, 197
Desertion from Polish forces (1831), 176, 178

Diebitsch-Zabalkansky, Field-Marshal Ivan (Johan), mission to Berlin, 119, 142, 163; counter-attack at Ostrołęka, 212; death, 213 and n.
Diet of the Kingdom of Poland, 45–7; approval of the rising, 138–9, 161–2; establishment of the Small Quorum, 170–1; debates on the peasant question, 189–93; discussion of form of government, 231; government changed, August 1831, 246–7; final meeting, 254
Distilling, exclusive rights of the manor, 62–3, 189
Dwernicki, General Józef, victory at Stoczek, 166; campaign in Volhynia, 169–70, 197; activities in emigration, 270–1

Emigration, post-1795, 37; post-1831, 257–60
Finance, in the Kingdom of Poland, 90–1; in 1831, 225–8
Flottwell, Edward, 261
Frankfort Conspiracy of 1833, Polish part in it, 273
Freemasonry, 105–6, 110

Giełgud, General Antoni, sent to Lithuania, 213–14; establishes Lithuanian government, 215; march on Vilna, 216; forced over the Prussian frontier, murdered, 216–17
Goszczyński, Seweryn, 103, 116; advice to the Polish Democratic Society, 277–8
Grabowski, Count Stanisław, minister of education, 99–100
Grain shortage, 1831, government questionnaire, 178–9
Grochów, battle of, 164
Gurowski, Count Adam, 156, 164, 170, 184, 270

Hauke, General Maurycy, 122n
Heltman, Wiktor, 275–6

Iganie, victory at, 192, 194–5
Industry, of Łódź, 88

Jabłonowski, Prince Antoni, betrayal of the Patriotic Society, 114
Jankowski, General, military failure, 233–4; murdered August 1831, 244

INDEX

Jełowicki, Alexander, 200–1, 235, 252
Jews, 7–8, 35, 196, 207, 208; Szaniecki's proposal for extension of rights to, 185–6
Jezierski, Count Jan, 136; envoy to St. Petersburg, 144–5, 146
Joseph II of Austria, legislation for Galicia, 67

Kingdom of Poland (1815), 43; population, 46
Kołłątaj, Father Hugo, the 'Forge', 22, 24, 32–3; attitude to the peasant question, 65–6
Kościuszko, Tadeusz, 32; Połaniec manifesto, 68–9
Krasiński, Adam, bishop of Kamieniec (Kamenets), 18, 21
Krukowiecki, General Jan, 131; governor of Warsaw, 167; complaints of harbouring deserters, 176; quarrel with Skrzynecki, 229; quietens the mob, August 1831, 244–5; elected head of the government, 246–7; in favour of accepting Russian terms, 248–50; interview with Paskevich, 251; resignation, 252–3
Krzyżanowski, Colonel Seweryn, 113–14

Labour services, increase in sixteenth century, 52–4; types, 56; incidence, 57–8
Land Credit Society, 91–3, 98, 191–2
Land ownership, 63–5; constitution of 1791, 67; in Galicia, 67–8; in Prussian Poland, 69; in the Duchy of Warsaw, 69–71
Ledóchowski, Count Jan, 73, 148, 156–7, 230
Legions, in Italy, 38; plan of revival, 271
Lelewel, Joachim, historian, 103–4; consulted by Wysocki, 121, 129, 140, 147; arrested by Chłopicki, 150, 156; elected member of the government (1831), 160; views on the peasant question, 182; anxiety for Lithuania, 212n; attacked by Skrzynecki, 230; quarrel with Czartoryski, 237–8, 243; in emigration, 269–70
Leszczyński, Stanisław, anti-king, 10, 17
Levée-en-masse, 227–8

Liberum Veto, 9, 23, 24, 27
Lithuania, 2, 55, 71, 86, 109; address of Lithuanians to the diet, 175; rising, 202; peasant *jacquerie*, 207; hostility of Lithuanians to Giełgud, 215; Ukaz of April 1831 for, 217; admission to rights and privileges of Kingdom, 217–18; effect of confiscations in, 267
Lubecki, Prince Ksawery Drucki–, minister of finance, 88–91, 93–4, 120, 124, 129; interview with Nicholas I, 143–4
Łubieński, Felix, minister of justice, 80, 83
Łubieński, Henryk, 93, 148–9
Łubieński, Tomasz, 93, 132, 141, 149, 157; chief of staff in charge of a corps, 210–11; remained in Poland after 1831, 264
Lubowidzki, Mateusz, 107; escapes from Warsaw, 148–9
Łukasiński, Major Waleryan, 109; conspiracy discovered, 112–13

Madaliński, General Antoni, precipitates revolution (1794), 31
Małachowski, Count Gustaw, minister of foreign affairs (1831), 127, 160; resignation, 218
Małachowski, General Kazimierz, 242; appointed acting commander-in-chief, 248; concludes military convention, 253
Manifesto of Połaniec (1794), 68–9
Manifesto of 1831, published without Chłopicki's approval, 147–8
Marriage laws, 99
Metternich, Prince, Austrian chancellor, advice to Andrzej Zamoyski, 223
Mickiewicz, Adam, 101–2
Middle Class, weakness in Poland, 7–8, 122
Mochnacki, Maurycy, 103, 128, 129; attack on Chłopicki and attempt at *coup d'état*, 130–1, 155, 158, 164; views on the social question, 184–5, 247; in emigration, 274
Morawski, General Franciszek, minister of war, 168, 254, 264
Morawski, Teodor, writer, 221

INDEX

Morawski, Teofil, member of government (1831), 140, 159, 235; resignation, 251

Nabielak, Ludwik, 246

National Government of 1831, 159–60 efforts to gather food supplies, 179–81; rejection of agrarian reform, January 1831, 183–4; debate on constitutional reform, 231; reformed August 1831, 246–7

Nicholas I, emperor of Russia, 117; attitude to the July revolution in Paris, 118; postpones Polish mobilization, 120; reaction to Polish revolution, 141–2; reception of Lubecki and Jezierski, 143–4, 147; deposed by the Polish diet, 157; strategy, 210

Niemcewicz, Julian Ursyn, 101, 124, 129, 222

Niemojowski, Bonawentura, 97–8, 137, 193, 218, 235–6, 249, 251–3; head of the government, September 1831, 253–4; in emigration, 270

Niemojowski, Wincenty, member of the government (1831), 97–8, 102, 137, 149; elected member of the government, 159; criticism of Skrzynecki, 235, 238, 269

Novosiltsev, senator, commissioner in Poland, 48, 109

Nowa Polska (New Poland), 149

Olizar, Count Narcyz, 197, 235

Organic Statute of 1832, 262–3

Orthodox Church, 5, 17, 267

Ostrołęka, battle of, 212

Ostrowski, Count Antoni, commander of the National Guard, 135, 153, 244

Ostrowski, Count Władysław, marshal of the diet, 127, 129, 138, 139–40, 149, 156, 161, 246

Oszmiana, Massacre of, 205

Pac, Count Ludwik, 125

Partitions of Poland, of 1772, 6, 17; of 1793, 30; of 1795, 34–6; of 1815, 43–5

Paskevich-Erivansky, Field-Marshal Count Ivan, 213, 234, 250–1; viceroy, 263

Patriotic Society, of Łukasiński, 110–11; established in Warsaw (December 1830), 128; suppressed, 132; revived, 154–5, 157–8; active members join the army, 164–5, 198; meeting of 15 August 1831, 241

Peasants, depressed condition, 51; types 56–8; obligations of landlords towards, 64–5; Kościuszko's appeal to, 68; committee of inquiry concerning, 71; Prussian Edict of 1823, 75–7; hostility to authorities in 1831, 178; rewards for peasant soldiers, 185; government proposals for Crown peasants, 187–8; debates on the peasant question (1831), 189–93; Small Quorum's scheme, 191–2; resistance to the *levée-en-masse*, 227–8; problem shelved by the Russians, 268–9

Permanent Council, 18–19

Płock, conditions in the *województwo* of (1831), 174, 180

Polish Democratic Society, 270, 275–7

Poniatowski, Stanisław August, King of Poland, 12, 20, 26

Potocki, family of, 11–12

Potocki, Franciszek Salezy, 11

Potocki, Ignacy, 12, 20, 26–7, 32

Potocki, Stanisław Kostka, 99, 106

Potocki, Stanisław Szczęsny, 11, 19, 29, 36

Prądzyński, General Ignacy, 110, 241, 249–51; quartermaster-general, 168; dismissed for intrigue, 236

Prices, inflation (1791–1805), 79; deflation, 84–5; in Warsaw (1830), 122, 180

Protestantism, 2, 17

Prussian Policy towards Poland (1789), 20; application of Prussian law in annexed territories (1799), 69; re-application in Poznania, 75; emancipation edict of 1823 for Poznania, 75–7; trade war against the Republic, 78–9; against the Kingdom of Poland, 87; cordon established, 1831, 223–4; Flottwell régime in Poznania, 261

Puławski, Father, 243–4

Radziwiłł, Prince Antoni, viceroy of Poznania, 75–6

Radziwiłł, Prince Michał, 124, 141; reasons for election as commander-in-chief, 151–3; resignation after Grochów, 166–7

INDEX

Ramorino, General Girolamo, 248–9, 254, 273
Republic of Poland (*Rzeczpospolita*), 1–2
Roman Catholic Church, 4; in White Russia, 6; defence by confederation of Bar, 17–18; attitude to marriage laws, 99
Romanticism, 101–5
Różycki, Karol, 200
Rybiński, General Maciej, last commander-in-chief, 253–5
Rzewuski, Seweryn, 23, 29

Sandomierz, conditions in the *wojwodztwo* of (1831), 176–7
Sanguszko, Prince Eustachy, 197
Sanguszko, Prince Roman, 198
Sapieha, Prince Leon, 91n, 198, 239, 272
Savoy expedition of 1834, 273
Saxon dynasty, 10
Serfdom, 54–5, 64
Skrzynecki, General Jan, appointed commander-in-chief, 167; effort to discover Russian intentions, 168; counter-attack, 194–5; attack on the Guards, 209–10; instructions to Chłapowski, 214; letter to Archduke Charles, 224n; quarrel with Krukowiecki, 229; complaints against the government, 230; complaints against Czartoryski, 232; decision to defend the Bura, 236; removed from post, 240
Sołtyk, Count Roman, 154, 252
Staniewicz, Ezechiel, 204, 209
Staszic, Father Stanisław, 21, 23, 65
Supreme National Council of 1830–1, 140–1
Szaniecki, Jan Olrych, 73, 85–6, 127, 141, 161, 190–1
Szembek, General Jan, 126, 141, 150, 152, 166
Szlachta: aristocracy, 11, 13, 18–19; medium *szlachta*, 13; petty *szlachta*, 14–15, 22n, 29–30, 46

Targowica, confederation of, 29
Tarnopol, region of, economic results of cession to Russia (1809), 71
Temporary government of the Kingdom of Poland, 130

Trade and Commerce, 78–80, 82; of Odessa, 86; crisis of 1822, 86–7; Russo-Polish agreement of 1822, 88; Warsaw as emporium, 94; cancellation of 1822 agreement, 265
Tyszkiewicz, Count Józef, 205, 215

Ukraine, Polish weakness in 1831, 195–6; confusion owing to Chróściechowski's circular, 197–200; defeat of Polish insurgents at Dashov, 201
Uniate Church, 4–6, 196, 200n, 267

Vienna, treaty of (1815), Polish attitude to, 43–4, 139, 147, 262–3

Wałchnowski, Andrzej, 198
Walewski, Alexander, 222
Warsaw, Duchy of, 41–2, 69–70
Warsaw, town of, 47; Lubecki's plans for, 94; in 1830, 122; supply of food for in 1831, 179–80; fall to the Russian army, 253
Węgrzecki, Stanisław, town president, 125, 163
Wielopolski, Marquis Alexander, 218, 222, 246
Worcell, Stanisław, 197
Wyleżyński, Tadeusz, envoy to St. Petersburg, 141; received, 145–6
Wysocki, Piotr, 115, 118, 121, 131, 198

Zajączek Józef, viceroy of Poland, radical during revolt of 1794, 33n, 39; in favour of French constitution, 41; viceroy, 48; attitude in the Rupiński case, 72
Zaliwski, Józef, 118, 214, 268
Załuski, Count Józef, 206, 208–9
Zamoyski, Andrzej (1716–92), chancellor of Poland, 66
Zamoyski, Count Andrzej (1800–74), opinion of Czartoryski, 159; conversation with Metternich (1831), 223; leadership in Congress Poland, 265
Zamoyski, Count Stanisław, obeyed summons to St. Petersburg, 136
Zamoyski, Count Władysław, 124 and n, 265, 271